SEBASTIAN COUNTY ARKANSAS

Biographical and Historical Memoirs

Goodspeed

Heritage Books
2026

HERITAGE BOOKS
AN IMPRINT OF HERITAGE BOOKS, INC.

Books, CDs, and more—Worldwide

For our listing of thousands of titles see our website
at
www.HeritageBooks.com

A Facsimile Reprint
Published 2026 by
HERITAGE BOOKS, INC.
Publishing Division
5810 Ruatan Street
Berwyn Heights, MD 20740

Previouly published:
Mountain Press
Signal Mountain, Tennessee
2006

International Standard Book Number
Paperbound: 978-0-7884-9875-6

HISTORY OF SEBASTIAN COUNTY

NATURAL HISTORY.

Location and Boundary.—The county of Sebastian lies near the middle of the western tier of counties in the State of Arkansas, and is bounded on the north by the Arkansas River, which separates it from Crawford County; on the east by Franklin and Logan Counties; on the south by Scott County, and on the west by the Indian Terrritory. According to the system of public land surveys, it embraces portions of Townships 4 to 9 inclusive north of the base line, and portions of Ranges 29 to 32 inclusive west of the fifth principal meridian, and has an area of 520 square miles, or 332,800 acres of land, divided into the following classes: Mountain and high ridge, prairie, timbered uplands, river and creek bottom lands. The thirty-fifth parallel of north latitude passes through the southern part of the county, and the ninety-fourth degree of longitude west from Greenwich, or the seventeenth degree west from Washington, runs along or near its eastern boundary.

Climate.—The climate is mild and pleasant, and of a comparatively even temperature throughout the year. The mean average temperature of the atmosphere, as observed at the United States Signal Service Station at Fort Smith, since it was established there, has been as follows: 1883, 60 degrees Fahrenheit; 1884, 59 degrees Fahrenheit; 1885, 58 degrees Fahrenheit; 1886, 58 degrees Fahrenheit; 1887, 61 degrees Fahrenheit, thus making the average for the five years, 59½ degrees.

The mean maximum and minimum degrees of temperature for each month of the year 1887 is shown in the following table;

	Mean.	Maximum.	Minimum.
January	38	73	4
February	45	75	20
March	54	76	28
April	64	91	30
May	70	92	50
June	76	95	57
July	82	104	65
August	78	101	57
September	74	97	45
October	60	90	32
November	50	79	17
December	38	72	8

The first column shows the mean or average temperature during the month, the second the temperature of the hottest day, and the third the temperature of the coldest day. It will be observed that the two extremes were reached in the months of January and July—the mercury going four degrees below zero in January,and rising 104 degrees above it in July. These extremes each existed only for a few hours. By deduction from the above table it is found that the mean temperature for each of the four seasons was as follows: Spring, $62\frac{2}{3}$ degrees; summer, $78\frac{2}{3}$ degrees; fall, $61\frac{1}{3}$ degrees; winter, $40\frac{1}{3}$ degrees. These figures are official, and prove conclusively that the climate of this section of country is mild and pleasant. It is safe to take these figures as applicable to the counties treated of in this work lying south of the dividing ridge of the Boston Mountains. North of that ridge the climate is somewhat colder. The average annual rain-fall in this section of the country, as ascertained by the Signal Service Station at Fort Smith, is thirty-eight inches.

Topography.—The surface of Sebastian County is composed of mountain ridges, table lands, rolling prairies, undulating timbered lands and valleys. The elevation of the St. Louis & San Francisco Railroad track at its intersection with Garrison Avenue, in the city of Fort Smith, is 417 feet and nine inches above the level of the sea. This point is on the bank of the Arkansas River, about 350 feet therefrom, and 1,300 feet below the mouth of the Poteau River. It may be taken as the elevation of the valley of the Arkansas, while the other lands range therefrom to a height of 1,500 feet at the top of the highest mountains. The Poteau Mountain Range lies in the extreme southern part of the county, and its course is a little south of west. About six miles north of this, and mostly in Range 32 west, are the Sugar Loaf Mountains, running nearly parallel with the Poteau range. Six miles east of the Sugar Loaf Mountains is the southwestern extreme of Black Jack Ridge, which crosses Range 30 west, and lies astride of the boundary line between Sebastian and Scott Counties. Two miles north of the right of this ridge is Pleasant Ridge, which extends east and west about two miles. On and near the line between Townships 5 and 6 north, and extending through Ranges 29 and 30 west, lies the range of the White Oak Mountains. The Washburn Mountains form a ridge in the northern part of Township 6 north, Range 29 west, five miles in length, bearing a little south of west. The Backbone Ridge, the longest one in the county, commences near the center of Township 5 north, Range 31 west, and extends five miles north, bearing slightly to the west; thence thirteen miles east, bearing slightly to the north, to the eastern boundary of the county. Griffith Mountain, which is nearly round and between one and two miles in diameter, lies mostly in the southwest corner of Township 6 north, Range 31 west. Sand Ridge extends about three miles east from Hackett City. Backbone Ridge commences west of the county line, and extends into the county in an easterly direction about seven miles. It lies in the northern part of Township 6 north. River Mountains lie in the extreme northeast corner of the county, in Township 9 north, Range 29 west, and form a range with a northeasterly bearing three miles in length.

These mountain ridges, together with some smaller ones not here enumerated, are estimated to compose about 10 per cent of the area of the county, and are mostly unfit for cultivation, although some good farms are found on their tops and sides. With the exception of a portion of Backbone Ridge, the mountain ridges in the county all have nearly the same bearing, which is east, bearing slightly to the north.

Prairies.—Mazzard Prairie, only a few miles southeast of Fort Smith, is from three to four miles square. Long Prairie lies ten miles south of Fort Smith, and covers several sections of land. Hodge's Prairie lies in the northeastern part of Township 5 north, Range 31 west, and contains about five square miles. Beautiful mountain scenery can be seen from it in every direction. Sorrell's Prairie, surrounding Sugar Loaf Post-office, lies in the east central part of Township 5 north, Range 32 west, and contains about two sections of land. Cherokee Prairie, containing three sections of land, lies in the southern part of the county, in Township 4 north, Range 31 west. From it a splendid view of the Poteau Mountains can be had. "The other prairies are mostly under a square mile in extent rather than over, though possibly a few years ago they were much larger, for the timber is gradually growing into them from their borders."* The area of the prairie lands is not equal in extent to that of the ridge and mountain lands. After deducting the prairie, ridge and mountain lands, the balance of the surface of the county consists of valley lands and of what are called timbered uplands in about equal proportions. There are no real swamp lands in the county, but some tracts are subject to overflow in season of high water.

Drainage.—The natural drainage of the county is most thorough, having the Arkansas River on the north and the Poteau on the west, and their various tributaries. The James Fork of the latter river is formed by the conjunction of streams from the Poteau Mountains, and into it, from the extreme southwest portion of the county, flows West Creek, and from the valley north of Black Jack Ridge flows Prairie Creek. This fork then flows in a northwesterly direction, receiving the waters of many smaller streams, and finally leaves the county near the center of its western boundary line. It drains nearly all that portion of the county lying in Townships 4 and 5 north. Sugar Loaf, Big Branch, Cedar, Mill and other creeks flow from the western portion of the county into Poteau River. The central part of the county is drained mostly by the Vache Grass and its many tributaries. These tributaries empty into the main stream from all points of the compass. The Vache Grass empties into the Arkansas near the line dividing Ranges 30 and 31 west, also near the center of the northern boundary of the county. The eastern portion of the county north of the Washburn Mountains is

* Notes on Western Arkansas, by John Carnall.

drained in a northerly direction by Big Creek and its numerous tributaries. Big Creek empties into the Arkansas two miles above the northeast corner of the county. The Mazzard, Little Vache Grass and other streams also flow into the Arkansas on the north. The extreme eastern portions of the county, lying in Townships 5 and 6 north, are drained by Washburn and Little Washburn Creeks forming the head waters of the Petit Jean Creek, which empties into the Arkansas three counties below.

Chalybeate springs, from which pure, sparkling waters flow in great abundance, are found in many places throughout the county. Sulphur springs are also found in several localities. At one of the latter, on Sugar Loaf Mountain, a number of cottages have been erected and the place fitted up for a summer resort. Good well water is obtained at a depth of twenty feet and upward. In some portions of the county it is obtained at an average depth of thirty-five feet. The depth is governed more or less by the elevation of the locality where the wells are sunk. For culinary purpose, cistern water is generally preferred and considered the most healthful. Upon the whole the water supply is abundant, and of the best quality.

Forests.—The following pertaining to the forests of Sebastian County is taken from Mr. John Carnall's valuable "Notes on WesternArkansas:"

Post oak is the most common growth, and red oak and black oak are almost everywhere interspersed. There is more red and black oak on the red soil, and post oak on the yellow soil. Then we have blackjack, hickory, dogwood, etc., on all the hills, and in all the bottoms, cottonwood, sweetgum (now extensively used in making furniture), walnut, sycamore, elm, maple, cypress, white oak, ash — seventy or eighty kinds in all — specimens of nearly all of which, dressed and undressed, may be seen at the State capital.

Coal.—The following is compiled from the geological report of Prof. David Dale Owen made some years ago:

The most important locality of coal in Sebastian County lies on the southern edge of Long Prairie, known as the Jennie Lind coal, in the northwest and southeast quarters of Section 33, Township 7, Range 31 west. The following is a section of this coal as it occurs at Greene's bank in the northwest quarter of the above mentioned section of land:

Rusty, ferruginous gray shales, with segregations of iron ore, 5 feet, 6 inches.

A streak of black shale.

A few inches of coal.

A few inches of black shale.

Upper member of the main coal, 2 feet 5 inches.

Clay parting, 1 inch.

Lower member of main coal, 2 feet 2 inches.

Coal rash (a few inches).

This coal is therefore 4 feet 7 inches in thickness, and is said sometimes to attain a thickness of 5 feet and over.

The following is a chemical analysis of a specimen taken from the upper member:

Volatile matter, 13.75 (water 1.40, gas 12.35); coke, 86.25 (fixed carbon 82.25, ashes, flesh color, 4.00). This coal swells up considerably in coking.

At Long's opening, on the southeast quarter of Section 32, Township 7 north, Range 31 west, the coal has the same thickness. The only difference is that the clay parting is from half an inch to an inch thicker than at Greene's bank. The dip is nearly the same.

A specimen from this bank yielded by analysis: Volatile matter, 14.50 (water 3.80, gas 10.70); coke, 75.50 (fixed carbon 84.10, ashes, light brown, 1.40).

This coal swelled up a great deal in coking, and gave off a gas which burned with a strong flame.

These analyses prove this coal to be semi-bituminous, like some of the coals in George Creek Valley, Maryland, and are far richer in fixed carbon than most of the coals in the western States, and, therefore, of course, almost twice as durable in the fire, with proper access of air. It contains just enough volatile combustible matter to keep it ignited without the artificial blast required for anthracite. If it can be mined free from pyrites and shale, it is one of the most valuable kinds of coal that can be offered in the market, especially for manufacturing purposes, if it be properly managed under a knowledge of its composition.

The Jenny Lind coal is situated from eight to ten miles from the Arkansas River. Both its quality and thickness must exercise a most important influence on the future prospects of Sebastian County, especially in the location of lines of railroad in the valley of the Arkansas River.

On Big Creek there is a three-foot vein of coal, probably equivalent to the Jenny Lind coal, which is well spoken of by blacksmiths.

In the ridge south of Jenny Lind coal, judging by the dip of the strata and character of the rocks, the coal must run out. A sudden reversal of the dip, however, brings the coal in again on James' Fork, and in Hodge's Prairie. The summit level between Long Prairie and James Creek is 240 feet, and is composed of shale capped with sandstone, dipping at an angle of 30° south 10° to 20° east. A cellular sandstone is intercalated in the mass of the shale of this ridge, which rock I find persistent throughout this part of Arkansas, and is, undoubtedly, when deep-seated in the synclinal troughs, a siliferous or salt-bearing sandstone.

The coal on the Sand Ridge branch of James' Fork, in Section 22, Township 6, Range 33 west, is owned by G. B. Morrow on the McMurtry estate. This coal, as far as entered, is three and a half feet, and seems to be increasing in thickness as it is followed into the bank. It is divided into two members of about equal thickness, by a shale parting of one inch, and rests on a bed of white clay. The succession of the strata in the ridge between the Jenny Lind and the James' Fork coal, appears to be as follows:

Thin-bedded and flaggy sandstone.

Heavier-bedded sandstone (the Greenwood building stone).

Cellular or saliferous sandstone.

Thinner-bedded sandstone with argillaceous flakes, containing equisetaceæ and other fossil plants.

Variegated shales.

These strata, which geologically belong under the coal, must have a thickness of 500 feet or more. A measurement was made by the aneroid barometer, on June 20, 1859, of the peak of the Sugar Loaf Range, near the Line road, in the vicinity of

Taylor's. It was found to be 1,230 feet above Taylor's, and 1,410 feet above Thomas Hicks'.

The structure of the mountain was found to be approximately as follows:

Schistose sandstone with intercalated bands of sandstone, 340 feet.

Conspicuous bench of heavy bedded sandstone, 90 feet.

Dark gray and variegated shales (easily decomposing), 800 feet.

From the summit of the Sugar Loaf Mountain there is an extensive prospect into the Indian country on the west, with a perfectly conical peak in the foreground, a few miles beyond the Indian boundary, of considerable greater elevation than the peak measured. On West Creek, a branch of James' Creek, a two-foot vein has been opened by the blacksmith at two different localities about two and a half miles apart.

A thick bed of coal occurs on James' Fork, one mile north of west of Sugar Creek Post-office, known as the More coal-bank. It is supposed to be six feet thick. Three and one-half miles east of More's mill there is a good coal, on the property of J. R. Smoot, on the water of James' Fork. Also at 'Squire Sorrell's, three miles south of James' Fork, of which coal there is only about one foot exposed in the bed of the stream, but extending to an unknown depth below. The probable thickness is about two feet. Here the coal dips at an angle of 40° to 50° north 10° to 20° west.

There are a number of coal banks in this vicinity, all within eight miles of each other. I had an opportunity of examining a good natural exposure of coal three-quarters of a mile below More's mill, on James' Fork. It crops out under a bank of variegated ferruginous shales, with numerous thin bands of slaty and kidney hydrated oxide of iron.

The coal is three and one-half to four feet in thickness, and dips at an angle of nearly 10°. There are block shale and coal rash, measuring about nine inches, insinuated between the coal and the fire clay. The coal lies fifteen feet above the waters of James' Creek. A section of this bank is as follows:

Sandstone with calamites.

Variegated shales with iron ore, twenty-one feet.

Coal, three feet six inches.

Block shale and coal rash, one foot.

Fire clay, one foot.

Flaggy sandstone with calamites.

This coal lies very conveniently for mining, as it can be worked without being incommoded by water, which is apt to be the case with most of the coals in this part of Sebastian County.

On the northeast part of the northwest quarter of Section 26, Township 5 north, Range 31 west, is a four-foot coal, on Cherokee Creek. This coal is covered with three or four feet of gray shale, and dips nearly 45°.

Coal also shows itself on the southeast corner of Section 24, Township 5 north, Range 31 west; also on the southwest corner of Section 23, the same township, and can be traced for about half a mile, maintaining a thickness of about four feet. On the southeast of Section 9, Township 4 north, Range 32 west, coal is again visible, on the property of Timothy Bloodworth; also on Section 27, Township 5 north, Range 31 west. This latter bank is from twenty to twenty-five feet above the bed of the creek, and has never been properly opened so as to show its whole thickness.

It is probable that the whole of Hodge's Prairie, north of these coal out-crops, is underlaid by this bed of coal, which could be reached by shafts of moderate depth.

The following, which is supplementary to the foregoing, is copied from Mr. Carnall's "Notes on Western Arkansas:" We were acquainted with Mr. Owen, afforded him some facilities for finding the beds, and got from him much valuable information; but there are now five beds open, and their thickness and extent known, where there was one when he made his reconnoissance. Numerous banks near Jenny Lind, all four to seven feet thick, are now open, and where he speaks of a thick bed of coal on James' Fork, the whole country, mountain and valley, is found to be underlaid with coal four to eleven feet thick, and we sent a block six feet thick from there to the Louisville Exposition, so that instead of Jenny Lind being the most important locality, it may be near Sugar Loaf Mountain, twenty-five miles from Fort

Smith. Mr. Owen says if it can be mined free from pyrites and shale it is one of the most valuable kinds that can be offered in the market. We say it can be, and has been for twenty years, mined free from pyrites and shale, and there is no trouble to do this. Sometimes a piece of shale sticks to it, but in mining it is struck off and cast aside; and any pyrites, so far as our information extends, is in blocks or lumps, readily distinguishable by appearance and weight, and never comes to market with the coal. This coal is universally used by the people for fires, and hauled twelve miles it is cheaper than wood, if you have to cut the wood. It is used for making steam, and is, we believe, equal to the Pittsburgh coal for that purpose, and if there is any coal better for heating, steam, coking, etc., we do not happen to know it, and it has this advantage, unknown to us to be common to any other western coal, it has no smoke.

The following is an extract from the geological report of Prof. C. B. Gannaway, made in June 1883:

By reference to the table showing the mines opened, it will be seen that the coal extends throughout the entire county.

Coal banks opened are: Claybourn, thickness of coal (?) feet; Harris, 6 feet; Gwyn, 6 feet; Noblet, 3 feet; West, 3 feet; Patterson, 3 feet; Pulliam, 3 feet; Martin, 4 feet; Kersh, 7½ feet—200-foot tunnel, 8-foot vein, with two 3-inch shale partings; Edmonson, 6 feet; Spessard, 6 feet; Dale, 4 feet; Douglas, 5½ feet; Emor, 5 feet—shaft 50 feet to coal, hoisted by engine; Sparks, 5 feet; Petty, 5½ feet—two tunnels, 100 and 300 feet; Mendenhall, 5 feet; Smart, 4 feet; Bostic, 5 feet; Cambell 1½ feet.

Wells in which coal have been found: Brewster, thickness of coal, 7 feet; well near Chocoville, 8 feet; Parson Young, 4 feet; Gwyn, 16 feet; Gwyn's shaft, 7 feet; Anthony Lewis, 7 feet; Armstrong, 7 feet; James Chastine, 10 feet; Widow Clayton, 3 feet; Hackett City public well, 3 feet; Yount's, 5 feet; Izell's, 2½ feet; J. H. Kirby's, (?) feet; S. W. Dale's, 14 feet.

Iron.—The same authority gives the following pertaining to the iron ore deposits:

The iron deposits of Sebastian County are co-extensive with the coal. It is a rare exception to find a bed of coal that is not overlaid by numerous strata of spathos iron ore. These strata often occur in great numbers, varying in thickness from one to eight inches at cropping. These strata are separated by from one-half to ten feet of ferruginous shale. A series of strata is reported on the southwest quarter of Section 24, Township 5 north, Range 31 west, some numbers of which measure fourteen inches in thickness; number of strata not known. Skirting Mazzard Prairie is a succession of slate hills with heavy deposits of spathic iron; in fact this is the only mineral we may look to as a source of iron in this region, as iron in the presence of carbonaceous matter (coal) is invariably found in the form of carbonate. I have examined numerous specimens of clay iron stone (an argillaceous carbonate), but generally they are too poor in iron to attract the notice of an iron master. The spathos ore, occurring as black-band, is the prevailing ore, and owing to its property of easy reduction this ore is profitably worked in many sections."

Building Stone.—Prof. Gannaway further says: "The numerous ridges which traverse Sebastian County furnish the best of freestone (sandstone). In color it is from gray to blue in some localities, but the prevailing color is gray, sometimes tinged with yellow, from presence of quantities of peroxide of iron. This stone is compact, easily worked when first taken out, hardens on exposure to weather, suffers no disintegration when exposed to moisture and cold; in fact it is as staple for building purposes as the best granite. The point which attracts most universal attention is the regular form in which the stone occurs. At Greenwood, sixteen miles southeast from Fort Smith, a quarry has been opened, showing strata from one-half inch to one foot thick, having a perfectly smooth bed, requiring no dressing whatever. Each stratum is uniform in thickness, and may be taken out in regular forms containing 100 square feet of surface. Should a railroad penetrate this section flagging would be quite an item of export. Quarries have been opened south and east of Fort Smith, southeast of Salem, and, in fact, near every small town in the county."

There is on exhibition in the rooms of the chamber of commerce, in the city of Fort Smith, specimens of the different qualities of coal, iron ore, slate and other natural productions found in

Sebastian County, the site of which will well repay a visit to their rooms.

Soil.—The best information concerning the soil and its productiveness is furnished by Mr. John Carnall, an old and well posted citizen of Sebastian County, in his "Notes on Western Arkansas," as follows: "Our soil from the west line of the State, extending east, say 100 miles, and from the benches of the Boston Mountains on the north to those of Poteau and other mountains on the south, say forty to fifty miles wide, and through which the Arkansas River flows, and which we call the Arkansas Valley, is most generally a light yellow, called a mulatto soil, but in many sections it is a light red. It will ordinarily produce, with good cultivation an average of three-fourths of a bale of cotton, twenty-five to thirty-five bushels of corn, ten to fifteen bushels of wheat, twenty to forty bushels of oats, two to three tons of millet hay per acre.

"This, it is to be understood, is the general upland soil of the country, not including creek or river bottoms, and there is a great similarity in it all through this valley; the woodlands and the prairies not differing greatly in quality of soil, and the level, undulating and hilly is in soil much the same, the hilly having some rock intermixed.

"The river bottom lands on the Arkansas River are among the best in the world, and will produce, with good cultivation, from $1\frac{1}{2}$ to 2 bales of cotton, 75 to 100 bushels corn, 30 to 40 bushels wheat, 3 to 5 tons millet per acre, and the creek bottoms will average a mean between the uplands and river bottoms. A peculiar feature of the uplands of this whole country is the remarkable retentive quality of its fertility. This is owing to the sub-soil of clay, which retains the fertilizing qualities, and at the same time prevents the lands from washing. * * * Many of our farmers are now making two crops a year on the same land. This is quite noticeable in and around Fort Smith, where market gardening is carried on; two crops of potatoes, two of millet, or a crop of potatoes and one of turnips, of wheat or oats, and then peas or millet, etc."

ORIGINAL OCCUPANCY.

Mound Builders.—It is believed by scientists and archæologists, that away back in the dim, shadowy past—" a time to which the memory of man runneth not to the contrary "—in an age prehistoric, that this country was inhabited and occupied by a race of people known as the Mound Builders—this name being attributed to them on account of the various kinds of earthworks, and their contents which they left behind them. Evidences of the existence of such a race of people on the American continent, before it was occupied by the Indians, have been found in all portions of the United States, but the question as to whether they were a race of people that long ago became extinct cannot be discussed here, for the reason that it is not profitable to discuss a subject about which little or nothing can be definitely known. There are some earth formations in Sebastian County supposed by some to have been made by the Mound Builders, but so far as they have been explored nothing of interest leading to a certainty as to whether they were formed by nature or by man has been found.

Indians.—There is positive history, however, that the Indian or Red Man occupied this country when it was first discovered and encroached upon by the present race of white people. When the United States obtained title from France to the territory lying west of the Mississippi, it became necessary to treat with the Indians to secure their titles also, not that it was recognized that such savage, untutored beings had any title to the lands more than belonged to the wild animals that also inhabited them, but for the purpose of getting peaceable possession of them and to secure safety, if possible, for the early settlers.

That numerous and powerful tribe of Indians known as the Osages claimed the territory from the Missouri River on the north to the Red River on the south, and the Quawpaw tribe of Indians also inhabited and claimed Central or Western Arkansas, and after their removal from Georgia and other States the Choctaws and Cherokees inhabited and claimed a part of Western Arkansas. The original Indian occupants, however, were the Osages and Quawpaws. These Indian titles were finally extinguished by treaties at the following times and places, to wit: With the Great and Little Osages on the 10th of November, 1808, at Fort Clark, on the Missouri; with the Quawpaws in August, 1818, for a portion of their claim, and again in November, 1824, for the balance; with the Choctaws on the 20th of October, 1820; and again with the Great and Little Osage tribes on the 25th of September, 1825, at St. Louis.

Wild Animals and Game.—When the settlement of the Territory composing Sebastian County began, all the wild animals native to this part of the continent were found roaming at large. The buffaloes, however, were not very numerous, and lingered only a few years after being pursued by the white hunter. Bears, wolves, panthers, catamounts, wildcats, deer, elk, antelopes and the smaller animals were here in great numbers. The bears were hunted and killed by the pioneers, who used their meat for food and their skins for bedding and raiment, but they have become almost extinct, except as one is now and then found strayed away from their mountain fastnesses in the counties farther south. The wolves have ceased to be troublesome, but still a few remain in the mountains remote from the settlements. Likewise with the other savage animals. Now and then a deer is found in the mountain retreats. In the early days they were extensively hunted and killed, and their flesh was extensively used for food, and their skins for men's clothing. The elk and antelopes have become extinct. The smaller animals remain in considerable numbers. Wild turkeys were originally very abundant, and were extensively used for food. They are now found only in limited numbers. Ducks and other wild fowl are still found along the water courses.

SETTLEMENT.

Fort Smith Military Post.—The authentic date of the first settlement of the territory now composing Sebastian County is that of the establishment of the military post at Fort Smith, in October or November, 1817. That there were white settlers, farmers and traders here before that time there is no doubt, but if so their names and history, except that of Capt. John Rogers, the first white settler on the site of Fort Smith, have not been preserved. He came soon after the battle of New Orleans terminated the War of 1812, and was afterward appointed first sutler to this post. Some of the soldiers who first came to garrison the post became permanent settlers. Among them was Aaron Barling, the father of Mrs. Jerry Kannady, now living in Fort Smith. After leaving the garrison, about the year 1828, he settled on the military road nine miles east of Fort Smith, and there for many years kept a house for the entertainment of travelers. The following letter, addressed to the committee appointed to collect historical matter for the centennial celebration held at Fort Smith in 1886, and embraced in Col. Ben T. Duval's address on that occasion, is of much interest pertaining to the settlement of this part of the country:

BILLINGSLEY P. O., ARK., June 26, 1876.

Sir: In answer to your note of June 21, I have this to say: My father, with two other families, moved from Middle Tennessee—Charles Adams and Samuel Williams, six in each family, making in all eighteen persons. It was in 1814 we came to the post of Arkansas in a flat-boat. There we found a small French and Creole village. The Quapaw Indians lived on the south side of the river. There we exchanged our flat-boat for a keel-boat with an old Indian trader; there was nothing like steamboats on the Mississippi River then. We made our way the best we could until we got to the Cadron, where we found one of my father's brothers, who had moved from Kentucky in an early day. We stayed there one year, then there was a treaty made with the Cherokees. They then lived on the Illinois and Point Remove Creeks, on the north side of the river. Some of them lived also on the south side of the river, on Shoal Creek—that is Boal's Village. They moved to Texas, to Cherokee County. Then we moved to Big Mulberry in 1816. We numbered about eighteen families, and lived there two years, in all the luxuries of life that a new country could afford, such as buffalo and bear, deer and elk meat, and fish and honey. And we had pound-cake every day, for we beat all the meal that we eat in a mortar; and the first year our corn gave out about six weeks before roasting-ears came in; the substitute for bread was venison, dried by the fire in a mortar and made in small cakes and fried in bear's oil; that *hoap* us out until forward Irish potatoes came in. We had all things in common. We had no doctors nor lawyers in those happy days. The first Legislature was held at the post of Arkansas. My father was a member. We had no tax to pay but county tax, the General Government paid all the balance. About that time Maj. Bradford came to Fort Smith and set up that post, and we furnished him with buffalo meat for the soldiers, and then we got some flour from him, which was a great treat to us. All the way Maj. Bradford got the mail then was by sending a soldier to the post of Arkansas in a canoe, which took him about three weeks to make the trip. Then the Government made another treaty with the Indians, and we moved to the south side of the river, and commenced settling all along the river from Fort Smith to the present seat of government; first some in McClain's Bottom, some at Dardenelle, some on Shoal Creek, and so on. And we soon got strict enough to hold camp-meetings, and everybody went and left their houses for a week at a time, and when they came back everything was all right. We then generally built our chimneys up to the mantel-piece, and hung our meat outside on the ribs of the house.

If any man had a lock on any of his doors in those days he would have been looked on with suspicion. We, about this time, began to get some mail contracts, and soon after that some law mixt in. We had some old fashioned brake-downs on a dirt floor, and if any of us lost a toe-nail we never said anything about it. You must excuse bad writing, etc. In haste,

JOHN BILLINGSLEY.

N. B. I have a little more time, and will go a little further. The county of Crawford at that time contained all of Washington and Sebastian, and the first court that was held in Crawford was at Fort Smith, by Judge Bates, of Batesville. All offices were filled by appointment of the governor. The first clerk that was appointed was George Pickett, and the first sheriff was James Wilson, and the first esquire was McClane, of McClane's Bottom. Well, the way men dressed themselves in those days was by dressing their deer-skins and making full suits of the same. There was occasionally a French trader came up the river in large canoes and brought domestics, calico and checks, and some earthenware and cutlery. We paid them 50 cents per yard for calico, 37½ cents for domestics, and 40 cents for checks. I gave $4 for the first set of teacups I ever owned, and very common at that; and $2 for a small dish, such as you get now for 50 cents, and $4 for a set of knives and forks, and common at that. We paid for all things in beaver, otter, bear and deer-skins and bear's oil and beeswax. The first settler was Capt. Rogers, and he got very rich. So I close at this time.

J. B.

Other Settlers.—In addition to the early settlers mentioned who settled in and around about Fort Smith were the following, viz.: Clark Landers, H. A. Quesenbury, the father of the eccentric genius, William Quesenbury, William Tichenal, Matthew Moore, Robert Sinclair, George S. and Charles A. Birnie, Matthew Moss, Gen. Nicks, Robert Gibson, Curry Barnett, James McDavid, Alfred Ray, Dr. David D. Williams, Stagner and William Duval, father of Col. Ben. T. Duval, who in 1825 came from Virginia, and ascended the Arkansas River in a keel-boat, and established a trading post on the land afterward owned by his son, Dr. Elias R. Duval. In 1829 he moved his family from Virginia to Fort Smith, and resided there until his death, which occurred in 1851, from an attack of cholera. In the extreme early days of Fort Smith, William Quesenbury, W. H. Rogers and Ben. T. Duval were the only boys in and about the place. Maj. Ben. Moore, from Virginia, settled in 1821, at Moore's Rock, on the Arkansas River, about eighteen miles below Fort Smith, on the farm now occupied by John B. Luce. At his own expense he cut a channel for the passage of vessels through the bed-rock which extended across the river at his place. He was the first individual who raised cotton and tobacco in this part of the county, and built the first grist-mill between Fort Smith and Little Rock. John Penn Dillard, a lawyer, came from Lynchburg, Va., in 1822, and settled at Old Crawford Court-house, and in his log cabin he entertained the lawyers who came there from a distance to attend court. In 1823 James Griggs settled near Sulphur Springs. Judge James Woodson Bates, brother of the renowned Frederick and Edward Bates, and who presided at the first court ever held at Fort Smith, settled on a farm near Moore's Rock about the year 1830, and lived there until his death, which occurred in 1846. He married a daughter of Maj. Ben. Moore, and sister of Mrs. Dillard, now of Fort Smith. Judge Hugh Knox settled on what is known as the "Knox Farm," on the Arkansas River, about eight miles below Fort Smith. Gen. Matthew Arbuckle, who, as colonel of the Seventh United States Infantry, was the second commander of the post of Fort Smith, settled on Arbuckle's Island, on the Arkansas River, twenty-five miles below Fort Smith. William Moore and Ben. Moore, Jr., settled at Moore's Rock the same time that Maj. Ben. Moore settled that place. Jack Tittsworth settled on the Little Rock road, at Short Mountain, and kept a house for the entertainment of travelers, his being the first house of entertainment on that road next below Aaron Barrings. Judge Jesse Turner, who now resides at Van Buren, was an early settler of Old Crawford Court-house, and has followed the county seat of Crawford County from place to place to its final location.

Among the later early settlers of Fort Smith were Capt. Nat. Gookin,* who was also one of the first school-teachers in the place; Jerry R. Kannady, who for many years was a prominent and much respected citizen, settled here in 1836, where he resided until his death, which occurred April 25, 1882. His widow survives him, and is still a resident of the place. Dr. Joseph H. Bailey and John Stryker were also early citizens of Fort Smith. Dr. J. H. T. Main settled here in March, 1838; and

*He married the Widow Kannady, mother of Jerry Kannady and sister of Capt. John Rogers.

the only citizens of the place of that date who now survive with the Doctor are John Stryker, Col. Ben. T. Duval, William H. Rogers and Mrs. Jerry Kannady, and perhaps one or two other ladies. Michael Manning, a resident of Fort Smith, now over eighty years of age, and who unfortunately has lost his sight, but still has a bright intellect and a wonderful memory, hired himself to a government agent in New Orleans to come here and work on the fort. He arrived May 10, 1840, and has resided here ever since. Col. Samuel M. Rutherford, the first representative in the General Assembly from this county, and afterward judge of the county and probate courts thereof, was also an early settler. He died April 1, 1867. Maj. Elias Rector was an early settler, and a citizen of the Fort Smith vicinity for over forty years. He died at his residence in 1878. Another old settler was Joseph Armorer, who came here some time in "the thirties." W. H. Mayers came from Maryland in 1841, settled in Fort Smith, and was for many years engaged with his brother, M. Mayers, in mercantile business.

Eaton Tatum, at whose house Sebastian County was organized, came from Missouri and settled at Jenny Lind in 1843; at that time there were settlements, in addition to those named, at Greenwood, Hodge's Prairie, Mazzard Prairie and in the Sugar Loaf Valley. The only settlers then at Greenwood were Reuben Coker and his two brothers, Henry and John, and Coleman Norris, and Dr. Allen was the only one in Sugar Loaf Valley. On Mazzard Prairie were Jesse Ross and Samuel Caldwell. James J. Baker, now a merchant in Greenwood, settled at Jenny Lind in 1845. His nearest neighbors were then Maj. Tatum, of that place; John G. Little, who lived less than a mile east thereof; the widow Welty and her sons, John and Henry, who lived on the Vache Grass, two and a half miles northeast; W. O. Hunter, who lived one mile east; —— Donaldson, who lived two and a half miles east; Judge James Clark, who lived the same distance northeast; Henry Ross, who lived two miles north, and Jesse Ross (already mentioned), who lived four miles north on Mazzard Prairie; and between the latter and Long Prairie, and on Long Prairie, was a little colony of Germans: Christopher Grober, Peter Euper, Casper Euper, Gottlieb Ellichen and Julius

Richards. Perhaps these were not all there in 1845, at the date of Mr. Baker's settlement, but were either there then or came soon thereafter. The first settlers on Mazzard Prairie, in addition to those already named, were Jesse, Thomas and Seaburn Standifer and Samuel B. Stevens. The early settlers were very fond of horse-racing, and near the residence of Samuel Caldwell, on the south edge of Mazzard Prairie, they prepared and maintained a race-track on which they trained their horses for speed.

James Rogers settled one mile east of Greenwood, and Coleman Norris immediately south. Reuben Coker lived where Judge C. B. Neal now lives, at Greenwood; Henry Coker near by, and John, his brother, a little to the north. Anderson Tinker settled a short distance southwest of Greenwood, and John Miller two miles due south, and beyond him James Morris. The latter two were stock raisers. Jordan Smith settled one and a half miles west of Greenwood; James and Mason Fletcher three miles north; Leonard Spradling six and William McAllister eight miles north. Farther down on the Vache Grass were the settlements of W. L. Seaman, William Price, William Ward, Grandy Ake and Judge Charles Milor; the latter at the mouth of Vache Grass.

Among the early settlers in the vicinity of the present village of Salem (Witcherville) were Walter T. Woodson, who came from Virginia in 1846, and settled one-half mile southeast thereof; Ransom Pilley, who came from North Carolina in 1849, and settled one mile southeast thereof; George Maynard, a Baptist preacher, who came from Tennessee some time prior to 1850, and settled one and a half miles west of the site of the village; John Martindale, who came from Missouri, and settled one and a half miles northwest thereof; Churchill Jones, one mile south; Joel Allison, one mile northeast; John Robins, from Tennessee, two miles west, and Joseph Evans, from Alabama, between one and two miles west. All of these are dead except, probably, Joel Allison, who moved away. William J. Witcher came from Virginia in 1850, and settled on the site of Salem, and afterward established the village, and still resides there, and as a servant of Uncle Sam distributes mail to his subjects. The same year Thomas Powers came from Indiana, and settled near Witcher's place, and afterward moved to California. Benjamin French and Thomas Sprouse, some time in "the forties," came from Alabama, and settled in the same neighborhood, and afterward moved to Texas. Also in "the forties," James T. Gillim came from Tennessee, and settled where he still lives, one and a half miles west of Salem.

In 1851 Levi Barrett came from Georgia, and settled on Horse Shoe Ridge, one the site of the present town of Huntington, where he and his aged wife still reside. Eli Shackleford, James Wilson. Charles Burton and Samuel Brown, all now deceased, were among the first settlers in this vicinity. Blany Harper, deceased, settled the place south of the ridge where Joseph Martin now lives. John Nelson, now deceased, came from Tennessee, and settled two miles west of the present town of Huntington. Squire Frazier came from North Carolina, and settled where he now resides, about three miles from Huntington. Abe West, now deceased, came from Tennessee, and settled between the present towns of Huntington and Mansfield. The early settlers of the extreme southern part of Sebastian County, in the valley between the Sugar Loaf and Poteau Mountains, known as the Sugar Loaf Valley, who settled there in "the forties," were James, Jack and Ned Tucker, who came from Mississippi; Earley Bales, Glenn, Fleming, Bloodworth, Squire Stafford, Dr. Allen, Daniel Dees, Rev. Snedley, Nicholson, Casey, Gist, Hart, O'Neal, Mayes and Norton. All of these, who settled there prior to 1846, are now dead. Dr. Walker, who lives in the same valley, but in the edge of Scott County, and who now practices law at Mansfield, settled there in 1846, and is the only surviving settler who resided there at that date. Later early settlers in the vicinity of the town of Hartford were C. E. Goddard, who came from Washington County in 1858; William Barnes, John Patton, Thomas Chronnister, William Woodson and Dr. J. D. Williams.

The early settlers of the vicinity of Hackett City and of the west central portion of the county were as follows: In 1839 William Tichenal settled at the place now called Jenson, and subsequently about a mile south of the present town of Hackett, where he lived until 1851, and then went to California, where he is believed to be still living. About the year 1830 William H.

McMurtry came from Missouri and settled near the line of the Indian Territory, and two miles west of the site of Hackett City, and near the same time William Fleming settled on the James Fork, two miles south of the latter place. Fleming moved away, and about the year 1851 his place was occupied by Matthew Moore. About the year 1839 Jacob Bender, formerly a soldier in the United States Army, settled one mile west of the site of Hackett City. James Green settled on the place where Mr. McMurtry, son of William H. McMurtry, now lives, at Hackett City. Thomas Patton, a blacksmith, settled on the site of this town, on the west side of the branch, some time prior to 1845. About the year 1843 a Mr. Pulliam settled a mile and a quarter southeast of the site of Hackett City, and Thomas Patton, the blacksmith, moved onto the same place about the year 1847, and lived there until he was killed in a cyclone a few years ago. Carbon Howell settled a little farther east. Samuel Sorrells and Lewis Brewer settled on Sorrells' Prairie over fifty years ago. Jeremiah Hackett came from Ohio in 1841, and settled on the place where he now lives, one mile southwest of Hackett City. In 1851 J. M. Hicks settled on the line five miles south of Jenson, and established a trading place for the Indians, the article mostly purchased by them being whisky. The Weltys and Reasoners and Ned Moore settled at the base of the Sugar Loaf Mountain, on the north side. In 1840 Harmon Mickell settled about seven miles south of Fort Smith, and about the same time John McMurtrey settled six miles north of Hackett City. Elzie Hano settled two miles northeast of the latter place, and P. Evans about a mile farther east. The latter was a soldier under Gen. Jackson in the battle of the Horseshoe, and during the late Civil War he was killed by a Confederate soldier after he had been captured.

By reference to dates it will be observed that the settlement of the territory of Sebastian County began at Fort Smith in 1817, and then followed down the river; that the portion bordering on the river was first settled, and that the central and southern portion of the county was not settled to any considerable extent until after the year 1840. Prior to 1850 the country was settled very slowly, after that more rapidly.

Referring to the early settlers of the county Col. Duval, in his historical address of 1876, said:

In those days there was a close sympathy and brotherhood among the people. Persons living fifty miles apart were neighbors in all the term implies. A camp-meeting, a funeral or a dance would bring them together. The ladies, young and old, would often travel over a great distance, on a visit or to a dance. They had to travel on horseback, for even in my day a buggy or carriage was unknown. The young ladies would pack their party finery in a satchel or saddle-bags, mount their steeds and joyfully ride fifty miles to a dance. There are some here to-day of both sexes who have attended parties under these circumstances, and they will tell you, with the sparkle of other days in their eyes, that those dances, often prolonged till "broad daylight," and repeated for several nights, on the rude puncheons, by the light of a tallow dip or pine knot, to the music of the fiddle and tambourine, were merrier and afforded more genuine pleasure than you can enjoy with the luxurious surroundings of a full band of music in a splendid hall.*

COUNTY ORGANIZATION.

Creating Act.—The act of the General Assembly creating the county of Sebastian was approved January 10, 1851, by Gov. John Seldon Roane. It provided as follows:

That all that portion of the county of Crawford lying south of the Arkansas River, and also all that portion of the counties of Scott and Polk included in the following boundaries, viz.: Beginning on the western bouudary line of Crawford County at low water mark, on the south side of the Arkansas River, running south with said western boundary line to where said line intersects the northern boundary line of Scott County; thence south with the western boundary line of Scott County to where said line intersects the northern boundary line of Polk County; thence south with the western boundary line of Polk County to the base line; thence east with said base line to the range line between Ranges 30 and 31 west of the fifth principal meridian; thence north with the said range line to where it intersects the Black Jack Ridge; thence in the middle of the top of said ridge, to where said ridge is crossed by the range line between Ranges 29 and 30 west; thence north with said range line to where it intersects the township line between Townships 5 and 6 north; thence east with said township line to where it intersects the range line between Ranges 28 and 29 west; thence north with said range line to the southern boundary line of Franklin County; thence west with the said boundary line of Franklin County to where said line intersects the eastern boundary line of Crawford County; thence north with said line to the middle of the main channel of the Arkansas River; thence west up the middle of the main channel of the Arkansas River to where the main channel of said river is intersected by the western boundary line of Crawford County; thence south to the place of beginning.

*For a description of the "pioneer's cabin," "pioneer weddings" and other customs of the settlers, see "History of Benton County" elsewhere in this work.

According to this description Sebastian County originally extended clear across, and included the western part of Scott, and also a small portion of the northwestern part of Polk County. The act creating the county was drawn up by the Hon. Ben. T. Duval, one of the original surviving settlers of Fort Smith, who was at that time clerk of the House of Representatives, and was presented by Harvey Steward, a member from Crawford County. In the convention of 1861 the southern boundary of the county was fixed, by ordinance, on the top of the Poteau Mountains, and the territory taken from Scott and Polk Counties was restored. A more definite description of the boundary lines of Sebastian County, as now recognized, is as follows:

Beginning at the point where the middle of the main channel of the Arkansas River intersects the western boundary of the State of Arkansas, thence running south on said western boundary line to the township line between Townships 3 and 4 north; thence east on said township line to the range line between Ranges 30 and 31 west; thence north on said range line to the township and correction line between Townships 4 and 5 north; thence west on said township and correction line (a mile and a quarter more or less) to the corrected range line; thence north on said range line to the middle of Black Jack Ridge; thence in a northeasterly direction along the middle of said ridge to the range line between Ranges 29 and 30 west; thence north on said range line to the township line between Townships 5 and 6 north; thence east on said township line to the range line between Ranges 28 and 29 west; thence north on the range line (five miles more or less) to the southern boundary of Franklin County; thence west with the southern boundary of that county to the middle of Range 29 west; thence north on section lines and on western boundary of Franklin County to the middle of the main channel of the Arkansas River; thence up the middle of the main channel of said river to place of beginning.

Seat of Justice.—The act creating the county located the temporary seat of justice at the house of Eaton Tatum, who afterward laid out a town there, which, upon the suggestion of Charles A. Hinkley, a member of the bar, was named Jenny Lind, in honor of the celebrated songstress of that name. The county, as it was then composed, embraced Big Creek, Upper and Sugar Loaf Townships of the parent county, Crawford. The first election for county officers was held on the 27th of January, 1851, and resulted in the selection of James Clark as county judge, Samuel Brooke Stephens, sheriff, both of whom died many years ago, and John Carnall, formerly sheriff of Crawford

County, as clerk. At the same time two commissioners for the county at large, and one from each civil township, were elected to select a site for and locate the county seat. John D. Arbuckle and Reuben Coker were elected at large, John Jones from Big Creek, Samuel Edmondson from Upper, and William Stafford from Sugar Loaf.

These commissioners met at Jenny Lind in May, 1851, and located the seat of justice on forty acres of land lying in Section 12, Township 6 north, Range 31 west, and donated by Reuben Coker for that purpose. They also named the place Greenwood. Fort Smith was then a rival point for the county seat, and was preferred as such by its citizens, as well as by many citizens in the northwestern part of the county. A contest immediately arose between those preferring the respective places named, as to where the public buildings should be constructed. This contest resulted, the following year, in the removal of the county seat to Fort Smith, where it remained until 1854, when it was taken back, by a majority vote of the people, to Greenwood. The following quotations are taken from the historical address of Col. Ben. T. Duval, delivered at Fort Smith July 4, 1876:

> The contest over, the location of the county seat increased in bitterness, and the town and country were arrayed in open hostility to the great detriment to the public interests. It engendered mutual hatred and distrust between the sections, and had its influence upon all the elections. In 1861 John T. London, who lived at Greenwood, and myself, then as now a resident of Fort Smith, were members of the House of Representatives, and Green J. Clark, who was also a citizen of Greenwood, was the senator. We agreed upon an act dividing the county into two judicial districts. The Fort Smith District to have two terms a year of the circuit court and four terms of the probate court, to be held at Fort Smith, and a like number of each at Greenwood. This act removed the sting from the vexed question, and was accepted as a fair compromise. The county organization, as to its revenue and general business, was left intact, and the county court for the whole county was still to hold its sessions at Greenwood.
>
> After the reconstruction in 1864, under the proclamation of President Lincoln, the circuit court was held at this place for the whole county. But, after the restoration of peace in 1865, the courts were held at both Greenwood and Fort Smith, as provided for under the act of 1861. In 1868 the county seat question was again revived, and under an act of the Legislature of that year an election was held. After an angry and bitter contest over the result, the records were removed to this place, and all the courts for the county were held here for a short time. At the session of the General Assembly of 1871 an act was passed dividing the county into two districts, with separate revenue, and,

in fact, making two distinct counties in one. This act was declared by the supreme court to be unconstitutional, and they also held that the act of 1861 was still in force, notwithstanding the election of 1868. The courts were again divided. The Constitutional Convention of 1874, by a provision inserted in the Constitution, provided that this county should be divided into two judicial districts, with separate county courts, separate revenue, and each paying its own expenses. So now we have two separate districts, with county, circuit and probate courts for each as distinct as of two counties, yet under one general organization.

As divided into districts Upper Township, including the city of Fort Smith, comprises the Fort Smith District, and the Greenwood District includes all the balance of the county.

Public Buildings.—The first court-house built by Sebastian County was erected on the public square at Greenwood in 1856–57. It was a two-story frame structure, fifty feet square, with the county offices on the first floor, and the court-room above. It was built by Peter K. Beam. Prior to that time the courts were held in private houses. This court-house was burned down in 1881. The county offices, and the records that were saved from the conflagration, were moved to a mercantile building standing on the east side of the street, a short distance north of the northwest corner of the public square. The following year this building was also burned. In these conflagrations many of the early records were entirely destroyed, and others so damaged as to render them nearly worthless. Soon after this the citizens of Greenwood contributed about $2,500 toward paying for the construction of a new court-house, and the county court made an order for the erection of the present building, which cost, in its present unfinished condition, $5,555. It is a two-story brick house set upon a rock foundation, and it is in size 50x54 feet. The first story contains the hall, stairs and county offices, and the second the court-room. About the time that the first court-house was erected, a jail eighteen feet square was built for the county by Coleman Norris, the contractor. It stood where the Harper House now stands. It was constructed with three walls made of logs, and stood upon a stone foundation. The logs of the outer and inner walls were placed in a horizontal position, and those of the middle wall in a perpendicular position. These three walls were closed together, thus making a combined wall of three logs in thickness. A jail constructed in this manner, upon a rock foundation and floor, and ceiled with logs crossed in manner similar to the side walls, with the inside face of the walls and ceiling driven full of spikes, will hold prisoners as safely as any that can be composed of rock, iron and steel, and constructed with all modern facilities. This jail was used until about the year 1886, when it was abandoned, and at the present writing the county has no jail.

Prior to the building of the court-house and city hall, which is now under construction, the Fort Smith District of the county has erected no public buildings for county purposes. Prior to 1872 the officers of the district occupied rooms in a building on the corner of Walnut and Second Streets, and in 1872 this building burned down. The offices were then moved to a building on the corner of First Street and Garrison Avenue, where they remained until March, 1875, when they were moved to their present location in the Kannady Block, on the south side of Garrison Avenue. The new court-house and city hall, now nearing its completion, located on Block 515, South Sixth Street, is a two-story brick and stone building, with a basement and attic.

The walls of the basement story are made of Eureka (Ark.) stone, and the face of the brick walls above is made of St. Louis brick. The balance of the brick work is made of home-made brick. The entire building is 84x102 feet in size, and the tower extends to a height of 148 feet above ground. The tower clock has four dials, each four feet in diameter, and the dials are placed about 100 feet above ground. A massive bell on which to strike the time is attached to the clock. There are ten rooms in the first story above the basement, and eight in the second. The city of Fort Smith will occupy all of the first story except the offices of county treasurer and county recorder, and the county will occupy the balance of the building. There are three fire-proof vaults in the building for the protection of the public records. The building is to be heated by the Ruttan system of warm air. Messrs. Nier and Byram are the architects, and M. J. Brennen, Esq., is the contractor. The cost of the building completed will be $55,000. It is a magnificent structure in appearance—made for the future as well as the present—and will stand as a monument of beauty and utility, and an ornament to the city of Fort Smith.

Since the United States District Court for the Western District of Arkansas was located at Fort Smith, it has occupied the central building in the old fort, utilizing the basement story as a jail. In 1887 $75,000 was expended by the Government in the erection of a handsome and commodious jail attached to the building used by the court, and at the present writing (fall of 1888) a magnificent new court-house and post-office is being completed by the Government. It stands on the west side of the street, directly opposite the new county court-house. The contract for its erection was let to Harris & Co., of Newport, Ky., for $70,770. One hundred thousand dollars was appropriated by the Government for its construction, all of which will be required to erect the building and provide the necessary plumbing, water works, heating apparatus, etc. The building is three stories in height, besides the basement and attic. The first story will be used for post-office, and the balance for United States Court purposes.

Poor.—The county of Sebastian has never purchased a farm and fitted it up as a "poor farm" or asylum for her dependent poor, yet the poor have been cared for. At present the county court appoints a commission, which provides for the support of the paupers by contracts with individuals, who care for them at a stipulated price; and upon the order of this commission the county clerk draws his warrant upon the county treasurer for the necessary funds.

Taxation and Finances.—The taxable property of Sebastian County, in 1880, was valued for taxation as follows: real estate, $1,245,372; personal property, $836,762; total, $2,082,134.

The whole property for the year 1887 was valued for taxation as follows: Fort Smith District, real estate, $3,354,867; Fort Smith District, personal property, $788,449; total, $4,143,316. Greenwood District, real estate, $1,449,188; Greenwood District, personal property, $784,666; total, $2,233,854. Grand total of taxable property in the county, $6,377,170.

The increase of taxable property in the Fort Smith District for the year 1888 is $511,633. The amount of the increase in the Greenwood District cannot be ascertained at this writing, as the books have not yet been footed, but it is presumed to be proportionate to the increase in the Fort Smith District. These figures by no means give the real value of the taxable property of the county, for the reason that it has been assessed for taxation at only about one-third of its actual value, so to ascertain the real value when it was assessed in 1887, the total, as then given, must be multiplied by three, which produces $19,377,170, and this may be taken as a safe estimate of the actual value at that time, but the increase since makes it about $21,000,000 for the year 1888. By comparing the total amounts for which the property was assessed for the years 1880 and 1887, it will be seen that in the time intervening, only seven years, the taxable property of Sebastian County more than trebled.

"The utmost limit of taxation is two and one-half per cent, and that upon an assessment which does not exceed one-third of the true value of the property, so that if the the full taxing power under the constitution of the State were put in force the total tax on true values would only be three-quarters of one per cent.

"This taxing power is limited by the constitution as follows:

"For all State purposes, one per cent; for all county purposes, half of one per cent; for all city purposes, half of one per cent; for all special school tax, half of one per cent.

"The latter tax can only be levied in the several school districts in which a majority of the electors vote for it at the annual school elections held in the month of May, at a time when there is no political election held. At the present time the State tax is only half of one per cent, two-fifths of which are for school purposes. It will be seen that outside of cities and towns the taxes amount to only one and one-half per cent. From this it will be seen that the taxes in the country districts (presuming that all the school districts vote for the special school tax, and as a rule they do), are on real values but forty-five one-hundredths of one per cent.

"Arkansas, however, can go still further in the statement regarding taxation. This is not only the rule now, but so it must remain so long as the present constitution of the State remains in force, for it is provided in the constitution that no town, city or county can loan its credit, or issue any interest-bearing evidences of debt. This provision prevents the counties, towns and cities from loading themselves down with debt, which the immigrant would have to contribute to pay off."

The Bonded Debt.—In 1880 the bonded debt of the county, as reported in the United States census, was $61,034, and the floating debt $17,337, making a total indebtedness of $78,371. The sinking fund reported on hand was $2,277, leaving a net debt of $76,094. The bonded debt has all been cancelled, and nearly all of the floating debt. The financial condition of the two districts composing the county, at the close of the fiscal year ending June 30, 1888, was as follows: In the Greenwood District at the beginning of the year there were warrants outstanding, on account of the revenue fund, to the amount of $7,199.20, and the amount of warrants issued during the year amounted to $14,569.12, and the treasurer's fees amounted to $326.12, making a total of the liabilities of $22,094.44. There was received during the year, from taxation and other sources, the sum of $16,316.19, all of which was paid out on the liabilities, thus leaving at the end of the year only $5,778.25. In the same district at the beginning of the year there was on hand, of the common school fund, $8,569.11, which, together with the sums received during the year, amounted to $28,285.92. This was all expended for the benefit of the schools, except $10,810.31, which remained on hand at the close of the year.

The Permanent Funds.—In the Fort Smith District there was on hand, of the revenue fund, at the beginning of the year, $17,975.62, which, added to the receipts from taxation and other sources during the year, amounted to $68,538.32. At the cloes of the year there was currency in the treasury to the amount of $13,605.41, and the orders outstanding amounted to $7,769.32, thus leaving net cash on hand, after redeeming the outstanding orders, amounting to $5,835.09. In the same district the amount of common school fund on hand at the beginning of the year, and the receipts during the year, amounted to $11,339.27, all of which was expended for the benefit of the schools, except $2,440.62, which remained on hand at the close of the year. From these figures it will be observed that the only indebtedness of the county at the close of the last fiscal year, June 30, 1888, was the amount of the outstanding orders in the Greenwood District. By comparing the taxes collected with the vast amount of taxable property in the county, it is apparent that the rate of taxation is very low.

Population.—The population of Sebastian County at the close of the three decades prior to the present one, as shown by the United States census reports, was as follows: For 1860, white, 8,555; colored, 681; Indian, 2; total, 9,238. For 1870, white, 11,545; colored, 1,354; Indian, 41; total, 12,940. For 1880, white, 17,970; colored, 1,541; Indian, 49; total, 19,560. According to these figures it is seen that the colored population increased from 1860 to 1870 nearly 100 per cent, while the white population for the same time increased only a little over 33 per cent, and that for the next decade—from 1870 to 1880—the colored population increased a little less than 15 per cent, while the white population increased a fraction over 55 per cent. During the first decade mentioned there was a large immigration of negroes to the county, and during the latter a large immigration of white people. In 1880 the population of the county by townships was as follows: Bates, 1,090; Big Creek, 2,030; Center, 2,516; Cole, 1,100; Dayton, 975; Hartford, 1,040; Marion, 1,649; Mississippi, 671; Prairie, 927; Sugar Loaf, 1,338; Sulphur, 1,229; Upper (including Fort Smith), 4,292, and Washburn, 683, making the total of 19,560. The population of Fort Smith in 1880 was only 3,099.

The population of the county by townships and towns, as estimated and published last year in E. L. Hayes & Co.'s County Atlas, was as follows: Bates, 1,200; Beverly (unorganized), 500; Big Creek, 2,000; Bloomer (unorganized), 1,000; Center, 3,000; Greenwood (town of), 1,000; Cole, 2,500; Hackett City (town of), 1,500; Dayton, 1,000; Hartford, 1,500; Marion, 2,000; Mississippi, 750; Prairie, 1,000; Rogers (unorganized), 300; Sugar Loaf, 2,000; Sulphur, 1,500; Upper (including Fort Smith), 18,000, making an aggregate of 41,750, which is more than double the number given in the census reports of 1880. This estimate was made about a year ago, and was then probably a little too high, which would make it about right in the aggregate for the present time. The rapid developments now being made in Sebastian County, and the many natural advantages which she possesses, is rapidly bringing in a foreign population, and the prospects are that this rapid increase of population will continue until the mineral, agricultural and horticultural resources of the county will be thoroughly developed, and she becomes a very wealthy county.

Post-offices.—The following is a list of the names of the several post-offices and of the postmasters, with the dates of their appointment, in the county of Sebastian, from its earliest settlement to the present time.

Actus: Lemuel B. Howard, April, 1880; Noah H. Stewart, November, 1880; George W. Harper, November, 1881; James R. Key, November, 1883; L. A. Greenlee, December, 1886; John W. Lambert, January, 1887.

Auburn (late Langston): Ethelbert Paddock, November, 1886.

Backbone: Henry A. Gouger, March, 1856; Dennis Frammel, April, 1857; discontinued June, 1866; re-established January, 1878, Wilson B. Manners; discontinued December, 1878.

Beltville: Joel C. McKinney, June, 1884; discontinued July, 1884.

Bethell: Ann Kelly, September, 1880; discontinued September, 1880.

Beverly: Thomas H. Carter, April, 1877.

Black Jack: L. P. Fuller, September, 1877; discontinued November, 1877.

Bloomer: Andrew J. Brooks, August, 1851; discontinued June, 1866; re-established September, 1867, Anderson Brooks; George H. Carson, April, 1887; Fleetwood Morris, February, 1883; John W. Washburn, October, 1885.

Breckenridge: William Bunch, May, 1858; discontinued June, 1866.

Brunner: John Eppler, March, 1852; J. C. Morgan, January, 1854; David L. Cormack, December, 1854; James G. Wootten, February, 1857; discontinued February, 1867.

Burnville: R. H. Crukmore, April, 1879; James T. Reding, August, 1883; W. S. Seamans, September, 1885.

Cavanaugh: Thomas S. Groover, July, 1886.

Central (late Montrose): Benjamin F. Campbell, May, 1883; Oliver H. Phillips, May, 1888.

Chocoville: Blancy Harper, July, 1852; William Chadwick, December, 1855; Blancy Harper, August, 1860; discontinued July, 1866; Joseph W. Harper, December, 1866; Mary S. Riley, July, 1867; Marion J. Watts, February, 1869; Blancy Harper, January, 1873; Peter M. Browning, February, 1874; Marion J. Watts, October, 1875; J. M. Pauley, August, 1876; Marion J. Watts, November, 1877; William Corlett, December, 1879; Dom C. Mickle, October, 1884; John M. Pauley, November, 1884; discontinued December, 1887.

Dayton (late Hodges Prairie): Thomas C. Miller, May, 1873; William H. Crawford, October, 1873; William Harp, March, 1874; Nancy E. Harp, February, 1877; Robert W. Ferguson, May, 1877; J. D. Benson, October, 1885; William A. Marquess, December, 1885; George W. Goodwin, June, 1888.

Enterprise (late Long Prairie): Robert S. McFarlane, December, 1871; Benjamin H. Bailey, February, 1876; John Dunn, August, 1877; John T. Booth, March,

1878; Robert S. McFarlane, May, 1878; discontinued September, 1878; re-established October, 1878, Benjamin H. Bailey; John Dunn, April, 1879; George Truschel, October, 1879; R. S. McFarlane, January, 1886; George Truschel, March, 1886; John Dunn, September, 1886; Henry McMurtry, February, 1887; William H. McMurtry, March, 1887; Abey S. Smith, August, 1887; Albert L. Nolen, November, 1887; William R. Booth, September, 1888.

Excelsior: W. J. McCheser, July, 1882; James T. Elmore, October, 1882.

Fort Smith (late in Crawford County): John Rogers, October, 1829; Samuel H. Montgomery, June, 1885; William A. Porter, March, 1857; Abraham G. Mayers, January, 1857; Francis E. Adams, February, 1864; re-appointed March, 1865; Francis M. Johnson, March, 1867; S. W. Murphy, September, 1867; James E. Bennett, April, 1869; Thomas G. Scott, July, 1870; Belle C. Shumard, February, 1873; Valentine Dell, December, 1873; J. H. Clendening, March, 1875; re-appointed January, 1879; James K. Barnes, February, 1883; William J. Fleming, May, 1886.

Greenwood: Lucas Willey, April, 1852; Samuel H. Payne, December, 1852; James Johnston, May, 1853; William Awalt, April, 1857; Isham T. Beck, May, 1857; Joseph W. Head, September, 1859; discontinued July, 1866; re-established August, 1866, Laurel Gee; Samuel H. Payne, May, 1867; Jonathan N. Hewes, December, 1867; Thomas McCord, April, 1869; John Bell, September, 1869; James S. Hukill, November, 1869; James A. Clemm, November, 1873; Mark T. Tatum, April, 1876; John M. Neal, April, 1881; Henry M. Tate, November, 1882; W. B. W. Heartsill, June, 1885.

Hackett (late Hackett City): Joel B. Mackey, June, 1887; George T. Harrel, September, 1887; Callie F. Stalcup, November, 1887.

Hackett City (late James Fork): William F. Belt, April, 1877; Thomas B. Bailey, May, 1878; Thomas P. Hackett, March, 1882; Joel B. Mackey, December, 1885; changed to Hackett June, 1887.

Hartford: Joseph B. Forrester, November, 1874.

Hodges Prairie: Samuel Johnson, September 1853; William G. Woodson, September, 1854; Rufus B. Woodson, May, 1857; discontinued February, 1867; re-established January, 1870, John M. Ferguson; Thomas C. Miller, April 1872; changed to Dayton, May, 1873.

Huntington: George S. Mahaney, October, 1887; Charles Knoble, July, 1888; Joseph W. Young, September, 1888.

Iris: David M. Jones, October, 1882; discontinued August, 1883.

Ipava: Ann Kelly, September, 1880; Henry N. Payton, June, 1881; James Y. Payton, December, 1882; William D. Kelly, April, 1886; Henry O. Wilcox, November, 1886.

James Fork (late in Crawford County): Jacob W. Bender, May, 1850; James W. Woodruff, December, 1853; A. B. Gaylor, May, 1854; Francis M. Moore, February, 1855; discontinued February, 1857; re-established April, 1858, Jacob W. Bender; discontinued July, 1866; re-established December, 1866, Eli N. Crawford; John Henderson, August, 1867; discontinued December, 1869; re-established January, 1870, Thomas B. Bailey; Daniel B. Johnson, December, 1873; William F. Belt, January 1877; changed to Hackett City April, 1877.

Jenny Lind: Thomas Yadon, May, 1851; James J. Baker, September, 1854; discontinued July, 1866; re-established May, 1868, George R. Fultz; Henry T. Caldwell, January, 1869; John H. Caldwell, December, 1870; Samuel Douglass, July, 1872; discontinued November, 1872; re-established April, 1873, John C. Yadon; John W. Venney, September, 1873; Benjamin F. Webb, February,

1874; discontinued February, 1875; re-established June, 1877, Maria A. Long; discontinued July, 1879.

Jenson: Jesse M. Duncan, January, 1887; Lewis A. Greenlee, June, 1888.

Langston: John P. Langston, January, 1886; changed to Auburn November, 1886.

Lavaca (late Military Grove): James B. Harwood, August, 1881; Albert Phillips, February, 1884; Eugene Bates, December, 1885; Charles F. Ivey, February, 1886.

Liverpool: Samuel H. Crow, April, 1887; Edmond B. Baker, September, 1887; Myron R. Cory, August, 1888; discontinued October, 1888.

Long Prairie: Alex. D. Scott, August, 1855; William Sigarson, July, 1856; Julius Reickerts, September, 1856; discontinued July, 1866; re-established September, 1868, Hubbard Stone; discontinued November, 1868; re-established April, 1871, Nathaniel B. McNabb; Robert S. McFarlane, October, 1871; changed to Enterprise December, 1871.

Mansfield (late Chocoville): John B. Pauley, December, 1887.

Mark: Bailey Tucker, September, 1885; J. J. Tucker, May, 1886; Bailey M. Tucker, July, 1886; discontinued August, 1887.

Massard: John D. White, June, 1877; discontinued January, 1885; re-established July, 1886, Joseph M. Moody.

Military Grove (late Myers Landing): George B. Harwood, February, 1879

Milltown: James H. I. Burke, August, 1880; Henry C. Earnest, November, 1883.

Milor: Volney V. Milor, February, 1860; discontinued July, 1866; re-established June, 1871, John W. Riggs; discontinued July, 1875.

Montrose: Bernard S. Seybert, May, 1876; Andrew D. Chaney, February, 1877; A. Phillips, April, 1878; changed to Central May, 1883.

Myers Landing (changed to Military Grove February, 1870): James B. Harwood, April, 1877.

Neal (late Rye): James H. Neal, March, 1888.

New Market: Daniel Williams, October, 1853; A. C. White, June, 1854; Thomas E. Stirman, August, 1854; B. F. Davidson, December, 1854; William M. Bradshaw, March, 1855; James D. Treadway, May, 1857; William Bunch, October, 1857; discontinued January, 1858; re-established April, 1870, Thomas F. Crossland; Jerry Bell, April, 1871; discontinued February, 1872.

Peoria: Francis J. Dean, April, 1878; Amos P. Robinson, March, 1887.

Randolph: Munsey Rogers, June, 1886.

Round Knob: Leonard Spradling, May, 1855; discontinued July, 1856.

Rye: Andrew A. Muse, June, 1886; Sallie Bourland, April, 1887; George Wood, May, 1887; changed to Neal, March, 1888.

Sugar Loaf (late in Crawford County): Francis W. Daniels, March, 1851; Charles W. Bishop, October 1860; Henry L. Brown, January, 1861; William H. Ware, February, 1861; discontinued July, 1866; re-established November, 1866, Samuel G. Benedict; Simon Stanton, June, 1867; George W. Sorrells, March, 1878; Charles W. Bishop, January, 1880; R. A. Bishop, January, 1880.

Vache Grass: Lawrence Thompson, July, 1858; discontinued July, 1866.

Valley: William Stafford, April, 1858; discontinued July, 1866.

Washburn: James McKelvy, April, 1875; G. N. McKelvy, August, 1876; James T. Elmore, September, 1876; Jeremiah Bell, September, 1878.

Witcherville: George W. Graves, September, 1875; Henry M. Graves, May, 1877; John H. Caldwell, April, 1880; George Fenry, March, 1881; Samuel E. Smith, July, 1885; William J. Witcher, February, 1888.

The number of post-offices now (1888) existing in Sebastian County is twenty-seven, as follows: Actus, Auburn, Beverly, Bloomer, Burnville, Cavanaugh, Central, Dayton, Enterprise, Excelsior, Fort Smith, Greenwood, Hackett, Hartford, Huntington, Ipava, Jenson, Lavaca, Mansfield, Massard, Milltown, Neal, Peoria, Randolph, Sugar Loaf, Washburn, Witcherville.

COUNTY OFFICERS.

Clerks of the County Court.—John Carnall, 1851–56; C. C. Burton, 1856–62; J. A. Brown, 1862–64; S. H. Payne, 1864–66; William Patterson, 1866–72; G. N. Spradling, 1872–74; J. H. McClure, 1874–78; W. J. Fleming, 1878–80; J. B. Forrester, 1880–82; J. H. McClure, 1882–88; Jesse A. Bell, 1888–.

Clerks of the Circuit Court.—A. Williams, 1872–80; W. J. Fleming, 1880–82; J. P. Stallcup, 1882–88; A. A. McDonald, 1888–.

Sheriffs.—S. B. Stephens, 1851–52; J. J. Baker, 1852–54; C. Norris, 1854–58; C. D. Pryor, 1858–60; W. A. Porter, 1860–64; V. V. Miller, 1864–66; G. F. Bethel, 1866–68; T. H. Scott, 1868–72; J. H. McClure, 1872–May, 1874; Henry Carnall, May, 1874–September, 1874; H. I. Falconer, 1874–84; J. F. Williams, 1884–88–.

Treasurers.—S. Norton, 1851–54; J. R. Kannady, 1854–56; J. M. Morrow, 1856–58; William Kersey, 1858–60; N. D. Osborn, 1860–64; George Wooten, 1864–66; Thomas Dunn, 1866–68; B. F. Hackett, 1868–72; H. M. Muekill, 1872–73; Jacob Baer, 1873–74; R. B. Morrow, 1874–84; Jesse A. Bell, 1884–86; J. P. Durden, 1886–88, 1888–.

Coroners.—William McAllister, 1851–52; H. E. Holliman, 1852–54; A. J. Singleton, 1854–58; T. H. Smith, 1858–60; W. H. Butler, 1860–62; M. J. Watts, 1862–64; J. B. Holliman, 1866–68; William Blaylock, 1868–72; Eli Leflar, 1872–74; Jesse Little, 1874–76; F. Luce, 1876–78; G. W. Dodson, 1878–80; William Green, 1880–82; A. J. Coleman, 1882–84; J. T. Booth, 1884–86; W. P. Graham, 1886–88; James Kelleam, 1888–.

Assessors.—D. E. Sutiliffee, 1864–66; W. A. Riley, 1866–68; J. A. Davey, 1868–74; T. F. Crossland, 1874–76; J. P. Durden, 1876–82; R. W. Gordon, 1882–86; W. L. Euper, 1886–88, 1888–.

Surveyors.—F. E. Williams, 1851–52; B. F. Davidson, 1852–54; J. R. Smoot, 1854–58; J. O. Brewer, 1858–62; J. R. Smoot, 1862–64; C. H. Drake, 1866–68; J. R. Smoot, 1868–74; B. H. Pearson, 1874–76; R. W. Gordon, 1876–80; S. F. Lawrence, 1880–82; G. H. Warren, 1882–84; R. H. Eliason, 1884–86; T. H. R. Johnson, 1886–88–.

County Judges.—James Clark, 1851–52; Samuel Wilson, 1852–54; S. M. Rutherford, 1854–56; Charles Milor, 1856–60; William McAllister, 1860–64; John Howard, 1864–68; C. P. Swift [date not given]; C. Perkins, 1874–78; R. B. Rutherford, 1878–82; B. J. H. Gaines, 1882–88; W. F. Blythe, 1888–.

Representatives and Senators.—Ninth Legislature (1852–53): Senate (Sebastian and Crawford), George W. Clark; House, S. M. Rutherford. Tenth Legislature (1854–55): Senate, J. J. Green; House, Samuel Edmondson. Eleventh Legislature (1856–57): Senate (Sebastian and Scott), Green J. Clark; House, Samuel Edmondson and R. H. McConnell. Twelfth Legislature (1858–59): Senate, Green J. Clark; House, R. H. McConnell, B. T. Duval. Thirteenth Legislature (1860–62): Senate, Green J. Clark; House, John T. Loudon and B. T. Duval. Fourteenth Legislature (1862–63): Senate, Green J. Clark; House, J. Carnall and C. B. Neal. Fifteenth Legislature (1864–65): Senate, Charles Milor; House, J. R. Smoot and J. Snyder. Confederate Legislature (1864): House, John Carnall and C. B. Neal. Sixteenth Legislature (1866–67): Senate, H. L. Holliman;* House, J. Hackett and B. Harper. Seventeenth Legislature (1868–70): Senate, Eighth District, Valentine Dell; House, Eighth District, J. B. C. Turman, D. H. Divelbiss, A. J. Singleton and A. Gunther. Eighteenth Legislature (1870–72): Senate, Valentine Dell; House, J. M. Pettigrew, C. B. Neal, J. B. Stevens, J. P. Grady. Nineteenth Legislature (1872–74): Senate, J. D. Arbuckle; House, J. A. Davie, C. E. Berry, L. C. White, S. L. Strong. Twentieth Legislature (1874–75): Senate, Twenty-eighth District (Sebastian and Scott), J. F. Wheeler; House, R. H. McConnell and R. T. Kerr. Twenty-first Legislature (1876–77): Senate, R. T. Kerr; House, W. M. Fishback and C. Milor. Twenty-second Legislature (1878–79):

*Thrown out, and T. H. Scott seated.

Senate, R. T. Kerr; House, W. M. Fishback and R. H. McConnell. Twenty-third Legislature (1880–81): Senate, J. P. Hall; House, E. F. Tiller and Jesse Martin. Twenty-fourth Legislature (1882–83): Senate, J. P. Hall; House, R. H. McConnell and S. E. Smith. Twenty-fifth Legislature (1884–85): Senate, R. H. McConnell; House, W. M. Fishback and J. S. Little. Twenty-sixth Legislature (1886–87): Senate, R. H. McConnell; House, J. B. McDonough and James A. Williams. Twenty-seventh Legislature (1888–89): Senate, A. J. Washburn; House, James A. Williams and J. F. Weaver.

ELECTIONS.

Following are the returns of the election held in 1844 for State and county officers in that part of Crawford County which was afterward cut off to form the county of Sebastian. This territory was then subdivided into three municipal townships: Big Creek, Upper (or Fort Smith) and Sugar Loaf. For governor: Thomas S. Drew (Dem.), 165; Dr. Gibson (Whig), 144. For Member of Congress: A. Yell (Dem.), 176; D. Walker (Whig), 146. State senator: Hans Smith (Dem.), 161; Jesse Turner (Whig), 151. Representatives: A. G. Mayers (Dem.), 165; John S. Roane (Dem.), 167; W. J. Duval (Dem.), 163; J. F. McKinney (Whig), 141; J. A. Simpson (Whig), 137; —— Collins (Whig), 120. Sheriff: Eli Bell (Dem.), 139; J. R. Kannady (Whig), 166, Clerk: —— Gibson (Dem.), 97; A. McLean (Whig), 207.

According to these figures it seems that the Democratic candidates, except for the offices of sheriff and clerk, were successful. There were 165 votes cast for the Democratic candidate for governor, and 144 for the Whig candidate, thus making 309 votes in all, which shows that the population was then very small. Multiplying the total vote cast by five, a result of 1,545 is obtained for the population of the county; but as the whole vote was not cast it is safe to say that the population of the county at that date numbered 2,000.

In consequence of the burning of the public records and papers, it is not possible to give the result of the succeeding elections of Sebastian since its organization, but the following, which have been gleaned from the files of newspapers still preserved, will be given. In the published returns the first names of candidates have sometimes been omitted, and hence will be omitted here:

1858—For Congress: Rust, 387; Drew, 797. Prosecuting attorney: Gregg, 595; Mansfield, 424. Representatives: Mendenhall, 298; Pitman, 128; Mayers, 518; McConnell, 605; Duval, 668. For clerk: Burton, 649; Porter, 457; Awalt, 123. For sheriff: Morrow, 396; Pryor, 491; Bethel, 329. For county judge: Milor, 455; Drum, 376; Long, 342. For surveyor: Brewer, 527; Smoot, 407; Spaulding, 239. For commissioner: Jones, 552; Marshall, 452. For county treasurer: Osborn, 422; Kersey, 707. For county assessor: Coffee, 169; Tatum, 115; Allison, 402; Harper, 136; Hendry, 260; Payden, 87. For coroner: Baurbyte, 289; Smith, 492.

1860—Governor: H. M. Rector, 1,038; R. H. Johnson, 662. Member of Congress: E. W. Gantt, 1,123; C. B. Mitchell, 540. State senator: A. G. Mayers, 900; G. J. Clark, 736. Circuit judge: J. M. Wilson, 639; J. J. Green, 1,008. Prosecuting attorney: L. Gregg, 1,274; J. R. Cox, 375. Representative: J. T. Loudon, 1,126; B. T. Duval, 912; J. H. Mendenhall, 760; J. W. Vandever, 148; William Bunch, 68. Sheriff: W. A. Porter, 787; H. Young, 586; A. Chandler, 83; H. L. Holleman, 35; J. M. Morrow, 193. County judge: William McAllister, 641; G. W. Sorrells, 477; J. J. Baker, 224; Thomas McCarron, 173; M. W. Leonard, 92. County treasurer: William Kersey, 768; N. D. Osborn, 834. Surveyor: J. O. Brewer, 1,101; M. J. Wilcox, 74. Assessor: J. C. Allison, 344; G. F. Bethel, 684; W. Condry, 245; J. A. Eno, 299; F. M. Moore, 81. Coroner: William Deason, 330; W. H. Butler, 382; J. Donahoe, 372; William Ward, Sr., 350. School commissioner: John Jones, 736; C. H. Wheeler, 507; J. Long, 342.

1864—in favor of new constitution, 1,080 votes. Governor: J. Murphy (no opposition), 1,080. Lieut.-governor: C. C. Bliss (no opposition), 1,032. Congress: J. M. Johnson, 903; E. P. Perkins, 132. State senator: R. D. Swindell, 363; C. Milor, 328. Representative: J. R. Smoot, 518; H. L. Holleman, 344; J. W. Spradling, 225; G. W. Sisson, 352; Jacob Snyder, 440. Circuit judge: S. Edmondson, 339; A. N. Hargrove, 384; I. Groves, 131; Thomas Pounds, 61. Prosecuting attorney: L. J. Barnes, 161; M. J. Leonard, 225; J. R. Steel, 142; — Williamson, 17. County judge: John Howard, 689; V. Dell, 189. County clerk: W. H. Lewis, 414; A. Hammersly, 110; L. Gee, 315. Sheriff: John H. Weir, 374; V. V. Milor, 409; A. J. Fry, 142. Coroner: M. J. Watts, 395; J. Holleman, 355; Ed. Murphy, 388; J. H. McClure, 384. Treasurer: A. J. Sleighton, 623; J. D. Treadway, 116.

Soldiers' Vote.—The following shows how the Union soldiers stationed at Fort Smith voted at the presidential election in 1864: Thirteenth Kansas Infantry: Lincoln, 347; McClellan, 3. Twelfth Kansas Infantry: Lincoln, 411; McClellan, 0. Second Kansas Cavalry: Lincoln, 211; McClellan, 0. Sixth Kansas Cavalry: Lincoln, 209; McClellan, 0. Fourteenth Kansas Cavalry: Lincoln, 179; McClellan, 0. Second Kansas Battery: Lincoln, 51; McClellan, 0. Detached men: Lincoln, 94; McClellan, 0. Eighteenth Iowa: Lincoln 404; McClellan, 0. Total: Lincoln, 1,906; McClellan, 3.

1866. The test oath prescribed by the Legislature of the State in 1864, to be taken by individuals as a qualification for voting, was declared unconstitutional by the supreme court, so that in 1866 all persons over twenty-one years of age, not otherwise disfranchised, were allowed to vote. On July 7, 1866, the Republicans of Sebastian County held a convention at Greenwood and endorsed the civil rights bill, the policy of Congress on reconstruction, and favored the free-school system. The vote of the county for that year for the public offices stood as follows: For Congress: J. M. Johnson (R), 423; A. B. Greenwood (D), 324. Representative: B. Harper (R), 383; John Carnall (D), 344; Jerre Hackett (R), 456; John King (D), 339. County judge: John Howard (R), 448; William McAllister (D), 333. Sheriff: G. F. Bethel (R), 433; W. A. Porter (D), 378. County clerk: J. N. Spradling (R), 380; J. R. A. Hendry (D), 328; S. H. Payne (R), 84. Treasurer: T. Dunn (R), 402; N. H. Osborne (D), 321. Assessor: W. A. Riley (R), 453; J. H. Reid (D), 256; N. D. Osborne (D), 78. Coroner: John Holleman (R), 402; M. Bunch (D), 56. Surveyor: W. Condon (R), 326; C. H. Drake (R), 229.

The Convention of 1866.—On December 13, 1866, a State convention was held at Fort Smith in response to what was entitled: "A call to the Loyalists and Unionists of Arkansas," etc., signed by some forty or fifty persons in Sebastian, Scott, Crawford and other northwestern counties of the State. Four hundred delegates were present, and Hon. LaFayette Gregg presided. Resolutions were adopted approving the reconstruction policy of Congress, advocating the adoption of the proposed fourteenth amendment to the constitution of the United States, and advocating universal suffrage of loyal men, and the disfranchisement of a certain class of men who had opposed the government during the late war. On these questions political excitement was then at a high point. The Legislature of Arkansas failed to ratify the fourteenth amendment to the constitution. The feeling of many and probably the majority of the Republicans, then so familiarly called "Radicals," on the question of suffrage is best expressed in the following quotation from the Fort Smith *New Era* of the issue of March 13, 1867: "What we want, what the country wants, just what it wants, neither more nor less, is the disfranchisement of every man who has at any time voluntarily aided or abetted the Rebellion."

1870. The number of votes cast for the various candidates at the general election in Sebastian County, in the year 1870, was as follows: Congressman: Boles, 720; Edwards, 653. Representative: Fishback, 683; Neal, 528; White, 88; Pettigrew, 405; Hackett, 355; King, 92; Grady, 521; Abernathy, 584; Stevens, 755; Snider, 205; Patterson, 153; Pritchard, 16. Sheriff: Bethel, 370; Falconer, 305; McClure, 668. County Judge: Howard, 334; Hightower, 190. Coroner: Field, 204. Treasurer: Hendry, 235; Vaughan, 166; Tilles, 425; Rattafee, 255. The multiplicity of candidates for some of the offices shows that it was "a free for all race."

The following shows the vote of Sebastian County, by townships, at the presidential election in 1872: Upper (D) 181, (R) 354; Marion (D) 44, (R) 33; Sugar Loaf (D) 98, (R) 120; Washburn (D) 18, (R) 33; Bates (D) 11, (R) 47; Big Creek (D) 66, (R) 61; Center (D) 44, (R) 307; Mississippi (D) 53, (R) 12; Sulphur (D) 25, (R) 41; Cole (D) 30, (R) 26. Totals (D) 570, (R) 1,034.

The following table shows the result of the election for county officers in Sebastian County for the same year: Representatives: William M. Fishback, 539; L. C. White, 1,005; J. B. Stevens, 563; S. L. Story, 1,007; W. R. Felker, 528; J. A. David, 1,004; G. C. Alden, 537; C. E. Berry, 1,013. Sheriff: Henry Falconer, 534; J. H. McClure, 1,011. Clerk: B. F. Hackett, 551; G. N. Spradling, 1,007. County Judge: M. D. Frazier, 569; J. Howard, 1,002. Treasurer: B. H. Borling, 535; M. M. Hukill, 924. Coroner: J. C. Pettit, 533; Eli Leftar, 924. Surveyor: J. K. Burnham, 549; J. R. Smoot, 972. Assessor: T. F. Crossland, 516.

1876—For governor: W. R. Miller (D), 1,659; A. W. Bishop (R), 720. State senate: R. T. Kerr, (D) 1,264; S. D. McDonald (R), 884. Representatives: W. M. Fishback (D), 1,237; B. F. Hackett (R), 619; R. H. McConnell (D), 1,034; Charles Milor (R), 1,084. Sheriff: Henry Falconer (D), 1,638; W. S. Hood (R), 564; J. W. Buzan (R), 292. Clerk: J. H. McClure (D), 1,264; G. N. Spradling (R), 1,146. County judge: Charles Perkins (D), no opposition. County treasurer: R. B. Morrow (D), 2,001; B. H. Pierson (R) 219. Assessor: J. P. Durden (D), no opposition. Surveyor: R. W. Gordon (D), no opposition.

1880—For governor: T. J. Churchill, 1,833; W. P. Parks, 194. Prosecuting attorney: J. S. Little, 1,816; W. M. Melette, 1,290. State senator: J. P. Hall, 1,874; A. J. Simer, 127; B. Harper, 1,100. Representatives: E. F. Tiller, 1,929; Jesse Martin, 1,715; J. W. Price, 126; T. C. Miller, 1,182; J. Steven, 133. County and probate judge: R. B. Rutherford, 1,869; R. P. Claborn, 1,272. Circuit clerk: W. J. Fleming, 1,938; John Patterson, 1,283. County clerk: J. B. Forrester, 2,025; W. J. Seamans, 1,122. Sheriff: Henry Falconer, 1,882; J. H. Mershon, 1,246. Treasurer: C. O. Frye, 1,108; R. B. Morrow, 1,991. Assessor: J. P. Durden, 1,930; John M. Ferguson, 1,194. Surveyor: S. F. Lawrence, 1,947; J. R. Smoot, 1,169. Coroner: William Breen, 1,707; S. M. Turner, 1,021. Those receiving the largest votes were, perhaps one or two exceptions, Democrats, and those receiving the lowest vote, Republicans.

In 1884 the vote of Sebastian County for public officers stood as follows: For State senate: R. H. McConnell, 2,535; E. L. Compere, 1,935. Representatives: William M. Fishback, 2,584;

J. S. Little, 2,574; A. J. Webb, 76; H. H. Waters, 1,787; W. J. Branden, 1,810. County judge: B. J. H. Gaines, 2,612. Sheriff: John F. Williams, 2,604; W. H. Bell, 1,917. Circuit clerk: J. C. Stalcup, 2,638; B. P. Davis, 1,885. County clerk: John H. McClure, 2,601; J. D. York, 1,886. County treasurer: Jesse Bell, 2,641; E. P. Payne, 1,851. Assessor: R. W. Gordon, 2,316; J. C. Pettus, 1,919. Surveyor: R. H. Eliason, 2,598; W. R. Tatum, 1,923. Coroner: Dr. J. T. Booth, 2,608; J. J. Short, 1,920. Hon. Thomas Boles, of Fort Smith, was the Republican candidate in 1884 for governor of the State, against S. P. Hughes, the Democratic candidate, the latter being elected.

1886—For governor: S. P. Hughes, 2,760; LaFayette Gregg, 1,270; C. E. Cunningham, 56. Circuit judge: J. S. Little, 2,734. Prosecuting attorney: C. A. Lewers, 2,565; John J. Boles, 1,395. Representatives: James A. Williams, 2,511; J. B. McDonough, 2,651; C. M. Barnes, 1,262; H. W. Fannin, 1,240. Sheriff: John F. Williams, 2,652; B. F. Hackett, 1,339. Circuit clerk: J. C. Stalcup, 2,724; J. C. Floyd, 1,264. County clerk: John A. McClure, 2,668; E. Haglin, 1,239. County judge: B. J. H. Gaines, 2,772; G. F. Bethel, 1,157; Assessor: W. L. Euper, 2,720; Silas K. Robinson, 258. Treasurer: J. P. Durden, 2,464; J. M. Tate, 1,520. Surveyor: Thomas Johnson, 2,618; J. D. Foreman, 1,342.

1888—Governor: J. P. Eagle (D), 3,305; C. M. Norwood (R), 2,138.* Secretary of State: B. B. Chism (D), 3,360; George W. Terry (R), 2,006. Attorney general: W. E. Atkinson (D), 3,352; W. J. Duval (R), 2,105. State treasurer: W. E. Woodruff (D), 3,469; ———, ——. Chief justice: S. R. Cockrill (D), 3,352; O. D. Scott (R), 2,007. Auditor: W. S. Dunlop (D), 3,351; A. W. Bird (R), 2,101. Land commissioner: P. M. Cobbs (D), 3,354; R. H. Morehead (R), 2,104. Superintendent public instruction: W. E. Thompson (D), 3,355; P. B. Baker (R), 2,101. Prosecuting attorney: J. B. McDonough (D), 3,311; J. H. Huckleberry (R), 2,140. State senator: A. G. Washburn (D), 3,340; Thomas Boles (R), 2,101. Representative: James A. Williams (D), 3,274; Thomas B. Latham (R), 2,119; J. F. Weaver (D), 3,322; R. P. Claborn (R), 2,100. County judge: W. F. Blythe (D), 3,274; James R. Norcott

* State ticket nominated by the Wheelers, and supported by the Republicans.

(R), 2,159. Circuit clerk: A. A. McDonald (D), 3,367; I. M. Dodge (R), 2,102. County clerk: Jesse A. Bell (D), 3,419; Tom P. Hackett (R), 2,086. Sheriff: John F. Williams (D), 3,289; J. S. Hammer (R) 2,159. Assessor: W. L. Euper (D), 3,332; W. E. Gilleam (R), 2,092. Treasurer: J. P. Durden (D), 3,182; W. G. Graves (R), 2,046. Surveyor: T. H. R. Johnson (D), 3,390; J. H. Kirby (R), 2,100. Coroner: Dr. James Kelleam (D), 3,452; Richard Stratham (R), 58.

For liquor license, 2,404; against liquor license, 1,350. For convention to amend State constitution, 1,268; against, 1,878.

AGRICULTURE AND HORTICULTURE.

In reference to agricultural products in the Arkansas Valley in general, Judge John Carnall, of Fort Smith, speaks as follows, in his "Notes on Western Arkansas:"

> The general products of this valley are corn and cotton. The staple production is cotton, but almost every farmer now raises wheat enough for home consumption. Oats is a universal crop; millet and sorghum are very generally raised, enough of the latter, or very nearly so, to supply the county with molasses. Tobacco is raised only to a limited extent, but we take this occasion to say, from our own personal knowledge, that it thrives very well here, and we believe it equal to Kentucky or Virginia to grow the weed. Of course, every vegetable from Maine to Texas grows and thrives here, and they are not cut short by * * * chinch bugs or grasshoppers, which are not known to Arkansas. For grapes, Italy itself is not superior. The vines grow wild all over the ridges and tops of the mountains in this country, and many wild grapes are found equal in size to the Concord. There are thousands of gallons of wine made near Fort Smith, some farmers making 100 and 200 barrels, in this county, a year.

According to the United States census, there were in Sebastian County in 1880, 2,421 farms with 72,049 acres of improved lands, valued at $1,500,976. The value of the farm implements and machinery was $85,085, and the value of the live-stock was $455,437, and the estimated value of all farm products for the year 1879 was $867,130. The cost of building and repairing fences for 1879 was $20,265, and the cost of fertilizers was $521. The vegetable production for the county, for the year 1879, were as follows: Corn, 553,513 bushels; oats, 53,976; rye, 55; wheat, 31,157; hay, 574 tons; cotton, 11,112 bales; Irish potatoes, 6,053 bushels; sweet potatoes, 8,985; tobacco, 8,576 pounds. In the production of corn Sebastian ranged as the sixth county in the State, and in the production of oats and wheat the eighth. According to the same census the number of head of live-stock in the county was as follows: Horses, 4,347, mules and asses, 1,627; working oxen, 157, milch cows, 6,486; other cattle, 11,835; sheep, 3,759; swine, 33,382. In the item of "other cattle," Sebastian County then ranked as the first in the State, and in milch cows and horses as the third.

Stock.—The raising of fine blooded horses was introduced here before Sebastian County was organized. The father of Col. Ben. T. Duval, an early settler, brought out from Virginia some thoroughbred horses. He was an ardent lover of fine stock, and was fond of regular turf racing. He laid out the race track near Fort Smith, and a jockey club was organized here. Similar clubs were organized at Van Buren and other places, at which regular spring and fall meetings, lasting several days, were held. Large purses were offered, and stables of fine horses were brought here from other States. Races of long distance were then in vogue. Maj. Rector, Col. Drennen and William Duval were then the principal raisers of fine stock in this section of country. Among the principal raisers of fine stock in Sebastian County, at this writing, are Paul Euper, J. C. Wilkinson and J. W. Pelley. An old paper published in 1843, and still preserved, contains an announcement of a race to be run on the race-course of the Fort Smith Jockey Club, on the 2d of May of that year, between horses owned respectively by A. Webster and T. G. Moore, for $300 a side, distance two miles. The next day there was to be a three-mile heat race for $1,000 a side, and on the 10th of the month a two-mile heat race was announced for sweepstakes for three-year-old colts. The announcements were signed by Samuel Caldwell. Horse racing is now usually carried on in connection with the fairs.

Crops.—The agricultural resources of Sebastian County have been but slightly developed. The virgin soil has generally yielded fair crops without having had much labor expended upon it. Shallow plowing and constant cropping, usually with the same commodity, constantly taking from the soil and returning nothing to it, has been the general practice among the farmers. When lands are not being used for cropping, they are allowed to exhaust their fertility by growing weeds. This method of farming will wear out the best of lands in the course of time. In riding over the country the observer will frequently see tracts of land that have been thus worn out, abandoned and thrown out to public. The reason for this, in part, is because the lands have been so cheap, and have been owned in such large quantities, that the farmers, after exhausting a piece of land, abandon it, and cultivate a new piece instead, and in this manner get rid of keeping their lands in order. It is, however, an expensive way of farming. But little clean farming has been done; the fence corners are generally allowed to grow up with briars, weeds and bushes. Deep plowing, clean and thorough cultivation, a rotation of crops, and the growing of the grasses and clover for refertilizing the soil and the feeding of more stock thereon, is what is wanted. A few individuals have recently introduced and are now practicing scientific farming, and when the masses adopt their methods and practice them, the lands will be made to grow richer instead of poorer, will produce double in return for the labor expended, and give a satisfaction to the farmer that he cannot otherwise enjoy. It seems that the wonderful resources of the county have only been recently discovered, or at least their development has only recently been commenced. This is due in a great measure to the fact that, until recently, the people have had no railroads for shipping their products to market. The soil and the climate is here, railroads have entered the county and others are under construction, and the time is not far distant when she will be rich in agriculture and horticulture, as she is also in mineral wealth.

Horticulture.—Almost every settled farmer has his fruit trees. Large orchards are not as yet very common, because there has as yet been no way of disposing of the fruit profitably. Now, since the advent of the railroads, farmers are enlarging their orchards, and we have plenty of good nurserymen who keep up with the late varieties and best sorts, and are doing a thriving business. Fruit trees grow very rapidly in this country, attaining in one season a growth of two in Illinois or Pennsylvania, and bear much earlier. A year-old grafted peach set out in November or December, and cultivated next year, will bear fruit the second summer. Many of the farmers have, however, large and well-managed orchards of best northern and southern varieties. It having been ascertained that the winter apples grown north of the middle belt of the United States are more apt to drop in our long summer than those of the middle and southern, the latter are generally preferred, but all the summer and early fall apples of the north do well here. Many new seedlings, indigenous to the southern country, and very fine and valuable, are now extensively grown in this region of the Arkansas Valley and south of here. *

Since the above extract was written, fruit evaporators and canning factories have been erected at Fort Smith, Van Buren, Ozark and many other places in Western Arkansas, and thus the market for fruits has been largely increased. There are three varieties of leading winter apples in the North, the Ben Davis, Winesap and Northern Spy, which are also raised in Western Arkansas, and do equally well here. The Shannon, a native of Arkansas, and the most popular fall apple here, is a very large greenish yellow apple, of unexcelled beauty and flavor. It is scarcely known in the North. The writer, who has attended the State fairs of Michigan and Indiana, and many county fairs, attended the fair at Fort Smith this month, October, 1888, and is free to say that at the latter place he saw a display of the largest and handsomest apples that he ever beheld. Peaches, plums, pears and nearly all the varieties of smaller fruits, such as grapes, blackberries, raspberries, strawberries, etc., can be raised in great abundance in Sebastian County. Grapes are raised in great abundance and extensively made into wine. Berries are also extensively raised and shipped to distant markets. The resources are here for the development of agriculture and horticulture to a limitless extent.

Fair Association of Western Arkansas.—This association was organized at Fort Smith in 1880, and on the 21st day of April, of that year, the following directors were elected, to wit: Gen. D. P. Upham, George Sengel, P. K. Roots, S. A. Williams, Frank Parke, J. R. Kannady, J. S. Williamson, R. S. McCarty, G. C. Falconer, G. D. Redwine, R. T. Kerr, J. H. Alexander, H. Stone, B. Baer and C. B. Neal.

P. K. Roots was chosen president; G. C. Falconer, vice-president; J. S. Williamson, secretary; H. Stone, treasurer, and Gen. D. P. Upham, superintendent. The territorial limits of the district were defined to embrace the counties of Crawford, Franklin, Logan, Scott and Sebastian, of the State of Arkansas, and the Indian Territory contiguous thereto. At the opening of the sixth

*Carnall's Notes on Western Arkansas.

annual fair October 13, 1885, Col. Duval delivered an address at the fair-grounds, from which the writer has obtained the above information. The first exhibition of the association was held in 1880, and annual exhibitions have since been held, the ninth having just closed. The present officers are Dr. J. H. T. Main, president; T. H. Barnes, vice-president; H. Stone, treasurer; C. M. Barnes, secretary; W. M. Fishback, superintendent of grounds. The directors, in addition to the officers named, are J. C. Wilkinson, S. A. Williams, John Matthews, J. H. Livingston, James A. Williams, William J. Johnston, Marshall Gaines, J. J. Little, B. T. Duval, C. M. Cook, William Breen, Thomas Rogers and Henry Kuper, Jr.

The Fair Association owns forty acres of land two and a half miles northeast from the center of Fort Smith, one-half of which is enclosed and fitted up with a first-class race track well fenced in, an ample supply of stables and sheds for animals, a large amphitheater, a large shed for the exhibition of buggies, wagons, and agricultural implements, a large art, floral and agricultural hall combined, a large octagonal hall especially for the display of fruits, and other necessary buildings.

THE COURTS.

COUNTY COURT.

Preliminaries.—Section 14 of the act of the General Assembly creating the county of Sebastian provided that the sessions of the county court should be held on the second Mondays of January, April, July and October of each year, and that the sessions of the probate court should be held on the second Tuesdays of the same months. The general law provided that the judge of the county court should be judge also of the probate court, and such has always been the case with the exception of a period of less than two years, during "the seventies," when the judge of the circuit court was given probate jurisdiction. The county and probate courts were established in accordance with the provisions of the act creating the county, and for a list of the names of the judges of these courts, see elsewhere.

Jurisdiction.—The county court has "exclusive original jurisdiction of all matters relating to county taxes; in all matters relating to roads, the appointment of viewers, receivers and overseers of roads; to order the erection of bridges, and directing the repairing of the same; to superintend all ferries, paupers, bastardy cases, vagrants and the apprenticeship of minors; to fix the places of holding elections; to designate apportioning justices; to audit, settle and direct the payment of all demands against the county; to have the control and the management of all property, real and personal, for the use of the county; to have full power and authority to purchase or receive by donation any property, real or personal, for the use of the county, and to cause to be erected all buildings and all repairs necessary for the use of the county; to sell and cause to be conveyed any real estate or personal property belonging to the county, and appropriate the proceeds of such sale for the use of the county; to disburse money for county purposes, and in all other cases that may be necessary to the internal improvement and local concerns of the respective counties." [Act February 5, 1875.]

PROBATE COURT.

The probate court has "original jurisdiction in the following cases:

"First. In all matters relating to the probate of last wills and testaments, the estate of deceased persons, executors, administrators, guardians and persons of unsound mind, and their estates.

"Second. In the settlement and allowances of accounts of executors, administrators and guardians.

"Third. To hear and determine all controversies respecting last wills and testaments, the rights of executorship, administration or guardianship.

"Fourth. To issue process and cause to come before such court all persons whom they may deem it necessary to examine, whether parties or witnesses, or who, as executors, administrators or guardians, or otherwise, shall be interested or in any wise accountable for any lands, tenements, goods, chattels, moneys or effects belonging to any minor, orphan, or person of unsound mind, or to the estate of any deceased person." [Act January 7, 1875.]

An act passed March 8, 1877, provided that the probate court for the Greenwood District of Sebastian County should be held on the third Mondays of January, April, July and October of each year, and that in the Fort Smith District it should be held on the fourth Mondays of the same months.

CIRCUIT COURT.

The sixteenth section of the act creating the county of Sebastian provided that the county should form a part of the Fourth Judicial Circuit, and that the circuit court should be held on the third Mondays of January and July of each year. Afterward, from time to time, as population increased, the State was redistricted for judicial purposes, changing the number of counties embraced in the several districts, and also changing the number of the circuits. The act of March 8, 1877, above referred to, made the Twelfth Judicial Circuit consist of the counties of Scott, Sebastian, Crawford and Logan, and so it stands at this writing. The first judge of this new circuit was J. H. Rogers, who served from April 20, 1877, to October 2, 1882, when he was succeeded by R. B. Rutherford, who served until October, 1886. The latter was succeeded by John S. Little, the present presiding judge. Judge Little was the first prosecuting attorney for the present Twelfth Judicial Circuit, and served three terms, until September 20, 1884, when he was succeeded by A. C. Lewers. The latter served until October 30, 1888, and was then succeeded by James B. McDonald, the present incumbent.

Time of Meeting.—The county court for the Greenwood District meets, under the present law, on the first Mondays of January, April, July and October of each year, and for the Fort Smith District it meets on the second Mondays of the same months. At the October terms of the county court, each year, the full quorum court, consisting of all the justices of the peace, meet in each district for the purpose of levying taxes and making appropriations. The circuit court for the Greenwood District meets on the sixteenth Mondays after the last Mondays of February and August in each year, and for the Fort Smith District it meets on the sixth Mondays after the last Mondays of the same months.

THE BAR.

The local bar of Sebastian County has always been noted for its ability and intelligence. Among its members are some of the ablest lawyers in the United States. Since the location of the Federal court, first at Van Buren and subsequently at Fort Smith, certain members of this bar have been the leading practitioners therein, and are there so constantly engaged that they have but little time to practice in the local courts. It is probably on account of the Federal court that so many lawyers are located in Fort Smith. Following is an alphabetical list of the names of the attorneys constituting the Sebastian County bar: A. H. Boles, J. J. Boles, Thomas Boles, James Brizzolara, J. K. Barnes, W. F. Blythe, T. W. M. Boone, T. L. Brown, J. C. Byers, E. C. Boudinot, P. D. Brewer, A. L. Brewster, William M. Cravens, J. H. Clendening, W. H. H. Clayton, M. J. Casey, C. M. Cooke, W. A. Cooper, John Carroll, Ben. T. Duval, T. M. Downs, William Duncan, M. M. Edmiston, C. H. Eberle, C. J. Frederick, E. J. Fannin, J. B. Forrester, George A. Grace, J. A. Green, John T. Hurley, F. C. Humphreys, P. E. Hileman, J. L. Hendrick, T. H. Humphreys, J. M. Hill, W. J. Horton, John H. Holland, R. E. Jackson, W. C. Jackson, J. W. Johnson, R. T. Kerr, J. A. Kale, Campbell Leflore, T. B. Latham, B. Luce, Thomas Marcum, P. J. M. MacGreevy, W. M. Mellette, J. B. McDonough, W. R. Martin, W. S. Murphey, N. L. Marmon, D. C. Morgan, R. W. McFarlane, C. B. Neal, George E. Nelson, T. S. Osborn, R. T. Powell, R. B. Rutherford, James F. Read, W. B. Rutherford, James G. Ralls, R. A. Rowe, S. T. Rowe, M. H. Sandles, S. H. Sherlock, S. H. Scott (colored), Julius Silverman, B. H. Tabor, William Walker, T. P. Winchester, J. S. Wheeles, C. E. Warner, W. S. Wolfenberger, F. A. Youmans.

CRIMINAL RECORD.

Sebastian County has had her share of crimes and excesses committed within her borders, but in this respect she is no worse than the average counties in the State. A number of offenses are herein reported, but the killing of defenseless men during the war, and the fighting of duels herein mentioned, must not be charged against the character of the citizens of the county, for the reason that the persons killed within the war period was the result of that unhappy struggle, and the duels were fought by non-residents outside of the county.

Fighting Duels.—In 1844 Mr. Borden, editor of the *Gazette*, published at Little Rock, and Solan Borland, editor of the *Banner*, published at the same place, the former a Whig and the latter a Democrat, got into an altercation, and Borden challenged Borland to fight a duel. The challenge was accepted, and the parties, after choosing their seconds, boarded a steamer and took passage for the Cherokee Nation, where, on the 6th day of May of that year, they fought a duel at a point across the river directly opposite Fort Smith. Both displayed unwavering coolness throughout the affair. Mr. Borden fought in his customary dress, but Dr. Borland threw off his outer garments. Borden's pistol was fired first, the ball falling short of his antagonist, while the latter's fire took effect in Borden's person, striking the breast, and making only a slight flesh wound, from which he soon recovered. The duel was fought at a distance of twelve paces. Several citizens of Fort Smith witnessed the affair.

Another duel was fought at the same place in August, 1848, between Albert Pike (since general) and John S. Roane (since governor). Both of them had been officers in the army in the Mexican War, and after returning home one of them severely criticised the military conduct of the other. A challenge was passed and accepted. Col. Robert W. Johnson and H. M. Rector were Roane's seconds, and Dr. Philip Burton, of Little Rock, was his surgeon. Luther Chase, of Little Rock, and a gentleman from Van Buren were Pike's seconds, and Dr. Thurston, of Van Buren, was surgeon and also a second for Pike. Roane, Johnson, Burton and Rector traveled to Fort Smith on horseback, and tarried two days for rest and recreation at the house of Maj. Elias Rector, who lived in the vicinity, before the duel was fought. Both parties were considered experts with the pistol. The morning was bright and balmy; the ground was stepped off, and the positions were chosen by lot. The distance between the combatants was ten paces. Both seemed cool and collected, and three shots were exchanged by them, but neither took effect. A reconciliation then followed, and all parties adjourned to a banquet in Fort Smith. Pike and Roane were afterward friends and companions.* Happily the barbarous custom, practiced even by men such as these combatants, of settling difficulties by fighting duels, has been abandoned.

Murder of Seaburn Standifer.—In September, 1847, a man named Hadley deliberately and in cold blood shot and killed Seaburn Standifer, a citizen of the county, living about seven miles south of Fort Smith. He was tried for the offense at Little Rock and acquitted.

The Killing of Jesse Merritt.—On the 19th of February, 1848, Jesse Merritt, a pardoned convict, was killed at Fort Smith by Samuel Edmondson. Some difficulty existed between the parties, and in the morning they met and quarreled, and about 3 o'clock P. M. Merritt walked into Edmondson's office to see Esquire Hudspeth, and after getting through with his business, and being in the act of leaving, Edmondson fired at him from the outside through the back door of the office. The ball entered his right breast, and came out under the right shoulder-blade. Merritt fell upon the floor, uttered one short groan, and was dead. Edmondson fled, and went to the residence of Maj. Elias Rector, about two miles from town, where he sent for the sheriff. He was afterward tried for the murder and acquitted.

Killing of William Thompson.—In 1859 Jacob Pittman was keeping a hotel in Sebastian County, and William Thompson was one of his boarders. Pittman became jealous of Thompson, and charged him with being unduly intimate with his (Pittman's) wife. A quarrel ensued, and Pittman shot and killed Thompson. The former was arrested, tried for the offense, and found guilty. An appeal was then taken to the supreme court, and, pending the decision, James Rudd and two or three others went to the jail ostensibly for the purpose of taking him out, but really for the purpose of shooting him as his head appeared above the trap-door. But instead of putting his head up he put up his hat, at which they fired, doing him no damage. He then climbed out and escaped. He was gone until 1862, when he returned and got his family, and with them went to Texas, where he was afterward captured by the Confederates for the purpose of forcing

*Hallam's History of Arkansas.

him into the army, and was there shot by a guard. Pittman had also killed a man in Fort Smith. The man attempted to shoot him, when he cut him down in self-defense.

Killing of Barnes and Matthews.—On one Sunday evening in 1859 or 1860 John Barnes and Daniel Matthews quarreled on the street in Greenwood, and shot and killed each other with pistols. Barnes was a cattle dealer on a visit to this county from Texas.

Murder of Tyler, and Lynching of Dumas and Walls.—In 1872 Thomas Walls was indicted for the murder of William Tyler, a farmer living twelve miles south of Greenwood. Walls and Tyler were together one evening, and went to the house of one of them, where they indulged in drinking spirituous liquors. Having thus crazed their brains, they became engaged in a quarrel, and Walls struck Tyler with a gun, and broke his skull, from the effects of which he died. Walls was arrested, and put into jail at Greenwood to await trial, and was there about twelve months. Meanwhile Charles Dumas, a negro, had been arrested and put into jail for striking an old man named Garner, at Fort Smith, on the head with a rock. Having by some means obtained the necessary articles, he dressed himself as a woman, and thus made his escape, securing and taking with him the jailor's pistol. In the fracas Walls also escaped with the negro. The latter fled into the "bottoms," and was followed by Jasper Blakely, who had just been appointed deputy marshal, and, being closely pursued, turned and shot his pursuer. Two negroes were then dispatched to capture and bring Dumas in, which they succeeded in doing that same evening. Meanwhile an alarm was given by firing guns, in response to which about 200 citizens assembled, took Dumas out after he had been returned to the jail, and dragged him about fifty yards to the rear thereof, where they hung him on the limb of a walnut tree while it was yet daylight. Walls remained out a day or two before he was recaptured and returned to the jail, and, on the second night after the hanging of Dumas, the crowd (or mob) re-assembled and took him out also and hung him, and this ended the whole tragedy.

Killing a Prisoner.—In 1874 a man named Barrett had

been placed in jail at Greenwood, on a charge of having stolen a suit of clothes in that town. On a certain occasion the jailor, R. T. Fuqua, took the prisoner out to empty some slops, and when the prisoner was engaged emptying the buckets the jailor shot him with a pistol. On trial before a jury of inquest the jailor claimed that the prisoner was trying to effect his escape. This was denied by witnesses, but the jury acquitted the jailor.

Killing of Dr. Waters.—A year or two after the foregoing transaction Dr. Waters, of Salem, was killed by William Belt, a merchant. Waters was a good physician, but was overbearing and troublesome when drinking. He made an attack upon Belt, who shot and killed him with a shot-gun. Belt was tried for the offense, but was acquitted on the ground of self-defense.

Other Crimes.—The first execution that took place at Fort Smith under sentence of the Federal court occurred on August 15, 1873, when John Childers, a half-breed Cherokee, was hung for the murder of Reyburn Wedding on October 14, 1870. He was arrested soon after the murder, but made his escape and was re-arrested three months later. He was brought to Van Buren, but again made his escape, with six others, on May 3, 1871. He remained at Liberty until September, when he was brought to Fort Smith, arraigned in November, and admitted to bail. He reported promptly at the May term, but the case was not tried until the following November, when he was convicted.

On October 10, 1873, two Cherokees, Young Wolf and Tu-na-gee, were executed for the murder of two trappers on Grand River in the Cherokee Nation, whom they killed for a few traps and some other worthless articles.

The third execution occurred on April 3, 1874, when John Billy, John Painter and Isaac Fillmore paid the death penalty, for three several murders. Billy, while under arrest at Muskogee, shot and killed Perry DuVal, a guard, shot Deputy Marshal J. C. Wilkinson through the body, and Deputy Marshal Willard Ayres through the wrist, in for which he received a shot in the head. Before his execution he made a profession of religion, and was baptized into the Episcopal Church. John Painter, a young Seminole, was convicted of being accessory to the murder of a drover on Canadian River, Choctaw Nation, in the fall of

1873. Isaac Fillmore was a Choctaw boy, not more than seventeen years old, who murdered an unknown white man near Fishertown, in the Creek Nation, in June, 1873.

On January 15, 1875, a young Indian named McClish Impron was hung for the murder of an unknown white man in 1873. He confessed his guilt, and asserted that his father had urged him to commit the deed. He was the first man Judge Parker passed sentence of death upon.

On September 3, 1875, William Moore, Samuel Fooy, William Whittington, Daniel Evans, all white except Fooy, who was part Cherokee, Smoker Mankiller, a full Cherokee, and Edward Campbell, suffered death in accordance with the sentence of the court. Moore killed William Spivey on November 9, 1874. Fooy killed a man named Naff, near Webster, on July 11, 1872. Mankiller killed William Short in Flint District, Cherokee Nation, September 1, 1874, and died protesting his innocence. Dan Evans killed a young man named Seabolt, near Eufaula. Whittington, while drunk, cut the throat of an old man named Turner, and robbed him. This occurred in the Chickasaw Nation. Edward Campbell and his half brother, Edward Butler, killed a negro man and woman in the Choctaw Nation. Butler was sentenced with the others, but when being taken from the court room made a bold dash for liberty, and was shot and killed just as he reached the gate of the inclosure.

The sixth execution took place on April 21, 1876. This time five unfortunates were shot through the death trap to eternity. The victims were Aaron Wilson, a negro, for the murder of an old man named Harris, and his little son, in September, 1875, near Washita Agency; Isham Seely and Gibson Ishtanubbee both full Choctaws, for the murder of an old Indian doctor called Funny, and his cook, a colored woman; Orpheus McGee, for the murder of Robert Alexander, in the Chickasaw Nation, on April 20, 1875, and William Leach, a white man, for killing Henry Watkins, in March, 1875, in the Cherokee Nation. On September 8, 1876, Osey Sanders, Sinker Wilson, *alias* Flyer Wilson, *alias* Acorn, Sam Peters and John Valley, all Indians, were sent to the happy hunting grounds, Sanders, for the murder of Thomas Carlisle, in the Cherokee Nation, on August 16, 1875;

John Valley, for killing Eli Hatchet, in 1873, and Sam Peters, for the murder of Charity Hanson, near Stringtown, Choctaw Nation, on October 15, 1875. Sinker Wilson was convicted of the murder of Datus Cowan, at Van Buren, on November 30, 1867, and was sentenced to be hung. On December 3, of the same year, he escaped from the jail and was at large until 1875, when he was again arrested, and tried on his identity. At the time of his escape he was only about sixteen years old.

On December 20, 1878, James Diggs, a negro, and John Post Oak, an Indian, were hung. Diggs' case was a remarkable one. In the summer of 1873 he was traveling through the Indian Territory, near the Kansas border, with his employer, J. C. Gould, a stock dealer, and a fellow workman, Hiram Mann. On the night of August 4 they encamped at a deserted cabin, and early on the following morning Diggs startled some people in the vicinity by stating that two mounted Texans came to the cabin in the night and killed his companions. The bodies of the murdered men were found, showing that they had been killed with an ax. No horse tracks were to be seen, and $27 in greenbacks were found upon the negro. This led to his arrest, but as no witnesses appeared against him he was released. Five years afterward Deputy Marshal J. C. Wilkinson, hearing of the case, was convinced of Diggs' guilt, and set to work to get up evidence against him. He found that one of the supposed murdered men, Mann, after lying unconscious for thirty days, had recovered, and was living in Michigan, and upon his testimony Diggs was convicted.

On August 29, 1879, Henri Stewart and William E. Wiley, *alias* "Colorado Bill," were executed. The former was born in the Choctaw Nation, the son of a white man, was a graduate of Yale College and Harvard Medical College, and had traveled extensively as a ship physician. He was convicted of being accessory to the murder of Dr. Jones, at Caddo, C. N., on August 8, 1878. Wiley was an Ohian who came South during the Civil War, and led a reckless frontier life until he murdered a Cherokee named Brown, at Muscogee, on February 23, 1879. He was arrested and convicted at the following May term.

John Jacobs and Robert Massey were hung on April 13, 1883,

Jacobs, a full Choctaw, was convicted in November, 1882, of the murder of a Mexican, Lee Morralles, in December, 1881. The Mexican had stopped at Jacobs' house to spend the night, but had left before morning, taking a pair of boots belonging to his host. Jacobs and a companion followed and arrested him, but, to save the trouble of taking him back, shot him. Massey killed a young man, Edward P. Clark, in the summer of 1881. The two men went from Dodge City, Kas., to Dakota with a drove of cattle, and after making the trip started for their homes in Texas. While *en route* Massey killed his companion, concealed the body in a hole, burned up the clothing and saddle, turned his own horse loose, mounted his companion's horse and went on. Upon trial he put in the plea of self defense, but all the circumstances proved it to have been a cold-blooded murder.

On June 29, 1883, W. H. Finch and M. Joseph, colored, and Teolitse, a full Creek, were hung. Finch, in July, 1882, stole a horse at Fort Sill, and was arrested at Decatur, Texas, by the civil authorities. He was being taken back to Fort Sill by three negro soldiers, and on the way, while two of them were asleep and the third at a spring for water, he gained possession of a gun, killed the sleeping guards, and made his escape. He was re-arrested in Texas, and convicted at the March term, 1883. Joseph was hung for the murder of Bud Stevens and his wife in April, 1882, on Arbuckle Mountain. He had an accomplice, Henry Loftus, whom he also killed before his arrest. Teolitse killed a white man named Cochran in the Choctaw Nation, for the purpose of robbery.

Thomas L. Thompson, John Davis and Jack Womankiller were hung for murder. Thompson and James O'Haleran, neither of whom had a family, lived together near Stonewall in the Chickasaw Nation, and Thompson, to possess himself of the little property his companion had, killed him. Davis was a full Choctaw, who killed a white man named Bullock in June, 1883, for the purpose of robbery. The case of Jack Womankiller was similar. He was a full Cherokee, and killed a white man named Wyatt in the Cherokee Nation on May 10, 1883. He afterward, while drunk, boasted of the deed, and was arrested.

William Phillips, a white man, was hung for the murder of

his father-in-law, William Hill. The parties lived just across the river from Fort Smith, in the Cherokee Nation, and had had some prior quarrels. Phillips had attacked Hill, and was under indictment for an assault with intent to kill him, when he went at night to Hill's cabin, and, thrusting the muzzle of a shot-gun through a crack, blew his brains out.

On June 26, 1885, William Parchmeal and James Arcine, Cherokee Indians, were hung for the murder of Henry Feigel on November 25, 1872. Feigel was a Swede, and was killed and robbed near Tahlequah. For twelve years the assassins went unpunished, but "murder will out," and in 1884 they were arrested by Deputy Marshal Andrews. Upon trial they prosecuted each other. Each attempted to clear himself by charging the murder upon the other. They were tried twice, the first jury failing to agree.

In February, 1886, seven men were sentenced to be hung on April 23, 1886, but before that day arrived the sentences of all but two had been commuted. The two unfortunates were Joseph Jackson, a negro, convicted of killing his wife at Oak Lodge, Choctaw Nation, on March 9, 1885, and James Wasson, a white man, who participated in the murder of Henry Martin in 1872, but was not apprehended until he took a hand in the killing of a man named Watkins in 1884.

At the February term, 1886, there were three convictions of murder in the first degree. Calvin James, an Indian-negro, was found guilty of the murder of Toney Love, whom he killed for four gallons of whisky. The crime was committed in the Chickasaw Nation in August, 1885, and he was hung on July 23, 1886. At the same time Lincoln Sprole, a white man, expiated the murder of Ben Clark and his son, Alexander Clark, whom he killed on May 30, 1885, in Paul's Valley, Chickasaw Nation. Kit Ross, a Cherokee half-breed, was sentenced to be hung with James and Sprole, but was respited until August 6, 1886. He killed John Davis on December 20,1885. Two years before he had attempted to ride into Davis' house, and had been forcibly ejected. On the day of the murder they met in a store at Chateau, and without a word Ross shot Davis in the back, and ran away, but was soon captured.

On January 14, 1887, the scaffold claimed four more victims, John Stephens, a mulatto, being one. On the night of May 28, 1886, he entered the house of Mrs. Annie Kerr, who lived in the Delaware Nation, brained her and her son, Louis Winters, then went to the residence of Dr. James T. Pile, and attempted to murder the entire family. He struck the Doctor and his wife on the head with an ax, and severely injured the other inmates of the house. All recovered, however, but the Doctor. The evidence against Stephens was circumstantial, but conclusive. J. T. Echols, who met his death with Stephens, killed John Pettenridge near White Bead Hill, Chickasaw Nation, on February 16, 1886, in a cruel and wanton manner. He was mad at Pettenridge about a horse-trade, and, going to the woods where he was at work, shot him without warning. James Lamb and Albert O'Dell, the other victims of this execution, were hung for the murder of Edward Pollard, in the Chickasaw Nation, on December 26, 1885. Each charged the murder upon the other, and thus assisted in their own prosecution.

Pat McCarty, an Irishman, was sentenced to be hung on January 14, but was respited until April 8, 1887, when he was duly executed. His crime was the killing of John and Thomas Mahoney. The Mahoneys were young men who had been at work on a railroad in the Territory, and were on their way to Kansas. They had a good team and wagon, and McCarty and a companion obtained permission to ride with them. While in camp, on the second or third night, McCarty and his accomplice killed the young men, and proceeded on their journey to Kansas, where they sold the team and divided the money. When arrested McCarty stoutly declared his innocence, but the evidence, although circumstantial, was conclusive.

On October 7, 1887, Silas Hampton, a Chickasaw youth, was executed for the murder of an old man, Abner Lloyd, about ten miles from Tishomingo.

April 27, 1888, was the day set for the execution of seven men, but before that day arrived four of them had been otherwise disposed of. The three unfortunates were Jackson Crow, Owen D. Hill and George Moss. Crow was convicted of complicity in the murder of Charles B. Wilson, of Kulla Chaha, on

August 7, 1884. The killing was done on the way home from an election, in the presence of some ten or twelve persons, all of whom, with two exceptions, were considered accessories. All were natives but Crow, and the Federal court had no jurisdiction over them.

Moss was a negro convicted of killing George Taff, in Red River County, Chickasaw Nation, on November 26, 1886. George Moss, Sandy Smith, Factor Jones and Dick Butler, all colored, conspired to steal a beef by killing and butchering it, but, before attempting to carry out their nefarious scheme, they entered into an agreement that they would kill whoever discovered them. Taff, a farmer of the neighborhood, chanced to ride through the bottom where the men had just killed a steer belonging to him. As he approached them Moss shot him. Jones and Butler were citizens of the Nation, and were shot by a mob there. Smith was shot while attempting to escape from the jail at Fort Smith, and died a short time before the trial.

Owen D. Hill, a negro, was hung for the murder of his wife, from whom he had previously separated.

Gus. Bogles, a white man, was hung on July 6, 1888, for complicity in the murder of J. D. Morgan, a coal miner, at Blue Tink, I. T., on June 28, 1887.

UNITED STATES DISTRICT COURT.

The early history of the United States District Court for the Western District of Arkansas is given in that of Crawford County, elsewhere in this work. Up to the second Monday of May, 1871, it was held in the town of Van Buren, and since that time it has been held in the city of Fort Smith. Prior to its removal to this city it was a small institution in comparison with what it is now. "This is the largest court in the world, and not only has jurisdiction over Western Arkansas, but also over the five civilized tribes of the Indian Territory. To run this court, with its vast array of deputy United States marshals, and posse without number, requires an annual expenditure of more than $250,000, the greater portion of which is spent in Fort Smith. As a result of the large amount of criminal business done by this court, frequent executions occur, the news of which is heralded over the country to the detriment of Fort Smith. But all the hanging done here is done by the Federal court, and the Indian Territory, which lies immediately to the west of us, furnishes all this ripe fruit for the gallows. We refer to this as it is not understood by a great many people who have not taken the trouble to investigate it, and is put down to the detriment of Fort Smith. Here life and property are secure, and the law is enforced as strictly as any place in the United States." [From Fort Smith Chamber of Commerce.]

In this connection it is proper to say that the county of Sebastian has never hung but one man, and that was a colored man named George Green, for the killing of his wife, which occurred about the year 1883. The records show that from January 1, 1873, to January 1, 1886, there were seventy convictions in the Federal court for capital offenses, forty-two executions, three died in jail, twenty-one were commuted to imprisonment for life, and two to short terms, one unconditional, one shot while attempting to escape, and one pardoned after serving a short time. Of the prisoners confined in jail at this writing, thirty are charged with murder, forty for larceny, and fifty for peddling whisky, making 120 in all, and nearly all of them are from the Indian Territory.

The officers of the Federal court are as follows: I. S. Parker, judge; M. H. Sandels, district attorney; C. M. Cook, assistant district attorney; Stephen Wheeler, clerk; I. M. Dodge, deputy clerk; J. A. Hammersly, crier; John Carroll, marshal; W. H. Cravens, chief deputy marshal; J. C. Pettigrew, jailor.

REPRESENTATIVE MEN.

Among the representative men who have been citizens of the territory composing Sebastain County it is proper to make especial mention of the following individuals, of eminent notoriety:

Judge James Woodson Bates, brother of Frederick and Edward Bates, of national notoriety, was born in Goochland County, Va., about 1788, and died at his home in Crawford (now Sebastian) County, Ark., in the year 1846. He was educated at Yale and Princeton Colleges, and graduated in the latter about 1810. When quite young he attended the trial of Aaron Burr, at Richmond, for treason. Soon after leaving college he commenced the study of law, and not long after the organization of the Territory of Arkansas, in 1820, he located at the post of Arkansas, and there commenced the practice of his profession. Soon thereafter he was elected first territorial delegate to Congress. In 1823 he was a candidate for re-election, but was defeated by the Hon. Henry W. Conway. After leaving Congress, Bates removed to the newly settled town of Batesville, which was named after him, and there resumed the practice of law. In November, 1825, President Adams appointed him one of the territorial judges. On the accession of Gen. Jackson to the presidency, his commission expired without renewal, and soon thereafter he removed to what is now Sebastian County, and there married a daughter of Maj. Moore, and settled on a farm, where he remained until his death. In the fall of 1835 he was elected to the constitutional convention, and contributed his ability and learning in the formation of the organic law of the State of Arkansas. Soon after the accession of John Tyler to the presidency he appointed Judge Bates register of the land office at Clarksville. He discharged every trust and all the duties devolved upon him with the utmost fidelity. He was a most gifted conversationalist, and a writer of unusual vigor. His mind was richly stored with classical learning.

Maj. Elias Rector, the youngest son of Wharton Rector, one of the nine Rector brothers who were brave soldiers in the War of 1812, was born in Virginia, September 28, 1802, and died at his home in Fort Smith, Ark., on the 22d of November, 1878. Though born in Virginia he was reared in St. Louis County, Mo., and educated at Lexington and Bardstown, Ky. He came to Arkansas in 1825, as surveyor under his uncle, Elias Rector, the surveyor-general of Illinois and Missouri, and in 1837 he moved to Fort Smith, where he resided until his death, save an interim of four years during the Civil War. He was appointed by President Jackson as United States marshal of the Indian and Arkansas Territories, and successively held the position for sixteen years, being first succeeded in 1846 by his cousin, Gov. Henry M. Rector, under President Tyler's administration. He was again appointed marshal by President Pierce.

One of his greatest achievements in life was the removal, as the agent of the Government, of the Seminole chief, Billy Bowlegs and his followers from Florida to the Indian Territory, for which service Congress voted him a resolution of thanks and $10,000. He was superintendent of Indian affairs for many years, and held that position when the Civil War broke out. Being opposed to the dissolution of the Union, and also to the taking up of arms against the people of his own section, he sought refuge in Texas, where he found shelter until the war closed, and then returned home to find a fortune lost in the wreck of war, and the Federal authorities in possession of his once princely home. Age and accumulated misfortunes came, in the winter of life, to chill his declining years, yet he met the inevitable with a moral heroism, which imparted a charm to his manhood. In the discharge of his official duties he was ever distinguished for his fidelity, his scrupulous integrity, and although millions of public money passed through his hands no one could ever say that one cent was misappropriated, or used for selfish purposes. He lived respected, and died lamented by all who knew him.*

Gen. Bonneville.—Among the most noted of the officers of the infantry stationed at the post of Fort Smith was Maj. B. L. E. Bonneville. He was of French parentage, and had been educated at West Point. His service upon the frontier had brought him into contact with Indian traders and mountain trappers, and he became so excited by their tales of wild adventure, and their accounts of vast and magnificent regions as yet unexplored, that an expedition to the Rocky Mountains became the ardent desire of his heart, and an enterprise to explore untrodden tracts the leading object of his ambition. In August, 1831, he obtained a leave of absence until October, 1833, in order that he might carry into execution his design of exploring the country to the Rocky Mountains and beyond. On the 1st of May, 1832, he took his departure from Fort Osage, on the Missouri, with a party of 110 men. He was the first to use wagons for transportation on these great inland expeditions, instead of mules and pack-horses.

On the 27th of July of the same year he reached the head-

* The sketches of Bates and Rector are compiled mostly from Biographical History of Arkansas, by Hallum.

waters of the Colorado of the West, which emptied into the Pacific. He was the first to cross the Rocky Mountains with a wagon train, and was justly entitled to the credit of the discovery of the Southwest Pass. Fremont, however, afterward was accredited with its discovery. Capt. Bonneville remained in the mountains several years, and nothing was heard from him; his name was dropped from the rolls. He was subsequently restored to the army, with his proper rank, and served with distinction until he was retired with the rank of brigadier-general.

He entered a large body of valuable land near Fort Smith at an early day, and after his retirement returned to Fort Smith, where he married a young lady, a native of the city. He built a handsome house on an eminence on the prairie, beautified the grounds, and then enjoyed life with his young wife, surrounded by a large circle of pleasant and devoted friends. In 1878 he closed his long career by a peaceful and happy death, leaving his wife a large and ample fortune. His adventures in the Rocky Mountains were written by Washington Irving, and published under the title "Bonneville." It is an interesting book. In speaking of himself, upon his return from this expedition, he said: "He who, like myself, has lived almost from boyhood among the children of the forest, and over unfurrowed plains and rugged heights of the western wastes, will not be startled to know that, notwithstanding all the fascinations of the world on this civilized side of the mountain, I would fain make my bow to the splendors and gayeties of the metropolis, and plunge again amidst the hardships and perils of the wilderness." Gen. Bonneville, however, did not make another expedition. In 1849, when the first immigrants to California assembled at Fort Smith, he was assigned to the command of the troops to escort them across the continent. He came here full of pleasant anticipations of retracing the steps of his early life, but before the expedition started he was supplanted by another, and his high hopes were dashed to the ground. He was greatly beloved by the people among whom he lived, for his charity and scrupulous integrity, and his death was deeply mourned, although his life had reached beyond the allotted period.

Dr. Joseph H. Bailey, another army officer, acquired large property in and around Fort Smith, and for many years identified himself with the community. His son, also a physician, still lives there. The Doctor was a splendid physician, took an active interest in everything for the improvement of the town and country, and died respected by all who knew him.

Gen. Zachary Taylor, whose history is familiarly known by every intelligent school-boy, commanded the United States troops at the post of Fort Smith for two or more years, and left here to take command of the troops which invaded Mexico in 1846. Of him Col. Ben. T. Duval, in his historical address of 1876, spoke as follows: "Many of our citizens remember him well. He was remarkably plain and unpretending in his manners. His social and hospitable habits made him generally popular. No one, judging from his appearance, would take him for a military man. I remember a circumstance that will show how little of the pomp and circumstances of the military there was in his dress and deportment. A couple of young brevets, fresh from West Point, were attached to the army in this department, and arrived here on a steamboat about daylight. Gen. Taylor, being an early riser, went on board the boat about sunrise, as was his custom to go to the boats when they arrived to hear the news, he being a large planter in Louisiana, and our mail facilities then were limited to a semi-weekly mail. The young men had just arisen, and seeing the old gentleman, whom they took for a farmer, accosted him as follows: 'Good morning, old fellow, how's the crops?' Gen. Taylor responded, 'Purty good.' They pressed him to take a drink, and amused themselves at his expense for some time, and as he left they sung out, 'Give our love to the old woman and the gals,' which he promised to do. You can judge of their surprise when later in the day they called, in full dress, to pay their respects to the commanding general, and found him to be their 'old fellow' of the morning. Gen. Taylor presented his wife and his daughter, Miss Bessie, remarking to them, 'Here are the old woman and my gal.'"

MILITARY.

The Mexican War.—Sebastian County has not been behind in furnishing her quota of soldiers to participate in the wars of the country. A few of her early settlers were among the United States troops that garrisoned the post of Fort Smith in an early day, and two companies of soldiers for the Mexican War were raised in her territory before she became a county. One of these was organized at Forth Smith, under Capt. Felch, and joined Yell's regiment, and with it served through the war. The other was raised mostly in what was then Big Creek Township, and was organized under Capt. Brooks. The quota for the army being full, it was not received.

THE CIVIL WAR.

Preparations.—At the outbreak of the Civil War great excitment prevailed in Sebastian County, and naturally enough the great majority of the people were in full sympathy with the Southern cause. The first actual operations, or the beginning of hostilities, in this part of the State was the seizing of the United States post at Fort Smith by the State troops. On the night of April 23, 1861, the steamers "Frederick Nortrebe" and "Talequah" arrived at Van Buren from Little Rock, with about 300 State troops on board, eight pieces of artillery, and fully prepared with all the munitions of war necessary for taking possession of the post at Forth Smith, all under the command of Col. Solon Borland. He had with him a demand from Gov. Rector to Capt. Sturgis, the commander of the post, to surrender it to the State of Arkansas. Adjt.-Gen. Burgevin accompanied the expedition, as did also Capt. C. C. Danley, of Little Rock. On the arrival of these boats at Van Buren the company already organized, and known as the Frontier Guards, began active preparations for joining the expedition, and, after being diligently employed all night in fitting themselves for the service, left next morning for Fort Smith. Capt. Perkins' Company of cavalry also left, or passed through Van Buren, *en route* to Forth Smith. The boats with the troops on board started there some time in the night, but before reaching their destination Capt. Sturgis, who had anticipated the movement, and who had kept a spy, or spies, concealed on the south side of the river below Van Buren, to inform him of the approach of any vessel or vessels with State troops on board, evacuated the fort with the garrison, and took with him all the arms and other munitions of war that he could, crossed the river and fled into the Indian Territory on his way to Fort Washita. The State troops arrived some three or four hours after the fort was evacuated, and took quiet possession, and continued to hold it. Another boat, the "Lion," arrived early on the morning of the 24th, with a body of State troops, and others soon followed, so that by that night Fort Smith was occupied with several hundred soldiers, in armed opposition to the Government of the United States.

On this same day (April 24), in response to a previous call, a large number of citizens of all parties met at Greenwood, in Sebastian County, and organized a meeting to consider what course they should pursue in connection with the war then already commenced. On motion of Mr. Fishback the Hon. Francis Dunn was called to the chair, and James A. Brown was made secretary. A committee, consisting of Messrs. William Fishback, Joseph W. Head, J. T. London, M. T. Tatum, J. H. Treadway, W. J. Witcher, J. H. Mendenhall, Dr. Swindell and J. R. Smoot, was appointed to draft resolutions expressive of the sense of the meeting. After due deliberation the committee reported as follows:

> WHEREAS, The administration of Lincoln, with a spirit of duplicity equaled only by its total disregard of every patriotic duty, has inaugurated a policy of coercion and subjugation by force of arms, arraying brothers against brothers: therefore be it,
>
> *Resolved*, By the citizens of Sebastian County, of all parties, in mass assembled, that we will resist such policy on the part of the administration even to the death! And to this end we pledge our lives, our fortunes, and our sacred honor!!

Following this meeting men flew to arms as if by magic, and soon several companies of soldiers were organized within the county, and as time passed, and the war progressed, the excitement increased and the bitter feeling against the Federal administration became more and more intense, as evidenced by the following article, which appeared in the Fort Smith *Herald* of June 17, of that year:

"It behooves every man to be ready, as all of the fighting men of the State will be needed. Get all your rifles ready, and if possible have the molds made conical and shaped like the minie ball, as the rifle will carry twice the distance with more than double the force. Let every gun and pistol in the land be put in good order, and organize guerrilla bands throughout the mountains and swamps, so that the enemy can be removed if they invade the State. Don't delay; be ready!"

Gen. McCulloch's Proclamation.—On the 27th day of June, 1861, Gen. Ben. McCulloch, the Confederate general, then in command of the Arkansas department, issued the following proclamation:

> Citizens of Arkansas, rally to the defense of your frontier! The troops of Missouri are falling back upon you. If they are not now sustained your State will be invaded and your homes desolated! All who can arm themselves will at once rendezvous at Fayetteville, where they will await further orders. All those who have arms belonging to the State will march to the scene of action, or give their arms to those who will not desert their country in this hour of danger. All organized companies of infantry and cavalry which report at Fayetteville will be accepted, and at once formed into regiments and battalions. The necessary subsistence stores will be forwarded from this point. Rally promptly, then, citizens of Arkansas, and let us send this Northern horde back from whence it came! (Signed) BEN. McCULLOCH,
> *Brigadier-General Commanding.*

In response to this call for troops the volunteer companies then under organization soon filled up, and the formation of others began. The first company raised in Fort Smith was known as the "Fort Smith Rifles," commanded by Capt. J. H. Sparks, with W. J. Walton as first lieutenant. The next company was the "Belle Point Guards," a German company, commanded by Capt. Hertzig. Then came "Reid's Battery," commanded by Capt. Jack Reid, assisted by —— first lieutenant; M. S. Wilcox, senior second lieutenant, and James H. Reed, junior second lieutenant. About the same time another company was raised, and commanded by Capt. W. C. Corcoran; a company of cavalry was also raised, and commanded by Capt. Thomas Lewis. All of these five companies joined the State troops. The "Fort Smith Rifles" and Capt. Corcoran's company joined the Third Arkansas Infantry. "Reid's Battery" was attached to the Third Louisiana Infantry, commanded by Col. McCulloch. Capt. Lewis' company joined Col. DeRosey Carroll's regiment. All of these companies were organized in full before the close of July, 1861, and the citizens of Fort Smith and vicinity had subscribed

$1,000 per month for the support of the soldiers' families. The city then claimed a population of only 2,500; but that was probably an over-estimate. The following tribute to the ladies was published at that time in the *Parallel*: "Too much praise cannot be ascribed to the patriotic ladies of Fort Smith, for their untiring perseverance and zeal in the cause of Southern independence. They have made the uniforms for seven companies, and for a part of these companies they have made two suits, besides repairs and additions to uniforms of other companies. They have given every attention to the sick that ladies could personally give; they are willing to do more when an opportunity is offered."

Another company in addition to the foregoing was raised for the State service; it was a company of cavalry, commanded by Capt. H. C. Minehart. Capt. John Griffith organized a company of soldiers at Greenwood early in 1861. It went to Fort Smith in a short time after the evacuation by the Federal troops, and took charge of the fort. It belonged to the Third Arkansas, State troops. This regiment participated in the battle of Oak Hill (Wilson's Creek) August 10, 1861, and there suffered a considerable loss. Of the Fort Smith Rifles, Lieut. Walton and Privates D. Holdesby, R. Woodson, L. D. Harper, Meyer Levy, H. Goodchesux and J. C. Emmert were killed. In Capt. Corcoran's company Lieut. Donahoe was wounded; and in Capt. Griffith's company Lieut. Inge was wounded, and Henry Vought and R. J. McCytur were killed. Some other companies of this regiment suffered greater loss. J. R. Gratiott was the colonel of this regiment. The Second Arkansas State troops (Col. DeRosey Carroll's regiment), was also in the battle of Oak Hill, and Capt. Thomas Lewis' company lost two men killed. Soon after this battle was fought the State troops were disbanded, and some of those belonging to Sebastian County, afterward, in 1862, volunteered in the organization of Capt. J. M. Ward's company of Col. Rector's, subsequently Col. King's, regiment of Arkansas volunteers in the Confederate service, and others joined various other commands.

In December, 1861, Gen. Ben McCulloch was in command of the Confederate army at Fort Smith. The following table shows the several commands composing his army, together with the strength of each and the number present for duty on the 21st day of that month:

COMMANDS.	STRENGTH.	PRESENT.
P. O. Hebert, Third Louisiana Infantry........	757	584
E. McNair, Fourth Arkansas..................	587	397
Mitchell, Fourteenth Arkansas................	937	891
Churchill, First Arkansas Mounted Rifles......	882	682
McIntosh, Second Arkansas Mounted Rifles....	722	553
E. Greer, Third Texas Cavalry................	1,020	747
B. Warren Stone, Sixth Texas Cavalry	935	865
Whitfield, Texas Battalion, Cavalry...........	339	315
McRea, Texas Battalion, Infantry.............	358	228
Good, Texas Battalion, Artillery..............	109	103
Hart, Arkansas Battery, Artillery..............	75	75
Province, Arkansas Battery, Artillery..........	73	73
Bennett, Texas Company of Cavalry..........	83	78
Nine companies Arkansas Infantry being organized..	585	585
Ten companies Arkansas Infantry being organized..	650	650
Sim's Texas Cavalry (not reported)		
Yound, Texas Regiment Cavalry.......	850	850
Total strength, present and absent.........	8,964	
Total strength present....................	7,676	

FRANK ARMSTRONG, *Adjutant-General of Division.*

The foregoing is a recapitulation of the "morning reports" made by each respective command for that day. Such reports are made daily when an army is in camp, so that the commanding general may at all times know the number of men he has present for duty. After Capt. John Griffith's company of State troops was disbanded, he entered the First Arkansas Volunteers, and, after the battle of Elkhorn, became colonel of that regiment. Capt. Thomas Lewis, who commanded a company in Col. DeRosey Carroll's regiment of State troops, afterward commanded another Sebastian County company, in Col. Arthur Carroll's regiment of cavalry.

Other Troops.—In May, 1862, a company was organized at Greenwood with the following officers: Elisha Meers, captain; J. O. Hawkins, first lieutenant; N. H. Osborn, second lieutenant; M. T. Tatum, third lieutenant; Jesse Crosby, orderly-sergeant. It became Company D, of the Twenty-second Arkansas Infantry. About the same time another company was organized at Fort

Smith, of which John Dillard was captain, and James Ward, first lieutenant. It also joined the Twenty-second Arkansas Infantry, and was designated as Company G. Company H, of the same regiment, W. A. Parks, captain, was raised in Franklin County, but had a number of its men from Sebastian County. Capt. James Newhitt's company, of this regiment, was raised at Dardanelle, and Capt. John Wallace's at Van Buren. The other companies composing the regiment were also raised mostly in this part of the State.

The Twenty-second Arkansas Infantry was organized at Fort Smith in July, 1862, with the following officers: H. M. Rector, colonel; James George, lieutenant-colonel; James King, major. Col. Rector resigned in July, 1863, and Lieut.-Col. George was promoted colonel. About September following he resigned, and Maj. James King became colonel. King remained until the spring of 1864, when the regiment was re-organized, and new field officers were elected as follows: John Wallace, colonel; H. J. McCord, lieutenant-colonel; M. T. Tatum, major.

This regiment, upon its organization, remained at Fort Smith about two months, and then marched to Elkhorn (Pea Ridge), and remained there in camp about three months; then moved by way of Huntsville to Mulberry, on the Arkansas River, then back to Washington County, and there participated in the battle of Prairie Grove, then fell back to Fort Smith, thence to Little Rock, and from there by boat to Pine Bluff, and thence back to Little Rock, where it remained several months, and then went to Helena, and participated in the battle fought there July 4, 1863. It then moved to a point about 120 miles west of Jacksonport, but returned at once to Little Rock, where it remained until September 10, 1863, when that place was evacuated. It then moved to Arkadelphia, and thence to Camden, where it went into winter quarters. The next spring it went to Shreveport, La., thence back to Camden, thence to Jenkins' Ferry and participated in the fight at that place, losing about seventy-five in killed and wounded; then returned to Camden, and thence to Louisville, Ark., and remained there until the spring of 1865, when it went again to Shreveport, La., and thence to Marshall, Tex., and there surrendered to the Federal forces, the war having closed. Soon thereafter the regiment returned home in a body. It contained over 1,000 men when it entered the service, but returned home with only about half that number.

Other companies were raised in Sebastian County for the Confederate army, among which was one raised in June, 1863, and of this Benjamin Neal was captain, and another raised about the same time, of which J. H. Council was captain; the latter company was raised mostly in the southern part of the county. These companies both joined their regiment at Lee's Creek, in Crawford County. James Fitzwilliams, of Fort Smith, was first a captain and afterward lieutenant-colonel of a regiment which broke up at Prairie Grove. He then returned to Sebastian County, and raised a company of independent scouts. Capt. Joseph Head also raised a company of independent scouts, and the two companies ranged mostly together. Company F, First Arkansas Infantry, was partly raised in Newton County, and finished in Sebastian about August 1, 1863. John McCoy was the captain; G. W. Raymond, first lieutenant, and ——— Edmundson, second lieutenant. Company C, of Col. Brook's regiment of Arkansas Infantry, was raised in the vicinity of Salem, William J. Witcher being captain.

The foregoing companies were all in the State and Confederate service, and many individuals of the county served in companies not here enumerated. The State and Confederate forces held possession of Fort Smith from the time they occupied it in April, 1861, until September 3, 1863, the day on which the Federal troops under Gen. Blount first took possession of it. From this time until the close of the war it remained in the hands of the Union army.

The first Federal troops raised in Sebastian County was a band of forty men, who were enlisted in February, 1863, and taken to Fayetteville under Capt. G. N. Spradling, of Greenwood. The most of these men joined Company E, First Arkansas Federal Infantry, and the balance of them joined Company A of the same regiment. This regiment was raised and organized partly at Fayetteville, Ark., and partly at Springfield, Mo. The colonel was James M. Johnson, of Madison County, Ark. After being organized it moved to Fort Smith, where it was encamped most of the time until the close of the war. It was, however, encamped at short intervals at Greenwood, Waldron, Jenny Lind and Van Buren. A great many men, in addition to the forty enlisted by Capt. Spradling, subsequently enlisted in other Arkansas Federal regiments, and many joined the regiments of other States — Kansas, Iowa, Missouri, etc. There were several hundred in all who joined various commands of the Union army. The details of the part taken in the Civil War by the citizens of Sebastian County, and of the incidents that occurred here during that period, would fill a separate volume, and hence cannot be fully given here. Soon after the Union army occupied Fort Smith, on the 30th day of October, 1863, an "Unconditional Union" mass-meeting was held there.

F. W. Wolfe was called to the chair, and C. G. Foster, was made secretary. On motion, Valentine Dell and twelve others were appointed a committee to draft resolutions expressive of the sense of the meeting. After deliberation the committee reported the following resolutions, which were adopted:

Resolved, That we are in favor of prosecuting the war as long as there is a rebel found in arms against the United States.

Resolved, That we will, to the full extent of our ability, support the administration in all its measures, past and present, to suppress the existing rebellion.

Resolved, That we recommend that delegates be chosen to a State convention, to be holden at Little Rock, for the purpose of re-organizing the State government. And,

WHEREAS, The institution of slavery is an incubus upon the welfare and material interests of the State, therefore be it

Resolved, That Arkansas should take her place in the Union as a Free State, and that all laws tending to establish or perpetuate the institution of slavery should be abolished.

Judge C. Milor and Dr. R. D. Swindell were then appointed delegates to the proposed State convention.

Skirmish on Mazzard Prairie.—On the 27th day of July, 1864, a force of Confederate troops under Gen. Gano, consisting of the Thirtieth and part of the Thirty-first Texas Cavalry, Col. Wells' Battalion and Folsom's and Walker's regiments of Choctaws, of Cooper's brigade, all estimated to be about 2,000 strong, made an attack on a battalion of the Sixth Kansas Cavalry, consisting of about 200 men, commanded by Maj. Mefford of that regiment, on Mazzard Prairie, about seven miles from Fort Smith. The Union soldiers fought well, retreating slowly toward town, but were at last completely surrounded and overpowered, and a number taken prisoners. In this engagement the Federal troops lost ten killed and fifteen wounded, and the Confederates twelve killed and twenty wounded. As soon as news of the fight reached headquarters Col. Judson, of the Sixth Kansas Cavalry, hastened to the scene of action with the balance of his regiment, but on arriving there found that the enemy had departed.

Execution of Copland and Others.—In April, 1864, A. J. Copland, John Norwood, William Cary, James Rowden and twenty others, dressed in Federal uniform and pretending to belong to the Fourteenth Kansas Cavalry, approached a party of ten Union soldiers, who were herding horses near Fayetteville, Ark., and, when within convenient distance, rushed upon and killed eight of them. The four persons here named were afterward captured, and put into confinement at Fort Smith, where they were finally tried by a United States military commission for the aforesaid crime, found guilty, and sentenced to be shot. Early in the morning of July 29, 1864, the day appointed for their execution, Chaplain Francis Springer visited them in their place of confinement, and, when the hour arrived for their execution, they were taken out, released from their irons, and seated upon their coffins in wagons. A solemn procession was formed, Capt. C. O. Judson, of the Sixth Kansas Cavalry, provost marshal of the district, with his staff, taking the lead; then followed the music, and the firing party, consisting of sixty-four soldiers of the Thirteenth Kansas Infantry, the two wagons with the culprits and chaplains, and lastly a guard. Large crowds of people, in a state of subdued excitement, assembled to witness the affair. On reaching the place of execution, which was outside of the rifle-pits, the prisoners were arranged in a line, each one by the side of his coffin. Three sides of a hollow square of infantry had already been formed to keep spectators at a proper distance. The judge advocate of the district then read the charges and finding of the military commission, after which the men knelt, and the chaplain offered prayer; then all retired except the judge advocate, who remained until the eyes of the unfortunate men were bandaged, their hands tied, and all preparations completed. At the command, forty-eight of the sixty-four muskets, were discharged, and the four victims fell dead upon the ground. One-half of the guns of the firing party were loaded with balls, and the other half with blank cartridges, and no man knew whether his gun was loaded with a ball or a blank. The sixteen men who did not fire their muskets were held in reserve to complete the work in case either of the prisoners had been left standing after the forty-eight muskets were discharged. The prisoners were young men, who had deserted from the Confederate army and gone to "bushwhacking."

Skirmishes near Fort Smith.—On Sunday, July 31, 1864, a considerable force of Confederate troops appeared about four miles south of the town, and drove in the Federal pickets. A brisk fire was kept up for some time by the skirmishers, and the Confederates threw a number of shells from howitzers. A part of the Second Kansas Battery, under Capt. Smith, promptly took position about a mile in advance of Fort No. 2, supported by two companies of the First Kansas, colored troops, just in time to prevent the Confederates from occupying the same hill with their battery. The firing from Smith's guns was effective, and killed a number of the enemy, and all their battery horses except one. The Confederates then retired to the dense thickets of the Poteau bottoms, from whence they continued firing until the next day, and then left. The Union loss was one killed, one wounded and one taken prisoner. Confederate loss not ascertained.

On the first day of September, following, the Federal pickets on the Texas road were attacked by a Confederate force consisting of about 300 Indians, and one Union soldier, Henry Hirsch, was killed. On the 28th day of the same month a forage train belonging to the Federal army, supported by a portion of the Fourteenth Kansas Cavalry, was attacked at a point fourteen miles out on the Little Rock road, by a body of Indian guerrillas, and eight men of the escort were killed and one, Captain Henry, was severely wounded. Being overpowered, the balance were obliged to retreat, leaving the wagons and dead upon the ground. The dead, when found, had been stabbed and robbed.

Last Execution.—The last authorized execution that took place in Fort Smith during the war was that of Private Alexander McBroom, of the First Arkansas (Union) Infantry, who was executed April 21, 1865, for desertion, as per sentence of a court martial. He was executed under the direction of Provost Marshal Lieut. Thomas A. Pollock, Twenty-second Regiment Ohio Volunteers, witnessed by many people and the troops off duty.

Men Killed.—In the atrocities of war a number of defenseless men were killed in Sebastian County, among which were the following: Gus Rutherford, a Union man, was hung by some State or Confederate troops at or near Greenwood. One McGoins, a Union soldier, who lived in the eastern part of the county, was caught and hung near Greenwood, while in the county recruiting soldiers for the Federal army. He was charged with having led a company of Union men, who had hung a Southern sympathizer by the name of Martin, because he was reporting Union men. Logan, a boy sixteen years old, Bridges and two men named Robins, all young men, were hung. After the Union army took possession of Fort Smith, John J. Johnson, a citizen thereof, and a Confederate, was called from his house and shot in his own yard. John Roland, who lived within three miles of town, was killed by a Confederate bushwhacker lying out and watching his opportunity. John Looman and Daniel Norton, Union men, while in camp one night about a mile from Fort Smith, were killed by Confederate scouts. In June, 1864, Capt. Turner and two men belonging to the Home Guards were killed near Greenwood by bushwhackers. The same month A. Paden, Thomas Paden and George H. Hill, Union men, were killed by bushwhackers near Fort Smith, and Patrick McKinzie, an original secessionist, but who had taken the oath of allegiance to the United States, was killed eight miles southeast of Fort Smith by a bushwhacker. Jasper Kersey was shot near Salem because he had joined a company in the Nation, and came out to see his folks. Other persons not herein named were also killed. Some desperate outlaws were executed by the citizens for their mutual protection.

Execution of Capt. Hart and Lieut. Hays.—These men were Texans, and had, as it is claimed, become outlaws, and, at the head of a band of men dressed in Federal uniform, were carrying on a sort of guerrilla warfare. They and their party were surrounded and captured by Confederate forces, and brought to Fort Smith. Hart and Hays were charged and tried by a military commission, for the killing of Col. Carroll and a Mr. Richardson, both citizens of Franklin County, and both of whom were killed at or near their respective residences. According to the evidence they were found guilty as charged, and were executed early in 1863, by order of Col. Phil. Crump, then in command of the Confederate forces at Fort Smith. They were hung to the limb of a tree at the old fort. Afterward an account was published in a Union paper to the effect that Hart and Hays were loyal Texans, who were on their way to Texas to recruit soldiers for the Federal army when captured, and were executed as Federal spies. Good citizens of Fort Smith now living, who had opportunities for knowing the truth, claim that the latter account is not correct, but that Hart and Hays, at the time of their capture, did not belong to either army, and that the first account above is correct.

CITIES, TOWNS AND VILLAGES.

FORT SMITH.

The following is from the records of the War department:* A military post was established at Belle Point, Missouri Territory, in October or November, 1817, by Brevet-Maj. William Bradford, commanding Company A, rifle regiment. The site for the post was selected by Maj. Stephen H. Long, topographical engineer, and is thus described in his report to Brig.-Gen. Thomas A. Smith, commanding the Ninth Military Department, dated May 16, 1818: "This place (Belle Point) is situated in north latitude 35 degrees, 23 minutes, 12 seconds, at the junction of Poteau, 460 miles from the mouth of the Arkansas, pursuing its meanderings, and about twenty miles above the Osage boundary line.

"The situation selected for the garrison is secure and healthy, and affords a complete command of the rivers above mentioned. Its elevation is about thirty-five feet above the water, from which it is accessible by an easy ascent. The point is supported upon a basis of stratified sandstone, well adapted for building, and is

*Address of Col. B. T. Duval.

surrounded by a woodland affording an abundance of excellent timber. The soil of the adjacent country is exuberant, producing corn, cotton, etc.

"In selecting the position a particular regard has been paid to your instructions, which required a site as near to the point where the Osage boundary line strikes the Arkansas as circumstances would permit."

Maj. Long's report was forwarded by Gen. Smith to the adjutant and inspector-general of the army, under date of May 16, 1818, with the following remark:

"The season being so far advanced, at the time of Maj. Bradford's arrival at the point fixed on for the occupancy of his command, that he was unable to do more than erect huts for his men last season. It is, however, to be presumed that he has by this time made considerable progress in the work, but of this I have not yet been informed." In December, 1818, the post was named Fort Smith, and July 4, 1819, the southern part of the Missouri Territory (embracing Fort Smith) was constituted the Territory of Arkansas.

The post was continuously occupied from the date of its establishment in October or November, 1817, to April, 1824. Re-occupied March 22,1833; troops withdrawn June 16, 1834; re-occupied July 27, 1838; troops withdrawn July 2, 1850; re-occupied March 14, 1851; troops withdrawn March 1, 1858; re-occupied December 18, 1858; troops withdrawn June 10, 1859; re-occupied September 19, 1860; troops withdrawn April 23, 1861; re-occupied September 1, 1863; troops withdrawn September, 1871.

The military reservation was relinquished to the Interior Department for disposition under act of Congress approved February 24, 1871, by the War Department letter of March 25, 1871. The cemetery tract is, however, still held as a national cemetery.

COMMANDERS OF THE POST.

Maj. William Bradford, Rifle Regiment, Nov., 1817, to Feb., 1822.
Col. Matthew Arbuckle, Seventh Infantry, Feb., 1822, to March, 1822.
Maj. A. R. Wooley, Seventh Infantry, March, 1822, to June, 1822.
Col. Matthew Arbuckle, Seventh Infantry, June, 1822, to Jan., 1823.
Capt. William Davenport, Seventh Infantry, Jan., 1823, to May, 1823.
Col. Matthew Arbuckle, Seventh Infantry, May, 1823, to April, 1824.

Capt. John Stuart, Seventh Infantry, March 22, 1833, to June 16, 1834.
Capt. B. L. E. Bonneville, Seventh Infantry, July 27, 1838, to Oct. 24, 1838.
Capt. W. G. Belknap, Third Infantry, October 24, 1838, to Sept. 25, 1840.
Capt. W. W. Lear, Fourth Infantry, Sept. 25, 1840, to Sept. 17, 1842.
Capt. William Hoffman, Sixth Infantry, Sept. 17, 1842, to May 15, 1843.
Capt. J. D. Searight, Sixth Infantry, May 15, 1843, to Nov. 16, 1843.
Capt. William Huffman, Sixth Infantry, Nov. 16, 1843, to Aug. 30, 1845.
Maj. B. L. E. Bonneville, Sixth Infantry, Aug. 30, 1845, to Dec. 21, 1845.
Capt. William Hoffman, Sixth Infantry, Dec. 21, 1845, to Jan. 4, 1846.
Maj. B. L. E. Bonneville, Sixth Infantry, Jan. 15, 1846, to July 13, 1846.
Capt. E. B. Alexander, Asst. Q. M., July 13, 1846, to Oct. 13, 1846.
Lieut. I. W. T. Gardner, First Dragoons, Oct. 13, 1846, to May 10, 1847.
Lieut. F. F. Flint, Sixth Infantry, May 10, 1847, to Nov. 3, 1848.
Capt. C. C. Sibley, Fifth Infantry, Nov. 3, 1848, to July 2, 1850.
Capt. C. C. Sibley, Fifth Infantry, March 14, 1851, to June 7, 1851.
Capt. R. C. Gatlin, Seventh Infantry, June 7, 1851, to May 24, 1852.
Col. Henry Wilson, Seventh Infantry, May 24, 1852, to Oct. 14, 1852.
Maj. George Andrews, Seventh Infantry, Oct. 14, 1852, to May 13, 1853.
Col. Henry Wilson, Seventh Infantry, May 13, 1853, to July 18, 1853.
Capt. H. J. Hunt, Second Artillery, July 18, 1853, to Aug. 7, 1853.
Capt. T. H. Holmes, Seventh Infantry, Aug. 7, 1853, to Oct. 1, 1853.
Lieut. Franklin Gardner, Seventh Infantry, Oct. 1, 1853, to Nov. 26, 1853.
Col. Henry Wilson, Seventh Infantry, Nov. 26, 1853, to May 5, 1855.
Lieut. J. H. Potter, Seventh Infantry, May 5, 1855, to May 22, 1855.
Capt. S. G. French, Asst. Q. M., May 22, 1855, to Dec. 8, 1855.
Capt. R. C. Gatlin, Seventh Infantry, Dec. 8, 1855, to Jan. 27, 1856.
Maj. Isaac Lynde, Seventh Infantry, Jan. 27, 1856, to March 3, 1856.
Capt. R. C. Gatlin, Seventh Infantry, March 3, 1856, to Dec. 19, 1856.
Maj. Isaac Lynde, Seventh Infantry, Dec. 19, 1856, to June 23, 1857.
Capt. R. C. Gatlin, Seventh Infantry, June 23, 1857, to Aug. 1, 1857.
Capt. Lafayette McLaws, Seventh Infantry, Aug. 11, 1857, to Sept. 11, 1857.
Capt. S. G. Simmons, Seventh Regiment, Sept. 11, 1857, to Feb. 8, 1858.
Lieut. E. J. Brooks, Seventh Infantry, Feb. 8, 1858, to March 1, 1858.
Capt. D. D. Sackett, First Cavalry, Dec. 18, 1858, to June 24, 1859.
Capt. W. W. Burns, Com'ry Sut., June 24, 1859, to July 21, 1859.
Lieut. E. W. Crittenden, First Cavalry, July 21, 1859, to Sept., 1859.
Capt. S. D. Sturgis, First Cavalry, Sept. 19, 1860, to April 23, 1861.
Col. William F. Cloud, First Kansas Cavalry, Sept. 1, 1863, to Dec. 1, 1863.
Col. John Edwards, Eighteenth Iowa Inf., Dec. 1, 1863, to March 21, 1864.
Lieut.-Col. A. W. Bishop, First Ark. Cav., March 21, 1864, to May 19, 1864.
Col. W. R. Judson, Sixth Kansas Cavalry, May 19, 1864, to Jan. 3, 1865.
Lieut.-Col. J. B. Wheeler, Thirteenth Kan. Inf., Jan. 3, 1865, to Feb. 1, 1865.
Brig.-Gen. Cyrus Bussey, U. S. Volunteers, Feb. 1, 1865, to Sept., 1865.
Col. M. M. Trumbull, Ninth Iowa Cavalry, Sept., 1865, to Feb., 1866.
Col. Paul Harwood, Fifty-seventh U. S. C. T., Feb., 1866, to May 9, 1866.
Capt. R. W. Barnard, Nineteenth Infantry, May 9, 1866, to Sept., 1866.
Capt. S. S. Culbertson, Nineteenth Infantry, Sept., 1866, to Nov., 1866.
Col. William J. Lyster, Nineteenth Infantry, Nov., 1866, to Jan. 14, 1867.
Col. James B. Mulligan, Nineteenth Inf., Jan. 14, 1867, to Feb. 25, 1867.
Col. Delancy Floyd Jones, Ninteenth Inf., Feb. 25, 1867, to Oct. 22, 1867.
Lieut.-Col. Pinckney Lugenbeel, Ninet'th Inf., Oct. 22, 1867, to April, 1869.

Capt. John J. Upham, Sixth Infantry, April, 1869, to June, 1869.
Capt. Montgomery Bryant, Sixth Infantry, June, 1869, to Nov., 1870.
First-Lieut. F. W. Thibaut, Sixth Infantry, Nov., 1870, to Jan., 1871.
Capt. Montgomery Bryant, Sixth Infantry, Jan., 1871, to July, 1871.
Lieut. F. W. Thibaut, Sixth Infantry, July, 1871, to Sept., 1871.

GARRISON OF POST.

Company A, Rifle Regiment, Nov., 1817, to Feb., 1822.
Companies B, C, G, H and K, Seventh Infantry, Feb., 1822, to April, 1824.
Company C, Seventh Infantry, March 22, 1833, to June 16, 1834.
Company F, Seventh Infantry, July 27, 1838, to Jan. 9, 1839.
Companies B and H, Third Infantry, Oct. 24, 1838, to Sept. 25, 1840.
Company D, Third Infantry, Dec. 28, 1839, to July, 1840.
Companies F and K, Third Infantry, Dec. 28, 1839, to Sept. 25, 1840.
Company E, Fourth Infantry, Sept. 25, 1840, to Sept. 19, 1842.
Companies D and F, Sixth Infantry, Sept. 17, 1842, to July 13, 1846
Company D, First Dragoons, Aug. 10, 1846, to May 10, 1847.
Detachments, May 10, 1847, to Oct. 31, 1848.
Company B, Fifth Infantry, Oct. 31, 1848, to May 6, 1850.
Company E, Fifth Infantry, Oct. 31, 1848, to July 2, 1850.
Company E, Fifth Infantry, March 14, 1851, to June 7, 1851.
Company F, Seventh Infantry, May 14, 1851, to May 8, 1854.
Company M, Second Artillery, July 9, 1853, to Aug. 16, 1853.
Detachment Seventh Infantry, May 8, 1854, to Dec. 8, 1855.
Companies B and F, Seventh Infantry, Dec. 8, 1855, to Aug. 1, 1857.
Companies D and H, Seventh Infantry, Aug. 11, 1857, to Feb. 8, 1858.
Detachment Seventh Infantry, Feb. 8, 1858, to March 1, 1858.
Companies A and B, First Cavalry, Dec. 18, 1858, to June 10, 1859.
Detachment First Cavalry, June 10, 1856, to Sept., 1859.
Company E, Second Artillery, Sept. 30, 1860, to Oct. 3, 1860.
Company F, Second Artillery, Sept. 30, 1860, to Oct. 15, 1860.
Companies D and E, First Cavalry, Sept. 19, 1860, to April 23, 1861.
Volunteer Troops, various States, Sept. 1, 1863, to May 9, 1866.
F, Third Battalion, Nineteenth Infantry, May 9, 1866, to Oct., 1866.
Company G, Second Battalion, Nineteenth Inf., June, 1866, to Nov., 1866.
Company B, Nineteenth Infantry, Nov. 13, 1866, to May, 1867.
Company F, Nineteenth Infantry, Jan. 14, 1867, to April, 1869.
Company H, Nineteenth Infantry, Oct. 9, 1867, to April, 1869.
Company A, Nineteenth Infantry, Oct. 15, 1867, to April, 1869.
Company E, Nineteenth Infantry, Dec. 4, 1867, to April, 1869.
Company G, Nineteenth Infantry, Dec. 4, 1867, to April, 1869.
Company K, Nineteenth Infantry, Dec. 24, 1867, to April, 1869.
Company I, Sixth Infantry, April 26, 1869, to Jan., 1870.
Company K, Sixth Infantry, April 26, 1869, to Jan., 1870.
Company D, Sixth Infantry, June 9, 1869, to July 18, 1871.
Detachment Company D, Sixth Infantry, July 18, 1871, to Sept., 1871.

The original fort was located on the bluff just below the junction of the Poteau with the Arkansas River. It was inclosed with a wooden stockade and protected by large log block houses.

Scarcely a trace of this old fort can now be discovered. It was inside of the line of the Choctaw Nation, for in the treaty with the Choctaws, in 1825, it was provided that the line between that Nation and the United States should begin "on the Arkansas 100 paces east of Fort Smith and run thence due south to the Red River." In 1838 commissioners were appointed to select a site for a new walled fort. They chose the location where the walls and other remains of Fort Smith now stand. In the same year Capt. W. G. Belknap, of the Third United States Infantry, with two companies of his regiment, built on Section 16, in Township 8 north, Range 32 west, it being the land afterward conveyed to Bishop Byrne of the Roman Catholic Church, and is now a part of the site of the city of Fort Smith. The quarters on this land were called "Camp Belknap," and were used and occupied by the troops until about the year 1842, when the buildings in the new fort were completed. After the site for the new fort was chosen, the Government purchased of Capt. John Rogers 300 acres of land, including the site. This, save the lands inclosed within the walls of the fort and the National Cemetery, has long been known as the Reservation. In 1871 it was transferred from the "War Department" to the "Interior Department," and finally, by an act of Congress approved May 13, 1884, it was donated to the city of Fort Smith "for the use and benefit of the free public schools of the single school district of Fort Smith." [For further mention of it refer to the Fort Smith schools.] Of the original buildings erected inside of the walls of the fort, the only one that has escaped destruction by fire is the one now used by the United States District Court.

"Soon after the sale to the United States of the land upon which to erect the new fort, Capt. Rogers laid off the original town. The first buildings were erected on Front Street, which was on the river bank, and for several years all the business houses were on Front Street, or Commercial Row, as it was then called. Since then the original town has been enlarged by additional surveys of lots by Capt. Rogers, Griffith & Nicks, Dr. Elias R. DuVal and Bishop Fitzgerald. The business has extended up Garrison Avenue back from the river, and most of the residences are built on the high ground lying in the rear of the original town plat. The store-houses of Front Row have been long abandoned and gone to decay."*

The surveyor who laid out the town for Capt. Rogers was Herald, the county surveyor of Crawford County. The original town extended from the river along the line of the reservation to La Fayette or Seventh Street, thence out La Fayette to the section line, and thence to the river, and thence with the river to the place of beginning. Since the address of Col. Duval was delivered, in 1876, several additions to Fort Smith have been laid out, among which is Fishback's Addition, the Reserve Addition and others. The original town, together with the several additions thereto, now covers about three full sections of land. Among the early merchants and business men of the town were John Rogers, sutler of the garrison, William Duval, Lewis and Edward Cznarnikow, George and Charles Birnie, J. R. Kannady and George and Henry Beckel. Capt. Rogers kept the first, and for a long time the only, house of entertainment. The first church edifice (a frame building on a stone basement) was erected in 1847 as a union church, on the corner of Washington and Mulberry Streets. It finally went into the hands of the Presbyterians, who occupied it until their present church was erected. This old union church is still standing, and is now designated "Cleveland Hotel." When the town was first laid out there were various large ponds bordering on Garrison Avenue, where many business houses now stand. In winter these ponds were filled with wild geese, ducks and other wild fowl, and the early settlers had much amusement in killing them.

For many years Fort Smith controlled the principal trade of the whole Indian Territory, and was the chief depot for the supplies of western forts, and had the benefit of the trade of the officers, soldiers and employes of the garrison. However, the growth of the town was slow until some time during "the fifties," when it began to grow more rapidly. In 1852 it contained only from 400 to 500 people. Johnson & Grimes were then in the mercantile business, in a house where the railroad depot now stands. Sutton & Griffith, William J. Weaver, Michael Manning, Dotson & Lynch, R. M. Johnson and Michael Henry were mer-

*Address of Col. Duval.

chants about that time. The latter was a wholesale merchant. R. M. Johnson was a dealer in skins, and William Walker was a leading lawyer. From this time forward to 1860 the town grew much more rapidly, as will appear from the following business directory of that year, to wit: General merchandise, Sutton & Spring, M. Sparks, Bostick, Griffith, Pennywitt & Co., Reutzel & Emrich, J. & H. Beckel, O. C. Ward & Co., E. B. Bright, Lewis & Navra, Speier & Shane, D. W. Heard, J. B. Gridley and Brooke & Latham; groceries, Lynch & Dodson; clothing, J. N. Slosson & Bro.; drugs, Hamilton Cline; furniture, A. Haglin; boots and shoes, A. M. Callahan & Co.; liquors, Walton & Bourne, J. B. Gridley, John Horn and Cullum & Robinson; jewelry, James Battersby and W. H. Seward; hardware, J. C. Atkinson and Charles A. Birnie; house painter, Fred Gerber; hotel, City Hotel by J. K. McKenzie; manufacturers of carriages and wagons, Jerry R. Kannady, Poteau Mills, Boyd & Massey; livery, — Gardners; harness and saddles, John Gardner; Fort Smith Female Seminary, N. E. Shepard, principal; Fort Smith Academy, J. M. Ward and J. C. Stanley, principals; Fort Smith Male and Female Seminary, Valentine Dell, principal; select school, Mrs. P. E. Gardner; photography, G. W. Sisson; lawyers, Ben. T. DuVal, John King, J. W. Vandever, J. H. Sparks and Josephus Dotson; physicians, J. H. T. Main, N. Spring, E. R. DuVal, J. E. Bomford, William L. Beall and A. Dunlap; dentist, J. N. Perkins; press, Fort Smith *Times*, by Wheeler & Sparks. In addition to the foregoing there were several mechanics' shops.

During the war the business of Fort Smith, aside from what was occasioned by the military, was generally suspended. Much of the town was destroyed, and when the war closed it presented an appearance of general desolation. During that unhappy struggle many of the citizens sought refuge in the South, and upon their return beheld the spectacle of ruined homes. This desolation, coupled with the enormous prices of the various articles of food, was enough to discourage "the bravest of the brave." The following is a list of prices current, published in the Fort Smith *New Era* of January 28, 1865, to wit: Flour, when there is any, $50 to $75 per barrel, or as much more as the seller's conscience will allow him to ask; other articles per pound—corn,

12 to 15 cents; corn meal, the same; sugar, $1; coffee, $1.50; bacon, $1; salt, $1; candles, $1; soda, $1.50; tobacco, 50 cents; dried apples, per bushel, $10; shoe blacking (small box), $1; whisky, 50 cents a thimble full (some say this consists three-fourths of Arkansas water); gin, same as above; beef, per pound, 7 to 10 cents; wood, per load, $3 to $5. In view of these facts, it is a wonder that the people escaped death by starvation. None but those who experienced these privations can tell how they did it. However, the town soon recovered and began to grow and prosper, but its growth was not rapid until recently. In 1880 the population of the place was 3,099, and since then it has increased to 15,000, and the principal business houses, instead of being confined to the streets near the river, as they formerly were, are now located on Garrison Avenue. This avenue is 120 feet in width, and its fine business blocks compare favorably with those of much larger cities. There are located on the avenue, and on the cross streets near by it, the following number of business houses, to wit: Grocery stores, 46; dry goods stores, 22; clothing and gents' furnishing stores, 7; drug stores, 10; hardware stores, 10; furniture stores, 6; jewelry stores, 5; wholesale flour and feed stores, 6; wholesale liquor houses, 4; saloons, 37; restaurants, 22; boot and shoe stores, 4; auction store, 1; dollar store, 1; queens-ware, 2; merchant tailors, 3; harness and saddle horses, 4; undertakers, 2; meat shops, 8; hotels—Main, Le Grande, McKibben, City, Avenue, Walton, Commercial, Iowa, West Point and a number of others; musical instrument stores, 2; livery stables, 5; barber shops, 11; gun-shops, 2; hide stores, 1; wall paper, paints, etc., 1; marble works, 3; book stores, 2; toy store, 1; book bindery, 1; bakeries, 2; lumber, sash, doors, blinds, etc., 3; banks—Merchants, National and American National; express offices—Pacific and Adams; telegraph office—Western Union. In addition to the foregoing, there are a number of smaller business houses in the suburbs of the city, and also several cigar and confectionery stores and fruit stands. The boarding houses are "too numerous to mention;" real estate and loan offices are also numerous. There are also a number of millinery stores, several photograph galleries and many other business houses.

Manufactories. — Chief among the manufactories are the

works of the Fort Smith Oil and Cotton Compress Company. This company was organized in 1880, with a capital stock of $225,000, and immediately commenced the erection of its buildings. The cotton compress and oil mill is a huge stone building, 800 feet in length and 175 feet in width. The average number of bales of cotton compressed and prepared for shipment annually is 40,000. During the working season, usually from 1st of September to the 1st of April following, the company employs about 115 men. The building, containing the company's cotton gin, is also made of stone, and is 50x500 feet in size. The company gins from 10,000 to 12,000 bales of cotton per year, and in the manufacture of oil and meal they consume about 10,000 bushels of cotton-seed. The number of bales of cotton compressed by this company each year represents the amount of cotton annually handled at this point, the greater part of which is grown in Sebastian County. There are several large "cotton yards" in the city for the storage of the cotton as it is brought in from the country. One of these yards near the cotton compress reaches from First to Second Streets, and is inclosed with a high stone wall.

The Border City Ice and Coal Company was organized about 1882, with a capital stock of $50,000. The building in which they manufacture ice is made of stone, and is 60x90 feet in size, with a frame addition for the furnace and coal room. It stands between the railroads near the cotton compress. Twenty tons of ice per day are here manufactured, and sixteen men are employed during the season for manufacturing it, which is from April 1 to November 1.

The Ketchum Iron Company was organized in 1886, with a capital stock of $15,000, and their buildings were completed the same year. This establishment manufactures steam engines, boilers, saw-mills, sorghum mills, elevators, drills for boring for oil and gas, and all kinds of architectural iron work, and deals in all kinds of machinery, and gives employment to about thirty men. In consequence of the great demand for steam engines the company has begun the manufacture of fifty of these machines, ranging in capacity from twelve to thirty horse-power, to enable them to supply the increasing demand for the next few months.

On the 1st of January, 1889, the company intends to increase its capital stock to $35,000. Thomas Ketchum is president and N. L. Wickwire is secretary and treasurer. Their trade extends through Arkansas, Texas and the Indian Territory. The city is also supplied with four large saw-mills, three planing-mills, and several extensive lumber yards aside from those connected with the mills, three furniture factories, flouring mills, and many smaller manufacturing establishments and mechanical shops.

Other Items.—The city is well supplied with gas and electric lights by the Fort Smith Gas and Electric Light Company. It also has a complete system of water-works, and a fine sewer system is under construction. It has about eighteen miles of street railways built and building. Its sidewalks are principally made of flagstone. It has the largest and finest opera-house in the Southwest. It has also a large fruit evaporator and a large canning factory.

In addition to its numerous churches and religious societies it has a Young Men's Christian Association. This association has a gymnasium, reading room and parlor, all well furnished. The reading room is supplied with a valuable library of choice works and periodicals.

Natural Gas.—For some months past a company has been boring for oil or gas on Mazzard Prairie, at a point about five miles southeast of Fort Smith, Ark., and finally their hopes have been realized by finding what is believed to be an abundant supply of gas. The well was fired on Saturday evening November 24, 1888, in the presence of a multitude of the citizens of Fort Smith and the surrounding country. The citizens of Fort Smith are rejoicing in anticipation of utilizing the gas to light their city, and for other purposes. It is impossible to state the supply of the gas at this writing.

A United States Signal Service Station was established at Fort Smith in June, 1882, and is still continued there. Corporal R. Q. Grant, a competent and obliging young man, is the observer. The city is in the latitude 35° and 22′ north, and in longitude 94° and 24′ west.

The Fort Smith Chamber of Commerce, recently established, occupies rooms in the second story of a building on the south side of Garrison Avenue. Here may be seen specimens of the mineral, horticultural and agricultural productions of Northwestern Arkansas, the sight of which well repays the visitor to these rooms.

St. John's Hospital, at Fort Smith, was founded and established in the early summer of 1887, by Rev. George F. Degen, rector of St. John's Parish. It is under the control of a hospital guild, composed of citizens generally embracing all religious denominations, as well as having members outside of the religious denominations. "The officers of the hospital guild constitute a board of management. Any one can become a member of the guild by paying 25 cents a month, and all members have the privilege of attending its meetings and discussing its affairs. Jews and Gentiles, Roman Catholics and Protestants of every denomination represented in the city, are found in the list of members." The first annual report of the hospital was published in July, 1888, showing that the efforts of its founder and supporters were rewarded with eminent success, there having been sixty-seven patients treated during the year. A training-school for nurses is now connected with the hospital. Mrs. Florence Wilton is general manager of the hospital and school. The officers of the hospital guild are as follows: Rev. George F. Degen, master; Mrs. Edith M. Degen, superior; Miss Laura Mitchell, secretary; Mrs. Alex. Walker, treasurer.

*The National Cemetery** at this place includes the original burying ground selected when the post was first established. It is beautifully located upon a hill overlooking the Poteau. Here rest in fraternal proximity the dead of both armies in the late struggle, as well as many of the citizens whose bones lie there. The cemetery is surrounded with a substantial brick wall, has a comfortable house for the quarters of the officer in charge. Under the management of a war-worn sergeant it is kept in perfect order; the graveled walks, bordered by beautiful flowers, make it a fit resting place for the heroes who lie there entombed. The quiet which hallows that lovely spot, where those who wore the blue and gray sleep peaceably side by side, should admonish the living that the war is over, and that hands and hearts should be joined in

* From Col. Duval's Address.

oblivion of the unhappy strife. The ex-Confederates, by the permission of the Secretary of War, have recently erected a monument over the graves of Gens. McIntosh and Steen, both of whom were killed in battle. [Gen. McIntosh was killed March 8, 1862, in the battle of Elkhorn, and Gen. Steen was killed December 7, 1862, in the battle of Prairie Grove. The Confederate soldiers were mostly buried there before the United States Army took possession of the place in September, 1863. The officer in charge makes no distinction in his care of the graves. Of the Union soldiers buried in this cemetery, 521 are known, and 1,304 unknown.]

Incorporation.—Fort Smith was incorporated by an act of the General Assembly in 1842, and the first mayor or chief officer (according to the best information now attainable) was Smith Elkins, and John R. A. Hendry, Sr., was the first recorder. The records were lost or destroyed during the Civil War, thus making it impossible to give the names of the early municipal officers in the proper order. Mr. Birnie, Joseph Bennett, John Striker, Jerry R. Kannady, R. M. Johnson, W. H. Rogers and R. P. Pulliam are remembered as having at various times held the office of mayor. The town was re-incorporated March 9, 1867, and the corporate limits were extended so as to include the additons laid out by Capt. Rogers, Dr. E. R. DuVal, and Griffith & Nicks. Since that time, as the city has improved, the corporate limits have been extended. Under a general act of the Legislature approved March 21, 1885, the city was changed from a second to a first class city. It contains four wards, and its board of aldermen consists of two from each. The present city officers are as follows: Samuel A. Williams, mayor; James H. Hamilton, city clerk; Mat. Grey, police judge; John R. McBride, city collector; J. C. Peel, city attorney; John Kennedy and W. J. Johnston, board of public affairs; Henry Schneider, city weigher; T. H. R. Johnson, city engineer; A. C. Wyman, chief of police.

Transportation.—The Arkansas River is navigable from its mouth to Fort Gibson, sixty miles above Fort Smith, but it is only navigable for boats of ordinary size for from four to six months in the year. From the early settlement until a recent date the river afforded the only means of transportation, aside from pack-horses and the slow process of hauling on wheels. Prior to 1858 the mail service was very poor, as the boats did not make regular trips, even when the river was navigable. In that year the great Butterfield California Stage Line was put in operation, and thus the mail facilities were much improved. Afterward the Star Route lines were made available. Before railroads penetrated the Arkansas Valley the goods were shipped by water to the river towns, and from thence conveyed on wagons to the towns in the adjacent country. In 1876 the railroad was completed from Little Rock to Fort Smith, and thus the river towns between these points were furnished communication by rail with the "outside world." From Van Buren this railroad swung around the bend of the river, entered the Cherokee Nation, and terminated at a point on the opposite side of the river from Fort Smith. The goods and passengers were then ferried across the river to the city. A depot was built at the terminus of the road. After crossing the Cherokee line the railroad ran a distance of about a mile within that nation, the officers of which objected to its location in their territory, consequently in January, 1879, the railroad company took up the rails from Van-Buren to its terminus, and moved the road to the line it now occupies on the south side of the river. They also moved the depot from the former terminus of the road to its new terminus in the city of Fort Smith. The trains were then transferred on a boat across the river at Van Buren.

The St. Louis & San Francisco Railroad was completed to Fort Smith in 1883, and for the next two years, until the bridge was built at Van Buren, the trains crossed the river on a boat. In 1887 this road was extended south to Paris, Texas, and the Mansfield branch of it was built from Jenson to Mansfield, in Sebastian County. The Kansas & Arkansas Valley Road gives Fort Smith connection with Wagoner, on the Missouri, Kansas & Texas Road, giving connection with Kansas and the great Northwest. The Missouri Pacific system is building a line from Fort Smith southeast to Gurdon, on the Iron Mountain Road, and has the grading nearly completed from Fort Smith to Greenwood. The St. Louis & San Francisco has commenced building another line south of Arkansas River to Little Rock, and the Fort Smith &

Dardanelle Road is also being built. In a short time Fort Smith will be a railroad center. Several mails now arrive and depart to and from the city daily, and the Western Union and railroad telegraph lines give it "lightning" communication with all parts of the country. It also has telephonic communication with all near surrounding towns.

The Press.—In June, 1847, John F. Wheeler issued the first number of the Fort Smith *Herald*, a weekly newspaper, and continued its publication as sole editor and proprietor for a number of years. In 1852 he sold it to an association to be converted into a Democratic paper, and as such its publication was continued until the approach of the war. After the war it was issued again for a time as a tri-weekly, by its original founder, John F. Wheeler, and then changed back to a weekly. Mr. Wheeler remained with it until 1870, when he sold his interest to Frank Parke. Its publication was suspended in June, 1879, for want of sufficient patronage. In 1858 the Fort Smith *Times* was established by John F. Wheeler and William Perkins, and in March, 1861, it was consolidated with the *Herald*, and the new paper, the *Times and Herald*, was continued until some time during the war by John F. Wheeler. The latter died in March, 1880, at the age of seventy-two years. At the time of his death he was connected with the *Independent.*

The *Thirty-fifth Parallel* was established October 4, 1859, upon material of the Arkansas *Intelligencer*, previously published at Van Buren. The war coming on this paper also had a short life. Its editor was A. J. Mayers. About this time, or soon thereafter, the Fort Smith *Daily Argus* was established, but it suspended in October, 1861. Its editor was George M. Turner. On the 8th of October, 1863, which was soon after the Federal forces occupied Fort Smith, the first number of the Fort Smith *New Era* was published by Valentine Dell. This number was printed on the back of a sheet containing Washington's farewell address. Sometimes, until the lines of communication were opened up after the war, the paper was printed on foolscap paper, and on various other sizes. This was the first Republican paper published in the State of Arkansas. Mr. Dell continued its publication up to his death, which occurred October 10, 1885.

He was born November 8, 1829, in Baden, Germany, came to America in 1846, settled at Fort Smith in 1859, and soon thereafter opened a high-school, and continued teaching until he established his paper. After the war he held many positions of trust, among which were State senator, postmaster at Fort Smith, and United States marshal for the Western District of Arkansas. In 1861 he married Miss A. A. Hunt, who, with nine children, survives him.

The Fort Smith *Standard*, a Union paper containing four pages of seven columns each, was established April 2, 1867, by James V. Fitch. Its publication was not long continued. In 1872 the *Herald* and *New Era*, both tri-weekly, and the *Patriot* and *Western Independent*, both weekly, were published in Fort Smith. In March, 1873, the *Herald* suspended as a tri-weekly, and continued as a weekly until its final suspension, in 1879. Another paper of recent publication in Fort Smith was the *Times*, which suspended in October, 1888. The only papers now published in the city are the Fort Smith *Elevator*, the Fort Smith *Journal*, the Arkansas *Volksblatt* and the *Golden Epoch*. The *Elevator* was established by John Carnall & Co., and its first number was published November 1, 1878. It is now published weekly by Weldon & Weaver. It is a nine-column folio, and advocates Democratic principles. The *Journal*, issued both daily and weekly, was established in November, 1887, by the Journal Publishing Company, of which J. H. Clendening is president; Stephen Wheeler, vice-president; F. R. Conway, treasurer and manager, and James A. Miller and W. C. Van-Antwerp, editors. It is an eight-column folio, and advocates Republican principles. The *Volksblatt* is an independent, eight-column folio, published weekly. It was established in 1885, and is now published by Ernest Pope. The *Golden Epoch*, a weekly paper published more especially for the colored people, was established some years ago, at Helena, Ark., and was moved to Fort Smith in June, 1888. Messrs. Fisher & Clark (colored) are its editors and proprietors. It is a six-column folio, and advocates Republican principles.

Celebrities.—Fort Smith was once the home of the celebrated artist and sculptor, Miss Vinnie Ream. Before the Civil War her father, Robert L. Ream, was a member of the real estate firm of Carnall & Ream, at Fort Smith, Judge John Carnall being the other member. Miss Ream worked in this office and colored maps for the firm. It was here that her artistic skill was discovered, upon which Judge Carnall advised her father to send her to Italy to take lessons in the art of painting, etc. Her talents, however, were not limited to the art of painting, as she also turned her attention to sculpture, and afterward, as it is well known, made a bust of President Lincoln, for which Congress paid her a handsome price.

In 1860 Messrs. J. M. Ward and J. C. Stanley taught the Fort Smith Academy, as has been mentioned in the business directory of the city for that year. Afterward this same Stanley became captain of Company A, in Carroll's (subsequently Gordon's) Regiment of Arkansas Cavalry, and deserted therefrom at Roseville, Ark., about February, 1863. Good citizens of Fort Smith, some of whom are well posted, believe and claim that he was the veritable H. M. Stanley who has since gained so much renown for his explorations in Africa; but this, for various reasons, is extremely doubtful.

Societies.—The greater portion of the following Masonic history is taken from a pamphlet compiled by E. R. Duval and Henry Reutzel in 1871. On or about the 1st of December, 1847, A. L. 5847, a meeting of the Master Masons of Fort Smith was held at the house of Dr. Joseph H. Bailey, assistant surgeon United States army, and, after due consideration, it was determined to apply to the M. W. G. M. of the State of Arkansas for a dispensation to work. A petition was accordingly drawn up, and signed by the following Master Masons: W. Claude Jones, Leopold Loewenthal, Joseph H. Bailey, Samuel L. Griffith, John G. Reed, John Rogers and F. W. Daniels.

This petition was acted upon by Van Buren Lodge No. 6, and recommended to the Grand Master, who accordingly issued his dispensation, dated December 10, A. D. 1847, A. L. 5847, designating it Belle Point Lodge No. 20, and appointing the following officers: W. Claude Jones, W. M.; Leopold Loewenthal, S. W., and Samuel L. Griffith, J. W.

At 10 o'clock A. M., on Saturday, the 18th day of December,

1847, at the Presbyterian Church, Deputy Grand Master Thomas L. Johnson installed the officers, viz.: W. Claude Jones, W. M.; Leopold Loewenthal, S. W.; S. L. Griffith, J. W.; J. G. Reed, Secretary; George S. Birnie, Treasurer; Joseph S. Bailey, S. D.; F. W. Daniels, J. D.; C. F. L. Henne, Tyler.

The lodge held its first regular communication at the house of Joseph H. Bailey, then living in the brick quarters at the post near the town. On Tuesday, January 4, 1848, at a regular communication of the lodge, Dr. Nicholas Spring, Mitchell Sparks and Jeremiah R. Kannady were initiated.

It appears from the records and tradition that the appointment of W. Claude Jones as W. M. was unsatisfactory; so much so that the Grand Master, through his deputy, Thomas L. Johnson, authorized the lodge to make another selection; and by such authority on the 21st of March, 1848, the brethren unanimously elected Samuel L. Griffith for the position. From December 18, 1847, to November 7, 1848, the lodge met in the Quartermaster's Building, Garrison, and from the latter date until January 1, 1853, in the third story of the St. Charles Hotel, at the corner of Ozark and Walnut Streets. On January 1, 1853, the hall in the Rogers Building on Washington Street was occupied, and on May 2, 1871, the lodge room was removed to Kannady's Block. On Monday, October 29, 1888, Grand Master Gee, assisted by Belle Point Lodge, laid the corner-stone of Baer Masonic Memorial Temple, now under construction on the corner of Sixth and Sycamore Streets. When completed the building will be three stories in height, the second and third to be used by the Masons. For the construction of this temple $10,000 was donated by Bernard Baer, now deceased; $4,000 by Dr. J. H. T. Main, $500 by the First National Bank of Fort Smith, $500 by P. K. Roots and $2,000 by various members of the Masonic fraternity.

Bellevue Royal Arch Chapter No. 8 was organized on January 28, 1853, and received a charter on the 15th of November following. The first officers were R. P. Pulliam, M. E. H. P.; A. Montgomery, E. K.; R. M. Johnson, E. S.; Thomas Vernon, C. of H.; Samuel Reed, Principal Sojourner; Thomas Sparks, R. A. C.; S. L. Griffith, M. 3d V.; W. W. Perry, M. 2d

V.; F. H. Wolfe, M. 1st V. On February 3, 1853, the following members were initiated: Nicholas Spring, W. J. Weaver, C. F. L. Henne, George E. Bomford and Solomon F. Clark, and during the year there were admitted eleven others, viz.: H. McDonald, Francis N. Page, Jeremiah R. Kannady, Marcellus DuVal, W. W. Fleming, F. E. Williams, Asa Clark, Leonard Spradling, John Pearson, Nicholas Williams and A. J. Singleton.

Osiris Council No. 5, R. and S. Masters, was chartered by the Supreme Council, Twenty-third Southern Jursidiction, on November 23, 1858, A. Dep. 2858, with the following members: R. P. Pulliam, Th. Ill. G. M.; S. L. Griffith, D. Ill. M.; N. Spring, P. C. W.; W. W. Perry, J. R. Kannady, William J. Weaver, Thomas Vernon, R. M. Johnson, C. F. L. Henne, Alex. Montgomery, F. H. Wolfe, George E. Bomford. No communications of the council took place from its organization until reorganization, December 26, 1866, but a charter was granted by the Grand Council of Arkansas on November 6, 1860. The officers at the reorganization were E. J. Brooks, Th. Ill. G. M.; R. M. Johnson, D. Ill. M.; H. E. McKee, P. C. W.

Jacques de Molay Commandery was organized under dispensation in Fort Smith, January 25, 1869. This dispensation was granted December 30, 1868, by Sir Knight William S. Gardner, Grand Master of Knights Templar of the United States, upon the petition of Sir Knights H. F. Thomason, S. L. Griffith, J. R. A. Hendry, William Byers, R. M. Johnson, A. McDonald, E. J. Brooks, H. T. Morton and S. P. Crawford, and the following officers were named by the Grand Master: Sir Edward J. Brooks, Eminent Commander; Sir Hugh F. Thomason, Generalissimo; Sir R. M. Johnson, Captain General.

Sir Knight E. H. English, Post E. C.; with Sir Knights S. L. Griffith, James A. Dibrell, Samuel W. Williams, J. M. Oliver, R. L. Dodge and Fred Kramer, of "Hugh de Payens Commandery" No. 1 of Little Rock, kindly visited Jacques de Molay," and aided in the organization of the new commandery, fully exemplifying the work in the various degrees. The first officers installed were E. J. Brooks, Eminent Commander; Hugh F. Thomason, Generalissimo; Raphael M. Johnson, Captain General; John H. T. Main, Prelate; James W. Donelley, Senior

Warden; John W. Cunningham, Junior Warden; Thomas Lanigan, Treasurer; John R. A. Hendry, Recorder; Constant F. Bocquin, Standard Bearer; Jonathan Vaile, Sword Bearer; Benjamin F. Atkinson, Warder, and Franklin Rounds, Sentinel.

The origin of the foregoing Masonic societies has been given for the reason that the Masons were the first to organize lodges in the county, and many of them were prominent among the early settlers.

The Independent Order of Odd Fellows was the next to organize, and among them were also many prominent early settlers of Fort Smith and vicinity. The other societies have all been organized within the last few years, and are so numerous that space will not admit of an extended mention of each. Aside from the Masonic societies already named there are now the following lodges: Amity Council No. 555, American Legion of Honor; Oklahoma Lodge No. 25, Knights of Pythias; Fort Smith Lodge, Independent Order of Bnai Brith; Border City Lodge No. 1050, Knights of Honor; Fort Smith Lodge No. 4, A. O. U. W.; Fort Smith Legion No. 2, S. K. A. O. U. W.; Border City Lodge No. 21, A. O. U. W.; Humbolt Lodge No. 22, A. O. U. W.; Robert Emmett Branch Irish Land League; Thomas Williams Post, Grand Army of the Republic; Catholic Knights of America.

GREENWOOD.

This town originated with the selection of its site for the location of the seat of justice, as heretofore stated. The land on which it was located was entered by Reuben Coker, and was in its natural uncleared state when chosen for the county seat. The first house in the town was erected by John Carnall and James J. Baker, for the office of the county clerk, Mr. Carnall occupying that position. It was a log cabin sixteen feet square, the logs being hewed flat on the outside and inside. A double log house was built in 1852, on the corner of Center and Front Streets, on the northeast corner of Block 8, and was used for some time as a court-house. Thomas Kersey opened the first store in the town, in a log building on the northeast corner of the public square. The first "tavern" was kept by John Martin, in a log house where Mrs. McDonald now lives. Betts and Phillips each had stores on the west side of the square, and Awalt & Clark had a family grocery. W. B. Manuel, Turner & Young and Hall Bros. were also early merchants in Greenwood. Dr. S. H. Payne was the first physician in the place. He was soon followed by Dr. W. F. Blakemore, who still resides there.

The growth of Greenwood was comparatively slow, but upon the breaking out of the Civil War it had attained some importance as a business point, being the next largest town to Fort Smith in the county. During the Civil War, up to September, 1863, it was occupied frequently by Confederate troops, being all that time within the Confederate lines. From that time to the close of the war it remained within the Federal line, and was occupied part of the time by Union troops. Scouting parties of both armies entered the town from time to time and burned buildings, so that at the close of the war only eighteen houses, including dwellings, were left standing. The best houses were all burned. The town has been rebuilt, and its present business directory is as follows: General merchandise, M. T. Tatum, M. S. Gaines & Co., Thomas McCord, John T. Bell, Moses & Fieble and G. N. Spradling; drugs, Dr. J. W. Nichol, J. M. Tate; groceries, R. Morrow, R. Hocott, J. J. Baker; furniture and undertaking, Cawthorn & Tatum; groceries and hardware, Meek Bros.; Thomas Kersey and M. T. Tatum are the proprietors of the Greenwood Mills, cotton gin and carding machine; J. Burton & Co. are proprietors of a grist and saw mill and cotton gin; hotels, Central House by W. P. Graham, Harper House by Thomas Harper, Capitol House by G. Loomis; livery, G. Loomis, C. A. Davis; also three blacksmith and wood shops, and some other enterprises; physicians, W. F. Blakemore, Charles Davenport, J. W. Nichol; dentist, Charles Richardson; attorneys, C. B. Neal, R. T. Fowler, R. W. McFarland, R. A. & S. T. Rowe, John Holland. In addition to the foregoing, the town contains two churches and the public school.

Greenwood was incorporated November 13, 1884, including within the corporate limits the east half of the northwest quarter, and the west half of the northeast quarter, and the north half of the northeast quarter of the southwest quarter of Section 12, Township 6 north, Range 30 west.

Societies.—Greenwood Lodge No. 131, A. F. & A. M.—Upon petition of Green J. Clark, C. Norris, L. Spradling, J. Hackett, E. Spradling, John Henderson and Charles C. Burton, recommended by Belle Point Lodge No. 20, at Fort Smith, a dispensation was granted November 27, 1857, by the Grand Lodge of Arkansas to Greenwood Lodge. Under this dispensation the first meeting of the lodge was held April 20, 1858, with John Pearson, P. M., of Belle Point Lodge, presiding as W. M. The lodge continued to work under dispensation until it received its charter, dated November 10, 1859. The first officers elected under the charter were as follows: Green J. Clark, W. M.; John C. Head, S. W.; W. McAllister, J. W.; N. D. Osborn, Treas.; James A. Brown, Sec. The following is a list of the Worshipful Masters from receipt of the charter to the present time: Green J. Clark, 1859; C. B. Neal, 1860; Elisha Meers, 1861; Clark and Neal, *pro tem.*, 1862 to 1863 (no meetings from August, 1863, to December 21, 1865); William Blalock, 1865–67; C. B. Neal, 1867–72; M. M. Hukill, 1872 to December; W. F. Blakemore, December, 1872; G. N. Spradling, 1873; W. H. Bell, 1874; M. T. Tatum, 1875; Samuel Dunn, 1876; James W. Breedlove, 1877; M. T. Tatum, 1878; J. W. Breedlove, 1880; C. B. Neal, 1881; G. N. Spradling, 1882; J. B. Forrester, 1883–84; C. B. Neal, 1885; G. N. Spradling, 1886–88. In February, 1870, a committee, consisting of M. M. Hukill, Samuel Dunn, W. F. Blakemore and Thomas Kersey, was appointed to select grounds and solicit subscriptions for the erection of a hall. The hall, consisting of a two-story frame building, the first story being for a school-room and the second for the lodge-room, was completed in 1871. Prior to this time the lodge held its meetings in the court-house. For some time the different religious denominations held their services in the school-room, but now it is used exclusively for schools. Greenwood Lodge has now about fifty members, and the present officers are G. N. Spradling, W. M.; R. T. Powell, S. W.; R. S. King, J. W.; R. Hocott, Treas.; J. M. Tate, Sec.

Greenwood Lodge No. 3184, K. of H., was instituted on July 15, 1885, by M. Futrell, with the following named officers: W. B. W. Heartsell, D.; M. D. Howk, V. D.; C. C. Stalcup, Asst.

D.; John S. Little, P. D.; R. W. Gordon, Rep.; G. N. Spradling, F. R.; W. L. Lyles, G.; T. E. Little, Guard; J. M. Davis, Sentinel; W. F. Blakemore, Med. Ex. The lodge was organized with sixteen members, and on the 1st day of January, 1888, there were twenty-three members, and at this writing there are forty-three. They have lost but one member by death. They hold their meetings in the Masonic Hall. The present officers are A. A. McDonald, D.; T. E. Little, V. D.; M. L. Gaines, A. D.; R. W. McFarland, P. D.; W. B. W. Heartsell, R.; C. C. Stalcup, F. R.; J. P. Durden, Treas.; M. T. Tatum, Chaplain; R. A. Meek, G.; R. B. Morrow, Guardian; H. M. Tate, Sentinel; Heartsell, Tatum, McFarland, J. S. Little and McDonald, Past Dictators.

Owens Post No. 20, G. A. R., was organized in 1886, with the following officers: W. J. Seamans, Post Commander; G. N. Spradling, S. V.; John A. Nichols, J. V.; J. H. Kerby, Adj.; T. J. Hanna, Q. M.; J. H. Claunts, Chaplain; F. H. Bridges, O. D.

The Press.—The Greenwood *Argus* was established about the year 1872 by Mr. Powell, who continued its publication a short time, and then sold it to George W. Rice and his son, P. H. Rice, lawyers. These gentlemen, in June, 1873, changed the name of the paper to the *Standard*, and published it about one year, and then sold it to Mr. Allison, who moved it, together with the press on which it was printed, to Waldron. The next paper was the *Western World*, moved from Waldron to Greenwood by W. W. Woods, who, after publishing it a short time, sold it to Messrs. Leake & Lyles, and they changed the name to that of *The Plaindealer*, and soon thereafter the office was burned. J. P. Leake then established the Greenwood *Times*, and soon thereafter sold it to Reese & Embra, who continued its publication about three years, and then sold it to R. W. McFarlane, who, in 1886, sold it to H. T. Hampton. On the first day of January, 1887, the latter changed its name to the Greenwood *Democrat*, and in September following he sold a half interest to Jesse A. Bell, and together, under the firm name of Hampton & Bell, they continue to publish the paper. It is a seven-column folio, Democratic in politics, and is a well-edited and neat local newspaper. The press of Greenwood has always been Democratic.

This town is situated in the municipal township of Cole, on the Mansfield branch of the St. Louis & San Francisco Railroad, thirteen miles south in a direct line from Fort Smith, and one and a half miles from Jenson Junction. The first store on the present site of the village was opened about the year 1860, by A. B. Merrill. Another store was opened in 1872, or thereabouts, by B. F. Hackett and Christopher Swisher. At this time B. F. Hackett, who owned the land on which most of the town is located, conceived the idea of establishing a permanent town, and to this end he began to give away lots to individuals who would agree to erect buildings thereon, and continued thus to donate lots until about 1886, or until the town was permanently established. In 1872 the prospective town contained only one dwelling-house, one store and one blacksmith shop, and had only one mail per week, and that came from Fort Smith. In 1886 the town had a population of from 200 to 250, and it now has a population estimated by the best authority (the mayor) at 1,200. A general survey and plat of the town has recently been made by the Kansas & Texas Coal Company, now operating the coal mines of Hackett City.

Following is the present business directory of the town: General merchandise, Kansas & Texas Coal Company, McMurtrey, Akin & Co., Upchurch & Sons, Hale & Co., P. B. Cole, J. C. Welch, Doyle & Co.; groceries, by Nutter, Howell, M. W. Christopher; drugs, Savage & Son, Forbes Bros.; hardware, Buck Williams; furniture and undertaking, W. T. Quinley & Co.; restaurants, Samuel Beaty, C. T. Wilson; millinery, Mrs. McAllister and Mrs. Murphy; dress-making, Mrs. Williams; meat markets, Samuel Goode, Pruett & Son; saloons, W. L. Walker, Irvin & Co., Al. Belt, J. F. Surratt; livery, T. J. Jorden; hotels, Hackett City Hotel by J. F. Surratt, Southern Hotel by Mrs. Jorden; physicians, Gorden & McGinty, Savage, Watson, W. J. Brinks, H. W. Fannin, Forbes; dentist, J. Cash; attorneys, P. D. Brewer, J. A. Hale; real estate agents, Williams & Harrell; also one barber shop, two blacksmith and wood shops, the flouring mill and cotton-gin of Medlin & Miller, the post-office, and the planing-mill of the Bloomburg Lumber Co., who are also dealers in lumber, doors, sash and blinds. The town contains three frame church edifices, Cumberland Presbyterian, Methodist Episcopal, South, and Baptist, each erected at a cost of about $800, and two public school-houses.

The most important business of Hackett City is that carried on by the Kansas & Texas Coal Company. This company commenced operations early in 1887, opened up a mine and sunk a shaft 150 feet deep on the west side of the town. They employ about 125 men at this mine, and excavate and ship from ten to fifteen car loads of coal per day. They have at this writing (October, 1888) from fifteen to twenty men engaged opening a slope to another coal mine about one mile east of the town. The pay-roll of this company for the month of September last, not including the expense of running their general store, was $6,500.

Hackett City was incorporated as a town September 18, 1886. The officers at present are B. F. Hackett, mayor; M. W. Christopher, recorder; J. E. Hale, treasurer, and L. P. Davenport, marshal. The board of aldermen consists of P. D. Brewer, J. D. Bender, Thomas Eskridge, P. J. Medlin and A. H. Gorden. The financial condition of the town is good, its scrip being at par.

Societies.—Amity Lodge No. 267, A. F. & A. M., received its charter, dated November 8, 1871, from Grand Master S. W. Williams. The officers named on the charter were John McClure, W. M.; William H. Shoemaker, S. W., and Ezaas Baker, J. W. Other charter members were R. P. Pulliam, H. H. Mouser, William C. Brewer, T. A. Parrish, Samuel K. Smith, J. E. McBride and J. Windham. The present officers are James A. Williams, W. M.; P. D. Brewer, S. W.; Asa Perdue, J. W.; C. M. Bagwell, Secretary; J. D. Bender, Treasurer; I. S. Ray, Tyler. The lodge has seventy-seven members in good standing, and is out of debt and has money on hand. They own their hall, but contemplate building a new one soon.

Lone Five Lodge No. 43, I. O. O. F., was organized April 17, 1888, with Hugh Hetherington, N. G.; A. H. Gorden, Vice G., and John Milling, Secretary. It has about twenty members, meets in the Masonic Hall, and is in good financial condition.

Oklahoma Lodge No. 3362, Knights of Honor, was organized December 1, 1887, with the following named officers, to wit: H.

Clay, D.; L. W. Bryant, Past D.; W. L. Walker, V. D.; G. A. Belt, Asst. D.; M. W. Christopher, Reporter; T. F. Patterson, F. R.; E. W. Harper, Treasurer. The lodge has now twenty members, and its financial condition is good.

Horse Shoe Assembly No. 10685, Knights of Làbor, was organized August 27, 1887, with E. A. Holden as Master Workman, and John M. Kelley as Secretary. It has now about 100 members.

Prairie View Agricultural Wheel, No. 596, was organized recently. It meets on the second Saturday in each month, at 1 o'clock P. M., at Roxanna Hall. James J. Short is president, and J. W. Clark, secretary.

Excelsior Wheel, No. 1749, meets at the Christian Church on the first Saturday in each month at 7 o'clock P. M. W. J. Tramell, president; J. W. Loudermilk, secretary.

The Hackett City Building and Loan Association was organized May 2, 1887, with a capital stock of $100,000. Forty thousand of this amount has been taken up, and is being paid in. The officers of the association, are T. F. Patterson, president; J. D. Bender, secretary, and B. F. Hackett, treasurer. The board of directors include the officers, and P. D. Brewer, James A. Williams, G. A. Belt and W. T. Quinley. The association is meeting with good success, and several of its members are securing homes of their own through its operations.

The Press.—The Hackett City *Horse Shoe* was established May 7, 1886, by Capt. James A. Williams, who still continues its publication. It is an eight-column folio, neatly printed and ably edited in the interest of Hackett City and the surrounding country. In politics it is Democratic.

HUNTINGTON.

This is a mining town, and is situated on the Mansfield branch of the St. Louis & San Francisco Railroad, nine miles south in a direct line from Greenwood. The Missouri, Kansas and Texas Coal Company bought the site, 120 acres, of L. P. Barrett, the original owner, and surveyed and laid out the town in August, 1887. So it is only a little over a year old at this writing. Samuel Fellows, superintendent for the coal company, built the first house at Huntington, before it was laid out, in June, 1887, and opened up the coal mining works. Slope No. 19 and some surface mining was opened in August, and Slope No. 21 was commenced in December, following. Mine No. 24, one-half mile west of the town, was opened in the spring of 1888, and an addition to Slope 21 was commenced in August, 1888. Slope 19 extends into the bank nearly eighty rods. The company is now (October, 1888) working from 400 to 500 men, and ship on an average about thirty car-loads of coal per day. The vein of coal is six and a half feet, in alternate layers of slate, as follows: 1st. Coal, 2 feet; 2d. Slate, 6 inches; 3d. Coal, 6 inches; 4th. Slate, 1 foot; 5th. Coal, 4 feet.

The first store-house in Huntington was built by the coal company in the fall of 1887. It is 120 feet long by forty-eight feet wide, and forty feet of the rear is "double decked," thus making in all 160x48 feet of floor. It is constructed of stone, and is claimed to contain more store-room than any other store in the State. In addition to this store the town contains the following business houses, to wit: General merchandise, George Bros., Ben. Wolf & Co., John McKamey; groceries, J. W. Young, J. N. Luckett; drugs, McConnell & Brewster, J. W. Young, J. W. Riley, Dr. Callicoatt; hotels, "Fellows Hotel," containing twenty-six rooms, and built expressly for a hotel, Samuel Fellows, proprietor; Drummers' Home, J. N. Luckett, proprietor; clothing, J. W. B. Appleby; restaurant, kept by Mr. McGovern; restaurant and bakery, J. Renfro; meat shops, John Dagan, Vinton Goff; billiards, A. Belt & Co.; livery, R. A. Bonham; real estate agents, F. W. Tilley & Co; attorney, A. L. Brewster; physicians, T. N. Callicoatt, A. C. Brewster, R. M. Osborn. In addition to the foregoing there are two blacksmith and wood shops, two barber shops, five or six boarding houses, one boot and shoe shop, two church edifices under construction, Methodist Episcopal and Methodist Episcopal, South; and R. L. West & Co. have a planing-mill, sash, door and blind factory and lumber yard, and last, but not least, the Farmers' Alliance have established headquarters at Huntington, and have a "cotton yard" inclosed, containing a space of 200x300 feet, on which is erected a shed 14x300 feet and ten feet high, also an office, and an elevated platform on which to unload the cotton from the wagons. The Alliance have their own agent and ship their own cotton, and thus save the profits usually given to "middlemen." The cotton yard was fitted up and is owned by the coal company, but the farmers have and will have the use of it free of rent so long as they continue to use it for the purpose intended. The yard is connected with the main line of railroad by a side-track.

The Press.—The Huntington *Hummer* was published at Huntington from June 4 to August 20, 1888, by Charles Noble, and then suspended. The Huntington *Herald* was established in October, 1888, by Bedwell & Wilson.

Miscellaneous.—Martin's addition to Huntington occupies the ridge above the business part of the town, and is being rapidly built up with residences. From this ridge a splendid view of the surrounding mountains and country is obtained. Huntington has several good business buildings, some of them made of stone, and a large number of comfortable residences; its population is estimated at from 1,200 to 1,500, many being miners.

HARTFORD.

This village is situated in the municipal township of Hartford, on Section 17, Township 4 north, Range 32 west, being in the valley between Poteau and Sugar Loaf Mountains. It was established about the year 1868 by Dr. J. D. Williams. William J. Fleming and William Stevenson opened the first store in the place. It now consists of the following business houses, to wit: General merchandise—J. D. Williams & Son, J. B. Forrester, R. Y. Baldwin, J. C. White & Co.; four blacksmith shops, one boot and shoe shop. There is also a grist-mill and cotton-gin owned by J. B. Forrester, a union church edifice used respectively by the Methodists, Baptists and Cumberland Presbyterians, and a public school-house. The physicians are Drs. S. A. Brown and J. D. Williams. The population of the village is between 200 and 300. It lies in what is called the Upper Sugar Loaf Valley, and like other Sebastian County towns it is surrounded with beautiful mountain scenery. It is distant two miles from the western and three miles from the southern boundary of the county.

Society.—DuVal Lodge No. 249, A. F. & A. M., was instituted July 1, 1871, by Dr. E. R. DuVal, with the following officers: J. L. McCracken, W. M.; Sanford Berry, S. W.; W. J. Fleming, J. W.; N. A. Jackson, Treas.; C. E. Goddard, Sec.; S. M. Griffith, S. D.; W. P. Guyon, J. D.; J. P. Landers and C. H. Davis, Stewards; G. S. Tatum, Tyler.

MANSFIELD.

This town is situated at the present terminus of the Mansfield branch of the St. Louis & San Francisco Railroad, and at the corner between Townships 4 and 5 north, and Ranges 30 and 31 west. A portion of it lies in Scott County. It was surveyed and laid out in July, 1887, by John P. Hely, C. E., for the railroad company, and J. W. Harper. The latter was the original proprietor of the land on which the town is located, but sold 100 acres to the railroad company before the town was laid out. Mansfield is in plain sight of and only two miles distant from Huntington. The first business house in the town was built in October, 1887, by J. W. Harper, and the same month D. B. Johnson opened the first store in the place. Soon thereafter McKamey & Bonham and S. E. Smith opened their stores. Other enterprises soon followed, more buildings were erected, and the new town has already grown to contain the following business houses: General merchandise, D. B. Johnson, S. E. Smith, McKamie & Bonham, J. R. Frazier, J. R. Lane; groceries, Charles Humphrey, Parks & Bryan, B. Robinson; drugs, George Remley, T. B. Richardson; millinery, Mrs. F. J. Weymouth & Co.; livery, Thomas F. Martin; blacksmith and wagon shop, William Harp & Co.; planing mill, James Sloan; hotels, Barnett House, by T. B. Barnett, Frisco House, by C. H. Hackett; boarding houses, by Thomas Cherry, William Morris; sewing machines, W. O. Martin. In addition to the foregoing Hart & Hodges have a steam power flouring and grist-mill and cotton-gin; George E. Otis & Co. are wholesale dealers in flour, salt and all heavy produce; James W. Harper deals in cotton and real estate, and Jesse Martin is a farmer and real estate agent.

Bowman Hall stands on the Scott County side of the line, as does also a large portion of the town. It was erected about the year 1874, and is a large two-story frame building, well finished, with a Masonic hall above and a church room below; the former is used by Reed Lodge No. 163, A. F. & A. M., of which mention is made in connection with the history of Salem, and the latter by the Methodist Episcopal Church. Mansfield has one physician, Dr. J. W. Gray, and one lawyer, Hon. E. T. Walker. The latter is also a physician, but devotes his attention mostly to the law. Mansfield is situated on an even plain, inclining slightly toward the east, in Sugar Loaf Valley, and is 600 feet above sea-level. The Poteau Mountains are in full view on the south, the Sugar Loaf on the west, Huntington to the northwest, and the Black Jack Ridge to the northeast, the whole constituting a magnificent view of scenery. If Mansfield continues to be the terminus of the railroad it will remain an important distributive point of trade for several towns and villages lying south, east and west of it, and will undoubtedly become a large and prosperous town. The extensive beds of coal lying near and around it will, when utilized, add much to its prosperity.

SALEM (WITCHERVILLE POST-OFFICE).

This is a very pleasant village, located in the south-central portion of the county, five miles south on a direct line from Greenwood, and near Hodge's Prairie. It is very pleasantly located, and from it a magnificent view of the Poteau and Sugar Loaf Mountains and of the Back Bone and Black Jack Ridges is obtained. William J. Witcher, the original proprietor of Salem, came from Virginia in 1850, and settled on the land where the village is located, and has resided there ever since. In 1868 he laid out the town of Salem, and he and W. Simpson erected the first store-house and opened the first store in the place. William Belt built the next house and opened the next store. In 1870 Mr. Witcher put up the first steam grist-mill and cotton-gin in the place, and in 1880 John F. Williams erected a steam flouring mill and cotton-gin.

The following is a directory of the business of Salem at the present writing: General merchandise, W. G. Graves, George A. Graves, E. M. Davenport, J. F. Marshall; groceries, J. W. Johnson, B. A. Cross; drugs, N. D. Woods; hardware, John Caldwell;

grist-mill and cotton-gin, B. A. Cross; two blacksmith shops; one church; Buckner College; post-office, William J. Witcher, postmaster; physicians, J. H. Foster, L. C. Greer, E. M. Davenport; attorney, J. M. Hudson; hotel, Isaac Davis. [For history of Buckner College, see article on Education.]

Societies.—Reed Lodge No. 163, A. F. &. A. M., was organized in 1855, about a mile and a half southeast of the present site of Salem, and the same year a church and hall was erected there conjointly by the Masons, Methodists, Baptists and Presbyterians. It was a two-story frame, and the church room was below and the hall above. Soon after the war this lodge moved across the line into Scott County, and located at the present site of Mansfield, where it still exists.

Pulliam Lodge No. 133, A. F. & A. M., was organized under a dispensation dated in January, 1875. The first officers were George W. Graves, W. M.; George H. Council, S. W.; J. K. Bell, J. W.; J. W. Sorrel, S. D. *pro tem.*; J. R. Ford, J. D.; R. P. Pulliam, Sec'y; W. J. Williams, Treas.; M. L. Spessard, Tyler. About the time this lodge was organized they erected a hall at Salem, consisting of a two-story frame building, with the first story fitted for a school-room and the second for the hall proper. The present officers of the lodge are J. W. Young, W. M.; G. H. Council, S. W.; J. J. Holland, J.W.; W. G. Graves, Sec'y; J. H. Caldwell, Treas. The membership of the lodge is twenty-five in good standing.

EDUCATION.

For full information pertaining to the Arkansas school system the reader is referred to that subject in the history of Benton County. No adequate system for the education of the masses existed in Arkansas before the inauguration of the present school system, consequently the children of the poor in Sebastin County, as well as those of all other counties of the State, were compelled to grow up into manhood without an education. Only the children of parents able to hire teachers on the "subscription plan" were furnished with school facilities. Fort Smith, being the first place settled in the county, opened and supported the first schools. Col. Duval, in his historical address, says: "Our first school-master was a little Irishman. He was a cripple, but of genial nature. I can well remember him, and even now fancy I can see him as he limped, singing 'Ye banks and braes o' Bonny Doon.'" His name was Graham. In 1840 John Carnall, who ever since that time has been a prominent and honored citizen of the county, opened a school on the corner of Third Street and Garrison Avenue, and after teaching there for some time he opened his school in his own house, on Lot 8, in Block 17, and next he taught in a house built for the purpose on Block 22, near the present Episcopal Church. This house was afterward converted into a dwelling, and is still standing. Mr. Carnall taught from 1840 to 1846, inclusive. During the last two or three years of this time he was assisted by his sister-in-law, Mrs. Mary Pearce. In an old paper has been found one of his advertisements published in 1845, which reads as follows:

> FORT SMITH ACADEMY.—The second term of this institution will commence on Monday, September 30, 1845, and continue twenty-two weeks. The instruction of the younger pupils, male and female, will be by Mrs. Mary Pearce. * * * It has been and shall be the subscriber's endeavor to see that each pupil is thoroughly versed in everything he undertakes before he is suffered to leave it.
>
> JNO. CARNALL.

In the spring of 1844 Prof. Melvin A. Lynde took charge of the Cane Hill School, and following Mr. Carnall he and his sister, Mrs. Sabine, taught for a time in Fort Smith.

Prairie Female Seminary was located in the country between Van Buren and Fort Smith, and was taught by Rev. and Mrs. C. C. Townsend. The third session of this school opened in September, 1846. Soon after this Rev. Townsend taught school in Fort Smith. He was at one time chaplain of the garrison at Fort Gibson. He was a minister of the Episcopal Church, and as such did a great deal of missionary work. He preached for his denomination in Fort Smith, the first services being held in the buildings in the fort. His first sermon in Fort Smith, however, was preached in the dining-room of the old City Hotel, then kept by Capt. John Rogers. The most noted individual in connection with the schools of Sebastian County, and who is entitled to the most extended notice, is Mrs. Martha J. Walker, who has recently retired from the profession of teaching, and who is still living, at an advanced age, in Fort Smith. In the spring of 1838 she came from Tennessee and located at Mulberry, in Crawford County, where she commenced teaching in the fall of that year. After remaining there about two years she moved to Beatty Prairie, in Benton County, and taught there other two years. She was then employed to teach the Union Mission School in the Cherokee Nation, at a point twenty miles above Fort Gibson, on the Arkansas River, where she remained four years. She then went to Newton County, Mo., and taught two or three years, and in the spring of 1851 she moved to Fort Smith, when the dreadful disease of cholera was prevailing there, and, not being able then and there to open a school, she went to Biswell Springs, on the Little Rock road, and there taught a school during the summer of that year. In the fall she returned to Fort Smith, and opened a school in a log house on North Fifth Street. This house was then surrounded by pecan trees and vines, and was then in the suburbs of the city. It has since been weatherboarded and enlarged, and is now occupied by Mr. Givens. Miss Armorer, a sister of Mrs. Dr. Main, was teaching in Fort Smith at this time. The following year Mrs. Walker (then Mrs. Dr. Ake), bought lots and built a residence and school-house combined on the corner of Fifth and Ash Streets. Here she taught until 1859, having meanwhile lost her husband, and subsequently married Calvin Walker, her last husband. She then moved with her husband to Bee Prairie, on the Little Rock road, and there built a school-house, and taught there and at Charleston, in Franklin County, for the next two years, and then returned to Fort Smith.

She then leased the Christian Chapel for ten years, and taught school in it from 1861 to 1870. After this she taught several terms at Oak Grove, near Greenwood, then returned again to Fort Smith in 1876, and opened a school and taught for a time in her own house again. She also taught the first public free school in the city. Her assistants in this school were Miss Bettie Wegman (now Mrs. Henry Birnie), her own daughter, Miss Pinkie Ake (afterward Mrs. Pennington), Miss Henriette Byers and Miss Katie Wolf. Only two of these assisted her at a time. The school then consisted of over 300 pupils. It was taught in the Christian Chapel. Later Mrs. Walker taught in the public schools in the country until 1887, when she retired from the profession. Among other early teachers in Fort Smith were some of the ministers of the different churches.

On the 17th day of September, 1875, when the authorities were prospecting to establish public schools in accordance with the new law, an election was held in Fort Smith on the proposition of voting a five-mill school tax, resulting in 170 votes in favor of the tax and 120 against it. The free school system then began to grow into favor. Prior to this time, viz., in 1870, the school board had purchased of John Carnall the Belle Grove property. The house on this property then was a large dwelling, which had been built by W. H. Morton, a former owner. It was converted into a school-house, and used as such until a short time before the present building was erected, and it was then torn down and removed.

In 1869 there were but two public schools in the city, one white and the other colored. The white school was taught by Prof. Burnham, with four assistants, and the colored school by Prof. Lyman.

The following letter, recently published by the Fort Smith Chamber of Commerce, is here inserted by permission of its author.

To the Chamber of Commerce:

I cheerfully comply with your request to submit an article for publication relative to the affairs of the city schools of Fort Smith. By an act of Congress the Government donated to the city of Fort Smith, for school purposes, the military reservation adjoining the city limits on the southwest. The munificence of the gift will be duly appreciated when it is understood that up to the present time, sales of lots in accordance with the act of Congress have reached the sum of $259,220.17, the number of lots sold being 582, or not quite half of the whole number as laid off by direction of the city government. Considering the fact that the property has steadily enhanced in value, and that some of the choicest lots remain on hand, I think it is no extravagant estimate that $500,000 will be realized from future sales. The special act of our State Legislature, creating the school district of Fort Smith, restricts the directors to the use of the interest arising from the reservation fund, the idea being to create and preserve a permanent endowment. After paying for school sites and buildings we have had sums loaned at 8 per cent per annum sufficient to realize $15,189.82 interest for the year ending July 1, 1888. Our school sites and buildings are as follows: Belle Grove, $60,000; Belle Point, $30,000; Peabody, 10,000; Howard (colored) $20,000; total, $120,000.

Besides these we have now under contract and in course of erection, DuVal School building, to cost $20,000 for the building alone, and plans are maturing for finishing at least four additional rooms for colored children. There were employed in the schools last year one superintendent and twenty-seven teachers, at a cost of $19,479.82.

We think our corps of teachers will compare favorably with any in the country, the policy of our board having been to secure the best talent that could be had for the salaries we were able to pay; and while in order to keep pace with the progress of the age we have drawn largely upon our sister States for teachers, home talent has not been neglected, but duly appreciated and employed wherever found. Relying upon the opinions of practical school men, with many of whom my position has brought me in contact for the past year, I do not hesitate to say that for efficient practical instruction, firm though kind government, coupled with good and sound moral influences our schools are unsurpassed by any in the West or South. Appreciating the importance of other information than that contained in text books, the initial steps have been taken for the establishment of a public school library. Our congressman (Hon. John H. Rogers) having succeeded in having this designated as a depository for public documents, many of these have been received, which, being supplemented by purchases made by the board of directors, gives us already the nucleus for a good collection of books. Beside the public schools we have two convent schools, one Lutheran school, a business college, and several other private schools.

Very respectfully,

(Signed) JOHN L. HENDERSON,

Secretary Fort Smith School Board.

All of the school buildings mentioned in the foregoing letter, except the DuVal building, were erected in 1885 and 1886, and about $100,000 of the principal of the reservation fund was expended in their construction. The balance of this fund, about $159,000, is now accumulating interest, to be used in payment of teachers. The writer is familiar with the school systems of Indiana, Illinois, Missouri and Tennessee, and with amounts of permanent school funds controlled in the several counties in each of these States, but has never found a county having over $70,000 under its control, but here is a single school district, containing the city of Fort Smith, with $159,000 of a permanent school fund, and a prospect, as stated in Mr. Henderson's letter, for the additional sum of $500,000, making in all $659,000. This magnificent sum, if realized and properly managed, will in future years annually pour into the school treasury at Fort Smith, at the rate of 8 per cent per annum, the large sum of $52,720 for the benefit of the schools. All this will be realized if Fort Smith continues its present rate of growth and prosperity. It is proper to say, in this connection, that the idea of securing the military reservation to the school district of Fort Smith, for the benefit of her schools, originated with Judge John Carnall, who, with a few others, labored for many years to secure the passage of a bill by Congress to make the donation.

At this writing there are twenty-eight teachers and one superintendent, Prof. N. P. Gales, employed in the schools of this district. Seven of them are in the grade and four in the high-school department of the Belle Grove school, eight in the Belle Point school, four in the Peabody school, four in the grade and one in the high school department of the Howard (colored) school. According to the last enumeration there are 2,727 children of school age in the district, 2,138 being white, and 589 colored.

There are three school districts aside from Fort Smith District in Upper Township, or the Fort Smith District of the county, and in the Greenwood District there are over seventy school districts. In some of the districts there are more than one school, so that there are outside of the city of Fort Smith upward of 100 schools in the county. "Provision is made in the constitution of the State for the support of public schools, requiring an annual tax of 20 cents upon each $100 of taxable property, to be levied and collected for that purpose, in addition to a per capita tax of $1 upon each adult male inhabitant. In addition to the amount raised by State tax, each school district, by vote, can levy a tax not to exceed 50 cents upon the $100 for the support of its school. A large portion of the districts vote the full amount allowed by law, paying in the aggregate for this laudable purpose 70 cents on the $100 of taxable property, together with a poll tax of $1." The public fund thus raised in the country districts sustain the schools from three to four months, while in the towns and densely populated and richer districts it sustains them for a longer period. When the public funds are exhausted in the towns and villages the people usually subscribe enough in addition to maintain their schools for from six to ten months. The school district in the extreme northwest part of the county has a decided advantage over all other country districts by reason of a considerable income from the tax on the two railroads passing through it and on the railroad bridge across the Arkansas. This advantage enables the district to maintain its school six months in the year with its public fund.

Buckner College.—This college is situated at Salem (Witcherville) in a beautiful grove at the edge of Hodge's Prairie, and from its location the magnificent scenery of the Poteau and Sugar Loaf Mountains, and of the surrounding country, is beyond description. The college was founded in 1875 by Rev. E. L. Compere, a Missionary Baptist preacher, and named after Rev. Buckner, a missionary to the Cherokees. In 1883 the present college building, being a frame structure 60x120 feet in size, and three stories in height, was erected at a cost of $15,000. The money was raised upon subscription by the citizens of this and adjoining counties. The first school was opened in 1883 by Dr. A. S. Worrell, who taught four sessions. He was succeeded in 1885 by Dr. Reynolds, who taught one session. Following him Dr. R. S. James taught three sessions, and Dr. David McDonald one session, the latter closing in June, 1888. The college was erected under the supervision of the Missionary Baptists, but its use was transferred in 1887 to the Episcopal denomination. It has capacity for seating 200 students. Huntington, on the Mansfield branch of the St. Louis & San Francisco Railroad, lies in full view three miles south from the college site. Salem is a very pleasant and healthful village, and has none of the vices and allurements common to large towns or cities, and is, consequently, a very desirable location for a college. It is also sufficiently near to railroad communication.

RELIGION.

The Methodist Episcopal Church.—Upon the division of the Methodist Episcopal Church in America, in 1844, and the organization of the General Conference of the Methodist Episcopal Church, South, in May of the following year, the Methodist Episcopal Church found few adherents in Northwestern Arkansas, or, indeed, anywhere in the State. Nevertheless, there were a few ministers who refused to join the new conference. Among them were Thomas Norwood, J. K. West and James Hanan. These men, with a few of the faithful in Missouri, held a convention on

Spring River, in that State, on December 25, 1845, and decided to do what they could to re-establish the Methodist Episcopal Church in these States. The next year Rev. Mark Robertson, from Missouri, attended a camp-meeting in Arkansas, and there it was agreed that J. K. West should preach on what was styled Washington Circuit, and James Hanan, on the Van Buren Circuit. In 1848 these circuits were supplied by Revs. Anthony Bewley and Mark Robertson, respectively. In their work these ministers met with great opposition, and, as the slavery agitation increased just before the war, this opposition became greater, resulting, in many instances, in their forcible expulsion from neighborhoods.

In 1852 Arkansas Conference was separated from that of Missouri, and on October 26, 1853, it convened at Fayetteville, Washington County, Bishop Morris presiding. The next year it was held at Pugh's Chapel, Sebastian County, and Bishop Ames presided.

The passage of the Kansas-Nebraska bill, in 1854, renewed the slavery agitation, and as the ministers of the Methodist Episcopal Church were, without exception, classed among the abolitionists, their attempts to hold meetings in slave-holding communities were the signals for uprisings of the people and threats of mob violence, which, in some instances, were put into execution. The Arkansas Conference, however, still maintained an existence, and in 1858 again held its session in Fayetteville. Anthony Bewley presided, no bishop being present. At this time some work was being done in Texas, and at its next meeting the conference convened near Bonham, in that State. This was on March 11, 1859. As soon as it became known that the conference was in session, a meeting was held by the citizens of Fannin County, in Bonham, at which the following resolutions were adopted, and are here inserted, since they state the position of the people of Arkansas quite as well as of those of Texas.

WHEREAS, A secret force lurks in our midst known as the Northern Methodist Church, entertaining sentiments antagonistic to the institution of slavery, and the manifest intention of whose Northern coadjutors is to do away with slavery in these United States; and,

WHEREAS, The further growth of this enemy would be likely to endanger the perpetuity of that institution in Texas; and,

WHEREAS, Sentiments diametrically opposed to the interests of the South have this day been publicly proclaimed upon our streets by a minister of said Northern Methodist Church; therefore, be it

Resolved, That the Methodist Church having separated into divisions, North and South, the organization of a Northern branch of the church in our State, as a screen behind which to hide the emissaries of a Northern political faction known as abolitionists, is dangerous to our interests, and ought not, therefore, to be tolerated by the people of Texas.

Resolved, That a suitable committee be appointed to wait on the bishop and ministers now in conference assembled on Timber Creek, in this county, and warn them to withold the further prosecution of said conference, as its continuance will be well calculated to endanger the peace of this community.

Resolved, That our motto be, peaceably if we can, forcibly if we must.

Resolved, That we hereby bind ourselves to co-operate in the future to do all we can to suppress abolitionism in our midst, and that henceforth we will suffer no public expression of abolition doctrines or sentiments in our streets or county to go unpunished.

These resolutions were presented to the conference by a committee of fifty citizens, and on the following day the conference adjourned *sine die.* It met again, however, the next spring at Pleasant Hill Church in Franklin County, Ark., but the work of the conference in Arkansas was at an end for the time. All of the ministers and many lay members fled the State. In 1861 the Missouri and Arkansas Conference (the two having again united) appointed five preachers to Arkansas, namely: J. R. West, J. W. Murray, T. Reed, Hiram Hess and C. Baker, but none of them were allowed to assume charge of their circuits. Nothing more was attempted until 1865, when the Missouri and Arkansas Conference was reorganized, and Rev. Mr. Blackburn was appointed presiding elder on the Arkansas District, while W. H. Gillam was stationed at Fort Smith, and W. L. Malloy at Fayetteville. R. W. Hammett, who had been an itinerant in the Methodist Episcopal Church, South, united with the conference, and at this time was located at Fort Smith. Mr. Blackburn was succeeded as presiding elder by W. H. Gillam, and in 1868 two districts were formed. Of the Little Rock District Mr. Gillam was made presiding elder, while R. W. Hammett was appointed to the Fort Smith District, In 1872 the Arkansas Conference of the Methodist Episcopal Church was constituted by the general conference, and was organized by Bishop Thomas Bowman, at Little Rock, on January 1, 1873, J. W. Bushong, secretary. At this time there were thirty-three preachers appointed to circuits and stations, which were grouped into four districts, viz.: Southeast Arkansas District, W. H. Gillam, P. E.; Southwest Arkansas District, E. W. King, P. E.; Fayetteville District, T. B. Ford, P. E.; Batesville District, R. W. Hammett, P. E. The appointments for the Fayetteville District were as follows: Fayetteville, E. F. Reser; Bentonville, G. W. Hood; Elm Spring, to be supplied; White River, G. W. Taylor; Huntsville, to be supplied; Van Buren, O. R. Bryant; Ozark, Henry Flood; Boston Mountain, to be supplied; Arkansas, W. H. Crawford; Carrollton and Harrison, T. M. Kirkpatrick. At the close of the year there were in the district ten churches and 1,122 members. Fort Smith and Greenwood circuits were in the Southwest District. For 1874 the appointments in the Fayetteville District were as follows: Fayetteville Station, to be supplied; Fayetteville Circuit, O. R. Bryant; Bentonville, G. W. Hood; White River, G. W. Taylor; Huntsville, T. M. Kirkpatrick; Van Buren, A. N. Fields; Ozark, J. D. Stockton; Carrollton and Harrison, E. F. Reser. T. B. Ford was again the presiding elder. Of the Southwest District E. W. King was presiding elder, and Fort Smith and Greenwood Circuits, were J. W. Bushong and L. C. Aley, respectively. In February, 1875, the third annual conference was held at Russellville, and the number of districts was reduced to three. The appointments for the Fayetteville District were as follows. T. B. Ford, P. E.; Fayetteville Union, W. H. Gillam; Fayetteville (second charge) and Washington, E. Roberts; Fayetteville Circuit, L. C. Aley; Huntsville, G. W. Hood; Ozark and Bentonville, to be supplied; Van Buren, J. A. Conley; Arkansas, Henry Turner; Fort Smith, R. W. Hammett; Greenwood and Grand Prairie, J. M. McCoy; Waldron, M. S. Hyde. At the end of the year there were reported 1,098 members, 169 probationers, 23 local preachers, 17 churches valued at $6,450, and 14 Sabbath-schools with 568 officers and scholars.

The fourth session of the conference was held at Fayetteville, beginning on February 3, 1876, and to the Fayetteville District the appointments were made as follows: Fayetteville Union, W. H. Gillam; Fayetteville (second charge), T. H. Nonally; Fayetteville Circuit, M. S. Hyde and L. W. Elkins; Bentonville, W. J. Simmons; Huntsville, J. M. Kimes; Ozark, R. C. Moter; Van-

Buren, W. H. Crawford; Fort Smith, R. W. Hammett; Greenwood and Grand Prairie, C. D. Fry. The fifth session of the conference was held at Fort Smith in February, 1877, Bishop Wiley presiding. At this session the State was re-districted, and the territory formerly embraced in the Fayetteville District was divided between Fort Smith and Harrison District. Among the appointments in the Fort Smith District were T. B. Ford, P. E.; R. W. Hammett, Fort Smith Station; W. H. Crawford, Van Buren; C. D. Fry, Ozark; L. C. Obar, Charleston; G. W. Hood, Witcherville. On the Harrison District O. R. Bryant was presiding elder, while J. M. McCoy was assigned to the Fayetteville Union, Henry Flood to Huntsville, and L. W. Elkins to Cincinnati. The sixth session of the conference was held at Little Rock during the last week in January, 1878, when the membership on the circuit in Northwestern Arkansas was reported as follows: Fayetteville Station (two charges), 90 members, 12 probationers; Fayetteville Circuit, 90 members, 10 probationers; Cincinnati Circuit, 81 members, 35 probationers; Huntsville Circuit, 120 members, 10 probationers; Fort Smith Charge, 90 members; Witcherville Circuit, 173 members, 23 probationers; Charleston Circuit, 52 members, 17 probationers; Ozark Circuit, 100 members, 19 probationers, and Van Buren Circuit, 77 members and 27 probationers. At this session Arkansas Conference was divided on the following lines: "Beginning at Ultima Thule, on the State line, and running thence through Locksburgh, Epperson's Mill, Caddo Gap, Hot Springs, Lewisburg, Batesville, Pocahontas, and thence north to the Missouri line." The work west of this line was designated Arkansas Conference, that east of it Little Rock Conference. The Arkansas Conference was divided into two districts. Harrison District, to which O. R. Bryant was assigned as presiding elder, and Fort Smith, to which was assigned Thomas B. Ford. In the Harrison District Jesse P. Lowry was appointed to the Harrison Circuit, R. W. Hammett to Fayetteville, Burrell D. Jones to Huntsville, and James Lokey to Cincinnati, and in the Fort Smith District, Graham W. Hood to Fort Smith, George E. Cunningham to Alma and Van Buren, and James W. Shinn to Ozark, L. C. Obar to Bloomer, William J. Simmons to Dayton.

The presiding elders of the Fort Smith District since 1879 have been as follows: G. W. Hood, 1880 and 1881; W. J. Simmons, 1882 and 1883; Robert C. Moter, 1884; O. R. Bryant, 1885–86–87; B. T. Jones, 1888.

The Methodist Episcopal Church has in Sebastian County at this writing (October, 1888,) the following stations and circuits: The Fort Smith Station, consisting of Trinity Charge and Ebenezer Church; Hackett City and Huntington Station, Dayton and Bloomer Circuits. Rev. N. B. Brashear is pastor of Ebenezer Church. Rev. R. C. Moter, pastor of Trinity Charge, has recently moved away, leaving it unsupplied with a minister. Not many years ago this charge had from forty to fifty members, but the membership has now dwindled to a nominal figure. The church edifice belonging to it burned down a few years ago. Rev. Milton T. Brown, late pastor of the Hackett City and Huntington Station, has recently moved to Chattanooga, Tenn., leaving that station to be supplied. Rev. J. T. Gideon is pastor of the Bloomer Circuit, of which the two principal charges are Ames' Chapel in Sebastian County and Hickson Ridge in Franklin County. The Dayton Circuit consists of Dayton, Oak Grove, Nixon and Mansfield. The membership of the Methodist Episcopal Church in Sebastian County is small, and the members are generally possessed of but little of this world's goods. The bitter feeling that was manifested against this church before the Civil War still exists to some extent, though very much modified in form.

Methodist Episcopal Church, South.—This church had its origin, as has been stated, in the withdrawal of nearly all of the Methodists in the slave-holding States from the Methodist Episcopal Church in 1844 and 1845. Under the organization of the new church Sebastian County continued, as it had been under the old organization, a part of the Fayetteville District until the year 1851, when it was changed to the Clarksville District, and remained as a part thereof until 1868, and it was then constituted, as it still remains, a part of the Fort Smith District. The presiding elders of the several districts of which the county has formed a part, beginning with the year 1850, have been as follows: Thomas Stanford, 1850; William L. McAllister, 1851 and

1852; Thomas Stanford, 1853 to 1856 inclusive; L. P. Lively, 1857 to 1859 inclusive; Russel Reneaux, 1860; * * * M. B. Pearson, 1866; J. M. P. Hickerson, 1867; W. T. Noe, 1868; J. J. Roberts, 1869 and 1870; H. R. Withers, 1871; F. M. Moore, 1872; H. M. Granade, 1873 to 1875 inclusive; S. H. Babcock, 1876 to 1879 inclusive; V. V. Harlan, 1880 to 1883 inclusive; M. E. Butt, 1884 and 1885; Thomas M. C. Birmingham, 1886 and 1887; S. H. Babcock, 1888.

In 1842 Van Buren and Fort Smith Station was established by the old church, with Rev. Byers as pastor in charge. He was succeeded the next year by Rev. Mr. Moreland, and during the years 1844 and 1845 it was under the control of Rev. J. J. Roberts. His successors were Rev. Mr. Pogue in 1846, H. A. Sugg in 1847 and 1848, and J. Eastabrook in 1849 and 1850. Rev. Eastabrook was appointed to this charge again in 1851, and died from cholera on July 21 of that year. The earliest record of the Van Buren and Fort Smith Station is that of the first quarterly conference in 1850, which met in Fort Smith on January 12. Thomas Stanford, the presiding elder, and J. Eastabrook, the pastor in charge, were present. William M. Hunt was chosen recording steward, and James Maxfield, steward. At the fourth quarterly conference for this year, the presiding elder was requested to use his influence to secure a division of the Van Buren and Fort Smith Station. This was done, and Salisbury Charge was attached to the Fort Smith Station. At the quarterly conference, held December 14, 1850, a building committee was appointed, consisting of the following persons: S. D. McDonald, Harmon Mickle, William M. Hunt, William A. Jackson and Reuben Lewis. McDonald and Mickle in 1853 were replaced by John Harrell and S. S. Sanger, Sr. The corner-stone of the new building was laid by the Masonic lodge on April 15, 1853, and was completed the same year. The success of the undertaking was largely due to Rev. John Harrell, and the new building was named Harrell Chapel. From this time until the Civil War the church was prosperous.

The first report of the Sabbath-school was made in February, 1857, and was as follows: "The Sabbath-school of this station is in a healthy and prosperous condition; notwithstanding the inclemency of the weather during the last quarter the school is in a flourishing condition. We have at this time from twelve to fifteen teachers, nearly all of whom are members of the church; from sixty to seventy-five pupils, and a library of 450 to 500 volumes, 225 of which have just been received."

From 1860 to 1866 there is no record of any quarterly conferences, and it is probable that none were held. In 1865 the conference assigned Rev. T. B. Ruble to the Fort Smith Station, and, at the first quarterly conference, J. R. A. Hendry, Francis Parks and W. H. Bailey were elected stewards. Services were held in the Presbyterian Church until Harrell Chapel, which was still in the hands of the military authorities, was delivered up. At this time only about thirty of the old members remained, and during the next two or three years the church seemed to languish. In November, 1868, Rev. H. M. Granade took charge of the work, and in a report of the condition of the church at that time said: "I find twenty members, sixteen of whom are females, and of the latter eight are widows, most of them poor in this world's goods." Mr. Granade labored with great zeal during the year, and raised the membership from twenty to forty, and since that time to the present the church has continued to prosper.

Harrell Chapel stood on Fifth Street, between Walnut and Mulberry. The lot on which it stood was sold in 1886, and the old church edifice removed. The same year the membership was divided, and the portion going out from the original church built the Central Church (frame) which stands on the corner of Thirteenth and Mulberry Streets, and the portion remaining have under completion a large and handsome brick edifice, designated First Methodist Episcopal Church, South. It stands on the corner of Seventh and Walnut Streets. This property, including the cost of the lot and building completed, cost the church $25,000. The stations and circuits of this church in Sebastian County are as follows: First Methodist Episcopal Church, South, Fort Smith, Rev. James A. Anderson, pastor; Central Church, Fort Smith, Rev. J. L. Massey, pastor; Fort Smith Circuit, including the territory fifteen miles east and the same distance south of the city, containing charges at Lavaca, Spring Hill, Mazzard

Prairie, Eureka, Enterprise and perhaps other points, Rev. G. W. Damon pastor of the circuit; Greenwood Circuit, consisting of charges at Greenwood, Burnsville, Oak Grove, Center Ridge, Pierce Camp Ground, Milltown and Washburn, Rev. W. R. Gardner, pastor; Hackett City, Huntington and Mansfield Station, Rev. J. M. C. Hamilton, pastor; Hackett City Circuit, consisting of charges at Hackett City, one in the country north thereof, Bethel, Excelsior, Mt. Olive and Mt. Pleasant, Rev. J. W. DeShazo, pastor; Mansfield Circuit, with charges at Hartford, Mansfield, Salem, Center Bluff, Brewster's Chapel, Center Bluff, Center Point and Dayton, Rev. Irwin T. Harris, pastor. The Fort Smith Station, including the two churches, has a membership of 360; the Fort Smith Circuit, 375; Greenwood Circuit, 525; Hackett City Circuit, including Hackett City and Huntington Station, 400; Mansfield Circuit, 425, making an aggregate membership in the county of 2,085. The circuits as here named are as they stand in 1888, but they are subject to change at the meeting of every annual conference. The Methodist Episcopal Church, South, is a strong denomination and is having fair success in its labors.

St. John's Episcopal Church.—The edifice of this church at Fort Smith was erected in 1859–60, on the corner of Sixth and Mulberry Streets, and the parsonage connected therewith was erected in 1886–87; both buildings are frame. A mission was established here about the year 1845, and placed under the supervision of Rev. Charles Townsend, a chaplain in the United States Army, then located at Fort Gibson. He was succeeded by Rev. Daniel McManus and others. The mission continued until the church edifice was erected; then Rev. I. Sandels became the first rector of the parish, and continued as such until March, 1863, when the church was closed on account of the war. When it was opened again, January 7, 1866, Rev. Robert B. Croes became rector for a few months, and, following him, Bishop Lay, who resided here, took temporary charge of the parish until November of that year, when Rev. Sandels returned and served as rector until 1870. Then Rev. T. B. Lee took temporary charge until 1871, when Rev. D. McManus again became rector, and remained until 1878. The same year Rev. F. B. Gilbert held the position of rector a few months, resigning in the fall. Rev. C. H. Newman became rector in August, 1879, and in September, 1880, Rev. Edward Magee succeeded him. The latter was succeeded in March, 1882, by Rev. J. S. Berne, who resigned in 1885. In December, 1886, Rev. George F. Degen assumed the rectorship, and still retains it. The parish consists of 230 members. The Sunday-school is in a prosperous condition. When Rev. Degen became rector it was composed of 115 scholars, and now (1888) it has just twice that number. The estimated value of the church and grounds is $10,000; the estimated value of rectory $1,800, and estimated value of other church property $640, making a total of $12,440, with an indebtedness of only $550. The first missionary services were held in the garrison.

The Baptist Church.—The Baptist Church at Fort Smith was organized December 1, 1859, and perhaps other churches of this denomination were organized within the county prior to the Civil War, but the organization of most of them took place since the war. The church at Fort Smith was organized with seven members, among whom were William H. Byers and wife, Mrs. M. A. Singleton and Siley Ellis. The construction of a church edifice was commenced about the same time, but not fully completed when the war broke out. Nothing further was done until after the close of the war, and then the building in its unfinished condition was given, together with the lot on which it stands, to the colored Baptists, and they continue to use it. In 1868 the church purchased Lots 1 and 2, in Block 14, in Fitzgerald's Addition, being on the corner of Thirteenth and Hickory Streets, and in 1883 the present frame church edifice was erected thereon at a cost of $3,000. The first regular minister of this organization was Rev. E. L. Compere, who served until the Civil War began, and then left. At the close of the war he returned and assumed the pastorate, which he held for several years. Others followed him until 1882, when Rev. G. W. Reeves assumed the pastorate and held it until 1884. He was succeeded a few months by Rev. John Wise, and in November, 1886, Rev. A. J. Kincaid assumed the pastorate, and continues to hold it. This church has a membership of 175, and the attendance at its Sunday-school is from 90 to 135.

In 1871 the Concord Baptist Association was organized, and soon included nearly all of the Baptist Churches in Sebastian, Franklin, Scott and Logan Counties. In 1880, a division of the association took place by a number of individual churches, among which was the one at Fort Smith, withdrawing from it. The difficulty grew out of a scandal concerning a certain minister in charge of one of the congregations belonging to the association. The association, however, has continued to hold its annual sessions, and its eighteenth session was held this month, October, 1888, at the Mazzard Prairie Church, in this county. The minutes of this session have not yet been published. The churches of this county belonging to the association, as reported in the minutes of the session held in 1887 at Union Grove, in Logan County, are the following, to wit: Prairie Grove, Sulphur Springs, Greenwood, Mount Nebo, Mazzard, Oak Valley, Union, Mount Olive, Oak Bower, West Harmony, Judson and Union Grove. G. T. Matthews was reported as pastor of Mazzard, Union, Mount Olivet, Judson and Union Grove; M. A. Pillers, of Prairie Grove; J. W. Nobles, of Sulphur Springs; D. L. Moore, of Mount Nebo; A. L. Brown, of Oak Valley; J. D. Rasbury, of Oak Bower; William Holland, of West Harmony. There are some other Baptist Churches in the county, not belonging to the Concord Association.

Presbyterian Churches.—The first church of this denomination in Sebastian County was organized at Fort Smith in 1846, by Rev. J. K. Marshall, the first pastor. The original members were John F. Wheeler, Joseph Bennett, Mrs. Margaret H. Baird and others. Of those named the latter is the only one now living, and she is believed to be the only one of the original members now living in Fort Smith. Mrs. H. B. Sparks, widow of Mitchell Sparks, joined this church in 1847, and she still lives in Fort Smith. The members of this church worshiped in the old Union Church, now known as the Cleveland Hotel, which stands on the corner of Second and Mulberry Streets, from the time of its organization until their present church was completed. The new church, which is a handsome brick edifice, was erected in 1876, at a cost of $6,000. It stands on the corner of Eighth and Mulberry Streets. Rev. Marshall served as pastor of the church one or two years, and was succeeded by Rev. Cephas Washburn, who served until 1856. In 1859 Rev. W. A. Sample became pastor, and excepting one or two intervals—the longest one being in the war period—he served as such until 1888, when he was succeeded by Rev. E. D. Gregory, the present pastor. The church has had a prosperous career. It now has a membership of about 150, and its Sunday-school is well sustained. This denomination has another organization in the county, located at Jenny Lind.

Among the most noted pioneer ministers of the gospel in this section of the country was Rev. Cephas Washburn, who came to Arkansas about the year 1830, as a missionary under the American Board to the Cherokee Indians, and lived among them until 1840, when he settled on a farm in Benton County, Ark., where he remained until 1847, and then moved to Fort Smith, where he became pastor of the church, and remained as such until 1856, and then went to Norristown, where he remained until his death, which occurred March 17, 1860. He was a man of extraordinary talents and of the highest literary attainments.

Cumberland Presbyterian Church.—At the stated meeting of Arkansas Synod in 1868 the following proceedings relative to the organization of King Presbytery were had.

WHEREAS, A petition has been received from the Arkansas Presbytery, asking for the organization of a new presbytery in that territory of the Arkansas and Ewing Presbyteries lying south of the Arkansas River;

Resolved, That the prayer of the petitioners be granted, and that a new presbytery be organized, to be known as the King Presbytery of the Cumberland Presbyterian Church, including all of the territory of Arkansas and Ewing Presbyteries lying south of the Arkansas River, and including all of the ministers and congregations in said territory.

Resolved, That the synod appoint Rev. B. H. Pierson, D. D., moderator, and Rev. Richmond Cole clerk of King Presbytery, and that the moderator be and he is hereby required to convene a presbytery at Charleston, Franklin Co., Ark., on Thursday preceding the last Sabbath in November, 1868, at 11 o'clock A. M.

The presbytery met at the appointed time, and at roll-call the following ministers answered to their names: B. H. Pierson, G. W. Williamson and Richmond Cole; W. M. Lisk was absent. The congregations represented were as follows: Charleston by W. F. McDonough, Fairview by Thomas Cauthron, Hodge's

Prairie by E. J. Wollage, Cooper Prairie by E. P. Tolkington, Long Prairie by R. S. McFarlane, Mt. Pleasant by J. H. Counsel, The congregations not represented were Greenwood, Delaware and Gum Springs. At this meeting it was ordered that a new congregation, to be known as Piney Fork, be organized within the bounds of Gum Springs congregation.

The second meeting of the presbytery was held in April, 1869, at Fairview, in Scott County, at which time Winchester and Pilot Prairie congregations were admitted. The growth of the church within the bounds of the presbytery was quite rapid, and at the end of the first year after its organization the committee on church statistics reported 96 professions, 88 accessions, 10 dismissals, 12 suspensions, 30 infant baptisms, 26 elders, 8 deacons, 3 candidates, 6 ordained ministers and 463 communicants.

In October, 1871, there were reported 15 congregations, 7 ministers, 124 accessions and 643 communicants. Two years later there were 17 congregations and 800 communicants. At the fall meeting, 1873, a petition to the synod, praying for a division of King Presbytery, and the organization of a new presbytery from the counties of Sarber, Yell and Perry, and that part of Conway south of Arkansas River, was prepared and signed by all the members of the presbytery. This petition was granted, and on November 6, 1873, the new Presbytery was organized under the name of Magazine Presbytery, with the following ministers: Richmond Cole, J. S. Burt, W. J. McDonald and J. T. Buchanan. The congregations within its bounds were Gum Springs, Piney Fork, Fairview, Six Mile, Washburn, Lavinia, Mount Pleasant, Dardanelle and Delaware. There then remained in King Presbytery three ministers, B. H. Pierson, N. B. McNabb and D. B. Harrison; three licentiates, E. W. Mathes, I. A. Gaither and S. L. Alexander, and nine congregations, Coop Prairie, Hartford, Hodge's Prairie, Pilot Prairie, White Bluff, Charleston, Greenwood, Long Prairie and Winchester. These two presbyteries continued to work as separate bodies until 1876, when the synod, upon the request of both, consolidated them under the name of Union Presbytery, which held its first meeting at Fairview, Logan County, on March 1, 1877.

The statistics of the consolidated presbyteries were reported as follows: Ordained ministers, 11; licentiates, 2; candidates, 1; congregations, 24; elders, 82; deacons, 17; added by profession, 32; by letter, 13; baptisms, 24; infants, 8; total in communion, 600; officers and teachers in Sabbath-schools, 9; scholars, 232. At the October meeting of the presbytery, in 1877, a petition was sent to the synod, requesting a restoration of the old name of King Presbytery, which was granted.

In 1880 the number of congregations had increased to twenty-seven and the communicants to 852. At the same time there were 105 elders, twenty-three deacons and eleven ordained ministers. Since that time to the present writing, 1888, the number of congregations has increased to forty-six and the communicants to 1,305. There are now fifteen ordained ministers, one licentiate and 109 elders. There are 449 scholars in the Sunday-schools of the Presbytery, besides those belonging to Union Sunday-schools, and the funds contributed for Sunday-school work for the last fiscal year was $102. The church organizations in Sebastian County belonging to the presbytery are Hodge's Prairie at Salem, Long Prairie, Oak Bower at Lavaca, Hickory Grove at Hackett City, Mt. Harmony and Union Grove near Greenwood, Washburn, Fort Smith and Greenwood, aggregating a membership of about 372. The first church of this denomination organized in Sebastian County is that of Hodge's Prairie, which was organized September 13, 1860, by Rev. B. H. Pierson, with William J. Witcher and D. Belt as elders, and other members, consisting of Z. P. and John Reed, Dotson Belt, John Laster, Elijah Wallace, Martha Wallace, P. Belt, N. J. Leonard, Matilda Reed, Emily Laster, Mary E. Witcher and others. They worshiped in the building known as Reed Lodge until they built their present church house at Salem. The congregation at Fort Smith now worship in a hall, but have completed the basement story of a new stone church edifice now in process of construction on the corner of Ninth and Mulberry Streets. This building when completed will cost about $8,000. Rev. S. H. McElvane is pastor at Fort Smith, and Rev. J. C. Francis at the Hodge's Prairie Church.

Roman Catholic Church.—Michael Manning, a venerable citizen of Fort Smith, who is eighty years old to-day (October 11,

1888), engaged at New Orleans in 1840 with an officer of the Government to work on the United States fort at this place, and arrived here on May 10 of that year. He was the first Roman Catholic that became a permanent settler in Fort Smith. On arriving here he found that two Catholic missionaries, both of whom were Frenchmen, had already located in Arkansas. One of them, Father Boles, was situated at Little Rock, and among the points visited by him in his missionary work were Fort Smith and Fort Gibson, the latter being sixty miles farther up the river. The other, Father Paris, was situated at Arkansas Post, and his missionary labors were mostly with the Creoles. There were very few Catholics then in Northwestern Arkansas. In 1844 Bishop Andrew Byrne visited Fort Smith in company with Father Curry, and remained a short time at the house of Michael Manning. While here, on that occasion, he organized the first Catholic Church. A small log church edifice was immediately erected on the corner of Third and Hickory Streets, where Mr. Manning now resides. On the same lot a foundation for a rock church was laid, and some time thereafter this property was abandoned for church purposes and sold to Richard Kern, whose family still resides there, as also does Mr. Manning.

In 1847 Bishop Byrne, then of Little Rock, purchased of the school trustees, George Birnie, Elias Rector and another, Section 16, in Township 8 north, Range 32 west, for the sum of $5,250, all of which he paid in gold. A part of this section, as elsewhere explained, had previously been occupied by United States troops, and the buildings occupied by the commander and lower officers still remained on the land. About 1851, when the old church property was abandoned, the building which had been occupied by the lower officers was adopted as the house in which to worship, and in 1853 the quarters of the commanding general were converted into a convent under the control of Theresa Farrell, mother superior, and the Sisters of Mercy. This building was enlarged by the Sisters, and in December, 1875, it was destroyed by fire. The present church edifice, which stands at the head of Garrison Avenue, was constructed in 1867, and was dedicated August 18 by Bishop Fitzgerald, assisted by Father Smyth. Soon thereafter the building now used for the convent school, it being the largest one on the grounds, was erected. There is also a small school-house in which small boys are taught by the Sisters, and another house standing on Little Rock Avenue, west of the main buildings, has been used for the education of larger boys, but is now idle. It is expected to be again utilized for that purpose. In addition to the foregoing there is the convent, parsonage and other buildings, all belonging to the denomination.

The first stationed priest was Father Curry, who left when the church property on corner of Third and Hickory Streets was abandoned. He was succeeded by Fathers Welch, Monahan, Reilly, Shanahan, and Fathers L. Smyth and Michael Smyth; the latter two located at Fort Smith before the late Civil War, and have remained here ever since. The present officiating priest is Father L. Smyth. The purchase of the school section by Bishop Byrne was a very fortunate transaction for the good of the Catholic Church. From time to time the greater part of the section has been laid out into lots, streets and alleys, and is known as Fitzgerald's addition to the city of Fort Smith. About twelve acres have been reserved in the convent grounds. The business portion of the city already extends well into the addition, and the residence portion much farther. A large portion of the lots has been sold, from which the church has derived a very large revenue, which will be largely augmented by receipts from the sales of the remaining lots a tract of land a mile square in a growing city, that will soon utilize it all for business houses, manufactories and residences, is certainly a valuable property. During the Civil War the property was despoiled to some extent, much of the timber that was standing on it being cut down.

Another Roman Catholic Church, recently built, and known as the "German Catholic Church," stands on the aforesaid tract of land, on the corner of Nineteenth and Mulberry Streets.

Evangelican Lutheran Church.—An organization of this denomination was effected in Fort Smith about the year 1874, by Rev. Wyneken, and about two years later their large frame church edifice, which stands on the corner of Twelfth and Hickory Streets, was constructed at a cost of $3,000, or perhaps more. Rev. G. Germann is the pastor of the church at this writing.

There are sixty members belonging to this organization, and the average attendance at the Sunday-school is seventy-five. The members are mostly German.

Christian Church.--The church of this denomination in Fort Smith was organized about the year 1855, probably by or through the influence of Robert Graham, then president of "Arkansas College," Fayetteville, Ark. Prior to the war services were held in a small building on North Sixth Street. Elder E. M. Northam was the minister in charge in 1859. During the war period the church became disorganized. In 1871 it was reorganized, the property on Sixth Street was sold, and the building now used by the congregation, standing on the corner of Seventh and Sycamore Streets, was completed and first occupied December 25, 1886. It cost $3,500, exclusive of the lot on which it stands. The membership of the church is 120, and the number of scholars in the Sunday-school averages about fifty. Elder R. L. Lotz was engaged to take charge as pastor November 11, 1888.

Other Churches.—There are two colored Baptist and one African Methodist Episcopal Church in Fort Smith, and some other churches in the county, of which no particular mention has been made. Upon the whole the entire county is well supplied with churches.

Camp Meetings.—During the early days of the history of the county, before church edifices were erected, camp meetings were much more frequently held than they have been of later years. Then people met together in the "leafy groves," regardless of sects, to worship God. Now nearly all denominations, save the Methodists, have dispensed with the "camp meeting" mode of worship. This denomination still adheres to the old custom, and still maintains the annual camp meeting. The "Pierce Camp Ground," situated about three miles northeast of Greenwood, was established in 1885. It consists of ten acres of land, on which are two valuable springs, named respectively Wesley and Asbury. The tract has been laid out into lots, streets and alleys, and a large tabernacle and other buildings have been erected. The annual meetings are held so as to include the third Sunday in August, and are continued from six to twelve days. The original incorporators of the Camp Meeting Association, and the purchasers of the grounds, were Frank Parke, Judge J. S. Little, W. H. Bell, Maj. M. T. Tatum, W. B. W. Heartsell, M. S. Gaines, Thomas E. Little, W. T. Rye, J. R. Bassett and John A. House. The officers of the present board of trustees are J. R. Bassett, president; W. H. Bell, secretary, and S. D. Richardson, treasurer.

SEBASTIAN COUNTY.

Daniel S. Altstatt, farmer, was born October 4, 1840, in Franklin County, Ark., and is a son of Thomas and Mary (Covert) Altstatt, natives of Clark County, Ind., born March 17, 1806, and March 17, 1804, respectively. The father was reared on a farm in his native county, where he was married October 15, 1826. In 1838 he immigrated to Franklin County, Ark., where he died in 1840. Mrs. Altstatt died in the same county in May, 1875, and was the mother of seven children, of whom four are living: John W., Margaret E., Thomas F. and Daniel S. Rachel J., Indiana and America are the ones deceased. The paternal grandparents of our subject came to the United States from Germany and settled in Pennsylvania, where they reared their family, afterward moving to Clark County, Ind. The husband was a soldier in Jackson's war, and a blacksmith by trade. He died in 1849, at the age of eighty-seven, after a residence in Indiana of about thirty-two years. The maternal grandparents were natives of Pennsylvania, moved to Indiana, and bought land and remained there some time. The husband was in the Florida War, and about 1833 came to Arkansas, and died in 1849. He was a member of the A. F. & A. M., and belonged to the first grand lodge held in the State of Arkansas, and frequently went to Little Rock to attend lodges. Learning the blacksmith's trade when a boy, in Franklin County, our subject followed that business about twenty-one years. During the war he worked at his trade in the United States shops at Fort Smith, he being one of the first workmen in the place. After the war he settled where he now lives. He then owned but forty acres of land but partially cleared, but now has 210 acres, 100 being under cultivation. His farm is nicely situated and well watered, an iron spring being immediately in front of his house. December 27, 1864, Mr. Altstatt was united in marriage to Mary E. Jones, who was born in Sebastian County September 6, 1846. Her grandparents were early settlers of Tennessee, where her parents, John and Narcissus (Rutherford) Jones, were both born. They immigrated to Arkansas in 1833. Mrs. Altstatt's maternal grandparents were natives of Tennessee. The grandfather died in his native State, and his wife in Arkansas. To Mr. and Mrs. Altstatt ten children have been born: Pleasant J., Eliza J., Mary E., Hiram A. B., William W., George W., Robert D., Abbie L., Sarah L. (deceased) and Thomas F. (deceased). Mr. Altstatt is a Republican, and a member of the I. O. O. F. and Masonic fraternities. His wife belongs to the Methodist Episcopal Church.

C. C. Ayers, dealer in general merchandise, was born in Fort Smith, Ark., in 1849, and is the son of Willard and Caroline (Forester) Ayers. The father was a native of Vermont, born in 1814, and was a stone-cutter by occupation. He came to Fort Smith to work on the fort and other government works erected here, and after they were finished he located here. He was married in Crawford County, Ark., to Miss Forester, who was born in Tennessee, and who by her marriage became the mother of five children, two of whom are now living, C. C. Ayers being the eldest. The father is still living, and is residing with one of his sons in this county. C. C. Ayers grew to manhood in Fort Smith, and received his education in the subscription school. The Civil War cut short his education, and although he was too young to join the regular service he obtained a position in the quartermaster department, in the Federal army, where he remained until peace was declared. Soon after the war he engaged in mercantile pursuits in Crawford County with his uncle, J. B. Forester, and from 1871 to 1880 he was United States deputy marshal of the Western District of Arkansas. He was then appointed jailer, which position he filled for two years. His brother, Willard R., was killed while making an arrest of a man for larceny. After being jailer he was again in the Government employ for four more years, making fourteen years in all that he has been in the Government service. He engaged in his present business January 1, 1885, with William Feuerstine. In 1874 he was married to Miss Mattie Stephens, a native of the Cherokee Nation, and three children are the result of this union: Grant, Sherman and Mattie.

W. W. Bailey, M. D., physician and surgeon at Fort Smith, Ark., was born in Fort Gibson, Cherokee Nation, November 28, 1839, being the son of Joseph H. and Mary A. Bailey. The father was a native of the State of New York, and was a surgeon in the United States Army. The Bailey family were relatives of John Quincy Adams, and on the father's side one of his aunts was an associate and friend of George Washington. Joseph Bailey was a physician, as was also his father, grandfather, and as are also his four sons. Reading, Conn., was owned and named after the Doctor's maternal great-grandfather. The female line on his mother's side were French Huguenots. Dr. W. W. Bailey took his degree of M. D. from Ann Arbor, Mich., in 1861, and during the late Civil War he was surgeon of the First Missouri Cavalry, and was also on Gen. Steel's staff, and surgeon of Gen. John M. Schofield's body guard (Gen. Schofield now commands the United States Army), serving in the capacity of surgeon until mustered out in September, 1865. It was during this time that he gained such proficiency in surgery, which distinguishes him at the present day. He located at Fort Smith after the war, and has been here ever since. He is one of the leading business men of the city, as well as the leading surgeon. He owns some of the best property in the city, and has in course of erection one of the finest business houses on Garrison Avenue. He is a Republican in politics, and has been Master of Belle Point Masonic Lodge, Fort Smith. His father established the Masonic lodge at Fort Smith. Dr. W. W. Bailey was married to Miss Lillie Main, only child of Dr. Main, of Fort Smith. They have four children: Belle, William, Kate and John Main. Dr. J. H. Main, father of Mrs. Bailey, was born in Frederick County, Md., November 13, 1813; was graduated from Starling Medical College, Columbus, Ohio, in 1836, and from the University Medical College, New York, in 1858. He settled in Fort Smith between 1836 and 1840, and, except during short intervals, has been here ever since. He erected Hotel Main, which bears his name, and many other of the chief buildings of Fort Smith. Dr. Main was married, in Fort Smith, to Miss Isabella Armour, who was born in Pittsburgh, Penn., March 26, 1826. [For further particulars of Dr. Main read history of Fort Smith.]

Harrison Ball, farmer and stock raiser, was born in Davidson County, N. C., February 20, 1841, and is the son of William and Rebecca (Essex) Ball, and grandson of Spencer and Susannah (Hawkins) Ball. Spencer Ball was born in England in 1753, and when young came with his parents to America, and located in Greenville County, Va. The grandmother was born in Germany, and was brought to America by her parents when small. Spencer Ball went to North Carolina when a young man; was there married to his first wife, who bore him four children. After her death he married the mother of William Ball. She was at that time the widow of Mr. Bradley, and by her union to Mr. Ball became the mother of six children, three sons and three daughters. She had a daughter by her first marriage. This wife died, and Mr. Ball then married Mrs. Margaret Barker. He was a farmer by occupation, was an old-line Whig, and lived to be seventy-seven years of age. William, the only one of the family now living, was born in Rowan County, N. C., August 25, 1815, was reared on a farm, and never went to school a day in his life. When about eighteen years of age he began learning the blacksmith trade, but after working at the same for about eighteen months his eyes gave out, and he was obliged to abandon the business. He then turned his attention to farming. In 1837 he married Miss Rebecca Essex, who was born in Davidson County, N. C., January 25, 1820. Her father was a Revolutionary soldier. To Mr. and Mrs. Ball were born eight children: Lucy A., Harrison, Franklin, Margaret E., Henderson, Martha R., John E. and Rhoda C. During the latter part of the war William Ball served about six months in the Confederate army under conscript. He lived in North Carolina until 1867, when he came to this county and settled on the place where he now lives. He is the owner of 150 acres of land, with about forty acres under cultivation. He was a Whig until that party went down, since which time he has been a Republican. He and wife are members of the United Brethren Church.

Their son, Harrison Ball, was reared a farmer's boy, and received a very limited education. He remained at home until August, 1862, when he was conscripted in the Confederate army, and served until March, 1865, when he decided to serve that cause no longer. He deserted while on picket, under the fire of his own comrades, and went north. He stopped in Pulaski County, Ill., and there, November 15, 1865, he married Miss Ann Harper, a native of West Tennessee, but a resident of Arkansas, where she had gone for protection. In 1866 Mr. Ball and wife removed to Sebastian County, and have since made it their home. They are the parents of one child, Lizzie (deceased), wife of J. F. Stewart. Mr. Ball has an adopted child, Minnie L. Ball. Mr. Ball is the owner of 240 acres, of which about 120 are under cultivation; he is a member of the Masonic order, and is a Republican in his politics. Mrs. Ball is a member of the Methodist Episcopal Church. Mr. Ball has been a resident of this county for twenty-two years, and although he has no children of his own, he takes a great interest in schools and other worthy enterprises.

C. M. Barnes, general fire and life insurance agent, of Fort Smith, was born in Livingston County, N. Y., August 25, 1845. His father was a son of Henry Hogan, who was paymaster in the United States army, and was lost at sea during the War of 1812, after which he was adopted by Gideon Barnes, and was known as Henry Hogan Barnes. He was married to Samantha Boyd, a native of Massachusetts, where Mr. Barnes' ancestors had located prior to the Revolution. Mr. Barnes, the father of our subject, was a farmer and merchant by occupation. C. M. Barnes grew to manhood in Calhoun County, Mich., and in 1861 enlisted in Howland's company of Michigan volunteer engineers, in which he served three months. He afterward served in the telegraph corps of the quartermaster's department, and in 1864 was stationed at Little Rock. In 1868 he came to Fort Smith, where he remained two years, after which he lived in Little Rock until 1876. He then located permanently in Fort Smith, where he became one of the leading citizens. From 1876 until 1880, and from 1881 until 1885, he was Chief United States Deputy Marshal of this district, and for four years he has served in the town council. He assisted in the organization of the fire department of Fort Smith, is president of the Empire Lumber Company, of Ashton, Ark., a stockholder of the Barnes Lumber Company, of Little Rock, and is secretary of the Fort Smith (Ark.) Fair Association. He was married, at Little Rock, to Mary E. Bartlett, a native of Massachusetts, and daughter of Judge Liberty Bartlett, who went to Little Rock from Massachusetts, before the war. Mr. and Mrs. Barnes have two sons and one daughter, viz.: Cassius, a student in the Racine College at Racine, Wis.; Henry Cooper and Eliza Louise, both of whom attend high-school. Mrs. Barnes is the treasurer of the Ladies' Aid Society of St. John's Episcopal Church, to which she and her husband belong.

Joseph P. Bassham, farmer and mechanic, is a son of Jonathan and Delilah (Payne) Bassham, both of whom were born in Franklin County, Va. The father was a soldier in the War of 1812, and was a cabinet-maker by trade, and in connection with this calling followed the occupation of farming. After his marriage he moved to West Virginia, where he made his home until 1839, when he came to Johnson County, Ark., and here he and wife spent the remainder of their lives, dying in 1848, at the age of fifty-two, and 1857, at the age of fifty-five, respectively. Three of their eleven children are living, Joseph P. being the fifth of the family. He was born in Tazewell, West Va., May 12, 1827, and while growing to manhood was engaged in farming and learning the cabinet-maker's trade. He received quite an extensive education for his day, and in 1847 was married to Sarah A. Bell, a daughter of Henry P. and Susan (Holmes) Bell, and by her became the father of eight children: Elizabeth E., Henry J., Luretha A., William O., Donana A., Minnie L., Katie and James. Mrs. Bassham was born in Tennessee, and died in Little Rock, Ark., in 1865. Mr. Bassham was married the following year to Miss Emily Redding, by whom he has one child, Samuel. This wife died in 1868, and he took for his next wife Mrs. Mary J. Rachels, *nee* Morris, a daughter of Ira L. Morris. They have a family of ten children: Thomas L., Sarah D., Nannie B., Mary L., James A., Jesse I., Martha A., C. B., Alice C. and an infant. His son, William O., is a Methodist minister, and his wives have been members of that church. In 1849 he came to Sebastian County, and in 1852 went to California and engaged in mining and farming for about two years. He then returned to Arkansas, and he and a brother opened a cabinet shop in Clarksville, which they managed until

1857. Mr. Bassham then returned to Sebastian County, and October 8, 1863, enlisted in Company F, Second Arkansas Volunteer Infantry, United States Army, and was appointed orderly. He was made second lieutenant February 25, 1864, and was promoted to first lieutenant July 6, of the same year, which position he held until he was mustered out of service at the close of the war. He was at Jenkins' Ferry and Prairie De Hand. In December, 1866, he returned to Sebastian County, where he has since made his home, and has been engaged in farming. He owns 157 acres of land, with about seventy acres under cultivation, and is a Republican in politics, and a member of the Masonic fraternity.

William H. Bell. Among the prominent men of Sebastian County, Ark., who have throughout life been honest tillers of the soil, may be mentioned the gentleman whose name heads this sketch. He was born in Henderson County, Tenn., September 7, 1834, being the fifth of ten children born to to the marriage of Henry P. and Susannah (Holmes) Bell. The father was born in Wayne County, N. C., in 1797, and was first married to Mrs. Susan Shadden, *nee* Holmes, by whom he had two sons and one daughter. He moved with her to Tennessee, where she afterward died. He resided in that State until 1839, when he moved to Arkansas, and located in Johnson County, and ten years later took up his abode in Sebastian County, where he spent the remainder of his days, dying in 1863, and his wife in 1869. He became a prosperous farmer, and he and both his wives were active members of the Methodist Episcopal Church, South. In early life he was a Democrat, but afterward became a Whig. Their son, William H., was reared chiefly in Johnson County, Ark., where he received rather limited educational advantages, but has since made good the deficiency by reading and private study. He remained with and assisted his father until he was twenty-one years of age, then engaging in farming, which occupation he has followed up to the present time, with the exception of a few terms of school which he taught. In 1860 he was married to Nancy J. Johnson, a daughter of James and Jane D. (Tilman) Johnson. She was born in Bradley County, Tenn., February 24, 1839, and was brought to Sebastian County when about twelve years of age, where she met and married Mr. Bell, by whom she became the mother of three children: Charles W., John W. and James H. Charles is preparing for the medical profession, and the other two are farmers. Mr. Bell served in the late war, first as first sergeant and afterward as second lieutenant, Company H, Second Arkansas Cavalry Volunteers, and after the close of the war was a captain in Col. John F. Wheeler's regiment of Arkansas State Militia. He is a Republican in politics, and owns 180 acres of good land, with sixty-five under cultivation, all of which he has made by his own exertions. He and wife are members of the Methodist Episcopal Church, South.

William T. Blakemore, M. D., of Greenwood, Ark., is a native of Sumner County, Tenn., and was born in 1830, being the son of Lee C. and Charlotte (Johnson) Blakemore, and grandson of Thomas and Sallie (Douglass) Blakemore. Thomas Blakemore was a native of Virginia, and was one of the first settlers of Sumner County, Tenn., where he passed his last days. Lee C. Blakemore was born in Sumner County, Tenn., in 1800, and was of Scotch-Irish and English extraction. He was born in Sumner County in 1831, and afterward immigrated to the Territory of Arkansas, locating two miles from where Van Buren is now located. In 1832 he moved to Fayetteville, Washington County, where he received his final summons. He died in 1881. He was one of the first white men to settle in Northwestern Arkansas, and was a member of the State Legislature several sessions, being elected by the Democratic party. He was register of the land office of the State of Arkansas during President Pierce's administration, being appointed by President Pierce in 1853, and serving four years. He was justice of the peace for many years, and was a man of much influence in the community in which he lived. His wife, Charlotte (Johnson) Blakemore, died in 1851. After her death Mr. Blakemore married Mrs. Nancy Crawley, *nee* Wallace. She, too, is deceased, having passed away in 1857. Mr. Blakemore was the father of ten children, six now living. William T. was the fifth child in the order of birth. He was but a year old when his parents moved to Arkansas. He attained his growth on the farm, and in 1854 commenced the study of his chosen profession, his preceptor being Dr. William H. Douglas, of Memphis, Tenn. He was under the Doctor's advice for over two years, and in 1856 went to Nashville, Tenn., where he entered the University of Nashville, and attended one course of lectures. In the spring of 1857 he commenced his practice in Greenwood, Ark., Sebastian County, where he has since been located. During the late war he was in the service but two months, when he was discharged on account of disabilities. In May, 1858, he married Miss Nancy Trammell, who was born in Crawford County, Ark., in 1834, and who was the daughter of Dimis and Elizabeth Trammell. Mr. and Mrs. Blakemore are the parents of five children: Jesse Lee, M. D., graduated from Vanderbilt University at Nashville, Tenn., in 1888, and is now second assistant in the insane asylum at Little Rock; Kate, wife of James B. Forrester; Bessie A., Ora C. and William F. In 1876 Dr. William T. Blakemore graduated as an M. D. at the Kentucky School of Medicine at Louisville, Ky. He is one of the oldest physicians and surgeons in Greenwood, and is one of the leading practitioners of Sebastian County. He is a man whose character is beyond reproach, and whose good name is untarnished. He is a Democrat in politics, was postmaster at Fayetteville, Ark., for six months, is a member of the Masonic fraternity, having taken the Blue Lodge, Royal Arch and Commandery degrees. He is also an Ancient Odd Fellow and an honorary member of the K. of H. He is a member of the Sebastian Medical Association, and he and wife are members of the Methodist Episcopal Church, South.

Henry W. Blan, a farmer, residing in Prairie Township, near Witcherville, Ark., was born in Henry County, Tenn., in 1851, and is a son of George P. and Jane P. (Ashlock) Blan, and grandson of James Blan, who was of English descent, and died in Sebastian County in 1872. George P. was married in Henry County, Tenn., in 1847, and in 1859 immigrated to Sebastian County, Ark., settling on the farm of 240 acres now owned by John M. Thompson. He was born in Tennessee in 1826, and died in Arkansas in 1877. His wife was a native of Kentucky, born in 1834, and died in Arkansas in 1875. Five of her ten children are living: Henry W., Adaline, wife of Archibald W. Brewer; Tennessee, wife of Clinton T. Ary; James W., and Amanda, wife of William Witcher. Henry W. Blan was eight years of age when he was brought to Arkansas, and resided with his parents on the farm until he was twenty-one years of age. In 1872 he was united in marriage to Miss Nancy A. Nixon, who was born in Henry County, Tenn., in 1854, a daughter of James A. Nixon. To them were born five children: Mary Lillie, James Porter, Sophronia Lulla, Serenie Belle and John Henry. After his marriage Mr. Blan located on the old homstead, a portion of which he farmed for some time, and now owns 114 acres of land, sixty acres of which are under cultivation. In politics he is a stanch Republican, and he and wife are members of the Methodist Episcopal Church.

A. E. Bloomburg, manager of the Bloomburg Lumber Company, of this city, is a native of Sweden, and was born in 1844. In 1858 his father, who for some years had been successfully engaged in farming in America, lost his wife, and returned to Sweden for his children. While *en route* to America a second time the father died at Liverpool. Our subject had been educated in Sweden, and after coming to the United States, in 1858, began life as a farmer upon his father's place. During the war he went to Kansas, and after the close of the Rebellion continued to live in that State until 1868. In that year he married Miss Emma Strong, who has borne him three children: Charles A., Lucy L. and Augusta. Mr. Bloomburg then farmed in Sebastian County, Ark., for fifteen years, and spent two years in the Rocky Mountains. In 1887 he formed a partnership with Mayor B. F. Hackett and John Sunburg, in the lumber business. These gentlemen have a large saw and planing mill, which has a capacity of 10,000 feet per day, and they furnish employment for a large number of men. Mr. Bloomburg is an influential citizen, and is the owner of several town lots and houses. In 1866 he served as mayor of the city, and in 1887 was elected an alderman. He is a Mason, and a member of the Methodist Episcopal Church, South, to which his wife also belongs.

Hon. William Franklin Blythe, judge of the Sebastian County Court, was born at Ripley, Tippah Co., Miss., March 7, 1851, and is of English and Irish extraction. His great-grandfather, Absalom Blythe, with two brothers, William and John, came to Virginia from England prior to the Revolution, and afterward removed to Georgia. The father of our subject, J. J. Blythe, was born in East Tennessee, and was a contractor and builder by trade. He married Miss Cleo Ussery, a native of Mississippi, and daughter of Shelby Ussery, who was the first representative of Tishomingo County, Miss., in the Legislature, and who represented his county until his death in 1851. W. F. Blythe attended school at Jacinto and Iuka, Miss., during his youth, and afterward taught school. Coming to Arkansas in 1876, he followed that vocation in Scott County, at Waldron, and began the study of law in 1880 at Clarksville, Ark. In the spring of 1882 (May) he was admitted to the bar, after which he settled at Fort Smith, and began to practice. During the same year he was elected justice of the peace, which position he has filled from that time until this year, when he resigned, having been elected judge of the county court. Judge Blythe was married at Ft. Smith, October 10, 1878, to Miss Linnah G. Barnes, a native of Mississippi, and daughter of William and Margaret C. Barnes. The former was killed during the war at the battle of Kenesaw Mountain, on the Confederate side. Mrs. Blythe is a member of the Baptist Church, and has two daughters, Cleo and Margaret. Judge Blythe belongs to the I. O. O. F., and is a Royal Arch Mason.

Louis Bolin, a grocer of Fort Smith, Ark., was born in Fannin County, Tex., November 29, 1844, and is a son of George Barnett and Anna Bolin. The latter was born in Alabama, and when a small child was stolen from her mother and taken to Springfield, Mo., where she was again stolen and taken to Fannin County, Tex. In 1867 she moved to Fort Smith, Ark., where she died in 1883. Her son, Louis, spent his early life in Fannin County, Tex., and came to Sebastian County, Ark., with his mother. From 1863 until 1886 he was engaged in tilling the soil, and owns a good little farm of forty acres, in the county, besides eleven houses and lots in Fort Smith. Since 1877 he has been engaged in the grocery business, and as he is energetic, honest and accommodating he is doing a prosperous business. He is a Mason, a member of the Missionary Baptist Church, and in his political views is a Republican, casting his first presidental vote for U. S. Grant. On the 20th of November, 1869, he was married to Jennie Kemp, who was born in Sebastian County, Ark., in 1851, and a daughter of Dick and Betsey Kemp, and by her is the father of the following children: Louis, born February 26, 1875; Millie, born in July, 1877; Wheeler, born April 7, 1882, and Bessie, born in August, 1884. One son, John, is deceased.

Mrs. Martha A. (Dillard) Bomford was born in Arkansas in 1832, and is a daughter of John Penn and Sallie Price (Moore) Dillard, both of whom were born in Virginia. They came from Virginia to Arkansas by water, landing at the mouth of the Arkansas River, and from there went to Moore's Rock, on ponies and pack-horses, which place they reached in 1822. While in Virginia they followed merchandising, but after coming to Arkansas engaged in farming. In 1833 they commenced to keep a large boarding house at Fort Gibson, Chickasaw Nation, for officers, and continued it until 1840. The father represented his county in the State Legislature, and his union with Miss Moore was blessed in the birth of twelve children, four of whom are still living: Mrs. Elizabeth G. (Rosser), Mrs. Solomon F. Clark, Mrs. M. A. Bomford and Mrs. Sarah P. Bossert. Maj. Dillard, formerly of Fort Smith, was a brother of Mrs. Bomford, and served through the Mexican War as captain under Col. Yell, and as major in the late war, Confederate States Army, in Gen. Fagan's brigade. John and Lucy (Penn) Dillard were the grandparents of Mrs. Bomford, the grandmother being a branch of the family of the famous William Penn. The maternal grandparents, Benjamin and Polly (Price) Moore, were Virginians, and moved to Arkansas in 1818. Maj. B. Moore sent out the first bale of cotton from this part of the State, and raised the first tobacco. Mrs. Bomford spent her early life in Sebastian County, and attended school in Van Buren and Fort Smith, where she acquired a good English education. In 1851 she was married to Dr. George Erving Bomford, who was born March 31, 1820, in Washington, D. C., the son of Col. George and Clara (Baldwin) Bomford. The former was chief of ordnance at Washington, and the latter was a sister-in-law of Joel Barlow, the author. Dr. Bomford was reared and educated in his native city, read medicine under Dr. Wilson, and attended lectures at Boston and Philadelphia, and received his diploma. He practiced several years in Washington, then moved to Fort Smith, Ark., in 1848, and immediately began practicing in that town. He was post surgeon of Fort Smith before and during the war, and was a Royal Arch Mason, a Democrat, and a member of the Episcopal Church. He has three sons: George D. (of St. Louis, Mo.), Erving (a druggist of Fort Smith), and Henry (a plumber of Fort Smith).

Robert A. Bonham, liveryman, notary public and city clerk at Huntington, was born in Anderson County, East Tenn., in 1861, and is a son of Absalom T. and Eliza (McClure) Bonham. When nine years of age he accompanied his parents to this county, where he assisted with the farm work, and in the winters attended the country schools. After becoming twenty years of age he spent one year at Cane Hill College, and two years at Buckner College. He then dealt in cattle some time, after which he taught school several terms. He next went into the mercantile business in Scott County, with Robert McClure, and then spent one summer in Kansas, where he had taken some cattle. He then went into the drug business with Dr. J. W. McConnell, establishing the first drug store in Huntington, and remained in that business until 1888, since which time he has been in the livery business. He is one of the influential business men of the town, and at the last city election was elected city clerk, having been a notary public since February of this year. He is one of the promising young men of the township, and cast his first presidential vote for Grover Cleveland. His father is also a successful farmer of this township, and was born in East Tennessee in 1825. He is a son of Martin and Orpha (McDaniel) Bonham, who were born in Virginia in 1778 and 1780, respectively. They went from that State to East Tennessee, and had a family of thirteen children, four of whom are living. A. T. Bonham was educated at Clinton and Jacksborough Colleges, in East Tennessee, and in 1851 married our subject's mother, who was of Irish descent, and a daughter of Alexander and Sarah (Gollaher) McClure. She bore eight children, and died June 13, 1881. October 5, 1887, Mr. Bonham married Susan Neal, daughter of Charles H. and Margaret (Johnson) Neal. Mr. Neal was born in South Carolina in 1816, and died October 20, 1886. His wife was born in the same State in 1815, and died January 8, 1879. They lived in South Carolina until removing to Mississippi, and in 1872 went to Tennessee. Mr. Bonham came to this county in 1870, and now has a farm of 300 acres, 150 of which he cultivates. He is a Democrat and a Mason, and belongs to the Cumberland Presbyterian Church.

Mrs. Sue Bonneville. Among the people of more than local note who have made Fort Smith their permanent home, and whose manner of living gives to Fort Smith social circles the metropolitan tone so evident to the astute observer, none is better known than Mrs. Sue Bonneville, widow of Gen. B. L. E. Bonneville, of the United States Army. Her home, on Hickory Street, is one of the most beautiful in the city, and her household consists of herself, her niece, Miss Kate Emric, and her nephew, John Emric. Her niece and nephew were left orphans when mere children, and have been reared and educated with as great solicitation by Mrs. Bonneville as if they had been her own children. Miss Emric is a highly accomplished and educated young lady, and a favorite in Fort Smith with young and old. Mrs. Sue Bonneville was born in Fort Washita, Chickasaw Nation, May 24, 1846, and is the daughter of Anton and Catherine (Sengel) Neice. [See sketch of Anton Neice.] Mrs. Bonneville is an orthodox Roman Catholic, and was educated in a convent. She was married to Gen. B. L. E. Bonneville, in Fort Smith, November 30, 1871, and with the exception of a few years succeeding her marriage, spent in St. Louis, has made Fort Smith her home since that event. Her position in life as the widow of a Federal officer has brought her in contact with many of the most talented and noted men and women of our country. She is a patriotic and typical southern woman. Mrs. Bonneville has in her possession all the deeds of lands and property signed for Gen. B. L. E. Bonneville by the Presidents of the United States. She has also a letter written by Marquis de La Fayette to the mother of Gen. Bonneville, requesting that the latter be permitted to suspend his studies for a period, at West Point, and go with him upon a visit to France. The Bonneville family and the family of Marquis de La Fayette were intimate friends. Gen. B. L. E. Bonneville was born in Paris, France, April 14, 1796, and "his father," says Washington Irving, "was a worthy old emigrant, who came to this country many years since and took up his abode in New York. He is represented as a man not well calculated for the sordid struggle of a money-making world, but possessed of a happy temperament, a festivity of imagination and a simplicity of heart that made him proof against its rules and trials. He was an excellent scholar, well acquainted with Latin and Greek and fond of the classics." Gen. Bonneville inherited much of his father's temperament, but thorough discipline in the military school at West Point, from which he graduated in 1815, fitted him better to grapple with men and events than was the case of his worthy sire. On graduating from West Point he entered the army, and the nature of the military service led him to the frontier, where, for a number of years, he was stationed at various points in the far West. "Here," says Irving, "he was brought into frequent intercourse with Indian traders, mountain trappers and other pioneers of the wilderness, and became so excited by their wild tales of wild scenes and wild adventures, and their accounts of vast regions as yet unexplored, that an expedition to the Rocky Mountains became the ardent desire of his heart, and an enterprise to explore the untrodden rocks was the leading object of his ambition." By degrees he shaped his day dreams into a practical reality, and a leave of absence was granted him August 3, 1831, on condition that he would furnish the Government information for the war department concerning the wild tribes he met on his journey. Being possessed of no fortune except the soldier's boon, his sword, he repaired to New York, then the center of American enterprise, where there are always friends ready for any enterprise, however chimerical or romantic. On the 1st of May, 1832, Gen. Bonneville found himself in possession of the requisite means, and at the head of 110 men, most of whom were experienced hunters and trappers and ready for the expedition. It was upon his return from this expedition, in 1836, that he was met by Washington Irving, at the table of John Jacob Astor, in New York. His journal, edited and amplified by Washington Irving, was published in 1837, under the title of "Adventures of Captain Bonneville (U. S. A.) in the Rocky Mountains and Far West." So long had all communication been cut off between Capt. Bonneville and the United States Army while he was on his trip through the West, that his name was dropped from the army roll, and he was considered lost. He was afterward restored to the army, and served in the Indian Territory, and in Florida and Mexican Wars, becoming major in 1845 and brevet lieutenant-colonel in 1847. He became colonel in 1855, was assigned to the department of New Mexico, and in 1857 commanded the Gila expedition. In 1861 he was retired from active service for disability, and during the Civil War served as superintendent of the recruiting service and disbursing officer in Missouri. In 1865 he was made brevet brigadier-general. In 1871, soon after his marriage with the present Mrs. Sue Bonneville, he retired to Fort Smith, built a residence outside the city, and amidst books, flowers, shrubs and trees, and in the happy society of his young wife, passed the remainder of his days. He died June 2, 1878, and his remains were interred with martial honors in St. Louis, Mo.

Mrs. Luvicy (Malone) Booth, of Marion Township, Sebastian Co., Ark., was born in Randolph County, N. C., in 1826, and is one of three surviving members of a family of ten children born to John and Annie Malone, who were also born in North Carolina, and died in Arkansas in 1851. After leaving their native State they first located in Tennessee, going thence to Mississippi, and finally took up a permanent residence in Arkansas. Mrs. Booth spent her early life in Tennessee and Mississippi, and in 1842 became the wife of John P. Booth, a son of John and Nancy (Phelps) Booth, of Georgia; he was reared to manhood in Alabama and Mississippi. He removed from the latter State to Sebastian County, Ark., in 1853, and he and wife became the parents of eight children: Elizabeth (Petty), Mary Caroline (Lamb), David F., John, William, Rufus, Dock W. and Jerry P. Mr. Booth was a farmer throughout life, and at the time of his death, February 23, 1872, owned a fine farm, consisting of 300 acres, besides a gin mill, and handled a great deal of stock. Both he and wife were members of the Methodist Episcopal Church, and he was a Democrat.

William R. Bowen, farmer and stock dealer, is the son of John and Jane (Bridgeman) Bowen. The father was born in Tennessee in 1799, and when still quite young went to Virginia, where he married Miss Bowen, who was a native of Virginia, born in the year 1797. After marriage they settled in Grainger County, Tenn., and in 1831 they moved to Madison County, Ark., where the father died in 1844. The widow and children then came to Sebastian County, where the mother married William Troylor. She died in 1850. The father was a farmer in early life, but later ran a still-house. He was justice of the peace and county judge for eight years in Madison County. He was an old-time Democrat, a member of the Cumberland Presbyterian Church, and both were worthy and intelligent people. By her first marriage Mrs. Bowen became the mother of thirteen children, five sons and eight daughters, but had no children by her second marriage. The second child, William R. Bowen, was born March 12, 1825, in Grainger County, Tenn. He was reared to farm life, and received little or no education. After he had reached forty-six years of age he became converted, and learned to read the Bible. In 1847 he married Miss Mary A. Barnard, who bore him eight children, three now living: Mary E., Buchanan H. and Alexander. About 1855 Mr. Bowen separated from his first wife, and in 1856 married Miss Elizabeth Bradshaw, who bore him five children, three now living: Ahab, John and Rachel. Mrs. Bowen died in 1885, and two years later Mr. Bowen married Miss Ellen Doyle. Since first coming to this country, in 1844, Mr. Bowen has followed farming, and is the owner of 200 acres of land, 100 acres of which are under cultivation. During the war he served two years in the Union army, and his disabilities allow him a pension of $8 per month. The most of his work was in hospital service. He is an essential Baptist in his religious views, and is a true Federal in his politics. Mr. Bowen contributes liberally to all charitable organizations, and takes an interest in schools and churches.

Dr. William J. Brandon, physician and surgeon of Dayton, was born in Shelby County, Tenn., in 1837, his parents being Philip Brandon and Elizabeth Snell. The former was probably born in Alabama, and the latter was a native of Bedford County, Tenn., born in 1801. They were married in Alabama, whither Mrs. Brandon had removed with her people, and then went to Shelby County, Tenn., in 1830, where Mrs. Brandon died in 1864. Mr. Brandon was a farmer, and died in Alabama, while on a business tour, in 1842. The paternal grandparents of our subject were natives of North Carolina, and the grandfather, William Brandon, was a soldier in the Revolution, and of Irish parentage. The maternal grandfather, Stephen Snell, was of English descent, born in North Carolina, and served in the Revolution. He died in Texas in an early day. Our subject was left to help care for his widowed mother when a boy, and was the fourth of a family of five children. He attended the log schoolhouse in Western Tennessee, where he lived, and began the study of medicine upon attaining his majority. In 1859 he entered the Memphis Medical College, and after one course practiced with his former preceptor until 1861. He then joined the Fifteenth Mississippi Volunteer Infantry as lieutenant, but soon afterward became a soldier in the Twelfth Tennessee Cavalry, Company A, Confederate Army. In January, 1863, he was captured on the Mississippi and Tennessee line, near Colliersville, Tenn., but was afterward paroled. In 1863 he entered Bellevue Medical College at New York, and graduated from that institution the following year with high honors, since which time he has practiced his profession with success. In 1867 he married Medora Farned, a native of Mississippi, and daughter of Marshall Farned, by whom he has had two children. In 1868 the family removed from Mississippi to White County, Ark., in 1872 went to Texas and in 1881 came to Sebastian County. Since 1882 the Doctor has practiced medicine and engaged in the drug business at Dayton with success, and he is also the owner of 300 acres of good land. He is a public-spirited citizen and a prominent member of the I. O. O. F. In politics he is a Democrat, and his first presidential vote was cast for Douglas in 1860. His wife is a Baptist in religion.

Joab H. Bray was born in Chatham County, N. C., March 17, 1825, and is a son of Solomon and Sallie (Brooks) Bray, natives of the same county and State. The father was a man of education, and was a wagon-maker by trade. Both himself and wife died in North Carolina in October, 1848. They were the parents of ten children, of whom the following seven are still living: Joab, Leander, Ely S., Ruth, Julia, Ursula and Mary. Those deceased were named Charles, Samuel and Elizabeth. The grandparents on both sides were born and passed their entire lives in Chatham County, N. C. Joab learned the wagon-maker's trade of his father, and followed that business exclusively until coming to Arkansas. He received a good education, and in 1860 immigrated to Tennessee by wagon, settling in Hardeman County, where he conducted extensive wagon-works until 1879. In 1853 he married Emily Brooks, a native of North Carolina, who has borne him eleven children: Adelaide S., Lousena A., Ursula H., John B., Joab L., Charles G., Edwin W., Mary E. and Walter. Decimus and an infant are deceased. While in North Carolina Mr. Bray belonged to the militia, in which he advanced to the office of adjutant. He also served as justice of the peace and constable. Mr. Bray came to this county in 1879, and now owns 220 acres of land, eighty-five being under cultivation. In religion his wife belongs to the Missionary Baptist Church, and he to the Cumberland Presbyterian, and in politics Mr. Bray is a strong Democrat. He has been a member of the Masonic fraternity over forty years, and is a much respected citizen.

J. W. Breedlove, M. D., practicing physician of the regular school of physicians, at Fort Smith, Ark., was born in New Orleans, La., and is the son of J. W., Sr., and Maria E. (Winchester) Breedlove. The father went to New Orleans from Virginia in 1814, was a commission merchant, and was also a collector of customs at New Orleans under Gen. Jackson. He was the father of seven children, three now living, J. W., Jr., being the youngest of the family. He received a good classical education in the University of Nashville, Tenn., and afterward pursued the study of medicine, graduating from the University of Louisiana in 1849. He was for twelve years house surgeon of the United States Marine Hospital of New Orleans. He served four years in the Confederate army, and was medical inspector under Gen. Breckenridge. At the close of the war he returned to New Orleans, and became assistant physician in the quarantine station below New Orleans. After this he went to the "Lone Star State," remained two years, and then in the fall of 1869 he came to Sebastian County, Ark., locating in Greenwood, where he practiced his profession until April, 1886, when he moved to Fort Smith. He has been a copartner with Dr. Southard two years. Dr. Breedlove was married in New Orleans to Miss Emma Rawlings, who was born in Kentucky, and whose father was a Mexican soldier. Dr. and Mrs. Breedlove are the parents of one child, Charles T., who is now in Baltimore pursuing dental studies. Dr. Breedlove is a Democrat in his political views, and is a member of Lodge No. 20 of the F. & A. M.

Dr. Asbury L. Brewster, of the drug firm of McConnell & Brewster, and assistant physician and surgeon for the Kansas & Texas Coal Company, is one of the promising young men of Huntington. He was born in Lauderdale County, Miss., in 1857, and is a son of Christopher C. and Mary G. (Pogue) Brewster, natives of Florida and Alabama, respectively. They were married in Mississippi, where they attained their growth, and lived in that State until after the war. They then removed to Louisiana, and in 1868 came to Sebastian County, Ark., settling near the present site of Huntington, at what is now known as "Brewster's Chapel." There Mr. Brewster owned a fine farm, upon which the family lived after his death in 1878 until the winter of 1887–88. Mrs. Brewster now lives in Huntington, and both she and her husband joined the Methodist Church when young. Asbury L. is the eldest of three sons and two daughters now living. He passed his boyhood upon a farm, and received but a common-school education. In 1878 he began the study of medicine, and in 1879 attended one course of lectures at the Louisville University in Kentucky. He graduated from the Vanderbilt University at Nashville in 1881, and has since practiced his profession with increasing success in the vicinity of Huntington. He owns eighty acres of land two miles from Huntington, which contains coal deposits. During the past year he established himself in the drug business. In politics he is a Democrat, and his first presidential vote was cast for Hancock in 1880. He is a member of Pulliam Lodge No. 133, at Witcherville, and belongs to the A. O. U. W. He worships at the Methodist Episcopal Church, South.

Alpheus C. Brewster, attorney at law and notary public, was born in Lauderdale County, Miss., in 1861, and is a brother of Dr. Brewster. He also was reared on a farm, and received a common-school education. When sixteen he entered Buckner College, which he attended two years. He then passed nine months at the State University at Fayetteville, and graduated from the Emory & Henry College, Virginia, in 1886. While at college he took an A. B. degree. He then taught school one year at Charleston, since which time he has practiced law, being a member of the Sebastian County bar. He is a Democrat, and is a member of the Bell Point Masonic Lodge at Fort Smith. In religion he is a Methodist.

Howard H. Brown, farmer and stock raiser, was born in Pontotoc County, Miss., in 1843, and is a son of Usrey and Lucinda (Eaves) Brown, natives of Maringo County, Ala., where they lived until after their marriage. They then made a home in Mississippi until 1859, when they removed to Hempstead County, Ark. In 1872 they came to Sebastian County, Ark. The father was a successful farmer, and died in 1882, aged sixty-eight. His widow is still living, and is now seventy-two years old. The maternal grandfather, Howard H. Eaves, was a blacksmith and well-borer, and was born in Georgia. He was a soldier in the War of 1812, and bored many artesian wells in Mississippi. He was of Portuguese parentage, and his father fought in the Revolution. Howard H. Brown is the fourth of a family of eleven children, and in 1859 he accompanied his parents to Hempstead County, Ark. At the breaking out of the war he joined Company I, Twelfth Arkansas Infantry, with which he fought at Belmont, Mo., Island No. 10 and Farmington. He was discharged in August, 1862, on account of disability, but in March, 1863, re-enlisted and went to Texas, where he joined Gen. Magruder's escort company of cavalry, with which he remained until the close of the war. He was at the surrender at Houston, Tex., and served most of the time as a courier. After the war he returned home, and in 1868 he married Mary E., daughter of Willis W. Nolen [see sketch]. Mrs. Brown was born in Hempstead County, and her union with Mr. Brown has been blessed with six sons and two daughters, all living, and the oldest daughter married to A. M. Nowlen, of Hackett City. Mr. Brown came to Sebastian County in 1869, and although he began life at twenty-two, after the war, with nothing, he now owns 225 acres of well-improved land, and is a substantial citizen. He owns 500 acres of land in all, and has made the most of his property by selling and improving land. He is a Democrat, and a member of the Oak Bower Masonic Lodge No. 277. He is a member of the Missionary Baptist Church, and all of his family before him belonged to the same church.

Isaiah W. Bruce, builder, was born in Claiborne County, Miss., at Port Gibson, August 22, 1839. His father, Thomas Bruce, was born in Kentucky, whither his father, John Bruce, had emigrated from Scotland. The latter was a merchant and the former a builder by occupation. After the death of her first husband the mother of our subject married Thomas Vernon, who was also a builder. Isaiah W. accompanied his step-father to Arkansas when ten years old, and was reared in this city, and at the age of thirteen began to learn the builder's trade. During the Rebellion he served the entire time in the Confederate army. He married Miss Malvina, daughter of Asa Clark, a native of Maine, who died in May, 1882. In September, 1884, he was married to Miss Anna Dewees, daughter of Judge William Dewees, of Culloden, Monroe Co., Ga., a highly accomplished and most estimable lady, He is the father of four sons: Thomas, an architect and graduate of the Arkansas Industrial University; Wallace, a plumber; Hoyt and Henry, who are attending school. Mr. Bruce now holds the office of superintendent of school buildings, and among the buildings he has erected are the Hotel Maine, the Merchants' Bank, and H. H. Clayton's residence. Mr. Bruce and his wife are worthy members of the Methodist Episcopal Church, South. He is a K. of H. and a K. T. of Jacques D. Molay Commandery, No. 3.

Marion S. Buckley, commission merchant at Fort Smith, Ark., was born in Middle Tennessee in 1830, and is the son of William Hall and Rebecca (Johnson) Buckley. The father was a native of Virginia, and was a carpenter by trade, as was also his father. The mother was a native of North Carolina and of Irish descent. Her father brought his coat of arms to America, and after reaching this country took part in the Revolutionary War on the side of the colonists. William H. Buckley engaged in business in Statesville, Tenn., where he passed the remainder of his life. His son, Marion S. Buckley, grew to manhood in Tennessee, and there received his early education. He was married in that State in 1850 to Miss Mary P. Bratton, daughter of Col. Bratton, of Macon County, Tenn., who was one of the leading citizens of the county, and was a member of the Legislature from that county. The fruits of Mr. Buckley's marriage were five children: William H., Calvin V., Kentucky, wife of Andrew Muse; Alonzo and Homer. Soon after his marriage Mr. Buckley moved to Bowling Green, Warren Co., Ky., where he worked as a mechanic for a short time, and then engaged in the stock business, which he carried on in connection with mercantile pursuits for about five years. On leaving Kentucky he came to Franklin County, Ark., and was there engaged in the stock business until the time of the war, when the Confederates took 150 head of cattle and forty head of blooded horses from him. During that eventful period Mr. Buckley was placed in the commissary department, and when peace was declared he returned to Fort Smith and commenced business anew. He has followed mercantile pursuits, and is also in the commission business. He joined the Baptist Church when thirteen years of age, joined a temperance society at the same age, and has never tasted liquor in any form, and does not know the taste of tobacco or coffee. He has given thorough attention to the education of his children, and has had children in William Jewell College, Liberty, Mo., for the past twenty years, and his older sons have graduated from that institution. His daughter, Kentucky, attended the Baptist Female College at Lexington, Mo. Mr. Buckley has reared one of his nephews and a niece as his own children. Olive Buckley graduated from the female college at Winchester, Tenn., and Willie D. Buckley graduated from William Jewell College in June, 1888, with high honors. Virgil Buckley completed the law course at Columbia, Mo., and is practicing law at Springfield, Mo. Willie Buckley is a young man of much natural ability, and is at present studying law. Alonzo is a dentist of Fort Smith.

Harrison Buckner was born in Carter County, Ky., October 22, 1845, his parents being Overton M. and Elizabeth (Fults) Buckner. The father was born in Scott County, Va., November 9, 1812, and when sixteen went to Kentucky, where he grew to manhood upon a farm. In 1832 he married, and of his thirteen children but eight are now living, viz.: Martha J., Mary, Sarah, Emanuel, Harrison, Cornelius, Overton and Barney K. Those deceased were named James, John, William, Lafayette and Elizabeth. During the late war Mr. Buckner served three years in Company K, of the Twenty-third Kentucky Volunteer Infantry, participating in the battles at Stone River, Perryville and Woodberry. He was discharged at Madison, Ind., in 1864. Patrick M. Buckner, the grandfather, was of Irish descent, and born in Virginia, where he died. For some time he lived in Kentucky, and he was a soldier in the War of 1812. His wife, Mollie (Esteys) Buckner, was married in Scott County, Va., and for some time practiced medicine in Georgia County, Tenn., she being a disciple of the homœopathic school. The maternal grandparents, Obadiah Fults and wife, were natives of Virginia, who immigrated to Kentucky, where they died. Our subject was reared and educated in his native county, and at the beginning of the war enlisted in Company I, of the Twenty-third Kentucky Volunteer Infantry, fighting on the same side as his father and brother James. The latter was killed at New Hope, Ga., May 27, 1864. Mr. Buckner was discharged at Victoria, Tex., December 29, 1865, and had participated in the engagements at Atlanta, Resaca, Rocky Face, Peach Tree, Sweetwater, Kenesaw Mountain, New Hope, Jonesboro, Lovejoy, Columbia, Spring Hill and Nashville. He also accompanied Sherman on his march to the sea. After the war Mr. B. farmed in Kentucky three years, and then passed two years in Franklin County, Ark. He then came to this county, where he has a farm of 120 acres, 100 of which are cultivated. February 22, 1866, he married Martha C., daughter of John and Rachel (Black) Remy. The mother was born in Tennessee, but reared in Kentucky, the native State of Mr. Remy. John Black and wife were natives of South Carolina. Mr. and Mrs. Buckner are members of the Regular Baptist Church. They have had nine children, all save one now living: Geneva A., Rachel E., Mary C., Martha E., John W., Ava R., Louisa B., Jeanette M. and James O. (deceased). Mr. Buckner is a strong Republican and a member of the G. A. R.

Charles Burns, ex-United States Jailer, was born in County Fermanah, Ireland, in 1833. His father, Patrick Burns, was born in Scotland, on the River Clyde, and is a descendant of the poet, Robert Burns. He was a member of the Church of England, and was married to Rose McManns, who was born in County Fermanah, Ireland, and a member of the Catholic Church. In 1845 Charles Burns came to North America with his mother and brother (his father having died in Cork, Ireland, shortly before embarking for the New World, and is now reposing in Father Matthew's cemetery in Ireland), and located in Toronto, Canada, where the mother was taken ill a few months later and died. Charles Burns came to the United States in 1848, and began learning the saddler's trade, but at the end of a few months ran away and enlisted in the United States army, serving for twenty-three years. He was one of the soldiers who was sent to quell the Indians, and has traveled all over the Western States and Territories. He was appointed ordnance sergeant at Annapolis, Md., but resigned the position owing to ill health, and soon after located in Fort Smith, where he was appointed United States Jailer, and held the position fourteen years, but resigned when Cleveland was elected president. He was married in Fort Gibson to Catherine Lawrence, by whom he became the father of thirteen children, nine of whom are living: Charles, Mollie, Catherine, Willie, Francis, Henry, Thomas and Leo. Annie died at the age of eleven years; John died in Maryland when a small boy; Eddie, who was accidentally shot by a school-mate, died at the age of twenty-five years, and Joseph died when seventeen years of age, in Fort Smith. The family are members of the Catholic Church.

John William Buskamp was born in Westphalia, Prussia, in the Court District of Holtwick, near Bocholt, Munster, on October 2, 1832, and is a son of John and Theodora (Schmitz) Buskamp. The father was a miller by occupation. In 1853 our subject immigrated to the United States, and landing at New York, proceeded to Cleveland, Ohio, where he learned the carpenter's and joiner's trade. He then worked in Detroit, Mich., and on the Michigan Central Railway. He afterward went to Joliet, Ill., and there engaged at his trade, putting on the roof of the court-house, and being among the first to work on the State Prison. Contracting the chills and fever at that place, he was obliged to seek another climate, and he consequently came to Fort Smith in 1859, where he has been engaged in building. He worked for the Confederates here during the war until 1863, and then worked for the Union Government. Among the buildings he has erected may be mentioned, Gen. Bonneville's residence, the Belle Point School-house and the St. Boniface Roman Catholic Church. He was married in 1861 to Miss Theresa Ermann, daughter of Casper Ermann, and a native of Westphalia. Mr. and Mrs. Buskamp have two daughters and one son living, viz.: Dora, Henry and Adelaide, all of whom were educated at the Convent. Two sons died in infancy. Mr. Buskamp and family are members of the Roman Catholic Church.

Dr. Thomas N. Callicoatt, practicing physician and surgeon at Huntington, was born in Marshall County, Miss., in 1850, his parents being John B. and Sarah J. (Hall) Callicoatt, natives of Tennessee. The father was of Scotch-Irish descent, and served the last two years of the Civil War in the Confederate service. He died in Fayette County, Miss., in 1884, where his widow still lives. Paschal Callicoatt, the grandfather, was born in Virginia, was a soldier in the War of 1812, and died in Nevada County, Ark., in 1877. Our subject is the fourth of a family of seven children, and during his youth his education was received at the common schools, and at Oxford College, Mississippi. In the spring of 1865 he enlisted in the Confederate army, serving three months in Gen. Blythe's courier line. In 1868 he began life for himself by farming, and afterward engaged somewhat in photographing in Texas, Arkansas, and the Indian Territory. In 1872 he began the study of medicine, and in the winter of 1873 and 1874 attended the medical department of the university at Nashville, since which time he has practiced his profession. In 1881 he took a five months' course in the Larimie Theological College at Florence, Ala., having since 1876 been preaching in the Christian Church. For twelve years he has resided in different parts of Arkansas, such as Madison, Franklin, and Scott Counties, but in 1888 came to Huntington, where he owns a business block, and has a grocery and drug store. He owns 160 acres of land in Logan County. Dr. Callicoatt has been thrice married. In 1872 he married Mollie E. Flemm, who with two children, Ada Belle and Fader, were drowned in Madison County, Ark., July 6, 1886, in a water spout. In 1886 he married Mollie Richie, who died in September, of the same year. In July, 1887, the Doctor was united in marriage to Sarah J. Baker. Mrs. Callicoatt is a member of the Methodist Church, and owns 240 acres of land in Logan County.

Samuel P. Campbell was born in Cumberland County, Ky., July 6, 1832. Samuel Campbell, the father, who was born in Virginia, of Scotch parents, went to Kentucky when young, where he lived about twenty-five years, and engaged in farming, manufacturing tobacco and distilling. While there he married Miss Christina Pevehouse, whose parents had immigrated to that country from Pennsylvania. She was of German descent. They there became the parents of nine children: George W., Adam P., William J., Dudly F., Joseph F., Cyrus W., Louisa J., Chloe E., and Samuel P., the subject of this sketch, who is the youngest of the family. In 1834 they immigrated, with all their children, to the Territory of Arkansas, and settled on the bank of a river of the same name, in what is now Crawford County, a few miles below the town of Van Buren, where they lived ten years and opened a large farm, but unfortunately were broken up by the great flood of 1844, after which they moved to the south side of the river, where they both died within two years, well stricken in age. Benjamin Campbell, the grandfather, emigrated from Scotland in the days of the colonies, and was a soldier in the Revolutionary War, and had many fights with the Indians in the settling of Kentucky and Virginia. He once came to Arkansas, to visit his son, Samuel, while in his dotage, and soon after died, near Versailles, Mo., in his one hundred and sixth year. Samuel P., the son and grandson of Benjamin and Samuel, was but two years old when brought to Arkansas, and states that the first thing he can remember of this life was living in a camp on the bank of the Arkansas River, when his elder brothers wounded a deer and caught it with the dogs near the camp, giving him the worst scare he has ever had. During the ten years of his stay on the place he was taught to work at everything then necessary on a farm. During the time he was boarded out, and sent to several sessions at school. At the death of his parents he lived with a brother, going to school at times. At the age of nineteen he joined a band of gold seekers at Fort Smith, bound for the Pacific Slope, while the gold fever was at its greatest height. A few days later the train of 130 wagons and 300 men started on their 2,000-mile journey through what was then a wilderness, where there was nothing known but deserts, mountains, wild beasts and Indians. After a six months' journey and many hardships the survivors reached the settlements of California. When the winter was over Samuel P. took stock in the Bullion Fluming Company. The summer past, the next winter was spent in prospecting, the river claim being worked out, and some money was cleared. For five years Mr. Campbell engaged in different mining companies, lastly in the Lone Star Tunnel Company, and in 1857 sold his interest, and came back home by the way of Panama, Cuba and New York. After his return he engaged in trading and hauling bacon from Sebastian County to Fort Worth, Texas, for about two years, and on the 22d of January, 1860, he married Laura P., daughter of Dr. C. P. H. Ake. Mrs. Campbell was born January 8, 1840, and was a native of Arkansas. She became the mother of six children: Henry A., William A., Cyrus W. and Martha C. now living; Eugene P. and Ernest F. deceased. She died February 14, 1877. Mr. Campbell lived a widower about five years, and on the 23d of July, 1882, he married Tennessee McClendon, a widow, daughter of Wiley O'Neal, of Tennessee. She is the mother of two children, Oscar J. and Emmer C. McClendon. Mr. and Mrs. Campbell belong to the Missionary Baptist Church, and the former belongs to the Masonic fraternity and the Agricultural Wheel. He was one of the first settlers near Biswel Springs, now famous in Sebastian County as the great camp ground. Mr. Campbell settled near Union Grove, where he now lives, in 1867. He has 400 acres of land, 100 in cultivation and well stocked.

Joseph H. and Thomas Milton Cardwell, of the firm of Cardwell Bros., doing business at Fort Smith, are natives of Oxford, Miss. The father, G. W. Cardwell, was a tinsmith, and a native of Virginia, and of Scotch descent, and died in Mississippi in 1876. The mother, Naomi S. Cardwell, was born in Aberdeen, Miss., and married at Oxford, Miss. Joseph H. was born November 7, 1860, and when young learned the builder's trade at Oxford. In 1880 he came to Hot Springs, Ark., where he became identified with building interests, and in 1883 he removed to Fort Smith, where he is now in business with his brother. He was married in Senatobia, Miss., to Miss Mary L. Medders, a native of Illinois, and daughter of J. L. Medders, of Senatobia. Mr. and Mrs. Cardwell are members of the Baptist Church, and have two sons, Leslie and Burrell. Thomas Milton, the junior partner of the firm, was born at Oxford, Miss., June 25, 1863, and also learned the builder's trade during his youth. Coming to Arkansas he worked some time as a journeyman at Fort Smith, and then engaged in contracting. Among the many buildings Cardwell Bros. have completed are the Central Methodist Episcopal Church, South, four business blocks for S. P. Day, and two for P. Delorvin. The brothers are successful and enterprising citizens, and both belong to the City Fire Department.

Alexander B. Carruth was born November 4, 1820, in Lawrence County, Ala., and is a son of Alexander and Nancy (Elkins) Carruth, both of whom were of Irish descent. The father was born in South Carolina, and being reared upon a farm, devoted his entire life to agricultural pursuits. He immigrated to Georgia, and after living there some years went to Alabama, where he died at the age of seventy-four. Mrs. Carruth bore nine children, three of whom are living: James H., our subject and Eliza. Those deceased were named William, Jesse, Joseph, Thomas, Martha and John. Mrs. Carruth was born in Georgia, and died in North Alabama in 1862, where she had gone in 1818. Alexander was reared upon his father's farm in Alabama, and during his youth received a common-school education, and learned the shoemaker's trade, at which he worked twenty years. He began life for himself when eighteen by buying land in Alabama, and in 1844 married Jane Roberts, by whom he had ten children. Mary A., Joseph P., Jesse J., William, John, Nancy and Harriet are living, and Absalom, Harry and Matthew are dead. Mrs. Carruth died in Illinois in 1864, and the latter part of the same year Mr. Carruth married Sarah Balom, who came to Kentucky from England when small. She afterward moved to Illinois, and there was married. She is the mother of three children, Belle, Emma and George. After farming in Illinois two years, in 1857 Mr. Carruth settled in Sebastian County, Ark., where he has a farm of sixty-five acres in cultivation. Mr. Carruth is a Democrat in politics, and is greatly interested in the educational advancement of the county, being a school director. Himself and wife belong to the Methodist Episcopal Church, South.

Capt. Claiborn W. Cauthron, furniture dealer and undertaker of Greenwood, Ark., is a native of Logan County, Ark. He was born near the town of Boonville in 1832, and is a son of Col. Walter and Bashaway (Wilson) Cauthron, and grandson of Claiborn Cauthron. Walter Cauthron was born in Franklin County, Ga., in 1797, and was of Scotch-English descent. At the age of twelve years he moved with his parents to Kentucky, where they remained three years; they then moved to Southwest Illinois, where his father died about 1818. He subsequently went south by way of Natchez, Miss., and as far as New Orleans, La.; he then went up the Mississippi and Red Rivers as far as Shreveport, La., then going (by land) up the Red River to what was known as Lovelace's Purchase. He settled down there, and engaged in farming; here he met and married Miss Bashaway Wilson in 1822. She was born in Lawrence County, Ark., in 1803. Mr. Cauthron moved to Scott County in 1824, and settled on the Petitjean River, two miles west of French's Prairie. Walter Cauthron was one of the first white men to settle in Western Arkansas. He came here when there were but very few settlers in the western part of the State. Wild animals were in abundance, such as buffalo, elk, bear, wolf and deer. He was fond of hunting, and had many thrilling adventures with the wild beasts of this wild country; there were plenty of Indians here also. He left this first settlement in 1826 or 1827, and moved to a place near the town of Booneville. Settling in the woods, he soon opened a farm and engaged in farming and stock raising; he also sold goods one year, and built the first cotton-gin in Scott County. About this time the county seat was located on a plat of land adjoining his farm. The county militia was then organized; Mr. Cauthron was elected colonel, but owing to the dissipation of the town the Colonel became dissatisfied with his surroundings, having a family of boys growing up; he moved in 1837 eight miles southwest of Booneville, to what is known as Cauthron's Prairie, named in his honor, and here he opened a farm and engaged again in farming and stock raising. School and church facilities were rather poor; he succeeded, however, in giving his five boys and four girls a fair English education, all of whom lived to have families of their own. In 1849 his wife, Bashaway, died, leaving him a family of nine children, and in 1850 Col. Cauthron married Mrs. Elenor S. Burton, *nee* Garner, who was born in Kentucky. He still resided on his farm, and in 1852 he was elected county judge of Scott County, and served one term. In 1854 his eyes became sorely afflicted, which terminated in the loss of his right eye and almost total blindness. He was a man of much influence and public spirit. His unbounded hospitality was known throughout the country, and many of the pioneer itinerant preachers of the country have found food and shelter under his hospitable roof; indeed, his house was a place of public worship for many years, and it was a common thing for a large part of the congregation, who assembled at his house for worship, to take dinner with him after services, and spend a portion of the afternoon in social chat. Few of the people of the present age can appreciate the state of society in the early days of Arkansas; there was a degree of liberality and equality among all of the people which is to-day unknown among our citizens. In 1864, when the country was overrun with the Federal army, Col. Cauthron and family refugeed to Bowie County, Tex. At the close of the war he returned to his home on Cauthron Prairie, where he lived until the death of his second wife, which occurred in 1875; Col. Cauthron then broke up housekeeping, and lived with his children the remainder of his life. He was a stanch Democrat, always taking a lively interest in the politics of the country; had been a member of the Christian Church for many years before his death, which occurred in 1877. Capt. Claiborn W. Cauthron was born and grew to manhood on a farm.

In 1852 he went to California with the long train of gold seekers, going overland, and taking six months to make the journey. He here engaged in mining for about six years, and then returned by way of Panama, Aspinwall, Key West and New Orleans, and arrived at his old home in June, 1859, where he engaged with his father in farming and stock raising; they were making arrangements for an extensive stock farm. When the war broke out he was found defending his home and native State against the invaders. In October, 1861, he enlisted in Company A, Second Arkansas Mounted Rifles, and was in the engagements at Pea Ridge, Murfreesboro, Jackson, Miss., Dug Gap, Resaca, Atlanta, Jonesboro, Franklin, Nashville and others; was with Gen. Joseph E. Johnston in his last battle in North Carolina. He entered the service as a private, but before the battle of Murfreesboro he was promoted to the rank of second lieutenant. In 1864 he was given the command of his company, but was not commissioned as captain until the spring of 1865. He was wounded several times, the first time at Murfeesboro, where he was wounded in the right hip by a shell; again, at Jackson, Miss., he was wounded in the left leg by a shell, which fractured the bone, and he was wounded in the left hand with a shell at Franklin; had his haversack and canteen shot off of him in front of Nashville by an eighteen-pound shell, but was never hit by a lead ball. He was paroled at Greensboro, N. C., in May, 1865, and afterward went to Bowie County, Tex., where he found his parents, where they had gone during the war. In December, 1865, he returned with his father and step-mother to the old home in Scott County, and engaged in farming again. During the reconstruction period a new county was formed of territory from Scott, Yell, Johnson and Franklin Counties; Cauthron Prairie was in the act taken from Scott. This new county was first called Sarber County, but afterward changed to that of Logan. In 1869 Capt. Cauthron married Miss Louesa C. Moody, who was born in Walker County, Ga., in 1848, who bore him one son, Justin. In 1881 Capt. Cauthron moved to Sebastian County, Ark., and located one mile west of Greenwood, and in 1883 he moved to Greenwood, and in June, 1884, he lost his wife, and in December the same year he returned to Logan County; in 1887 he came back to Greenwood, where he engaged in the furniture and undertaker's business. He is a Democrat in politics, and a member of the Methodist Episcopal Church, South.

Hezekiah Chaney, a wealthy farmer, residing five miles south of Greenwood, Ark., was born in Jefferson County, Tenn., in 1829, and is a son of Charles and Phoebe (Brown) Chaney, both of whom were Tennesseeans, born in 1801 and 1805, and died June 8, 1877, and in 1843, respectively. The father was a son of William Chaney, and resided in Tennessee until 1873, when he moved to Hickman County, Ky., and in 1877 took up his residence in Logan County, Ark., coming to Sebastian County two years later, where he died at the home of his son, Hezekiah. After the death of his first wife he was married twice, and both of his later wives are also dead. Eleven children were born to his first union, Hezekiah being the fourth child. He was reared to manhood on a farm, and made his home with his father until he was sixteen years old, when he hired out in a brick-yard for $3 per month, and remained two seasons. He then began working on a farm for $11 per month for one year. December 16, 1852, he was married to Miss Debbie Brogdon, who was born in Williamson County, Tenn., in 1829, and by whom he became the father of ten children: James William; Phoebe Jane, wife of George Loney; Susan C., wife of Walter Cornett; George, Hezekiah, John F.; Alice, wife of Samuel Gooden; Robert, Lucy Lee, who died in 1874, at the age of eight years, and Luther Matthew. About 1865 Mr. Chaney moved to Hickman County, Ky., and three years later became a resident of Texas County, Mo., and nine months later located in Franklin County, Ark. Here he resided until 1879, when he became a citizen of Sebastian County, and in 1880 purchased ninety-five acres of land, sixty-five of which were under cultivation. He now owns 135 acres, and is doing well financially. He has been a life-long Democrat, and his first presidential vote was cast for Franklin Pierce. He is a member of the Methodist Episcopal Church, South.

Mrs. Margaret (Rogers) Chollar is a native of the county in which she now resides, and was born in 1838. Her parents were Capt. John and Mary (Flagg) Rogers. They had the following children: Mrs. Chollar, Mrs. Emma Johnson, William, Hickory, Thomas and Buckner. The sons live in the Indian Territory. Mrs. Chollar was reared in Fort Smith, and attended the St. Paul's Institute, of Baltimore, Md. She was first married to John Melvin, who was born in Pennsylvania, and was a steamboat pilot on the Arkansas River. He was a member of the I. O. O. F., and died in 1878, and she was afterward married to John Chollar, a native of York State. To her first union two children were born: Jane, who is now in the patent office at Washington, D.C., and William, a machinist at Fort Smith, Ark. John Rogers, Mrs. Chollar's father, was the founder of Fort Smith. He was born near Carlisle, Penn., and removed with his father to near Pittsburgh, where he was educated. When quite young he left Pittsburgh and went to Harper's Ferry, Va., where he remained until the breaking out of the War of 1812, and was then engaged in supplying the army of Gen. Harrison with provisions, serving in this capacity until the close of the war. He was appointed collector of the post of Detroit, Mich., and was appointed deputy paymaster of the United States Army, and in the winter of 1816 went south to New Orleans. In 1818 he became sutler of the army, and the following year became military commissary keeper, and acted as purchasing agent for the army, and also furnished provisions for Gen. Jackson's Florida expedition. In 1822 he came to Fort Smith, and was the first postmaster of the town, which position he held thirty years. He laid out the town, and the first two buildings were erected by him, the materials for which were brought from Pittsburgh, Penn., on keel-boats, by Capt. Rogers and George S. Birnie. Until 1842 his time was devoted to building up the town which he had founded, and he was a man of unusual business ability and sagacity, and was noted for his honesty and liberality to the poor. Owing to his enterprise and push, the county is largely indebted to him for its prosperity, and he is justly entitled to rank among the representative men of Arkansas.

Dr. Peyton B. Coker, physician and farmer of Big Creek Township, was born in Bibb County, Ala., in 1835, and is a son of Robert and Sarah (Myers) Coker, natives of Lawrenceburg District, S. C., and Georgia, respectively. They removed from Alabama to Mississippi in 1847, where their respective deaths occurred in 1881 and 1887. Philip Coker, the grandfather, was born in South Carolina, and died in Georgia. Dr. Coker is one of a family of twelve children, and being reared upon a farm his early education was received at a country school. He read medicine from 1856 until 1860, and the following winter attended the Memphis Medical College. He began to practice in Tishomingo County, Miss., and until 1870 practiced in that State. He then came to Sebastian County, and having taught school prior to the war continued that vocation one year, since which time he has devoted his attention to farming and medicine. In August, 1861, he enlisted as a Chickasaw Ranger, in Martin's battalion, of Steward's brigade, and served in the Virginia army until discharged on account of ill health the following December. He afterward served in different capacities, and he fought at the battle of Shiloh. In June, 1863, he married Elizabeth, daughter of Thomas and Sarah Rogers, natives of North Carolina and Georgia. Mr. Rogers died in 1886, but his widow is now living. Mrs. Coker was born in Georgia, and has borne the Doctor eleven children, of whom nine are living, and have enjoyed the advantages of a good education. Dr. Coker has been a prominent member of the Methodist Episcopal Church, South, for thirty-one years, having held many offices in the meantime, and his wife belongs to the same denomination. Dr. Coker owns a nice farm of 320 acres as a result of his labor. He has always been a Democrat, and for a short time served as justice of the peace. He is a demitted member of the Masonic fraternity.

Preslie B. Cole, proprietor of Cole's Dry Goods and Grocery Emporium, is a native of Georgia, was born in 1861, and is a son of Monroe Cole. The father was a native of Georgia, and for some time was second lieutenant of a company of Confederate soldiers. For some time during the war he was in charge of Andersonville Prison. His parents are living in Georgia, at an advanced age. Our subject attended the public schools in his native State, and then obtained a position as a clerk. Leaving home at the age of nineteen he came to Arkansas, and for two years clerked at Webb City. He then came to Hackett City, and for a year clerked for T. H. McMutrey, after which he traveled for Black & Co., of Fort Smith, a year. Returning to Hackett City at the end of that time he engaged in the mercantile business, in which he has since met with good success. He carries a stock of about $5,000 worth of goods, and his sales average $2,300. He is a substantial citizen, and owns several town lots. In politics he is a Democrat.

Abraham F. Coleman, farmer and stock raiser of Sulphur Township, was born in Rowan County, N. C., June 30, 1835, and is a son of James D. and Sarah E. (Mann) Coleman, natives of North Carolina, where they lived until 1860. They then removed to Newton County, Mo., and during the war came to Benton County, Ark. They afterward located in Sebastian County, where the mother died on January 9, 1884, and the father January 8, 1885. The grandfather, James Coleman, was born in Virginia, and was of German and Irish descent. Our subject is the oldest of a family of eight children, and during his youth his early education was received at the common schools of North Carolina. In 1855 he left home, and going to the Granby lead mines of Newton County, Mo., remained there until the war. In 1862 he joined Company H, Second Kansas Cavalry. He fought in the battle at Saline, and operated in Missouri and Arkansas until mustered out at Fort Gibson at the close of the war. He then went to Lawrence, Kas., and from there came to this county, where he has since made his home. In December, 1870, he married Lucy A., daughter of James and Eliza Crockett, who came to Missouri from Kentucky, where Mrs. Coleman was born, and then immigrated to Arkansas in 1859, settling in Sebastian County. Mr. Crockett is now living in Chickasaw Nation; his wife died here. The union of Mr. and Mrs. Coleman has been blessed with six children, all but two now living. Mr. Coleman owns 200 acres of land, forty being bottom land. He has improved and cultivated ninety acres, and is a self-made man. He settled upon his farm when it was surrounded by a wilderness, inhabited by wild animals, and when there were but five houses between his farm and Fort Smith. Mr. Coleman cast his first presidential vote for Buchanan in 1856. After the war he was a Republican until the Baxter trouble, when he again espoused Democratic principles.

Jerry H. Colvard was born July 26, 1845, in Carroll County, Ark. His father, Wade H. Colvard, was born in North Carolina, and when young went to Hardeman County, Tenn., in an ox-cart. In 1836 he went to Washington County, Ark., and in 1847 came to Franklin County, where he purchased land of Anthony Brown, and farmed until his death, December 7, 1864. He was one of the best and most successful farmers of the county. The mother, Latha (Gage) Colvard, was born in Tennessee, and when about grown went to Washington County, Ark., where she was married. She died in Sebastian County in 1863, and was the mother of ten children. Those now living are Melissa, Benjamin D., Jerry H., Lydia, Robert B. and George N. Those deceased are Andrew J., Nancy, Thomas J. and Columbia. The paternal grandfather of our subject was a native of England, and an early settler of North Carolina, where he died. His wife was born in Wales, married in North Carolina, and died at the home of our subject, aged ninety. The maternal grandfather was born in North Carolina, and served in the War of 1812. After living some time in Tennessee he came to Washington County, Ark., which he represented for several terms in the General Assembly of the State. He afterward located in Franklin County, where he died, and where his second wife, the grandmother of our subject, still lives. Jerry H. Colvard was reared on a farm in Franklin County, and received a limited education. When fifteen he enlisted in Company A, Fifth Arkansas Volunteer Infantry, Confederate States Army. After fighting at Wilson's Creek he was discharged, and then re-enlisted in Company A, of McCullough's regiment. He passed his time upon the plains until the following December, when he joined the Indian Department of the regular army, under Cooper, at Newtonia. Coming to Fort Smith he was assigned to Clark's regiment, and at the battle of Prairie Grove he lost his left leg, which was amputated below the thigh. The cannon ball which shot him is still in his possession. He was laid up in the hospital some time, and then returning home went with his father to Texas, where he remained two months. He then re-entered the Confederate army at Pine Bluff, and remained in service until he surrendered with the Southern army. Mr. Colvard afterward went to Franklin County, Ark., where, February 7, 1867, he married Mary A., daughter of S. B. Holder, a native of Greene County, Mo., who was reared in Greene County. To this marriage eight children have been born: Alice, Annie, Rufus, Sunnie S., Edward E. and Burt. Two children died in infancy. Mr. Colvard is the owner of eighty acres of land in Sebastian County, and has served several times as chairman of township conventions, besides having been a delegate to the State convention. He is a Democrat, and his voice is often heard in the behalf of his party. During the outbreak in Scott County, in 1879, he was captain of a company, and he has in his possession a letter from the adjutant-general of the State in commendation of his conduct.

Capt. George H. Council, farmer and stock raiser, was born near Knoxville, Tenn., in 1828. His parents, Howard and Lucinda (Gollihar) Council, were born in East Tennessee in 1801. The former died in Georgia, in 1838, and his widow afterward married again. She died in Logan County, Ark., in 1875. Mr. Council was of Irish descent and of North Carolina parentage. He became a well-to-do man, but during the gold excitement in Georgia was a heavy loser. Both he and the mother of our subject belonged to the Presbyterian Church. George H. is the second of a family of seven children. He attended the common schools of the neighborhood during his youth, and went to Hiawassee College, East Tennessee. He began life for himself at the age of eighteen, as a farm hand, and afterward taught school about six years. In 1856 he married Martha, daughter of David and Nancy Ragon, and a native of Hamilton County, Tenn., whose parents were natives of North Carolina. To Mr. and Mrs. Council nine children have been born, of whom all save one are living. In 1857 Capt. Council came to Sebastian County and entered the land he now owns, which was then unimproved, and which he proceeded to cultivate. This was laid waste during his absence in war times, but he has now converted it into a nice farm of 370 acres. Although he began life in humble circumstances he is now a successful and prominent farmer of Prairie Township, and one of its respected citizens. From June, 1862, until after the battle at Prairie Grove, he served as first lieutenant of Company G, Col. Brooks' regiment, but was then made captain, which position he held until the close of the war. He operated in Arkansas and Louisiana, participating in the engagements at Helena, Pleasant Hill, Mansfield, Jenkins' Ferry, etc., and was discharged when the company disbanded at Marshall, Tex. Capt. Council has given his children good educations. Himself and wife have been members of the Missionary Baptist Church since their youth. He is a Democrat, and since 1863 has been a member of Pulliam Masonic Lodge No. 133, at Witcherville.

Dr. John C. Daily, homœopathic physician, of Fort Smith, Ark., is a native of Jeffersonville, Ind., born in 1856. He received his academic education at Barnett Academy, Charleston, Ind., and first studied medicine in Indiana, but afterward attended Putte Medical College at Cincinnati, Ohio, where he remained for some time. In 1880 he came to Little Rock, Ark., where he practiced medicine for about three years with Dr. W. E. Green. He then returned to college, graduated in 1883, and then located at Fort Smith, where he has successfully practiced his profession ever since. He is among the leading homœopathic physicians of the city, and one of the representative practitioners of the county. Dr. Daily was married to Mrs. (Lanagan) Whitthorn, daughter of Thomas Lanagan, chief of the Treasury Department at Washington, D. C. To Dr. and Mrs. Daily have been born one child, Harry P. The Doctor is a member of the American Institute of Homœopathy, Southern Homœopathy Association, and is a member of the K. of H.

Dr. Edgar M. Davenport was born in Lawrence County, S. C., in 1850, and is a son of Dr. Thomas and Louisa (Huller) Davenport, natives of the same State. When Edgar was five years old the family came to Scott County, Ark., and in 1879 to Witcherville, where the mother died in 1880. The father died at Greenwood August 20, 1887. He graduated from the Transylvania Medical College, of Lexington, Ky., when twenty-six years of age, and also possessed a good literary education. He made medicine his life-long occupation, and for a short time during the war served as surgeon in the Confederate army. Both parents were of English descent. Dr. Edgar Davenport is the eldest of a family of seven children, and his early education was received at Cane Hill College. He began the study of medicine with his father, and in 1875 graduated from the Louisville Medical College after a two years' course, in a class of over 300, and about seventy graduates out of this number who passed their examination in all the branches of medicine. He then returned home, and on June 15, 1875, married Mollie, daughter of David and Pauline Moore, of Cane Hill. Mrs. Davenport was born in Washington County, and is the mother of two living children, Alberta and Marvin. The Doctor located at Waldron soon after this, where he had a very large practice, extending over an area of twenty-five miles, notwithstanding there were a dozen or more old physicians in the town and county.

Since that time he has practiced at Mansfield and Witcherville, coming to the latter place in 1878, and is the oldest practicing physician in Witcherville, where he owns a good house and two business houses, a two-story stone building and a one-story brick. The great-grandfather of our subject was a descendant of the English Davenports, and belonged to one of the best families of Virginia. He afterward removed to Lawrence County, S. C., where Birket, the grandfather of our subject, was reared, and died in the vigor of manhood, leaving a widow and four children. Thomas, the father of Dr. Edgar Davenport, began the study of medicine when twenty, and became a well-to-do and successful physician. Dr. Edgar Davenport is a member of the Knights of Honor, a member also of the Masonic fraternity, and one of the principal officers at this time. He is also a trustee of the Episcopal College, known better as Buckner College. He has entire control of the institution, although he is a member of the Presbyterian Church.

William Murphy Davis was born in DeKalb County, Ga., April 2, 1840, and is a son of William M. and Frances (Morton) Davis. His father was born in Virginia, and when young went to South Carolina, where he learned the blacksmith's trade, and grew up upon a farm. From South Carolina he went to Georgia, and in 1845 came to Arkansas. In 1852 he removed to Texas, and there died in 1855. He was a farmer by occupation. The mother was a native of Virginia, but was married in Pendleton District, S. C. She died in Jefferson County, Ark., in 1863, and was the mother of nine children, of whom our subject is the only survivor. The others were Miles A., Unity, Mary, Gabriel, Franklin, Caroline, Lewis and Frances. The grandparents on both sides were natives of Virginia, who went to South Carolina. The paternal grandparents died in that State, but the maternal grandparents died in Georgia. William Davis was but four years of age when brought to Jefferson County, Ark., where he grew up upon his father's farm. Being the oldest child he was needed upon the farm, and consequently received but a limited education. In 1861 he enlisted in Company I, of the Ninth Arkansas Volunteer Infantry, Confederate States Army, and served in that company until discharged in 1862. He was present at Grant's defeat at Belmont. He then enlisted at St. Charles, Ark., under Capt. Peoples, Confederate Army, and served until mustered out in 1865. The company was disbanded at Louisville, Ark., with other Southern troops. After the war he engaged in farming in Jefferson County, Ark., but in 1872 came to Sebastian County, where he bought eighty-four acres of land, fifty of which he cultivates. In 1869 he married Margaret, daughter of James Carr, a native of Gibson County, Tenn. Mrs. Davis came to this State when young, and has borne eight children, all save one now living: Dorah, Phœby, Marshall, Morgan Marches, Estelle, Motier, Ida L. and Morgan (deceased). Mr. and Mrs. Davis belong to the Methodist Episcopal Church, South. Mr. Davis has served his township as school director and overseer, and in politics is a straight Democrat.

Leroy Dawson is a worthy tiller of the soil in Sebastian County, Ark., and owns a fertile farm of 160 acres, 110 of which are under cultivation. He is the eldest of eight children, and was born in Jackson County, Ala., June 26, 1824, and from his earliest boyhood up has been engaged in farming. At the age of twenty he began the battle of life for himself, and June 26, 1847, was married in Missouri, whither he had moved with his parents, to Elizabeth C. Burtoff, by whom he became the father of four sons and three daughters. For his second wife he chose Miss Elizabeth Wilhite, who bore him one son and five daughters. Mr. Dawson is a Democrat, and since 1879 has been a resident of Sebastian County, Ark. His parents, Larkin and Lucinda (Williams) Dawson, were born in North and South Carolina, respectively, and when quite young were taken to Jackson County, Ala., where they married and lived until about 1842, when they took up their abode in Crawford County, Mo. They both died in 1864 at a good old age, their deaths occurring one day apart. The mother was a true Christian in every sense of the word, and was a devoted member of the Primitive Baptist Church. The father was a Democrat in his political views, and was highly esteemed and respected by all who knew him.

John Degen, butcher and fine stock raiser, of Huntington, is one of the first settlers of that place, having purchased the first corner lot. He was born on the Rhine, Germany, in 1838, and is a son of Hermann and Barbara (Eichorn) Degen, who, coming to the United States in 1848, spent one year in New

York City, and then lived until 1860 in Schenectady. They then immigrated to Fort Smith, near which place the mother is now living, and where the father died in 1869. He was a civil engineer, and followed that vocation while in New York. In his native land he was a prominent politician, having been a member of Parliament many years, and, being upon the unpopular side during the European trouble of 1848, he deemed it prudent to emigrate. John Degen, the subject of this sketch, was the seventh child in a family of five sons and five daughters, and received his English and German education in New York City, where he also learned the butcher's trade. After working in Schenectady, Syracuse, Utica, Detroit and Chicago he traveled farther west in 1854. He served throughout the Kansas War, and enlisted in the Government employ in May, 1854. He served five years in Company B, First United States Cavalry, as sergeant, and fought the Indians in Colorado, Montana and the Rocky Mountain district. He first visited Fort Smith in 1854, and taking up his residence at that place in 1860 he made it his home until coming to Huntington in 1887. Upon the outbreak of the Civil War he commanded a company under Gen. Pike, with whom he traveled through the Indian Territory, making treaties for the Confederate army with the Indians. He remained in service as military instructor for the trans-Mississippi Department until captured in Sebastian County in 1863. He was held a prisoner six weeks at Fort Smith, and was not exchanged. November 4, 1864, he married Bertha, daughter of Andrew Euper, who came from Germany when a child with her parents. This marriage has resulted in five children, four of whom are living. After the war until 1869 Mr. Degen traded in cattle, but since 1871 has been engaged in butchering and contracting with the railway. He assisted largely in the building of the "Frisco," Missouri, Kansas & Texas, and other lines in the Southwest. Since 1877 Mr. Degen has devoted a great share of his attention to the breeding of Poland China and Berkshire hogs and short-horn cattle. He has some fine herds, and has taken several premiums at different fairs, including the fairs of Fort Smith and St. Louis. He is well informed upon the subject of cattle raising and breeding, and has done a great deal toward the improvement of stock in the county. He is a large dealer, exporting cattle to Texas, Missouri, Indian Territory and other States.

Paul Alfred Delorvin, proprietor of the Border City Manufacturing Company, was born in Dantzic, Germany, July 18, 1857, and is a son of George and Adele (Juchanovitz) Delorvin. The paternal grandfather, George Delorvin, was a native of France, and the maternal ancestors were from Poland. Our subject grew to manhood in the land of his birth, and there received a good education and engaged in the grocery business. In 1873 he came to America, and for some time travelled as a baker and confectioner through Illinois, Missouri and this western country. In January, 1883, he located at Fort Smith, where he established himself in the confectionery business. He has a large factory, and besides candies manufactures baking powder, bluing, cider, etc. In 1887 he completed his present large factory, warehouse and store, on the corner of First and Second Streets, and built a large store next to the one occupied by Messrs Reynolds & Foster. He was married in St. Louis, Mo., to Miss Imogene Ellis, a native of that city. Mr. and Mrs. Delorvin have no children, but George, a son of our subject's brother George, is living and working with his uncle. Mr. Delorvin belongs to the Lutheran Church, and his wife to the Episcopal Church.

John Dodson, retired merchant and land agent of Fort Smith, Ark., hails from Belfast, Ireland, in which city, and in England and Scotland, he learned flax-spinning, by machinery, and became what he calls manager, and we call superintendent of a factory, a part of the business being the making of tailors' and other threads. Whilst in Ayrshire he went to the Burns' Festival, heard Prof. Wilson deliver his famous address, saw several noted writers, saw Burns' sons and some of his old neighbors, also a representation of "Tam o' Shanter," his mare, "Meg," and the "Witches," and saw "Cuttie Sart" pull Meg's tail off crossing the "Keystane o' the Brig." At a time of bad trade he left Ireland for New York, tramped over much of that State, New Jersey and Pennsylvania; got disgusted and dropped his trade, for if there were then any factories worthy of the name he failed to find them. He spent two years at common labor in a New Jersey woolen mill, and his wages were $8 per month. Three or four months before Zach. Taylor's election he was discharged, and between Philadelphia and Baltimore got into a crowd of

3,000 men that had been discharged from the Eastern mills to show that an increased "protective tariff" was necessary—seems this game is played every four years, whether trade be really good or bad. The crowd took everything eatable on the road, and sometimes took drinkables, so he left and headed for Ohio. It was a long walk to Beaver, or Fallston, over 300 miles of a rough country road, but he got work there at 50 cents a day, one-half cash and one-half in woolen cloth. Ere reaching Beaver, and at the foot of Laurel Hill, he was offered work, mining or digging iron ore at $18 per month. Here he worked five weeks, and received in full pay $2—some other of the workers got less. The two owners of the furnace refused to pay all tramps and strangers, and were habitually cheating. Some workmen were paid on head and ribs with the furnacemen's iron pokers. His work led him past the cottage of "Grace Greenwood" daily. She was young then, and making a name as a writer. She seemed fond of birds and flowers. Greenwood, of course, is not her real name. He tried next the blue-grass region of Kentucky, and would willingly have settled there, for the country and people suited him, but times were dull and work scarce, and in hunting for the latter he found himself at Little Rock, Ark. The capital of Arkansas is a fine city now, but when he first saw it it was a small town—land too plenty, people too few, money and work too little. Chopping wood and burning coal seemed all that was needed, and not much of that same. Here he lived two years, mostly as guard and inside keeper of the penitentiary. The next year he was a store clerk in Van Buren, and the following year in Fort Smith. After that he had a small interest in the store, and made much money for his partner and some for himself. The "Know-nothing" movement came up before the Civil War, and, being the Irish leader here, he found it harder than the war; his caution and the good understanding he maintained with the Germans helped much, and hardly any injury occurred to person or property. He never owned a slave, but he thought justice was on the South's side, and spent about $15,000 in supporting her. He lost two young sons and a brother, and his home and other things, and for two years after the war closed did not get enough to eat. But he wasted no time in grumbling, and luck turned with him as soon as he became a land agent. In 1886 he was worth $20,000 or $30,000, and in 1887 came a boom, and he made about as much more, and he has it and is not likely to waste it. He married three times. The first wife was a Miss O'Keeffe, of Wicklow, Ireland; the second, a Miss Murray, of his old town of Belfast; his third is a Chicago lady named Miss Brady. He has three children; one is a partner in a planing mill, another is studying law in Baltimore, and the third is a girl of seven years. He took Father Matthew's pledge, and keeps it. He never gambled; his leisure hours are spent in reading. He has many books on many subjects, and by the best authors—for some of them he sent to Ireland. He thinks he has the best Catholic library in Arkansas; if he lives long he will, for he is occasionally adding to it. He thinks Fort Smith will gradually enlarge; that as she has several railroads she will have others, and that, distances being far to Little Rock, Kansas City and St. Louis, this town has a superior location.

Dr. Albert Dunlap, physician of Fort Smith, and son of Joseph and Mildred (Jones) Dunlap, was born in Alabama December 8, 1828. Joseph Dunlap is a native of North Carolina, was a mechanic by occupation, is still alive, and a resident of Washington County, Ark. His mother, Frances Dunlap, is also living in Washington County, Ark., and is the oldest person in that county. She is ninety-seven years of age. Dr. Albert Dunlap came to Arkansas during his minority, and grew to manhood in Washington County. He received his education in Ozark Institute, and in 1850 he commenced the study of medicine under Dr. Pollard. He graduated from the medical department of the Transylvania University, at Lexington, Ky., in 1851, and with the exception of a short time he has since practiced medicine in Fort Smith, locating here in 1852. He is a member of the Sebastian Medical Society, Arkansas State Medical Society, American Medical Association and International Medical Congress. He has been president of the Sebastian County Medical Society, and vice-president of the Arkansas State Medical Society; was a member of the Fort Smith Board of Health for about twenty years. He was in the hospital department during the late war, serving the whole time in the trans-Mississippi Department. He is the oldest practicing physician in Fort Smith, and his family are members of the Episcopal Church. The Doctor was married to Miss Virginia Spring, daughter of Dr. M. Spring, formerly a physician of this place, and medical partner of Dr. Dunlap. Mrs. Dunlap is a member of the Ladies' Relief Union. Dr. Dunlap is a member of the pension examination board, and examining physician for several different life insurance companies. After years of experience in the country, Dr. Dunlap is about to retire from active practice in the city of Fort Smith, and is building up a health resort on the top of the Boston Mountains. This he considers the greatest enterprise of his life. The location is certainly a happy one, and has the sanction of the highest medical authorities in the South, besides being expressly chosen by Dr. Dunlap, who would certainly know its virtue if anyone would. The close proximity of the location to the Southern lowlands, the great altitude and the purity and variety of waters to be found on the location, make it expressly desirable. This is unquestionably destined to become one of the leading health resorts of the South. It is 2,000 feet above the level of the sea, and the highest temperature reached during the summer of 1888 was ninety degrees. The place chosen for the health resort is situated on both sides of the St. Louis & San Francisco Railroad, forty-two miles from Fort Smith, and two trains pass daily each way, making regular stops at the station—Winslow.

Jeremiah P. Durden, treasurer of Sebastian County, Ark., is a native of Muscogee County, Ga., and was born July 15, 1841, being a son of Asa R. and Nancy (Ransom) Durden. Asa R. Durden was born in Northeastern Georgia, in 1795, and was of Irish-English descent. He was a mechanic and carpenter in early life, but later followed the farmer's occupation. In 1849 he moved to Barbour County, Ala., where he passed the remainder of his life. He died in 1858. His wife was born in Northeastern Georgia, is yet living, and is residing with her children, in Sebastian County, Ark., coming here in 1885. Of the eleven children born to her marriage eight are now living, and Jeremiah P. Durden is the seventh in order of birth. He attained his growth on the farm, and remained with his mother until twenty-four years of age. March 10, 1862, he enlisted in Company A, Forty-fifth Alabama Regiment, Infantry Volunteers, and participated in the battles of Murfreesboro, Missionary Ridge, Chickamauga, Jonesboro, Resaca and Springhill, Tenn. At the battle of Murfreesboro he was wounded in the right leg by a rifle-ball, and was absent from command sixty days. He was again wounded at Springhill, Tenn., November 29, 1864, being struck in the left leg by a minie-ball below the knee, but the wound was so severe that in March, 1865, amputation was necessary to save his life. He was held in prison until June, 1865, when he was sent to the prison hospital at Nashville, Tenn. He remained there until the latter part of July, when he was released, and in the fall returned to Alabama. After the war he attended school, and in 1867 engaged in the teacher's profession, teaching in Alabama until 1872, when he immigrated to Sebastian County, Ark., and located six miles east of the county seat, where he resumed teaching. He continued this for two years, and in 1874 was appointed deputy assessor of Sebastian County, and in 1875 he was elected county assessor at a special election. He was re-elected in 1876, 1878 and 1880 to the same position, serving in all eight years. The four years after this he followed farming, and in 1886 he was elected county treasurer of Sebastian County, Ark., his majority being over 1,300, thus forcibly showing his popularity among the people. Mr. Durden is a fine business man and a good citizen. He is the owner of 300 acres of land, and is a successful farmer. In 1868 he married Miss Martha R. Thames, who was born in Sumter County, Ga., in 1844. Eight children were born to this marriage: Pruett (who was killed accidentally by being struck by a base-ball bat at Fayetteville, Ark., June 24, 1888, at the age of eighteen years), Harman, Reuben O., Eula F. (deceased, who died at the age of one year), John J., Lemuel P., Ida L. and Abbie M. Mr. Durden is a member of the K. of H., also a member of the Methodist Episcopal Church, South, and he is Democratic in his political views. Mrs. Durden is a member of the Missionary Baptist Church, and Democratic also.

Mrs. Angela Medora DuVal, widow of Dr. Elias Rector DuVal, was born in Van Buren, Ark., December 9, 1841, and is a daughter of Dr. J. A. Dibrell. She was reared in Arkansas, and educated in Richmond, Va., and on the 8th of May, 1860, was married to Dr. DuVal, and soon after took up her residence in Fort Smith, where she has since made her home, and in her commodious and handsome residence on Hickory Street is devoting her time and energies to the education and culture of her children, whose names are as follows: Annie

Medora, who was educated in the University of Arkansas, at Fayetteville; Ben. T., who is attending school in Tennessee; Dibrell LeGrande and Angela M. Elias R., another child, died in 1864, at the age of eleven months. Dr. J. A. Dibrell, the father of Mrs. DuVal, was born in Nashville, Tenn., August 15, 1817, and was educated in the university of that city. He studied medicine for three years under the instruction of Dr. Thomas R. Jennings, and graduated from the medical department of the University of Pennsylvania in 1839, and has been a practicing physician of Van Buren, Ark., for forty-one years, except during the late Civil War. His wife, Ann Eliza (Pryor) Dibrell, was also born in Nashville, October 8, 1825, and became the mother of five children : Angela Medora (Mrs. DuVal), James Anthony, J. A., Thomas H. and Ann Eliza. Mrs. DuVal's paternal grandfather, Edwin Dibrell, was clerk in the Federal Treasury under President Polk, and was a descendant of the French Huguenots. His wife, whose maiden name was Martha Shrewsbury, was of English lineage, and was born in Kentucky. The great-grandfather, Anthony Dibrell, was a wealthy planter and a member of the Virginia Legislature. He was a soldier in the Revolutionary War, and fought through the entire conflict for our national independence, being wounded in the fight at Guilford Court-House, and was carried off the field by the noted giant, Peter Francisco. The Pryor family are of Virginia stock, and are related to the Jefferson family by marriage. Dr. Elias Rector DuVal was born in Fort Smith, Ark., August 13, 1836, and received his literary education in the Arkansas College, Fayetteville, graduating with the degree of A.B. in 1854, at the age of eighteen. The next two years were spent in the Louisville and Philadelphia Medical Colleges, graduating from the latter institution as an M. D. March 6, 1858, also having the degree of A.M. conferred upon him. He served in Lieut. Steen's command in New Mexico as acting surgeon of the United States Army, but in 1859 retired to private life in Fort Smith, where he not only rose to be one of the leading physicians and surgeons, but became one of the leading men of the State. His talents were not limited to his profession, but extended over a large area, and much of his time was devoted to the improvement and development of the county and community in which he resided, the public schools testifying to his ability and discreet management. In medical circles no man in the State stood higher, and he was a member of the Fort Smith Medical Society; was president of the Sebastian County Medical Society in 1872; president of the State Medical Society during 1874–75, and was a permanent member of the American Medical Association. He was president of the Fort Smith Board of Health, and a member of the State Board of Health of Little Rock. In 1861 he was appointed assistant surgeon in the Confederate army, and the same year was promoted to the post of surgeon. In August, 1862, he was promoted to chief surgeon of the Second Division of the First Army Corps, of the trans-Mississippi Department, and in March, 1863, was appointed medical director for the entire department. Among his published writings, worthy of especial mention, are "Bucnemia Tropica," "Malarial Hæmorrhagic Fever," "Influenza," "Cerebro Spinal Fever," "History of the Cholera in Fort Smith in 1866," and "Eclampsia Puerperalis." Dr. DuVal had taken all the York Rite degrees of Masonry, and had been Worshipful Master, High Priest of the Chapter, Most Worshipful Grand Master of the State, and for two years successively was Grand High Priest of the State ; one year, Right Eminent Grand Commander of the Knights Templar, and was for a number of years chairman of committees on Masonic history, and is the author of the "History of Masonry in Arkansas." He voted against secession prior to the war, but afterward espoused the cause of the Confederacy, and throughout the remainder of his life was a consistent Democrat. He died on the 7th of October, 1885, lamented by a large circle of friends and acquaintances. He was a son of William DuVal, who was a direct descendant of the French Huguenots. His grandfather was of the Maryland line of DuVals. William resided for a number of years in Virginia, and came to Fort Smith, Ark., in 1825. He was much beloved by the Indians, with whom he traded, and was sent as their representative to Washington, D.C. Dr. E. R. DuVal, in his private life, was a refined Christian gentleman, in his family the center of every attraction, being idolized by all hearts. His distinguishing characteristics were charity for the feelings and opinions of others, and his firm convictions of right, ever in his lectures denouncing infidelity and showing the evil tendencies of skepticism. His sweet memory will live with us until we are carried to our last abode. While his noble deeds will diminish in the lengthening distance when viewed by future generations, yet in heaven they are written with imperishable characters, and the angel of light has brightened the page with a record of his noble deeds.

M. T. Dyke, of the firm of Miller & Dyke, at Fort Smith, Ark., was born in Indiana, in 1856, and is the son of Nathaniel and Emily M. (Trester) Dyke. The Dyke family are descendants of the early New England Presbyterians, and were tenacious of their religious belief, and Grandfather Nathaniel Dyke was a veteran in the War of 1812. Nathaniel Dyke, father of our subject, was married to Miss Emily M. Trester, in Indiana, and five children were the result of this union, two sons and three daughters, only two sons now alive. M. T. Dyke was educated in the graded schools of Indiana, and came to Arkansas in 1875, where he engaged in the lumber business, in the employ of J. G. Miller. Three years later he became a member of the firm, under the title of J. G. Miller & Co., remaining as such until 1887, when the firm title was changed to Miller & Dyke. Mr. Dyke was married, in Fort Smith, to Miss Myrtle M. Parke, daughter of Maj. Frank Parke, one of the oldest settlers of Fort Smith. This union resulted in the birth of two children: Mary Trester and Myrtle Parke. Mr. Dyke is secretary of the building committee for the construction of the First Methodist Episcopal Church, South, is church secretary, and is a member of the A. F. & A. M. Mrs. Dyke is a member of the Ladies' Aid Society, also a member of the Missionary Society, and has taken an important part in society work. Nathaniel Dyke, the third member of the firm of Miller & Dyke, came to Fort Smith in 1880, entered the employ of the firm, and became a member of the same January, 1888. He is a K. P., is a member of the Methodist Episcopal Church, South, being steward of the same, and is organist and instructor of the church choir. He was also educated in the high-schools of Indiana, and has unusual musical talent. The firm of Miller & Dyke manufacture all kinds of doors, sash blinds, etc., and do a general lumber business.

Henry Clay Earnest, farmer, miller and postmaster, at Milltown, Ark., is a son of David and Jennie (Smith) Earnest, the former of whom was born in Franklin County, Va., in 1781. His wife was born in North Carolina in 1785. They were married about 1802, and located in Ashe County, but in 1835 moved to Bradley County, Tenn., where the mother died in 1854. About 1861 the father went to Walker County, Ga., where he resided until his death, in 1865. For a great many years he held important official positions in Ashe County, N. C., filling the position of county and circuit clerk of Ashe County for forty years. He was a Henry Clay Whig, and throughout life was extensively engaged in farming. His father came from Germany at an early day, and followed the occupation of blacksmithing. Henry Clay Earnest is the only surviving member of a family of nine children, and was born on the 12th of May, 1823, in Ashe County, N. C. He received the education and rearing of the average farmer's boy of his day, and at the age of twenty began tilling the soil on his own responsibility. In 1844 he espoused Mary Melton, who was born in Cocke County, Tenn., in 1827, and in 1859 they moved to Walker County, Ga., and seven years later removed to Washington County, Ark., where they made their home until 1883, since which time they have resided in Sebastian County. Mr. Earnest's chief business through life has been farming, but since locating in Sebastian County he has operated a grist-mill and cotton-gin. In 1884 he was appointed postmaster of Milltown, and is a Republican in politics, and his wife is a member of the Missionary Baptist Church. They own sixty-eight acres of land in Sebastian County, and eighty acres in Washington County, and are the parents of the following children: Winfield S., Mary J., Mattie, Margaret, David, John, Thomas, Charles, Amanda, Henry, Minnie and Otto. The eldest son is a merchant of Milltown.

Robert H. Echols, farmer, is a son of Thomas and Mary (Harper) Echols, the former of whom was a native of Wilkes County, Ga., born April 21, 1801, though reared in Clark County. The Echols family was first represented in America by John Echols, who was born in England, and settled in Virginia, where he was married to Mary Cave, a Welsh lady. Grandfather Echols was married to Susan Sampson, and moved to Georgia, where he reared a family of five sons and two daughters, of whom Thomas is the third. The latter's brother Robert was a member of the Georgia Legislature for many years, and was president of the Senate for eleven years. Thomas Echols was married in Clark

County in 1821, his wife being born in 1806, and they resided respectively in Clark, Walton, Newton, Fulton and Paulding Counties, Ga., and in 1869 became residents of Crawford County, Ark., coming to Sebastian County eight years later. The mother died in Fulton County, Ga., in January, 1848, and the father has since been married twice. His two sons and two daughters were born to his first marriage. During the days of militia he held the offices of lieutenant and captain, and throughout his long and useful career has followed the occupations of farming and carpentering. He is a member of the Missionary Baptist Church, has been a Democrat all his life, and a Mason for thirty-four years. Robert H. Echols, his son, was born in Clark County, Ga., December 3, 1824, and up to the present time has made his home in the same localities in which his father has resided. While in Fulton County, Ga., he was married (in 1849) to Elizabeth Morris, by whom he had one son. After her death he married Mary A., her sister, who has borne him nine sons and two daughters. He owns eighty acres of land, and in politics is a Democrat.

William M. Ervin, farmer, was born December 10, 1830, in Lincoln County, Tenn. (now Moore County), his father being James Ervin, who married a Miss Merritt. The former was reared upon a farm in North Carolina, where he was born, and when a boy traveled by wagon to Tennessee, where he lived until his death in December, 1882, aged eighty-five. He enlisted as a captain in the late war, and arose to the office of major-general. The mother was born in the same county, and was a school-mate of her husband. She also went to Tennessee when young, and there married and bore seven children. Those living are Jonathan, William M., James and Thomas. Hezekiah and Milton were killed while in the Confederate service, and Lucinda is also deceased. Mrs. Ervin was of English descent, and her death occurred the day after her husband's, when she was eighty-six. The paternal grandparents emigrated from North Carolina to Tennessee, and from there to Cape Girardeau County, Mo., where they died. The maternal grandfather was born in North Carolina, and fought in the battle of New Orleans. He died in Tennessee. Our subject was reared upon the farm in Tennessee, and during his youth received a good education, and learned the tanner's, carpenter's and shoemaker's trades, at the latter of which he worked about twenty years. In 1849 he married Rebecca La Massey, who was born in Tennessee, and died October 6, 1887. She was the mother of the following children: Mary, James, William, John, Thomas, Henry, Alvin and Elizabeth (deceased). July 8, 1888, Mr. Ervin married Mary A. (Brewer) Lindsey, daughter of Zebedee and Amanda Brewer, and widow of Mr. Lindsey, by whom she had four children: Ada, Ida, Thomas and Rhoda. Mrs. Ervin was born and reared in this county, and is a member of the Baptist Church, to which Mr. Ervin also belongs. During the war Mr. Ervin served four years as shoemaker in the Confederate army. He participated in the battle at Prairie Springs, and surrendered at Houston, Tex., in 1865. In 1881 he settled in Sebastian County, where he has a farm of 380 acres, 215 of which he has finely cultivated. He is a prosperous citizen, a Democrat, and a member of the Masonic fraternity.

Anton Euper, a retail liquor dealer of Fort Smith, Ark., was born in the Kingdom of Prussia in 1836. His parents, Anton and Beatrice Euper, were born in Germany, the former being reared in the Kingdom of Wurtemburg. He was a wagon-maker by trade, and in 1849 came to America, landing at New Orleans, and came directly to Fort Smith, where he worked at his trade the first few years, and afterward kept a boarding-house. He was born in 1800 and died in 1869. Only two of his ten children are now alive. Anton, Jr., came with his father to the United States, and served an apprenticeship at the wagon-maker's trade, and has since been occupied in various callings, being now engaged in the retail liquor business. He is a member of the Roman Catholic Church. He was united in marriage to Pauline Grober, a daughter of Frederick Grober, one of the pioneer settlers of Fort Smith. His wife was born in the Kingdom of Prussia, and is the mother of five children: Tony, George, Frank, Ida and Rauling. The first child born to Mr. and Mrs. Euper died when an infant. Mrs. Euper is a member of the Lutheran Church.

W. L. Euper, assessor of Sebastian County, was born at Fort Smith August 2, 1852, and is a son of Melchior and Eva (Herold) Euper, natives of Wittenburg, Germany, and Vienna, Austria, respectively. The father was a glove-maker, and was married in Vienna. In 1849, with his wife and two sons and two daughters, he immigrated to America, landing at New Orleans the same year.

In 1850 the family came to Fort Smith, where Mr. and Mrs. Euper are now enjoying their old age. In this county our subject passed his youth, and after attending Cane Hill College, engaged in mercantile pursuits, in 1878 going into business for himself. In 1882 he was elected justice of Hartford Township, and in 1886 was elected county assessor, to which office he has since been re-elected consecutively. Mr. Euper married Miss Lena Refald, foster daughter and niece of the Hon. W. D. Carroll, and a native of Pine Bluff, Ark. Mr. and Mrs. Euper are regular communicants at the Church of the Immaculate Conception, and have a family of three children: Clayton, John Henry and Edna White. Mr. Euper is a Catholic Knight.

William Patrick Evans, M. D., of Excelsior, Ark., was born in Sebastian County in 1863, and is a son of William P. and Amanda (Tedford) Evans, and a grandson of Patrick and Sallie (Blevens) Evans. The grandfather was born in a fort in North Carolina in 1794, and at the age of six years was taken by his parents to Overton County, Tenn., and was married in Winchester of that State in 1817, moving to Jackson County, Ala., in 1822. Here he resided until 1850, when he took up his abode in Polk County, Ark., and the following year came to Sebastian County. He was killed in the Indian Nation. Three of his uncles immigrated to the Indian Territory at an early day, and his uncle James cut the first tree where the city of Evansville now stands, the town being named in his honor. Sallie (Blevens) Evans was born in Kentucky in 1800, and died in 1874, being a daughter of Elisha and Polly (Roberts) Blevens, who were born in England, the father dying in Illinois in 1833. William P. Evans, Sr., was born in Marion County, Tenn., in 1836, and in 1851 came to Sebastian County, Ark., and died in 1862. His wife was also born in Marion County in 1836, and died in 1877. They were the parents of three children: Goodson M., who is a medical student at Little Rock; Matilda, wife of George Tedford, and William P., M. D. The latter received his literary education in the schools of Excelsior and Hackett City, and in March, 1884, commenced the study of medicine under the instructions of Dr. J. W. McConnell, of Hackett City. In 1887 he graduated from the medical department of the Industrial University at Little Rock, and in April, 1885, began his first practicing at Brazil Station, Choctaw Nation, and eight months later located in Excelsior, one and a half miles from his birthplace, where he has since been practicing, meeting with good and well deserved success. He possesses a fine medical education, and is a young man of ability and enterprise.

Col. William Meade Fishback, presidential elector at large for Arkansas in 1888, is a native of Jeffersonton, Culpeper Co., Va., and was born in November, 1831. He is a son of Col. Frederick Fishback and Sophia A. Fishback, *nee* Yates. Col. Frederick Fishback was born in the same house as his father, and on February 14, 1813. The Fishbacks were originally from Germany, and made their first settlement at Fredericktown, Md. This town was named after the owner of the land on which it is situated, who was Frederick Fishback. Hagerstown, Md., was named after the father of his wife, Miss Hager, who owned the land upon which it was built. Sophia A. Yates was born near Appomattox Court-house, Va. Her mother was a Miss Stith, a descendant of one of the first historians of Virginia. Col. William M. Fishback grew to manhood in Jeffersonton, Va., was educated at the University of Virginia, and read law in Richmond, Va. He came west in 1857; on his way he stopped in Springfield, Ill., and made the acquaintance of Abraham Lincoln, who took a fancy to him and gave him his first legal business, and after he came to Arkansas, in 1858, Mr. Lincoln wrote to him suggesting his return to Illinois, offering to give him other business. In 1861 he was elected as a Union man to the secession convention, and when the State seceded he resigned and went north. He returned to Little Rock in 1863, and edited the *Unconditional Union*, at which he made considerable money. In 1864 he was elected to the United State Senate by the Union Government, organized under the proclamation of Mr. Lincoln, and under the assumption that the State had not seceded. It was the first case of reorganization of seceded States, and he and his colleague, Elisha Baxter, were denied admission, because the negro was not allowed the elective franchise. He was again elected to the constitutional convention of 1874, by the same county of Sebastian, and made his first attempt in that body to have the fraudulent bonds of the State repudiated by a constitutional provision, so that people could know which bonds the State recognized. The measure failed. In 1876 he was elected to the Legislature, and introduced the "Fishback Amendment" to the Constitution, forbidding the payment of these bonds; again he failed. In 1878 he was again elected, and again brought the matter up. This Legislature adopted and submitted the amendment to the people. It was carried by 40,000 majority, but was counted out. It was again submitted in 1884, and carried by over 100,000 majority. In 1888 he was a candidate for governor, but although he had more first and second choices than any of the four other candidates, he withdrew in the interest of Democratic harmony, and the convention in his absence elected him presidential elector for the State at large. In 1865 he accepted the office of treasury agent, under Andrew Johnson, and used his office to protect Southern people in their prosperty. After he had succeeded in this he resigned in 1865, and recommended that his office be abolished as useless. Two regiments were partially raised in his name for the Union army, although he was never in the service himself. He was a candidate for the United States Senate in 1885, against Hon. I. H. Berry and Poindexter Dunn. Berry was the successful candidate. He was married April 4, 1867, to Adelaide Miller, and has six living children. His wife died in 1882. He has not married again. He is a Democrat, and his family are members of the Episcopal Church. He is not a member of any church himself.

W. J. Fleming, postmaster of Fort Smith, is a native of Pope County, Ark., and was born March 29, 1845, his parents being Reuben R. and Melinda (Latimer) Fleming, natives of Tennessee. The father was a farmer by occupation; was married in Bedford County, Tenn., and about 1840 settled in Pope County, Ark., where he died in 1846. The grandfathers, William Fleming and Robert Latimer, were early settlers of Tennessee, whither the former went from England. Our subject attained his growth in Johnson County, Tenn., and when sixteen years of age enlisted in Company A, of the Sixteenth Arkansas Infantry, Confederate Army, He served from September, 1861, until taken a prisoner near the close of the war at Port Hudson, La. He then filled the office of sergeant-major. After his parole he returned to Clarksville, Ark., and served in the Indian Territory in the commissary and quartermaster's department until the cessation of hostilities. He then spent some time in Lawrence and Baldwin City, Kas., after which he lived six months at Springfield, Mo. After clerking eighteen months in the Indian Territory, in 1868 he engaged in merchandising at Hartford, Sebastian Co., Ark., continuing in business there three years. His next venture was in the milling business, at which he spent two years. After 1878 he served two terms as circuit clerk of Sebastian County, and then from 1882 until 1883 sold goods at Greenwood. In the latter year he became a resident of Fort Smith, where he has been engaged in mercantile life for two years. In 1885 he was appointed postmaster, which position he now holds. While in Hartford he married Sarah J., daughter of James T. and Rebecca M. Carter, a native of Tennessee. Mr. and Mrs. Fleming have the following children: Bertie M., Annie R., Willie R. and James T. Mrs. Fleming worships at the Methodist Episcopal Church, and Mr. Fleming is a member of the Blue Lodge in Masonry.

J. K. Foltz, a prominent fruit grower and dealer in real estate at Fort Smith, Ark., was born in the "Buckeye State" in 1853, and is the eldest of eight children born to the marriage of David Foltz and Susan Kimerer, and a grandson of John Foltz, who was born in Prussia, Germany, and immigrated to the United States many years ago, locating in Pennsylvania. He afterward moved to Ohio, where he spent his declining years and died at a ripe old age. David was reared on a farm near Wooster, Ohio, and there he and his wife, who was born in the Shenandoah Valley, Va., spent the remainder of their days. Their son, J. K. Foltz, was educated in Hiram College, and had Gen. James A. Garfield for a tutor. It was his early intention to adopt a profession, but the death of his father called him home, and being the eldest of the family he was obliged to take charge of the farm, which change caused him to give up his intentions of a professional life, and to follow agricultural pursuits instead. He was first married in Mount Vernon, Ohio, to Miss Mary Ewalt, who afterward died, having borne one child, Mary Helen, now the wife of D. W. Loney, of Olna, Ohio. Mr. Foltz afterward went to Mississippi, and while there was married to Miss Mary A. Rothell, who was born in Mississippi in 1844, and there made her home until ten years of age. She was sent to school at Mount Vernon, Ohio, where she graduated. After her marriage she returned with her husband to Ohio, where they made their home three years, and then moved to Memphis, Tenn., where they were engaged in farming until 1881. Since that time they have resided in

Sebastian County, Ark., where Mr. Foltz is engaged in fruit growing and the real estate business. He is an extensive land-holder, and owns stock in the Fruit Evaporator of Fort Smith. He and wife are the parents of three children: Joseph R., a law student at Ann Arbor, Mich.; Jennie O. and Fannie Frances, who are both attending school at St. Mary's Academy, Knoxville, Ill. Sarah, another daughter, died at the age of eight months. Both the Foltz and Kimerer families were of German descent, and the latter family was noted for their large statures, robust constitutions and great longevity. Mrs. Foltz's parents, A. G. and Mary (Cannon) Rothell, were both born in Maryland, the former moving to Mississippi at an early day, where he operated a saw, grist and planing-mill, and was an extensive dealer in lumber. Mrs. Foltz is the third of their five children. Her paternal grandfathar was Parrott Rothell, who was born in France, and established the first circulating library in Baltimore, Md. She is a member of the Episcopal Church and her husband is a member of the Christian Church.

Dr. Joseph H. Forbes was born in Barren County, Ky., in 1837, and is of Scotch and Dutch descent. His great-grandfather was a soldier in the Revolution, and his grandfather, James Forbes, was a soldier in the War of 1812. Joseph H. Forbes was educated at a private school in his native county, and in 1863 began the practice of medicine in Oregon County, Mo., but on account of the disturbed condition of the country during the war did not devote his attention exclusively to his profession. Having moved to Hackett City prior to 1871, in that year he again began the practice of medicine, and in 1877 he started a drug store in the city, which he conducted until 1885, then selling it to his sons. In 1880 he started a dry goods store in the city, but after 1885 devoted his attention to the practice of medicine. July 22, 1857, he was married at Thomasville, Oregon Co., Mo., to Elizabeth Woodside, daughter of John and Emily H. Woodside. Mr. Woodside is a lawyer, and held the office of circuit judge of Oregon County. Dr. Forbes' first wife died in 1861, leaving two children: Liegh and Alice. The Doctor was afterward married, in Oregon County, to Eliza A. Andrews, daughter of John and Matilda Andrews, farmers of Oregon County, who reared a family of twelve children. He and his wife belong to the Presbyterian Church. To them fourteen children were born, of whom the following are living: Lee W. (husband of Elizabeth Looman), Sarah Alice (wife of Dr. U. Marrow), William J. (husband of Julia Graves), Clemming (wife of Thomas E. Casey, of Hunt County, Tex.), Molly (wife of J. C. Welch, of this place), Emma, Ida, George, Daisy and Joseph. Dr. Forbes is a Mason, and a well-to-do citizen, owning several residences and business houses in town.

J. Bryant Forrester, postmaster and general merchant at Hartford, Sebastian Co., Ark., was born in Roane County in 1830, and is a son of Solomon and Sarah (Marney) Forrester, who were born in the "Palmetto State," in 1803 and 1807, and died in 1863 and 1852, respectively. They were married in their native State, and afterward removed to Tennessee, thence to Arkansas in 1833, settling in Crawford County, where they followed the occupation of farming. To them were born a family of nine children, three of whom are yet living: James M. (residing in California), B. F. (living in Texas) and J. Bryant. The paternal and maternal grandparents, Mark Forrester and Amos Marney, were of English and Scotch-Irish descent, respectively, the former being a native of South Carolina and a soldier in the Black Hawk War. J. Bryant Forrester, whose name heads this sketch, was brought to Arkansas when the country was yet a wilderness, his early days being spent in Crawford County. In 1855 he was married to Maria Shannon, who was born in Crawford County, Ark., in 1838. Her parents, Jeremiah and Elizabeth (Bryant) Shannon, were born in Tennessee, and located in Crawford County, Ark., in 1833, and engaged in tilling the soil. The former died in 1853, but the latter is still living, with her four surviving children, Nancy (Mrs. Clark), Mary (Mrs. Williams) Bryant, and Elizabeth (Mrs. Hight). Mr. Forrester's wife died in 1859, having borne two children: James B., of Fort Smith, and Haseltine (Mrs. Keeney), and in 1872 he married his second wife, Eliza, a daughter of Lucinda (Dalton) Forrester, who were Tennesseeans, and removed to Arkansas in 1850. Six children were born to his second union: Virginia, B. M., J. Bryant, W. B., Duvall and Mark. In May, 1862, Mr. Forrester enlisted in Company B, Col. Clarkson's regiment, Arkansas cavalry, as captain, and in September, 1862, was elected captain of Company D, of the same regiment, and participated in the battles of Elk Horn and Prairie Grove, serving until he received his discharge at the close of the war. He is a Mason, a member of the Missionary Baptist Church, and in his political views is a Democrat, and cast his first vote for James Buchanan.

John A. Forrester, farmer and prominent citizen of Hartford, Sebastian Co., Ark., was born in 1849 in East Tennessee. His parents, William and Lucinda (Dalton) Forrester, were farmers by occupation, and were born in Tennessee in 1825. After residing a short time in Arkansas and Texas they permanently located in Arkansas in 1867, and spent the remainder of their days in Franklin County. William Forrester still lives in Franklin County. His wife died November 17, 1885. William Forrester enlisted in the Confederate army in 1863, and operated on the frontier of Texas until the close of the war. Six of their eight children are living: Ephraim H., John A., Eliza, Thomas E., Maggie (Jackson) and Martha M. (Abbott). John A. Forrester was reared in Arkansas and Texas, and began life for himself as a farmer at the age of twenty years. In 1873 he espoused Miss Mary A. Simmons, who was born in Missouri on the 27th of December, 1849, and a daughter of William J. and Susan (Hahan) Simmons. The father was a minister, a teacher, a blacksmith and gunsmith, and was born in Tennessee in 1818, and died on the 30th of June, 1882. His wife was born in Missouri in 1823, and died in 1865. Their children are as follows: Naomi (Horn), Mary A. (Forrester), Elizabeth (Pyle), Barbara A. (Echols), Simon and Martha (Boling). In 1883 Mr. Forrester removed from Franklin to Sebastian County, and bought the fertile valley farm of 120 acres where he is now residing. He has 100 acres under cultivation, and is one of the prosperous and progressive farmers of the county. He is the father of six children, two of whom died in infancy: William, Thomas, George W., Addie R. and James Crockett. He is a Democrat, and cast his first presidential vote for Tilden. His grandparents, Alexander and Sarah Forrester, were of English and Irish descent, and were farmers by occupation.

Leander Foster, farmer and stock raiser of Hartford Township, Sebastian Co., Ark., is a son of George W. and Frances L. (Bishop) Foster, and was born in North Carolina in 1844. His parents were born in North Carolina in 1818, and he was subsequently removed by them from his native State to Georgia, thence to Missouri in 1855, and two years later came to Sebastian County, Ark., where his parents were engaged in farming and stock raising. He is one of seven surviving members of a family of eleven children, whose names are as follows: Elizabeth (Tucker), Martha (Bradley), Amanda (Tucker), Frances L. (Harris), Leander, George and Columbus. Leander Foster spent his early life in Arkansas, Kansas and Missouri, and in March, 1867, was married to Jane Wells, who was born in Platte County, Mo., in 1850, and a daughter of James and Ashby (Shirley) Wells. Mr. Wells and wife became the parents of twelve children, eight of whom are living: Charles, Joseph, Sanford, Ann (Robertson), Polly (McClintock), Julia (Brown) and Jane (Mrs. Foster). Leander Foster and wife became the parents of eleven children, only the following of whom are living: James, Sherman, Clarence, Walter A., Sidney, Horace G. and Ada. Charles and three infants are deceased. After residing a short time in Missouri Mr. Foster returned to Arkansas in 1869, and bought his present farm of 200 acres in 1872. He has 170 acres under cultivation, and a commodious and convenient frame residence. In 1863 he enlisted in Company I, Second Cavalry Regiment, United States Army, was in a number of engagements, and received his discharge in 1864. He is a Mason and Republican, and cast his first presidential vote for U. S. Grant.

Josiah Foster, of the firm of Reynolds, Foster & Co., of Fort Smith, was born in Crawford County, Ark., at Van Buren, May 13, 1849, and is a son of Riley and Luama (Snyder) Foster. The father was born in Howard County, Mo., and was a son of Josiah Foster, a native of Alabama. By occupation he was a farmer and trader. The mother was a native of Kentucky, and was a daughter of Cornelius Snyder, a native of Germany. Our subject grew to manhood in Van Buren, and since 1875 has been engaged in the mercantile business. He was a member of the Van Buren City Council five years, and was one of the originators of the Citizen's Bank and the Van Buren Ice & Coal Company, in both of which he was a stockholder and director. He was also director of the Crawford County Fair Association, and from 1869 until 1873 served as United States Deputy Marshal. He was married in Crawford County, Ark., January 30, 1872, to Miss C. D. Turner, a native of Missouri, and daughter of S. D.

Turner. To them two sons and one daughter have been born: John Edmund, Josiah and Ethel. Mr. and Mrs. Foster attend the Cumberland Presbyterian Church, and the latter is a member of the Ladies' Aid Society. Mr. Foster is a Mason, and was knighted in the Jacques DeMolay Commandery. He also belongs to the I. O. O. F. encampment, and has represented his lodge in the State councils.

Dr. James H. Foster, physician and surgeon at Witcherville, was born in Yell County, Ark., in 1858, and is a son of R. C. and P. C. (Parker) Foster, natives of South Carolina and Arkansas, who were born in 1828 and 1832, respectively. They were married in Yell County, where the mother died in 1881, and the father still lives. He is a farmer by occupation, and during the war served the entire time in the Thirty-sixth Arkansas Infantry, United States Army. His father, James Foster, was a native of South Carolina, and in 1842 came to Arkansas, where he died at the advanced age of ninety-four. He was of Irish descent. The maternal grandfather of our subject, John Parker, was born in Tennessee, and, after a long residence in Arkansas, died about 1858. Dr. Foster is the third of a family of nine children, and until grown he attended but the common schools of Yell County. He then passed a year in school at Dardanelle and attended the Fayetteville University one year. In 1882 he began the study of medicine, and in the winter of 1884–85 attended the Memphis Medical College. He has since been a practitioner of Witcherville, where he is widely and favorably known, and enjoys a lucrative patronage. He is of an enterprising nature, and intends soon to further complete his medical studies. In 1882 he married Willie Parker, who died in 1884. In 1886 he was united in marriage to Tama Farreer, of Memphis, Tenn., who has borne him one child. Dr. Foster cast his first presidential vote for James G. Blaine, and is a stanch Republican. In religion he is a member of the Episcopal Church, and his wife belongs to the Catholic Church. He is a member of Christian Masonic Lodge No. 394.

M. D. Frazier, farmer of Sebastian County, Ark., was born in North Carolina December 1, 1823, and is the fourth son of ten children, three living, born to the marriage of George Frazier and Sarah Russell, both of whom were North Carolinians, born in 1777 and 1782, and died in 1865 and 1851, respectively. The father was a farmer, and a son of George and Mary Frazier, natives of North Carolina. George Frazier was a farmer and stock raiser, a soldier in the Revolutionary War, and was at the battle of Cowpens and Guilford Court-House. The paternal great-grandfather, Thomas Frazier, was a Scotchman, and at a very early day crossed the Atlantic and settled first in Pennsylvania and then in North Carolina. The maternal grandparents, George and Rebecca Russell, were born in England and North Carolina, respectively, the former coming to the United States and settling in North Carolina at an early day. He also served in the Revolutionary War. M. D. Frazier, whose name heads this sketch, remained in his native State until twenty-four years of age, receiving but limited early educational advantages. In 1847 he was married to Miss Rebecca Curtis, who was born in North Carolina on the 26th of May, 1830, and a daughter of Harrison and Mary (Wright) Curtis. The father was a distiller in North Carolina, and died in 1845, his wife dying in 1832. Mr. Frazier and family moved from North Carolina to Little Rock, Ark., in 1848, and afterward to Searcy County, thence to Texas in 1859, and in 1860 came to Sebastian County and bought the farm of eighty acres where he now lives. He has since increased his acreage to 700, with 240 acres under cultivation. He served in the Home Guards for some time during the war, and was quite severely wounded in the skirmish at Salem. He is a Mason, a member of the Methodist Protestant Church, and a Republican in politics, casting his first vote for James K. Polk. His children, who are living, are as follows: Sally I. (Mrs. Keener), B. F., John R., Julia A., Susan E. (Mrs. Taylor), and George M.

Frank Freer was born in Dublin, Ireland, and when but fifteen years of age came to America. Since 1857 he has been interested in the Western country, and his first visit to Fort Smith, in 1868, resulted in his ultimately locating here, where he is now successfully engaged in business. During the war he served in the Federal army. He was married in this city to Miss Rosina Hess, a resident of Fort Smith, who has borne him one son, Edward, a young man of high ability and promise.

Benjamin J. H. Gaines, ex-judge of the county court of Sebastian County,

Ark.,is a native of Rhea County, East Tenn., and was born in 1817. His father, James S. Gaines, was of Welsh descent, and was born in Culpeper County, Va., in 1767. He was married in his native State to Miss Judith Easley, and after a short residence in North Carolina returned to Virginia, and in 1800 moved to Rhea County, Tenn., and in 1820 took up his abode in Southern Alabama, where he died two years later. His wife was born in Virginia, and also died in 1822. Benjamin J. H. is the youngest of their thirteen children, and was only five years old when his parents died. From that time until he was sixteen years of age he resided with his brother, John S. Gaines, and then became salesman in a store in Knoxville, Tenn., but at the end of one year returned to Southern Alabama, and engaged in pedagoguing, and also did some clerking in the courts. From 1839 to 1840 he taught school in the "Lone Star" State, and at the latter date returned to Alabama, and was married in 1848 to Miss Sallie Inge, who was born in Fayetteville, Lincoln Co., Tenn., in 1827, by whom he became the father of four children: Helen, wife of J. L. Duke, a jeweler of Fayetteville, Ark.; Thomas W., a merchant; Marshall S., a merchant, of Greenwood, Ark.; and John H., who clerks for his brother, Marshall. In 1849 Mr. Gaines was elected clerk of Sumter County, Ala., but the following year the law was changed and he was deprived of his office. At the same time, however, he was elected probate judge of the same county, serving in this capacity six years. In 1856 he moved to Monroe County, Tenn., and in 1859 took up his residence in Fayetteville, Ark., for the purpose of educating his children. He had commenced the study of law in 1848, and the following year was admitted to the bar, practicing his profession in Fayetteville until 1880, when he became a citizen of Greenwood, Ark. Two years later he was elected judge of Sebastian County, being re-elected in 1884 and 1886. He has always rendered his decisions with judicial fairness, and has made a capable and popular public officer. Previous to the late lamentable war he was a Whig in politics, but since that conflict has been a supporter of Democratic principles. He is a Royal Arch Mason, and a member of the Methodist Episcopal Church, South. His wife belongs to the Christian Church. His son, Marshall S. Gaines, a prosperous young merchant, of Greenwood, Ark., was born in Monroe County, Tenn., in 1857, and was educated in the schools of Fayetteville, Ark. At the age of sixteen years he began clerking in a store in Fayetteville, continuing four years, and then engaged in merchandising on his own responsibility in Greenwood, and in 1883 formed a partnership with Thomas E. Little, and the firm was known as Little & Gaines. In December, 1887, they dissolved partnership by mutual consent, and the firm has since been known as M. S. Gaines & Co. Their stock, which is valued at $15,000, is the largest stock of general merchandise in Greenwood, and is bringing in Mr. Gaines a handsome annual income. He is a man of sterling worth and of exceptionably good business qualifications, and commands the confidence and esteem of the citizens of the county. May 25, 1877, he was married to Miss Rebecca A. Hodgins, who was born in Mississippi in 1861, and died on March 20, 1887, having borne a family of four children: J. Bennie, Edmund P., Bessie and Helen. September 9, 1888, Mr. Gaines married Miss Sallie Whitworth, a native of Texas. He is a Democrat, and has been a member of the school board of Greenwood for six years; is a Master Mason, a K. of H., and he and wife are members of the Methodist Episcopal Church, South.

D. M. Gardner, M. D., a prominent practitioner of Fort Smith, Ark., was born in Tallapoosa County, Ala., in 1849, and is the son of William L. and Rhoda P. (Monk) Gardner. The father was an agriculturist, and died in Alabama when his son D. M. was a child. The Monk family were well educated, several of them being preachers, and fluent and eloquent speakers. Dr. D. M. Gardner took a literary course in the University of Mississippi, and graduated from the St. Louis Medical College in 1877. He then commenced the practice of his profession in Mississippi, and continued in this State for twelve years, where he gained a large practice. He was in partnership with Dr. Thomas D. Iron, the leading physician in Northern Mississippi. He came to Fort Smith in June, 1877, and here he has since remained engaged in the successful practice of his profession. He is now one of the leading physicians of the city. He was married to Miss Nettie Goolsby, a native of Lafayette County, Miss., and became the father of two children: F. Q. C. and D. M. Dr. Gardner is a member of the Masonic fraternity and of the K. of H.

Thomas Benjamin Garrett was born in Tyro, Miss., September 18, 1849, and is a son of James and Harriet R. (Sharp) Garrett, natives of Virginia, and descendants of one of its old families. James Garrett, the grandfather, was also born in that State, and was a member of the Baptist Church. Several ancestors of our subject fought in the Revolution and in the Mexican War. The mother was a daughter of Thomas Sharp, of Alabama, whose ancestors also were early settlers of Virginia Thomas Benjamin Garrett passed his boyhood upon his father's plantation, receiving a common-school education. He afterward attended the University of Mississippi at Oxford, graduating with the class of 1871-72. He then returned home, and occupied himself with mercantile life until 1873, when he was elected representative of Tate County in the Mississippi Legislature, which county he represented two consecutive terms. In 1881 he came to Arkansas and located upon a cotton plantation in Woodruff County, where he engaged in farming and merchandising until 1886. He then sold his property, and coming to Fort Smith invested his money in the livery and transfer business. He is a prominent business man of the town, a member of the city council, and is a stockholder in the Fort Smith Ice and Coal Company, also in the Fort Smith Land and Improvement Company. He also took an active interest in the organization of the Fort Smith Natural Gas Company, of which he is a director. While in Tyro, Miss., he married Miss Ella Brown, daughter of Jesse and Mary Brown, natives of Virginia. Mr. and Mrs. Garrett are the parents of the following three children: Luella, T. B. and Ollie.

Robert Bell Gartrell, farmer and miller of Center Township, Sebastian Co., Ark., was born in Lumpkin Co., Ga., in 1835, and is a son of William J. and Malinda (Hallum) Gartrell, the father being of French-Welsh descent. They were born in Georgia and South Carolina, in 1791 and 1819, respectively, and were married in Union County, Ga., soon after moving to Lumpkin County, Ga., where the father worked in the gold mines. He moved to Gordon County, Ga., in 1863, where he died four years later, followed by his wife in 1868. They became the parents of twelve children, five of whom are living at the present time, Robert Bell Gartrell being the eldest of the family. He was reared to manhood on a farm, and in the gold mines, the fall and winter seasons being spent in the mines. He made his home with his parents until thirty-three years of age, and in December, 1868, was married to Miss Mary Ward, who was born in Gordon County, Ga., in 1852, and by whom he became the father of seven children: Theophilus, Viola Gertrude, Lenora Irene, Charles Serastus, Martin Luther, Cora Sedalia and Robert Franklin. Mr. Gartrell resided in his native State until 1871, when he immigrated to Sebastian County, Ark., and purchased 327 acres of land in Center Township, about seven miles from the county seat, where he located and has since resided. In 1874 he purchased a horse gin, which he operated seven years, the last year converting it into a steam gin, the capacity of which was about 300 bales of cotton per year, and in the fall of 1888 erected a gin at a cost of about $180. He is considered one of the enterprising farmers of the county, and in his political views is a Democrat, casting his first presidential vote for James Buchanan. He is a Master Mason of Hackett Lodge. In April, 1862, he enlisted in Company H, Fifty-second Regiment Georgia Infantry, but was afterward transferred to Company I, Eighth Regiment Georgia Infantry. He went out as a private, but was promoted to second lieutenant, and participated in the battles of Missionary Ridge and Perryville, being wounded in the latter engagement by a falling tree, which was shattered by a cannon ball. He was honorably discharged at Cumberland Gap, and returned to his home and the peaceful pursuit of farming.

Gen. R. C. Gatlin was born in Lenoir County, N. C., on the 18th of January, 1809. He is the son of John Gatlin and his wife, Susan, the daughter of Richard Caswell, the first governor of the State of North Carolina. He entered the military academy at West Point as a cadet July 1, 1828, and graduated July 1, 1832, when he was appointed a brevet second lieutenant in the Seventh Infantry, then stationed at Fort Gibson. He joined the regiment in December, 1832, and served with it on the southwestern frontier until February 7, 1839, when he accompanied it to Florida, arriving at Tampa Bay in March. He had been promoted to be second lieutenant in 1834, first lieutenant in 1836, and was appointed adjutant of the Seventh Infantry in December, 1838. He served in Florida until the close of the Seminole War in 1842. In 1845 he accompanied the regiment to Corpus Christi, where it became part of the Army of Observation under Gen. Taylor. In September, 1845, he was promoted to be captain. He served in

Fort Brown during its bombardment by the Mexican troops, from the 3d to the 9th of May, and was engaged at the battle of Monterey, in which he was wounded, and for gallant and good conduct he was breveted a major in the United States Army. In consequence of his wounds he was sent home to recruit his health. In January, 1848, he joined his company in the City of Mexico. After the close of the Mexican War he served with his company at Jefferson Barracks; also in Florida, and again on the southwestern frontier, commanding Fort Smith from 1851 to 1857; then in Utah and New Mexico, when he commanded Fort Craig. He was promoted to be major of the Fifth Infantry in February, 1861, and resigned his commission in the United States army May 20, 1861, after which he went to North Carolina, and was appointed a brigadier-general of North Carolina troops, and assigned command of the coast defenses of Wilmington. He exercised the command until the 31st of August, 1861, when the North Carolina troops were transferred to the Confederate service, when he was appointed a brigadier-general, P. A. C. S., and assigned to the command of the Department of North Carolina. He was relieved from the command on account of ill health in March, 1862, and resigned September 6. In 1863 he was appointed adjutant-general of North Carolina, which office he held to the close of the war in 1865. He then came to Arkansas, and settled on the farm opposite Van Buren in January, 1866, where he remained until 1880, when he moved to Fort Smith, where he still lives. On the 20th of January, 1857, he married Mary A. Gibson, daughter of R. S. and Sarah P. Gibson, of Sebastian County, Ark. They have two children living, Susan Caswell and Mary Knox Gatlin.

Andrew J. F. Gist, a prominent farmer and stock raiser of Dayton Township, was born in Missouri, November 2, 1839, and is a son of Aaron and Elizabeth (Morrison) Gist, who removed to Missouri from Tennessee about that year, and in 1844 settled near Greenwood, Sebastian Co., Ark., where they lived one year, and then moved in the vicinity of where our subject now lives. The father is now seventy-seven years of age. He has always been an industrious farmer, and for some time was engaged at the carriage trade, which he learned when young. He is of Irish descent, and some of his ancestors fought in the early Indian wars. He has been thrice married. His first wife died December 25, 1846. She was the mother of five children, of whom Andrew J. F., and Lucy Ann, wife of Charles Smith, of Choctaw Nation, are now living. By his second wife he had two sons and two daughters, three of whom are living in different parts of the West. Mr. Gist is now living with his fourth wife. He has been a member of the Protestant Methodist Church many years, and has always been a Jackson Democrat, his first presidential vote having been cast for Gen. Jackson. He was a Union man during the war, and so left Arkansas during that time and lived North. He began to teach school when quite young, and followed that vocation to some extent until 1870, in Tennessee, Missouri and Arkansas. In 1860 he lost his left arm in a sorghum mill. Our subject was but five years old when he came to Arkansas. At the age of fourteen he began life for himself, and for two years worked for his board and clothes. He then clerked for a short time in a drug store at Fort Smith, and then until 1859 worked at various things. He was then united in marriage with Mary Ann, daughter of James and Elizabeth Hart, who came to Arkansas (this county) from Missouri, in 1844. Mr. Hart died before the war, but Mrs. Hart is still living. Mrs. Gist was born in this county, and died in Choctaw Nation in 1864. August 2, 1866, Mr. Gist married Elizabeth, daughter of William and Mary Cowen, a native of Tennessee. Mrs. Gist died September 9, 1880, leaving one child, who is now deceased. January 25, 1881, our subject wedded Mattie, daughter of Elza and Martha Harlow, natives of Missouri and Tennessee, respectively. In an early day they came to this county, where Mrs. Gist was born. Mr. Harlow was of Irish parentage, and died in Sebastian County, as did his wife.

Daniel B. Glass, another successful tiller of the soil, is a native of Henry County, Tenn., born April 26, 1848, and is the son of William and Elizabeth (Boone) Glass, natives of Georgia and Kentucky, respectively, and the mother a niece of the great hunter, Daniel Boone. When young the parents went to East Tennessee, where they met and were married. Soon after they moved to Giles County of the same State, and in 1833 moved to Henry County, of West Tennessee, where the father died at an advanced age. In 1850 the mother with some of her children went to Greene County, Mo., and eight years later to Scott

County, Ark. In 1867 she came to Sebastian County, where she died at Fort Smith soon after. She was a member of the Baptist Church, and was the mother of eleven children, nine sons and two daughters. The father was a carpenter by trade, although he made farming his chief occupation during life. He was a member of the Presbyterian Church. Their son, Daniel B. Glass, was but two years of age when he immigrated with his parents to Greene County, Mo. He moved around with his mother until 1867, when she came to Sebastian County. His education is very limited, he not having attended school more than twelve months altogether. In October, 1863, he enlisted in Company C, Second Arkansas Volunteer Infantry, United States Army, and served until August 28, 1865. He participated in the battles of Prairie Grove, Jenkins' Ferry, and a number of minor engagements. He was never wounded or taken prisoner, and received an honorable discharge at Clarksville, Ark. In 1867 he began learning the tanner's trade, at which he worked for about four years. October 4, 1868, he married Miss Mary E. Bunch, a native of Middle Tennessee, born March 17, 1849, and eight children were born to this union: James A., William A., Charles M., Lilly B., Stephen E. T., Jesse C., Daniel E. and an infant (deceased). After leaving the tan-yard Mr. Glass turned his attention to farming, and this he has since continued. During the administration of Gov. Miller, when the militia was called out to quell the trouble in Scott County, Mr. Glass was commissioned captain of a company. He has been justice of the peace of his township, bailiff of the township, and is now deputy sheriff of Sebastian County. In politics he has been a Democrat all his life, and has been a Mason since twenty-one years of age. He is the owner of 190 acres of land, with about 100 under cultivation. He has been a resident of this county for twenty-one years, and is accounted an honest, upright business man. He and Mrs. Glass are both members of the Missionary Baptist Church.

Dr. A. H. Gordon, senior partner of the medical firm of Gordon & McGinty, was born in Tennessee in 1850, and is a son of A. B. and Martha J. (Blassingame) Gordon. The father was a farmer by occupation, and now resides in Hunt County, Texas. He served throughout the entire war in Forrest's cavalry, but escaped without injury. After receiving a common-school education our subject entered the Savannah College, and later attended the Vanderbilt University at Nashville. He graduated from the medical department of the latter institution in the winter of 1875–76 with distinction, and immediately began the practice of his profession at Gravel Hill, Tenn., where he remained until 1881. He then became a resident of Hackett City, where his practice became so extensive that in 1887 he took Dr. McGinty as a partner. [See sketch.] In 1883 he became associated with Dr. McConnell, and in 1884 with H. W. Farnum. From 1882 until 1885 Dr. Gordon was a member of the medical examination board, and also served as alderman of the city. He is now the physician and surgeon of the Kansas and Texas Coal Company's works at this place. He is a well-to-do citizen, and owns two and one-half lots and a good residence. In 1876 he married Miss Mary E. McCoy, of Gravel Hill, Tenn., daughter of James McCoy, who has borne him four children, all now living: Pearl, Myrtle, Lillian and Montrose. Mrs. Gordon is a member of the Baptist Church, and the Doctor is treasurer of the I. O. O. F. lodge here, Master Workman of the A. O. U. W., and a member of the K. of L. In politics he is a Democrat.

John Goset is a prosperous farmer of Sebastian County, Ark., being a native of Union County, S. C., born on the 15th of November, 1831. He is one of the five surviving members of a family of nine children born to the marriage of Nathaniel Goset and Arena Bishop, the former born in North Carolina in 1809, and the latter in South Carolina in 1814. They were married in the latter State, and there the father died in 1873. His widow is still living, together with the following children: John, William, Mary (Mrs. Austin), Louisa (Mrs. Clark) and Laura Ann (Mrs. Stokes). The paternal grandparents, George and Mary (Boone) Goset, were of Scotch descent, born in Maryland, and died in South Carolina in 1811 and 1839, respectively. John Goset spent his boyhood days in South Carolina, and at the early age of seventeen years began to fight the battle of life for himself as a farm hand. In 1851 he espoused Ellen Clark, who was born in South Carolina in 1830, and died November 26, 1854, and the following year he married Mary E., a daughter of John and Mary (Thrift) Gregory. She was born in South Carolina in 1832, and died February 22, 1880, having borne a family of ten living children, who all reside in Sebastian County, Ark. Their names are as follows: Jennie (Reeves), Mary E., J. N., W. F., B. A., C. R., E. S., Mattie, Belle and Thomas J. October 9, 1880, Mr. Goset married Sarah A., a sister of his second wife. They have three children: Josie, Lillie, and an infant unnamed. In 1866 Mr. Goset removed with his family to Arkansas, and took up his abode in Jefferson County, thence to Roane County in 1867, from there to the Indian Territory in 1871, coming to Sebastian County in 1881, where he has since made his home. He is a Mason and a Democrat, and at the breaking out of the late Civil War enlisted in Company B, Eighteenth South Carolina Infantry, but was afterward transferred to Company K, Fifth South Carolina Cavalry, Confederate States Army, and was in the battles of South Mountain, Antietam, Petersburg and James Island, and served until the close of the war.

Judge Matthew Grey, judge of the police court of Fort Smith, was born in Ireland, County Cavan, Parish of Columbkill, July 14, 1833, and is a son of John and Rose (Ruden) Grey, also natives of Ireland, where they were well-to-do citizens and farmers. At the age of thirteen our subject crossed the ocean to America alone, and, locating in Philadelphia, learned the shoemaker's trade. Leaving that city to go west, he crossed the Mississippi River, and upon arriving at St. Louis enlisted in the United States regular service. He was stationed upon frontier duty in Utah and Mexico, and after serving ten years was honorably discharged, on account of disability, in 1860. Upon the outbreak of the Civil War he enlisted in the Home Guards. Having visited Fort Smith in 1851, while a soldier, he returned to this place in 1863, and engaged in trading with the Comanche and Wichita Indians. In 1870 he permanently located here, where he soon became a leading political power. He has served as mayor of Fort Smith, and since 1875 has been a magistrate. In 1887 he was elected police judge, and he is now discharging the duties of that office. Judge Grey married Miss Martha Evans, daughter of the late James P. Evans, M. D., and now has the following family of children: Mary Agnes, a graduate of St. Mary's Academy, of Fort Smith; John, who is at school; Kate, James and Lucy. Mr. and Mrs. Grey are members of the Church of the Immaculate Conception, and he belongs to the American branch of the Home Rulers' League.

Major B. F. Hackett, mayor of Hackett City, was born in Sebastian County in 1844, and is a son of Jeremiah and Sarah A. (Tichnal) Hackett [see sketch]. He received a limited public school education during his early youth, and in March, 1863, enlisted as a private in Company B of the Second Kansas Cavalry. This company was afterward put on detached service to command Hopkins' Battery, and in 1864 declared an independent battery, known as the Third Kansas Battery. He participated in the fights at Honey Springs, Fort Gibson and Weber's Falls, but escaped without any wounds. After the war Mr. Hackett attended school a year in Ohio, and upon his return to Arkansas served four years as treasurer of Sebastian County. He then engaged in the mercantile and stock business near Hackett City, on the line of the Indian Territory, and in 1872 located where Hackett City now is, which town he started, and which bears his name. This is now a flourishing town of 1,500 inhabitants, although in 1872 Mr. Hackett was obliged to give away lots in order to induce people to locate here. He owns a large number of town lots, and houses which he rents, and has about 600 acres of valuable land, which contains large deposits of coal. He is the leading business man of the town, and is interested in the saw-mill, lumber and cotton business. Mr. Hackett has served as assessor of the county three terms, and was deputy sheriff four years. In 1874 he was appointed by Gen. Armstead to raise a company of militia, of which he was first made captain. He was afterward commissioned major, and recruited and mustered in six more companies. Maj. Hackett is now serving his second term as mayor of the city. In 1872 he married Miss Helen Bradbury, of Ohio, whose father is a merchant and banker at Middleport. Mr. and Mrs. Hackett have two children, John T. and Samuel B. Our subject and wife belong to the New Church, and the former is a member of the American Legion of Honor and the Masonic order, of which he has been District Deputy Grand Master.

J. A. Hale was born in Georgia twenty-three years ago, and is a son of J. K. Hale. After receiving a public school education he entered the State University of Missouri, and began the study of law. He graduated from this institution in 1888, but was previously, in 1886, admitted to the bar, after studying under the supervision of Judge Little, of Greenwood. He came to Arkansas with his parents in 1870, and after graduating returned to Sebastian County and began the practice of his profession. He is rapidly establishing an enviable reputation, meeting with good success. He is considered one of the enterprising citizens of the township, and has served as deputy sheriff with satisfaction.

Elder R. W. Hammett, a grocery merchant of Fort Smith, Ark., was born in Marion County, Miss., March 4, 1829, being the son of James and Sarah (Head) Hammett, and grandson of William Hammett, who was a Revolutionary soldier and a captain in that war. James Hammett was a native of Georgia, born in 1787, and was a farmer by occupation. He located in Alabama, and there spent the greater portion of his life. He died at the age of ninety-six years. The Hammetts were Baptists, as were also the Heads, who were natives of Georgia. Sarah (Head) Hammett was the mother of ten children, three now living, Elder R. W. being the seventh in order of birth. His maternal grandmother was a Ray. Elder R. W. Hammett attained his growth in Alabama, and came to Arkansas with the intention of remaining a short time and then going back. He was educated in Salisbury Institute, Batesville, Ark., was converted in 1847, and the following year he commenced preaching, or exhorting. He was ordained deacon in 1853, an elder in 1855, and still keeps up his license to preach. He was for thirty-five years a traveling preacher in Arkansas and adjoining States, and now preaches occasionally. He was presiding elder of the Clarksville District when the war broke out, and was an uncompromising Union man. He stood manfully at his task and through all dangers, preached the Gospel. After the war he became a member of the Methodist Episcopal Church, and helped reorganize that church in the State. He was presiding elder in the church for many years, and has filled the stations at Fort Smith from 1855 to 1857, Helena in 1858 and Fayetteville in 1859. He was married in 1860 to Miss Elizabeth Dobson, a native of Cleveland, N. C., born August 1, 1842, and to them were born four living children: Ellis (a saddler by trade), James (tinner), Leonodia Dobson and Mattie P. Two children died in infancy: Richard and Myrtle. Mr. Hammett is the owner of a house and lot in the city, is a Mason, an Odd Fellow, a temperance man, and one who is universally respected.

Harvey T. Hampton, editor and co-proprietor of the Greenwood *Democrat*, is a native of Logan County, Ark., born in 1855, and is the son of James H. and Jane C. (McCormick) Hampton. James H. Hampton was born in Simpson County, Ky., November 2, 1822, and was of Irish descent. He was a farmer by occupation, and when a small boy went with his mother, Ann (Barker) Hampton, to Randolph County, Ill., his father, John Hampton, having died in Kentucky when James H. was quite small. James H. Hampton was married in Illinois in 1847, and two years later he moved to Napoleon, Ark., where he remained for one year, and then moved to Fort Smith. Four years later he moved to Booneville, or near the town, where he died in 1877. His wife was of Irish descent, and was a native of Randolph County, Ill., born in 1828, and died in 1861. After her death Mr. Hampton married Mrs. Martha E. Spindle, *nee* McCormick. She is yet living. Harvey T. Hampton is the fourth child by the first marriage, and was educated in the Fort Smith District High-school at Booneville, Ark. He worked on the farm until twenty-one years of age, and in 1876 entered a printing office, where he worked as an apprentice for four years and as a journeyman for three years. In 1880 he became editor of the Paris *Express*, at Paris, Ark., and in 1881 served as deputy circuit clerk of Logan County. From 1882 to 1883 he edited the *Express*. In 1884 he was elected tax assessor of Logan County, and served two years. In 1886 he became a citizen of Greenwood, Ark., and November 1 of that year he purchased the Greenwood *Times*, changing the name to Greenwood *Democrat* January 1, 1887. September 15, 1887, Jesse A. Bell became an equal partner, and has since been half owner of the paper. The motto of the *Democrat* is, "Under the Wholesome Influence of Democracy the Nation Prospers." It is a newsy sheet, and has a weekly circulation of from 800 to 1,000. In 1879 Mr. Hampton was united in marriage to Mattie V. Sipe, a native of Georgia, born in 1855. To them were born five children: Norma, Fay, Ora, Hymenus T. and Max C. On October 30, 1888, Mr. Hampton was appointed deputy circuit clerk and recorder of Sebastian County. He is a member of the Masonic fraternity, Master Mason, and he and wife are members of the Methodist Episcopal Church, South.

William J. Haug, one of the enterprising farmers of the county, is the son of Valentine and Joannah (Schafier) Haug, both natives of Wurtemburg, Germany. The Haug family are of Russian origin. When the Black Death depopulated such a vast part of the German Empire, a great many families emigrated from Russia, and among them were the Haugs. On the Schafier side they are purely German. The parents were married and lived in Wurtemburg until 1853, when they came to America, locating in Sebastian County, Ark., and here passed their last days. The father was a stone-mason by trade, and many of the buildings he helped erect are still standing in Fort Smith, as monuments of his handicraft. In connection with his trade he also carried on farming. He was a Republican in politics, and died April 13, 1871, and she died December 1, 1879. In their family were nine children, only two now living, a son and daughter. The father had been married previously, and had a son by his first wife. William J. Haug, the youngest but one by the second marriage, was born in Sebastian County, Ark., June 7, 1856, aided on the farm, and received a limited education in the country schools, being obliged to walk three miles to obtain a little learning. He remained and worked for his mother until December 17, 1876, when he married Miss Roxanna Yaden, a native of Sebastian County, born July 7, 1854. Two children were born to this union, both deceased: Thomas V., born March 10 1878, died October 18, 1880, and Frank J., born December 28, 1880, died August 11, 1885. Mr. Haug is a member of the Methodist Episcopal Church, and she of the Old School Presbyterian. Mr. Haug is a Republican in politics, and in September, 1888, he was chosen magistrate. He has lived in this county all his life, is the owner of eighty acres of land, forty-five under cultivation, has also other means, and is a Master Mason.

Thomas J. Hannah, a prosperous farmer of Sebastian County, Ark., is a son of Samuel W. and Rebecca M. (Gilliam) Hannah, both of whom were born in East Tennessee, in 1816 and 1820, respectively. They were married and resided in their native State until 1849, when they moved to Texas, and after residing in Hopkins, Hunt and Fannin Counties for about nine years, came to Sebastian County, Ark. The father was a soldier in the Florida War, a farmer by occupation, and was justice of the peace for many years both in Texas and Arkansas. He was a Democrat, and the last vote he cast was against the secession of his State, but from some unknown cause he had made enemies, and while returning home from a neighbor's one Sunday morning in 1863 was shot at from the brush along the road, and was afterward stabbed with a knife, from the effects of which he died. He was ever a man of peace, and had the confidence and esteem of his neighbors. His widow and four of his nine children survive him. Thomas J. Hannah was his third child, and was born in Bradley County, Tenn., October 29, 1846, being reared on a farm. January 10, 1864, he enlisted in Company F, First Arkansas Volunteer Infantry, United States Army, and served until August 10, 1865, being a participant in the battles of Prairie De Hand and Saline River. He was honorably discharged at Fort Smith, and returned to the peaceful pursuit of farming. In 1868 he was married to Susan J. Seamans, who bore him six children, two of whom are living: Albert W. and Jacob A. After the death of his first wife he married Parlee McNabb, by whom he has three children: Maudie, Thomas A. and James L. This wife died on the 29th of January, 1887, an earnest and devoted Christian and member of the Methodist Episcopal Church. Mr. Hannah is a stanch Republican, and a member of the G. A. R., and the owner of 163 acres of land, with ninety under cultivation. James M. Hannah, his brother, was born in Fannin County, Tex., February 16, 1857, and was educated in the common schools and by personal study. He owns a good farm of 160 acres, with sixty under cultivation, and, like his brother, is a stanch Republican in politics.

James W. Harper, cotton dealer and real estate agent at Mansfield, Ark., was born in Tennessee on the 15th of May, 1849. His parents, Blaney and Elizabeth (Griffey) Harper, were born in the "Old North Carolina State" in 1816 and 1814, and died in 1882 and 1880, respectively. They removed from their native State to Tennessee, thence to Arkansas in 1851, settling at Fort Smith, where they remained one year, then moving twenty-five miles south, where he made his home until his death. The father was a minister of the Gospel, belonging to the Methodist Episcopal Church, and was a member of the Legislature, being elected in 1867 for two years. He became the father of nine children, seven of whom are living: Nancy B. (Mrs. Bruce), Jesse C., Samuel H., Joseph W., Lenora Ann (Mrs. Ball), J. W., and Mary H. (Mrs. Gleason). James W. Harper spent his early life in Sebastian County, and received his education in private schools. After attaining his twenty-first birthday he began doing for himself, and has been a contractor for twenty years and a merchant for four years. He lives upon the old homestead, the present site of the town of Mansfield. He is a stanch supporter of the Republican party, and is a member of the Methodist Episcopal Church. In 1869 he was married to Miss Mary J. Dixon, a daughter of William H. and Mida (Short) Dixon, of Tennessee. She was born in Arkansas in 1847, and became the mother of seven children: William B., George, Joseph L., Graham, Nora and Myrtle. One child, Freddie, is deceased. Mr. Harper's grandfather, Haynes Griffey, was a soldier in the War of 1812.

Malachi B. Harrison was born July 23, 1835, in Benton County, Tenn., his parents being Malachi and Nancy (Baggett) Harrison. The father was born in Sumner County, Tenn., December 9, 1805, and there grew to manhood. He then immigrated to Benton County, and there married Miss Baggett, who was born in North Carolina in 1805. Mrs. Harrison came to Tennessee by wagon when young, and settled in Benton County during its early history. She died in 1846, and was the mother of the following children: Matilda, Henry W., Malachi B. and Cynthia J. now living, and Nathaniel, John, Julia A. and James M., deceased. The following year Mr. Harrison married Polly Tittle, daughter of Anthony Tittle, of West Tennessee, by whom he had six children: George W., Dora A., William C., Victoria, Priscilla and Margaret (deceased). Mr. Harrison died in Franklin County January 13, 1888, aged eighty-two years, but his widow is still living in that county. The Harrison grandparents were natives of South Carolina, who immigrated to Tennessee in an early day, and were of French descent. They belonged to the family of which Benjamin Harrison is a descendant. The maternal grandparents were also natives of South Carolina, and early settlers of Tennessee. Our subject left his native State when nineteen, having passed his youth upon a farm, and received an ordinary education. He farmed one year in both Benton County, Ark., and Franklin County, and then spent two years in Denton County, Tex., after which he traveled a year in Arkansas. Returning to Denton County he remained ten years. He then passed one year in Franklin County, three years in Sebastian County, and eight years more in Denton County. He permanently located upon his present farm of seventy acres in 1881. He cultivates all his land, and is a successful farmer. During the war Mr. Harrison served one year in Company I, Choctaw Regiment, and three years in Company E, of the Twenty-ninth Texas. He was disbanded at Hempstead, Tex., in April, 1865, and had participated in the battles at Pea Ridge, Bird Creek, Poison Springs, Jenkins' Ferry and Cabin Creek. During the war he served as sergeant, and since coming to this county he has been justice of the peace two terms, and also served as school director. In 1862 he married Sarah L., daughter of Nimrod B. Tolle, of Texas. Mrs. Harrison was born in Lewis County, Mo., and has borne eleven children. Those living are Sidney M., Minnie R., Nancy C., Daisy D., Sarah A. and Thomas C. Those deceased: James E., Nimrod, Annie M., Ervin and Herman. Mr. and Mrs. Harrison belong to the Missionary Baptist Church, and the former is a Mason and a Democrat.

Edward M. Harrison, M. D., was born in Nashville, Washington Co., Ill., in 1850, and is the son of Gen. M. LaRue Harrison, the present inspector of the money order system at Washington, D. C. Gen. M. LaRue Harrison was born in the State of New York, received his education in Yale College, and while there studied theology with a view to the ministry, his father being a Presbyterian minister. After leaving college he taught school in Southern Illinois, and was there married to Miss Axley, who became the mother of five children, only two now living. Gen. Harrison abandoned teaching, and engaged in railroad business until the breaking out of the Civil War, when he enlisted, in Illinois, as a private in the Federal army. He went through a series of promotions, and was finally raised to colonel of the First Arkansas Federal Cavalry, and was mustered out as general. In a few months after the war he was appointed special post-office inspector, and since the money order system was inaugurated he has been money order inspector, and has been in the mail service since 1865. He holds his position purely on the grounds of his being able to speak many different languages. His son, Edward M. Harrison, entered the army when quite young, and served three and a half years in the First Arkansas Cavalry. He commenced the practice of surgery during the war, and after cessation of hostilities studied medicine under a preceptor, practicing at the same time. He graduated from the Homœopathic College of St. Louis,

Mo., and practiced medicine in that city for a number of years. Afterward he was ten years at Lebanon, Mo., and then came to Fort Smith, Ark. Dr. Harrison was married when eighteen years of age to Miss Mattie Mitchell, of Tennessee, and nine children were the result of this union, four now living: Katie, Della, Eleanor and Edward M., Jr. Dr. Harrison is a Republican Prohibitionist in his political opinions, is a member of the A. O. U. W., and a Select Knight; is president of the Arkansas Telephone Company, and inventor of the Harrison Microphone and the Fire Alarm System of Fort Smith. He is a member of the Congregational Church. His father, Gen. M. LaRue Harrison, is a relative of President-elect Harrison. Dr. Harrison is also the inventor of the Electric Air Machine, which he believes will cure consumption and kindred diseases.

J. B. Harwood, dealer in general merchandise at Fort Smith, Ark., is a native of Henderson County, Tex., and was born in 1850, being the son of William T. and Nancy (Dodson) Harwood. William T. Harwood is a native of Tennessee, and at the age of eighteen he entered and served all through the Mexican War. Since that time he has been engaged in agricultural pursuits, and now resides near Huntsville, Madison Co., Ark. He was married to Miss Nancy Dodson in Tennessee, and she died when the subject of this sketch was but twelve years of age. The latter was the eldest of six children. William T. Harwood was married to Miss Eliza Boatwright, a native of Arkansas, and the daughter of James Boatwright. J. B. Harwood left home at the age of seventeen years, and engaged in merchandising at Myer's Landing, where he remained for about three years. He then engaged in the same pursuit at Military Grove, but subsequently came to Fort Smith where he opened business in the present house. He was married to Miss Sallie B. Myers. Mr. Harwood is a member of the Methodist Episcopal Church, South, is a member of the Masonic fraternity, and the town of Myer's Landing was named by him.

John Lawson Henderson, of the firm of Myrick & Henderson, was born in Williamson County, Tenn., December 24, 1841, and is a son of William and Mary (Scales) Henderson. The father was of Scotch descent, and a son of William Henderson, an early settler of Tennessee. The father was born in Rutherford County, Tenn., and was a merchant by occupation. The mother was a daughter of Joseph H. Scales, a native of North Carolina, and an early settler of Williamson County, Tenn. When sixteen years of age our subject left the paternal roof, and for some time worked as a shipping clerk in Memphis. At the commencement of the war he joined the Memphis Light Dragoons, which afterward became Company A of the Seventh Tennessee Cavalry. He served throughout the war, and surrendered with his company at Gainesville, Ala. He was wounded in the battle at Holly Springs. After the war he sold goods in Coahoma County, Miss., and subsequently went to New Orleans to accept the position of receiving teller in the United States Treasury Department. In 1871 he went to Helena, Ark., where he clerked until 1881, after which he engaged in the mercantile, flour, jobbing and commission business at Fort Smith. Upon the organization of the Ketcham Iron Company he served a year as treasurer and secretary. He is interested in the educational advancement of the county, and is a member of the school board. In politics he is a Democrat, and while in Helena he filled the office of city treasurer. He was married in Kenton, Miss., to Miss Maggie Dinkins, who died in Helena, leaving two children, John H. and Lula K., now high-school students. Mr. Henderson afterward was married in Natchez, Miss., to Miss Bessie Lambdin, who has borne him three children: Maggie, Willie and E. R. DuVal. Since early manhood Mr. Henderson has been identified with the Baptist Church, and he is a member of the board of directors of the Y. M. C. A.

Eli Hester, farmer, of Center Township, Sebastian Co., Ark., is a native of Randolph County, Ala., born in 1847, and is a son of Tapley and Mahala (Stone) Hester, who were born in North Carolina and South Carolina, in 1813 and 1814, respectively. The father is of Irish descent, and after reaching man's estate went to Randolph County, Ala., where he was married in 1833, and has since resided. He owns about 400 acres of land, and is one of the prominent old residents of the county. He did some service during the latter part of the late war. Eli Hester is the sixth of their eleven children, eight of whom are living, and was reared on a farm and remained with his parents until he attained his eighteenth year, when he was married to Mary E. Ware, a daughter of Thomas C. and Nancy (Lewis) Ware. She was born in Heard County, Ga., in 1844, and is the mother of eight children: John Henry, Olie Anna (deceased), Thomas Luther, Oliver Jackson, Edward Lovie Norman Ezra, Lennie Elizabeth and Cleveland Thurman. Mr. Hester resided in his native State until 1868, when he immigrated to Georgia, residing there until 1881, when he came to Sebastian County, Ark., and purchased 160 acres of land about three miles west of Greenwood, where he is now residing. In 1885 he erected a good frame residence, at a cost of $1,000, and has increased his lands until he now owns 240 acres. He is one of the solid, substantial and enterprising farmers of the county, and in his political views has always been a strong Democrat, casting his first presidential vote for Samuel J. Tilden. He and wife are members of the Methodist Episcopal Church, South.

John Hewett was born in Tuscaloosa County, Ala., in February, 1819, and is a son of George and Sophia (Dockery) Hewett. The father came to America from Holland when twelve years old, and first lived in the Carolinas. He afterward grew to manhood on a farm in Tennessee, where he was educated, after which he lived in Alabama. He was a soldier in the War of 1812. His death occurred in Alabama about 1854. The mother spent her early life in Tennessee, and was there married to Mr. Hewett. She died in 1853, and was the mother of eleven children: A. J., John, George, Israel, Eliza and L. R. now living, and Mary (Phillip), Calvin, Joseph, and W. H. H. deceased. John Hewett lived with his parents upon the Alabama farm until his marriage, in 1845, to Rebecca Johnson, a native of Alabama, and a daughter of Jacob and Rebecca Johnson, who went to Alabama from South Carolina. To Mr. and Mrs. Hewett ten children were born; those living are William H. H., Benjamin F., Laura, Almeda, John M., Cytha; those deceased were named Lucinda, Zada, Manda and Julia. After his marriage Mr. Hewett continued to live in Alabama for five years, and then removed by water to Texas. He lived five years in Washington County, Tex., and then moved to Falls County, Tex., and lived there ten years. Then he moved to Sebastian County, Ark., and has lived here for twenty years, successfully engaged in farming, and has 153½ acres of land, sixty of which he has under cultivation. In politics he is a Democrat, and during the war served in the Federal army for fifteen months, or until discharged at the close of the war. Mr. Hewett lost his first wife in this county in 1873, and he afterward married Eliza Beveans, who died November 22, 1887.

F. W. Hink, a prosperous farmer of Sebastian County, Ark., was born in Prussia, Germany, in 1828, and is a son of John and Elizabeth (Fisher) Hink, who were born in Prussia, the former in 1778. John Hink was captain of a body guard to Napoleon Bonaparte at the battle of Waterloo. F. W. Hink spent his early life in traveling through Germany, France, Italy and Switzerland, and served in the War of Rebellion in Baden and Holstein, Germany, under the late Emperor William, who was then commanding the Seventh Division of the German Army. In 1850 he crossed the ocean and landed in Connecticut, but two years later went to Philadelphia, and a year later to St. Louis, spending some time as pastry cook on a steamboat plying between St. Louis and New Orleans. In 1854 he went to Kansas, where he remained until 1858, when he located in the Cherokee Nation, Colorado, and drove a Government team for eighteen months during the war. He went to Fort Smith in 1863, where he worked at the baker's trade for the Union army until the close of the war, also running a private bakery. In 1866 he was married to Martha E. Spangler, who was born in Arkansas in 1842, and by whom he became the father of ten children: F. W., Elizabeth G., Iva J., Mary B., Onie, Anna, Tamar, Dollie, Hazel and Henry, all of whom reside with their parents. Mr. Hink located on his present farm of 180 acres in 1876. He has sixty acres under cultivation and eighty acres in meadow. He is a member of the I. O. O. F., and in his political views is a Democrat. Mrs. Hink's parents, George and Susan Spangler, were born in the "Buckeye State," and were farmers by occupation. Only three of their nine children are living: Mrs. Hink and two sisters—Mrs. Rebecca Nijong and Mrs. Ann E. Bourland.

James Hoey, hardware merchant, was born at Port Arlington, Queens County, Ireland, December 23, 1833, and is a son of John and Elizabeth (Bennett) Hoey. When seventeen James crossed the ocean to seek his fortune in America, and upon landing came west almost immediately. For a few years he engaged in carpentering at Leavenworth, and in 1860 he came to Fort Smith, where he worked as master mechanic for the Government. He enlisted for three months in the Third Arkansas Volunteer Infantry, as second lieutenant, and at the expiration of that time entered Company A of the Seventeenth Arkansas Infantry, Confederate Army, in which he served throughout the war. He was taken a prisoner at Iuka, and held seven months at St. Louis, Memphis and Fort Delaware. He was exchanged at City Point, Va., and then served on Gen. Feathertour's staff, as assistant inspector, until he could join his regiment at Crystal Springs, Miss., in the fall of 1863. After the war he was employed in the Government shops at Fort Smith, until the Government post was disbanded. He then worked at his trade in the Indian Territory, and finally engaged in the lumber business at Atoka until 1877, when he embarked in the sash, door and lumber trade at Fort Smith. In 1884 he abandoned the lumber business and started a hardware store, and is now furnishing builders' materials. While at Leavenworth, Kas., he married Miss Ann Reilly, a native of County Cavan, Ireland. Himself and wife are members of the Catholic Church. Mr. Hoey is a member of the board of sewer commissioners of Fort Smith, and an enterprising citizen.

John Alexander Hoffman was born in Greene County, Ill., July 26, 1841, and is a son of Nathan and Catherine (Gore) Hoffman. The father was born near Culpeper Court-House, Va., his ancestors having come from Germany and settled in Virginia prior to the Revolution. In 1844 he immigrated to Lamar County, Tex., and from there to Fort Smith, Ark., where he died in 1868. Our subject grew to manhood in Texas, and there learned the builder's and contractor's trade in Paris. He then joined the army, and for a year did active service in Company A, of the Ninth Texas Volunteer Infantry. He was then on post duty at Shreveport, La., for some time. After the war he followed his trade at Paris, Tex., until 1866, and then came to Fort Smith. He has built many of the stores and private residences in this city, and among the public buildings which he has erected may be mentioned the First Methodist Episcopal Church, Eberle Block and the old Music Hall. In 1863 he was married, in Texas, to Miss Mary Isabel Bishop, a native of Kentucky, and daughter of Daniel and Elizabeth Bishop. Mr. and Mrs. Hoffman have three children: Blanche, an accomplished musician; Claude, who is studying civil engineering at the John Hopkins University, Baltimore, Md., and Albert, who is just finishing a commercial course. Mrs. Hoffman belongs to the Baptist Church. Mr. Hoffman has been a member of the school board for about nine years, and has served in the town council two years. He is a member of the board of public works, and is a contributor to the *Building and Trades' Journal* of St. Louis. He also belongs to the K. of H.

John Howard, ex-county judge and farmer, of Sebastian County, is the son of John and Ellen (Claypool) Howard. The Howard family originally came from England. Two brothers came to America about the breaking out of the Revolutionary War. One entered the army and the other the navy. The one who enlisted in the army is the great-grandfather of John Howard, subject of this sketch. The latter's grandfather moved from Virginia to Kentucky at a very early date, being among the earliest settlers of that State. John Howard, Sr., was born in Virginia, and when his father moved across the mountains to Kentucky he and his sister were carried across a horse, one in each end of a sack. Ellen (Claypool) Howard was born in North Carolina, and when a child her parents also moved to Kentucky. In this State she met Mr. Howard, and they were married in Warren County in 1835. They afterward moved to Warren County, Ill., where the mother died in 1845 and the father in 1853. He was a farmer all his life, a Democrat in politics, and both were members of the Cumberland Presbyterian Church. Their family consisted of ten children, five sons and five daughters. John Howard, Jr., the eldest child living, and the eighth in order of birth, was born December 9, 1817. He attained his growth on a farm, and being obliged to work hard while young, as a consequence his education was neglected. At the age of twenty he began business for himself as a farmer, and March 15, 1838, he married Miss Phœbe J. Coy, who was born near Elizabethtown, Ky., April 17, 1820, and when a little girl her parents moved to Sangamon County, Ill., and later to Knox County, where she married Mr. Howard. They afterward located in Warren County, Ill., where they lived until 1847, when they moved to the "Lone Star State." They remained here but a short time, and then came to Arkansas, located in Sebastian County, and here they have since made their home. Mr. Howard was a Whig until after the war, and since then he has affiliated with the Republican party. Toward the close of the war he was appointed county judge by Gov. Murphy, which position he held for about six years. For many years he has been justice of the peace; has lived in this county for forty years, and is a highly respected citizen. Mr. and Mrs. Howard are the parents of two children, Nancy A., wife of James Blaylock, and Lemuel B., a farmer of the neighborhood. Mrs. Howard is a member of the Methodist Episcopal Church.

Sergeant Edward Hunt, of Fort Smith, Ark., was born in Frankenhausen, Fierstenthum, Schwarzburg, Rudolstadt, Germany, and is the son of John Gustave and Dora (Forderer) Hunt. John G. Hunt was born in the same place as his son, and died in 1858. Dora Hunt came to America about 1862, and died in Philadelphia in 1882. Her ten children also came to America. Edward Hunt came to this country in 1849, and followed the occupation of a shoemaker at Philadelphia, St. Louis, New York and Chicago. At the breaking out of the late Civil War he was keeping a saloon in St. Louis, and also a shoe-store, but left these with his brother and joined the three months' service, Second Missouri Infantry, under Col. Bornstein, and was at the battles of Camp Jackson, Boonville and Wilson's Creek. He was mustered out of the three months' service August 31, 1861, after serving four months and eight days. September 1, 1861, he re-enlisted in the Twelfth Missouri Volunteer Infantry, Company C, under the command of Col. Osterhause, and was promoted by him to the rank of sergeant. Mr. Hunt was first sent by Col. Osterhause to Chicago on recruiting service. He was successful, and returned to his regiment at Warsaw, Mo., November 8, 1861, and arrived in Springfield, Mo., November 20, of the same year. Here their general, Fremont, was superseded by Gen . Hunter, and shortly after they were ordered back to Rolla, Mo. February 2, 1862, they left Rolla, and went back to Springfied on the 13th of February, when the snow was from one to three feet deep on the ground. The Confederates had gone into winter quarters at this place, but were driven out by the Union soldiers, and on the following day the latter pursued the enemy, and reached the rear guards of Gen. Price's army near Keysville, and here a slight skirmish occurred. On the 17th of February they traveled through Arkansas, and on the 20th of that month they entered Camp Halleck, where they remained until March 2. March 6 they moved through Bentonville, which was only six miles distant, and the regiment which Mr. Hunt was in had the rear guard that day. By some means the enemy separated them from the main body, but by hard fighting they again regained it. On the following day three charges were made on the army, and they fought all day at Pea Ridge, or Elkhorn Tavern. The next day some hard fighting was done, but the Union army was victorious and captured many prisoners. They made many long, toilsome marches, and one day traveled thirty miles without water. They marched to Helena, Ark., and suffered greatly with hunger on the way. Afterward Mr. Hunt was sent to St. Louis on a commission, and there he remained until November 25. He then joined his regiment, which he found opposite Helena. From December 27 to December 31 the Union army besieged Vicksburg, but were not successful, and the army took boats and went up the Arkansas River to Arkansas Post, and the 11th of January they captured the post with about 6,000 prisoners. They left here the 15th of that month, after destroying the fort. January 15 they went to Bird's Point, opposite Vicksburg, and here the soldiers lived on bad water, a few miserable crackers and sow-belly. February 17 Mr. Hunt's regiment, with the Seventeenth Missouri Infantry, went back to Helena, but here Mr. Hunt was taken sick with rheumatism and swamp fever, and was left at the Adams Hospital. He left the same April 4 and went to Convalescent Camp, two miles below Memphis, but April 12 he joined his regiment at Young's Point. They left there soon, and marched through Louisiana. May 13 they had a battle, and captured a number of prisoners and a herd of sheep, the latter causing them to rejoice exceedingly. May 15 they captured Jackson, Miss. Flour sold here as high as $120 a barrel, potatoes at $30 a bushel, eggs $1.50 a dozen, and coffee could not be purchased. May 22 their brigade made a charge on Vicksburg, and here Mr. Hunt was knocked down by a cannon ball, the hearing of his left ear destroyed, and blood ran from his ears, nose and mouth. After this he was no longer in active duty, as the shock caused epileptic fits. September 5, 1863, he was declared unfit for duty, and was transferred to the invalid corps, and served out his time as guard to prisoners at Rock Island, Ill. November 1, 1864, he received an honorable discharge, and went back to St. Louis, where he was once more a citizen. February 9, 1865, he went down to Helena, and was sutler of the Thirty-fifth Missouri Infantry. Later Mr. Hunt took charge of the sutler's outfit of the Fifty-seventh Infantry, and went with the regiment from place to place until finally they came to Fort Smith. Mr. Hunt engaged in merchandising at this place in 1865, and here he has remained ever since. He was married in April of 1866 to Miss Amelia Griner, and eight children were born to this union: Lillie, Ella, Dora, Minnie, Anna, Edward, Herman and Irene. Mr. Hunt served as alderman in Fort Smith three years, and filled the position of treasurer of that city for two years. He is a member of the Lutheran Church. Mr. Hunt accumulated a great deal of real estate in and out of the city; is the owner of a fine block of twelve lots, 300 feet square, in the heart of the city, corner of Sixth and Maple Streets. At the time he was alderman the city expenses were $5,000 a year, and now they are $50,000. Lots which were sold at that time for $150 to $200, are now selling at $1,000 each, size 50x140 to the alley. The last discovery of natural gas will make the city the size of Kansas City in five years.

William Hunter was born in Tennessee in 1827, his parents being Squire and Rebecca (Burden) Hunter, natives of Tennessee, where they were reared and married. The father was well educated and a member of the Free-Will Baptist Church. From his native State he went to Missouri, settling near Springfield, Greene County. A short time after (about 1856) he came to Franklin County, Ark., where he died in 1861. Mrs. Hunter died at Fort Smith during the war. She was the mother of ten children. Those living are William, Marion and Elizabeth. Sarah, Charles, Ira, John, James, Mary and Squire are dead. The paternal grandparents were natives of North Carolina, who immigrated to Tennessee in an early day, and there passed the remainder of their lives. The maternal ancestors were founders and large property owners of Stanton, Va., where they were born. William Hunter, our subject, received but a meager education during his youth, which was passed upon a farm in Missouri. When eighteen he left home and came to Franklin County, Ark. Upon the outbreak of the Civil War he enlisted at Fort Smith in Company D, of the First Arkansas Volunteer Infantry, and served until discharged at the same place in 1865. He served on detached duty, and was wounded at the battle of Big Creek. After the war he was engaged in farming in this county, and he now owns 260 acres of good land, 120 of which he cultivates. In 1847 he was united in marriage to Barbara Powell, of Arkansas, who died in 1865. She was the mother of six children: Elizabeth, Rebecca, Matilda (deceased), Polly A. (deceased), Rachel (deceased) and an infant (also deceased). In 1866 Mr. Hunter married Sarah, daughter of Isaac Ellis, of Benton County, Ark. This marriage has been blessed with four children: Ellen, Annie, William and Sarah. Mrs. Hunter is an active member of the Christian Church, and Mr. Hunter is a Republican in politics.

William D. Hunter, undertaker at Huntington, has been engaged in his present business here since January, 1888. He was born in De Kalb County, Mo., in 1832, his parents being William and Mary (Grace) Hunter, natives of Kentucky and North Carolina, respectively. After their marriage, over seventy years ago, they immigrated to Northwest Missouri, being early settlers of what is now De Kalb County. In 1858 they removed to Texas, where the father died in 1863, and the mother in 1883. The former served as postmaster of Graveston many years, and served one term while in Tennessee as sheriff. He was a soldier in the War of 1812 under Gen. Jackson. The grandfather of our subject, Charles Hunter, was a farmer, and died in Missouri. William D. is the fourth child born to his parents, and during his youth, which was passed among the wilds of Missouri, he received but a meager education. He was married in 1856, in De Kalb County, Mo., to Nancy J., daughter of Michael and Minerva Moore, early settlers of Northwest Missouri, who came from Tennessee. In 1858 Mr. Hunter went to Texas, and there lived until 1871, when he went to Hackett City. Two years later he came to Huntington, and since January of this year his residence has been in the town. He owns five town lots, and a farm of eighty acres three miles southwest of the town, all of which is good valley land. He also has two houses and lots in Hackett City, all his property being the result of his own industry and good management. He has always been a Democrat, and is an alderman. He served three years in the Confederate army, first in Company F, Fifth Texas Rangers, and then in Martin's regiment of cavalry. He enlisted in 1862, and operated in the Indian Territory and Arkansas until the regiment was disbanded at Richmond, Texas. Mr. and Mrs. Hunter belong to the Free-Will Baptist Church, and two of their seven children are members of the same church. Mr. Hunter learned the cabinet trade when a boy, and followed the same until coming to this county. In connection with the undertaking business he deals in shingles.

George F. Hynes, M. D., physician and surgeon at Fort Smith, was born in Brockville, Canada, in 1848, and is the son of William M. Hynes, a native of Dublin, Ireland, born in 1792; he was educated in England, but returned to Ireland, and emigrated from there to America, and located in New York State, before he had attained his majority. He commenced life as a teacher, and followed this occupation in that State for several years. He moved to Canada about 1827, locating at Brockville, where he followed educational pursuits for over forty years. In 1855 he went to Montreal, and was there connected with Lower Canada College as professor of mathematics for one year, after which he returned to Western Canada, and became interested in the publication of a newspaper, Prescott *Messenger*, filling the office, in the meantime, of superintendent of county schools. Before his death he abandoned teaching. He was a stanch Protestant member of the Presbyterian Church, and was a strictly temperate man in all his habits. He died in 1866, at the age of seventy-four years. He was married twice, first to Miss Margaret Burrell, who died in Canada, leaving six children. Mr. Hynes was afterward married to Miss Mary Burrell, a sister of his first wife, and to them were born ten children. Margaret and Mary Burrell's father, William Russell, was a prosperous farmer of New York State, and was an elder in the Presbyterian Church. Late in life Mr. Hynes and wife went to Ohio, to live with their youngest daughter, and here passed the remainder of their days. His great-grandfather, whose name was Morgan, was in the Revolutionary War, and fought on the British side. Dr. George F. Hynes graduated from Cleveland College in 1879. After practicing in Cleveland for a year he came South, and located in Van Buren, Crawford Co., Ark., where he remained until March, 1888. While in that county he was associated with Dr. Dibrell. Dr. Hynes came to Fort Smith in March of 1888. He is a member of the Sebastian Medical Association, and although only a short time in the State he was made chairman of Arkansas State Medical Society for 1888. While in Van Buren County he was surgeon for the railroad and for the K. of P. He was married to Miss Sue Dibrell, daughter of J. A. Dibrell, Sr., and two children were the result of this union: Dibrell Pryor and Mary Russell. Dr. Hynes is a member of the Presbyterian Church, and is a prominent practitioner.

Dr. Lee H. Ingraham, farmer and stock raiser, and retired physician, of Lavaca, was born in McNairy County, West Tenn., in 1844. His parents, James M. and Elizabeth (Spencer) Ingraham, were born in Bedford County in 1815, and in Wilson County in 1817, respectively. They were married in Madison County in 1835, and afterward settled in McNairy County, where the father of our subject was reared. In 1869 they left that county to come to Sebastian County, Ark., where Mr. Ingraham farmed until 1879. He then established the first family grocery store where Lavaca now stands, where he has since continued to do business, being at present the oldest merchant in the town. His father, John S. Ingraham, was a native of Virginia, who accompanied his parents to Wayne County, Ky., when a child. After his marriage he settled in McNairy County, Tenn., where he was the third white settler subsequent to the sending away of the Indians. He died in that county in 1855, at the advanced age of seventy-one. Our subject is the fifth of a family of nine children. He received his early education in his native county, and at the age of seventeen enlisted in Company C, Fifty-second Tennessee Infantry, Confederate States Army, which, after the battle of Shiloh, was consolidated with the Fifty-first Tennessee. He served until the fourteen months of his enlistment had expired, and participated in the battles of Shiloh, Perryville and Stone River. He then returned home, and in 1867 began to study his chosen profession. In 1869 and 1870 he attended the medical university at Louisville, Ky., after which he practiced in McNairy County one year. He then came to Sebastian County, and for four years practiced in Big Creek Township. He then retired upon a farm four years, after which he passed three years in the practice of his profession again, being the only physician between Fort Smith and Charleston. September 10, 1874, he was united in marriage to Mrs.

Mary E. Carroll, daughter of John D. and Louisa Arbuckle. Mr. and Mrs. Arbuckle were born in Christian County, Ky., in 1808, and Cooper County, Mo., in 1817, respectively. After their marriage they lived in Cooper County a short time, and then removed to Henry County. In 1835 they came to what is now Sebastian County, and settling in Big Creek Township they passed their lives in the house they built at that time. They were among the early pioneers of the county, and died in 1872 and 1886. Mr. Arbuckle was a nephew of Gen. Arbuckle, who formerly owned Arbuckle Island, which is now the property of our subject. In 1872 Mr. Arbuckle was elected to represent this county in the Senate, but his death occurred before the Legislature convened. For a number of years he had served as justice of the peace. He was a member of the Cumberland Presbyterian Church and his wife of the Christian Church. He was of Scotch-Irish extraction, and a descendant of one of three brothers who came to America in an early day. Dr. Ingraham is one of the prominent citizens of the county. He is the owner of nearly 1,000 acres of land—the result of his own thrift and industry, and has cleared about 300 acres of land on Arbuckle Island. His wife owns 600 acres of choice land. To them one child has been born. In religion the Doctor and his wife are members of the Cumberland Presbyterian Church, and in politics the former is a Democrat, his first presidential vote having been cast for Tilden in 1876. He is a member and fills the position of secretary of Oak Bower Masonic Lodge, No. 277. He belongs to a long-lived family, his great-grandfather, James Ingraham, having lived in Wayne County, Ky., to the age of one hundred, and two of his sons also lived to be very old men. James Ingraham originally came from Virginia.

Matthew Jerome Irvin, one of the old settlers of Center Township, Sebastian Co., Ark., residing about one and a half miles west of Greenwood, was born in Lincoln County, Tenn., in 1833, and is a son of Charles Ellis and Malinda (Akins) Irvin, who were born in Dublin, Ireland, in 1771, and Kentucky, in 1801, respectively. At about the age of twenty-two years the father immigrated to the United States, locating in the State of Georgia, and afterward went to Lincoln County, Tenn., thence to Jackson, Madison County, where he died in 1844. He was a Methodist minister, and was engaged in preaching the Gospel until about 1820, when he gave up this calling, and spent the remainder of his days retired from the active duties of life. He was twice married, his last wife dying in Sebastian County, Ark., in 1876, having come here in 1857. She was the mother of eleven children, Matthew Jerome being the seventh born. From early boyhood he has been engaged in tilling the soil, and made his home with his mother until he was twenty-two years old, and after his marriage his mother made her home with him. In 1856 he left his native State, and immigrated to Sebastian County, Ark., where he was married in August, 1858, to Miss Mary Ann McCray, a daughter of Alexander and Keziah (Perkins) McCray, who came to Sebastian County in 1850, and were natives, respectively, of Georgia and Alabama. Mrs. Irvin was born in Tallahatchee County, Miss., in 1840. Ten children have blessed their union, only six of whom are living: Martha J. (wife of Robert H. Moore), William H., Lillie Eudora (wife of Sanford Caudle), John Matthew, Susan Ellen and Frank Tatum. In 1860 Mr. Irvin purchased 120 acres of land in Center Township, and from time to time has since increased his acreage, until he now owns 220 acres of fertile land. He and wife have been members of the Cumberland Presbyterian Church for the past twenty-five years, and he has been a ruling elder in the same for the past twenty years. In 1862 he enlisted in Company H, Eleventh Regiment Arkansas Infantry, Confederate Army, and served for about one year, though he was a Union man at the commencement of the war. He is a Democrat in politics, and cast his first presidential vote for James Buchanan.

Hon. James E. Johnson, practicing physician and surgeon at Lavaca, was born in Monroe County, Miss., in 1847. His parents, Rev. Samuel C. and Margaret (Jennings) Johnson, were natives of Georgia and Tennessee, born in 1804 and 1808, respectively. They were married in Greene County, Ala., and made that place their home until 1846, when they removed to Monroe County, Miss. The mother died in the last named county in 1871, and Mr. Johnson is now living in Lowndes County, with his second wife. He is a man of natural fluency of speech, and for over fifty years has been an active and energetic preacher in the Baptist Church. His father, Jesse Johnson, was a well-to-do farmer of Georgia. The maternal grandfather of our subject came to the United States from Ire-

****

land when young, and settled in Pennsylvania, where he was married. He was named Jesse Jennings, and died in Tennessee. James E. Johnson is the youngest of a family of five sons and four daughters. He was reared upon a farm, but received a common-school education during his early youth. During the latter part of the war he served in Company H, Twenty-eighth Mississippi Cavalry, Confederate Army, and after the war returned home. In 1869 he began life for himself as a farmer, and in 1872 began the study of medicine. In 1874 he studied with Dr. E. E. Winn, of Sherman, Tex., with whom he remained a year. He then studied in Polk County, Ark., with Dr. J. W. Gwinn as a preceptor, since which time he has practiced with success. He lived in Polk County until 1884, when he came to Sebastian County, and after spending two years at Central he became a citizen of Lavaca, where he has already a wide and extended practice. In politics he is a Democrat, and as such represented Polk County in the Legislature one term. He has been a member of the Baptist Church since 1871. At this time he is master of Oak Bower Lodge No. 277. In 1872 he was united in marriage to Mary, daughter of Samuel D. Ryan and Mary McKanse, natives of Georgia and Tennessee, respectively. Mrs. Johnson is a native of Georgia, and the mother of five sons. She also belongs to the Baptist Church.

Aunt Sophia Kannady, of Fort Smith, Ark., was born in Fort Gibson, Cherokee Nation, August 16, 1826, and is the daughter of Aaron and Rebecca Borling. Aaron Borling was born in London, England, June 4, 1792, and his father, Moses Borling, sailed for America August 31, 1793, and landed on American soil November 5 of the same year. He brought his family with him, and lived in Baltimore the balance of his life. He was born April 29, 1767, and died in 1796. He was married in England to Miss Mary Cooper, March 7, 1787, and she died in Baltimore, at the age of twenty-six years. Aaron Borling was one of five children born to his parents, and was by trade a sail-maker. Being left an orphan at an early age, he was reared by an aunt. When quite a boy he went to sea, and followed a seafaring life for twelve years. During this time he was married to Miss Rebecca Tucker, a native of Maryland, born October 14, 1781. After his marriage, Mr. Borling followed the sea until he joined the United States army, and with the first troops came to Arkansas, where he helped locate Fort Smith. He was in the Federal service for about five years, when he finally received his discharge. He was promoted to the rank of sergeant. His family had previously joined him at Fort Gibson, and of the six children born to his union, three are now living: Sophia, subject of this sketch; Henry and Robert. After resigning his position in the army Mr. Borling bought a farm in what is now Sebastian County, and upon this farm the family was reared. About 1835 Aaron Borling was employed by the Government to issue supplies to the Seminole Indians, and in the spring of 1841 he moved back to his farm. In 1853 he moved with his family to Fort Smith, and here Mrs. Borling died July 27 of the same year. On March 22 of the following year Mr. Borling also died. May 19, 1847, the subject of this sketch married Jerry R. Kannady, and their marriage was the first one published in the first newspaper of Fort Smith. They were also married by the first Episcopal minister of the place. Jerry R. Kannady was a native of Pennsylvania, and was born at Beaver, Beaver County, on February 11, 1817, and moved to Ohio with his family while yet an infant, their home being in Ohio, at Hebron. He came to Fort Smith in the last of February, 1836. He came with his uncle, Capt. J. Rogers, the founder of Fort Smith, for whom he kept store until he engaged in mercantile pursuits for himself, and then engaged in various kinds of business. At the time of his marriage he was sutler for the United States troops at Fort Smith, for many years. During the Civil War, Mr. Kannady manufactured different kinds of implements. He owned several slaves, and about 1863 he took his wife and negroes south, remaining in the "Lone Star State" until the close of the war. He then returned to Fort Smith in the summer of 1865. During the latter part of the war he was in the employ of the Confederate Government, erecting public buildings. He was born in 1818 and died in 1883. Mrs. Kannady has an oil painting of Fort Smith as a garrison, and this is valued at $700, and is the only one in existence.

Thomas J. Keener, merchant, was born November 23, 1859, in Denton County, Tex., his parents being Miles and Alcy (Lenley) Keener. The father was born in Lincoln County, N. C., and is now engaged in farming, milling and ginning at Waldron, Ark. During the Civil War he served three years in the

Union army, participating in numerous engagements, and was discharged at Holly Springs, Mo. The mother is a native of Jasper County, Mo., and when about grown she moved to Texas, where she was married. She is the mother of ten children, the following now living: Thomas J., Lizzie, Fannie, Grant, Sarah and Dora. Thomas J. passed his youth, after becoming ten years of age, in Scott County, Ark. He received a good education for those days, and after leaving school taught ten terms. He now holds a first grade certificate. In February, 1883, Mr. Keener embarked in the mercantile business at Waldron, procuring his stock on credit, as he had no capital but a good name. He continued business successfully at that place until 1866, and then sold out and came to Lavaca. Here he has the largest stock of general merchandise in town, and does a thriving business on the general supply plan. October 16, 1883, he married Lulu Bell, daughter of J. C. Bell, of Waldron. Mr. Keener was left a widower December 19, 1885. In politics he is a Republican, and while at Waldron served the town as postmaster. He belongs to the I. O. O. F. and the Masonic fraternity, and is a much respected citizen.

J. M. Kelleam, M. D., and coroner of Sebastian County, was born in Franklin County, Ark., November 6, 1858, and is a son of Dr. W. L. Kelleam, a native of Johnson County, Ark., where he practiced over thirty-five years. Our subject lived in Franklin County until sixteen years of age, and then entered the literary and scientific course of the Cumberland University, in Tennessee. Returning to Arkansas, he attended the University at Fayetteville one term, and then entered the University of Louisville, Ky. He graduated from the medical department of that institution in 1882, and then located at Fort Smith, where he has been actively engaged in the practice of his profession since, and is meeting with well-deserved success. He is a member of the County and State Medical Society, and also of the Medical Association. In 1888 he was elected coroner of the county, and he is now filling that position with credit to himself and the community. While in Louisville, Ky., he married Miss Emma Wier, a lady of education and ability.

Allen A. Kersh, farmer and blacksmith of Diamond Township, was born in Orangeburg District, South Carolina, in 1817, on March 31, and is a son of William and Rachel (Shuber) Kersh, natives of South Carolina, who lived in that State until 1833. They then removed to Rankin County, Mo., where they passed the remainder of their lives. Mr. Kersh was a farmer and blacksmith. His father, Andrew, came to America with his parents, from Germany, prior to the Revolution, and, his parents being poor, he was bound out in order that he might support himself. The maternal grandfather of our subject was born of German parents in South Carolina. Allen A. Kersh is the third of a family of eleven children, and during his youth he attended the country school of his neighborhood. At the age of sixteen he accompanied his parents to Mississippi, where he was married, in 1842, to Elizabeth, daughter of James H. and Barbara W. Riddlespirger, natives of Collenton District, South Carolina, where Mr. R. died when Mrs. Kersh was but an infant. His widow afterward became the wife of Mr. Griffith, and when Mrs. Kersh was ten years old removed to Lauderdale County, Miss. In 1859 the family came to Sebastian County, where Mrs. Griffith died in 1861. Mrs. Kersh's grandfather, David Riddlespirger, was born in South Carolina, and his father, Abram, was a native of Germany. Mr. and Mrs. Kersh have three sons and six daughters, viz.: Rachel M., wife of David Bishop, of Benton County; Eliza R., wife of Wiley R. Gwyn; William Horton; Samuel R., of Texas; J. Timothy; Sarah B., wife of George Bishop; Elizabeth M.; Susan L., wife of Cooper Hayes, and Viola A., wife of Wiley Martin. Our subject has had fifty-nine grandchildren. In 1858 Mr. Kersh came to Sevier County, and the same year located near Huntington, in Sebastian County, on the Brewster farm. He engaged in farming and blacksmithing, and became the owner of 1,400 acres of land. He now owns about 500 acres. He was one of the pioneers of the county, and remembers paying $13 for 250 pounds of salt, and $11 per barrel for flour, at which time the nearest trading point was either Fort Smith or Little Rock. Mr. Kersh has been a member of the Methodist Episcopal Church, South, since his youth, and his entire family belongs to that denomination. He is a Democrat, and cast his first presidential vote for Van Buren in 1840. He belongs to Pulliam Masonic Lodge No. 133.

Thomas J. Kersey (deceased) was one of the oldest and most highly esteemed citizens of Sebastian County, Ark., and was born in Davidson County, Tenn., in 1819. At an early day he came to the State of Arkansas and settled in Logan County, where he was married to Peggy A. Shelby, who afterward died, having borne two children: Jane, widow of L. Gee, and George Huston, who was eighteen years old at the time of his death. In 1847 Mr. Kersey was married to Mary Ann Williford, who was born in Montgomery County, Ill., the daughter of Jordan and Sarah J. Williford. Mrs. Kersey came to Arkansas when only thirteen years old, and was married to Thomas Kersey at the age of fifteen. She is the mother of fifteen children, only four of whom lived to be grown: Amanda V., who married, during the war, Mr. A. J. Fry, and was the mother of six children, four boys of whom are living, Grant, Charles, Baty and Mathew; the two youngest are living with their Grandma Kersey, their mother having died when the youngest, Mathew, was only one year old; Baty, who is now thirteen years of age, has lived with his Grandpa since last May, his father having died; the other two are grown. The next child of Thomas Kersey, a son, I. N. Kersey, died when twenty-one years of age; he was an excellent young man in every way, and was much beloved by all who knew him; he was a student of Cane Hill College, Washington County, Ark., and would have graduated the spring he died. A daughter, Mollie, was married very young to Dr. N. D. Woods, Jr.; she is the mother of four children: Mary E., Susie, George Newton and Annie Tribue, the first and last of whom are living. Georgia is the wife of A. J. Chandler. Of these four children, who lived to maturity, only two are living: Mollie Woods and Georgia Chandler. Thomas J. Kersey made a trip to California in 1849 with the long train of gold seekers, and was absent fifteen months, meeting with good success and returning with a large amount of gold. Soon after coming back his dwelling was set on fire at night during the absence of the family, and a heavy loss sustained. He suffered considerably by fire (having been burned out three times—once losing a hotel), but this only increased his determination to accumulate more property. Mr. Kersey was for many years one of the foremost citizens of Greenwood, and was ever ready to assist all laudable public enterprises, and was largely interested in a dry goods store, and owned a mill in the town. He was known throughout Western Arkansas for his honesty, integrity and liberality, and although uneducated, save by his own exertions, was a man of powerful mind and good judgment. He was successful in all his business enterprises, a man of quick perceptions, and possessed considerable personal magnetism, which drew around him a large circle of friends. He was for many years a consistent member of the Methodist Episcopal Church, South, and was one of its most liberal supporters. He was a member of the A. F. & A. M., Lodge No. 131, and was buried by the members of his lodge with impressive ceremonies. He commenced life a poor man, but at his death, October 11, 1888, was a large land-holder, and possessed a large amount of personal property. Of keen observation, he absorbed a great deal by travel, and for fifteen months, when a young man, lived in Texas among the Indians. His house was the home of the orphan, and he partly reared five orphan children. Mrs. Kersey has been a member of the Methodist Episcopal Church, South, since she was thirteen years of age.

R. B. King, M. D., another successful physician and surgeon of Fort Smith, Ark., was born in Little Rock, of that State, October 17, 1845, being the son of George B. and Jane (Walker) King. The father was born in North Carolina, but came to Arkansas, and lived near Little Rock for many years, where he died in 1862, at the age of sixty years. He was of Scotch descent. The mother was born in Arkansas, while it was still a Territory. She is the daughter of Col. Alexander Walker, one of the noted men of the early days of Arkansas. Dr. R. B. King received his literary education in Arkansas, and graduated from the medical department of the University of Louisiana (New Orleans) in 1868. He located in Little Rock, where he practiced medicine for several years, and then made an extensive trip over the Western States and Territories. In 1882 he came to Fort Smith, where he has since gained a lucrative practice. While in Little Rock he was united in marriage to Miss Onetha Badgett, daughter of N. H. Badgett, one of the pioneer merchants and one of the leading business men and citizens of Little Rock, Ark. He was one of the extensive property owners of that city, and the Badgett Block, which is still in possession of the family, bears his name. Dr. R. B. King is the father of two children, Grace and Edwin. He is a member of the Episcopal Church, and belongs to the I. O. O. F.

Henry Kuper, Sr., merchant tailor, of Fort Smith, Ark., was born in Westphalia, Prussia, October 8, 1832, and is the son of B. H. and Mary Ann Kuper. The father was a weaver by trade until late in life, when he engaged in the general produce business. He died in 1860 at the age of sixty years. He was forced into the army under the first Napoleon. After his Russian campaign he joined the regular army, and fought against him at the battle of Waterloo. B. H. and Mary Ann Kuper were the parents of three children, Henry being the only one who has crossed the ocean to America. He served an apprenticeship at the tailor trade while in his native country, and was a journeyman for four years before coming to America. He arrived in this country in 1854, and was seven weeks and three days in making the voyage. He worked at his trade for seven months in New York City, and went from there to Waterloo, of the same State, where he remained four years engaged in his business. In 1859 he came to Fort Smith, where he has been in business for himself since 1861. This is the oldest tailoring establishment in the city. He was married in Waterloo, N. Y., in February, 1855, to Miss Gertrude Ermann, daughter of Kasper and Gertrude Ermann, her father being a stone-mason and contractor by trade. By his marriage Mr. Kuper became the father of eight children, seven of whom grew to maturity, and six are now living: Mary, wife of Henry Limberg; Henry, the present partner with his father in the tailor business, and who married Miss Lizzie Theurer, who bore him three children (Henry, Martin and Bernard); Lizzie, wife of Antone Kasberg; Ann (deceased), who was the wife of B. Upton; Theresa, wife of Paul Guenzel; Agnes and Clara; Gertrude died in infancy. Mr. Kuper and family are members of the Roman Catholic Church, and he is a member of the Catholic Knights of America, of which he is treasurer, and of which his son, Henry, Jr., is recording secretary.

John H. Lairamore was born December 25, 1828, in Morgan County, Mo., and is a son of Obadiah and Emily (Esteys) Lairamore. The father was born in Greene County, Ky., July 8, 1800, and lived there until eight years of age. He afterward lived in Franklin and Sangamon Counties, Ark. and Ill., when these States were inhabited by Indians and wild animals, and he was of great assistance in driving the former to the Indian Territory. He grew to manhood in Petersburgh, and volunteered in the Black Hawk War from Illinois. He also enlisted in the Mexican War, and during the late war served as a Government scout and spy. He settled in this county, which was then Crawford County, over sixty years ago, when there were but two log cabins at Fort Smith. The mother was born in Sangamon County, Ill., where she was reared and married. She bore nine children. Those living are Nelton L., John H., Obadiah and Wiley. Those deceased: William, Martha J., Rebecca, Samuel, who was killed in the war, and Elijah. Mrs. Lairamore died in Sebastian County in 1862, and Mr. Lairamore afterward married Polly Cordin, a native of Coffee County, Tenn., who came here in 1858. She is the mother of two children, Mary Doney and Elizabeth (deceased). The paternal grandparents of our subject were natives of Maryland, who immigrated to Kentucky, and the maternal grandfather was a resident of Illinois. John H. Lairamore came to Sebastian County when three years old, and here grew up with but a limited education. He lived with his parents until his marriage, in 1846, to Jane, daughter of Lewis Pinnell and wife, formerly a Miss Turney, early settlers of this county. Mrs. Lairamore was born in Illinois, and bore three children: Elizabeth, Mary and Clarinda (deceased). Mrs. Lairamore died March 12, 1858, and in 1860 our subject was united in marriage with Ann P., daughter of Theophilus and Elizabeth Petty, natives of Tennessee. Mrs. Lairamore was born in Missouri, and is the mother of six children: John H., Milford, Frances P., William, Martha and George W. (deceased). Mr. Lairamore is an ordained minister in the Free Will Baptist Church, and his wife belongs to the same denomination. In 1863 Mr. Lairamore enlisted in the First Arkansas Volunteer Infantry, and served in Company H until discharged at Fort Smith, August 10, 1865. Since then he has lived in Sebastian County, with the exception of two years spent in Missouri. He owns 155 acres of land, and cultivates sixty. In politics he is a Republican. Six months before the conscript law Mr. Lairamore sold 200 acres of land, taking it all in property, with a view of trying to get north. His position south of the Arkansas River was a most trying one, and the sufferings he, in common with other Union sympathizers, underwent, can better be imagined than described. At one time several of them were obliged to lie concealed in the brush until a favorable opportunity was afforded for reaching the Federal lines. When it became known that Mr.

Lariamore had left the country, the jayhawkers entered upon a course of indignities toward his family wholly unwarranted. Everything obtainable was taken, his wife and children being left so destitute that the former found it necessary to travel fifty miles on foot to find a place of safety among friends. A return of peace was hailed with sincere joy, and harmony and good feeling have since prevailed.

John W. Lamb, farmer, is a son of Nathan and Rebecca (Simpson) Lamb, who were born, reared and married in Alabama. Soon after the consummation of the latter event they moved to Nashville, Tenn., where the mother died. Mr. Lamb moved to Arkansas about 1834, locating in Greene County, where he married Eliza Simpson, a sister of his first wife. They afterward moved to Jackson County, Ark., and there the father died at the age of fifty-nine years. He was a farmer by occupation, and he and both his wives were members of the Methodist Episcopal Church, South. Two sons and one daughter were born to his first union, and two sons and six daughters to his last. John W. Lamb was born in Nashville on the 17th of April, 1835, was reared on a farm, and received a very liberal education. At the age of eighteen years he began farming for himself in Jackson County, Ark., and in July, 1862, enlisted in Company C, Thirty-second Arkansas Volunteer Infantry, Confederate States Army, and served nearly three years, participating in the battles of Prairie Grove, Pleasant Hill and others. After his return home he resumed farming, and in 1871 moved to Franklin County, Ark., where they resided about eight years, and then came to Sebastian County, locating on the farm of 153 acres where he now lives. He has 100 acres under cultivation, and is doing well financially. He is a stanch Democrat in politics, belongs to the Masonic fraternity, and throughout life has been identified with all the farmers' movements, being a member of the Wheel, Alliance, etc. He was married in 1856 to Martha J. Patterson, a native of Alabama, and by her is the father of nine living children: Mary P., William N., Andrew, Joseph, Palmyra, Sophronia, John, Nancy and Mattie. Samuel and an infant are deceased. Only one of the sons, William N., is married, and all are farmers.

J. R. Lane, general merchant, of Mansfield, Ark., was born in North Carolina on September 9, 1836, and is a son of J. F. and Catherine (Ballenger) Lane, who were born in North Carolina June 6, 1812, and Indiana in 1808, and died March 10, 1885, and June 25, 1880, respectively. They were married in North Carolina, and in 1857 moved to Arkansas, settling in Dallas, Polk County, where they engaged in farming. The father was elected to represent Polk County in the State Legislature in 1871, and served with credit to himself and to the entire satisfaction of all concerned. Four of his nine children are still living: Rebecca, Mrs. White; Eliza, Mrs. Pirtle; Isaac N. and J. R. The latter removed with his parents to Arkansas when he was nineteen years of age, and attended New Garden Boarding College, or Quaker College, for twelve months. After attaining his majority he engaged in farming for himself, and also clerked in a store for some time. He was married in 1859 to Mrs. Nicy Jane Cunningham, a widow, who was born in Mississippi in 1837, and is a daughter of Preston and Ellender (Lawson) Ward, and by her became the father of six children: J. P., Mary, Mrs. Wallace; D. G., H. C., Martha and Joseph R. In September, 1888, Mr. Lane moved from Dallas to Mansfield, and has since been engaged in merchandising in the latter place. In 1861 he enlisted in Company H, Fourth Arkansas Infantry, Confederate States Army, and at the battle of Pea Ridge, Ark., was appointed lieutenant, receiving his discharge in 1865. While residing in Polk County he served as sheriff for six years. He is a Mason and Democrat, and his first presidential vote was cast for John C. Breckinridge. His grandfather, Isaac Lane, was born in North Carolina in 1764, and died in 1871, at the age of one hundred and seven years. He was a teamster in the Revolutionary War. The maternal grandfather, John Ballenger, was a North Carolinian.

Richard D. Lewis, agent of the Little Rock & Fort Smith Railway, was born in Wales June 13, 1844, his parents being Benjamin and Mary Lewis. In 1848 they immigrated to America, settling at Kaneville, Kane Co., Ill., where our subject grew to manhood. In 1861 he enlisted in Company D, Nineteenth Illinois Volunteer Infantry. He then turned his attention to railroad work, entering the Chicago & Northwestern office at Chicago as a clerk. After three years had elapsed he accepted a position as clerk with the Union Pacific Railway at Omaha and Uintah, where he remained a year. He afterward passed two years at St. Louis with the St. Louis & Iron Mountain Railway, one year at Poplar Bluff, eleven years at Little Rock, and nearly three years at Dallas, Tex. He then became a resident of Fort Smith, where he has been employed now about two years. Mr. Lewis was married at Sterling, Ill., to Miss Emily Elsey, who is now the mother of three daughters: Laura, Alice and Dora. Mr. Lewis is a member of the K. of P. and K. of H

John Jesse Little, member of the council and school board of Fort Smith, was born in Jackson, Butts Co., Penn., October 24, 1845. His father, J. C. Little, was born in Putnam County, Penn., and became a merchant of Jackson at an early age. His mother was Elizabeth Loyall, daughter of Jesse Loyall, a merchant of Monticello, Jasper Co., Penn., and a native of that State, of Scotch descent. Our subject grew to manhood in his native State, and at the age of eighteen enlisted in the Confederate service, in Company E, of the Thirtieth Pennsylvania Infantry. He served throughout the war in the commissary department, and then returned to Pennsylvania. He then took a position as first salesman in one of the leading houses in Griffin, where he remained until 1883, when he became a citizen of Fort Smith. While in Griffin he was united in marriage to Emily, daughter of Fleming Mobley, a merchant of that place. This union was blessed with two sons and three daughters. While in Griffin he served as chief of the fire department eleven years, and was alderman of the city seven years. Mrs. Little is a faithful member of the Baptist Church. Mr. Little is one of the best known citizens of Fort Smith, having always served as chief of the fire department, which he helped to organize and raise to its present efficiency. He is alderman of the city, is now serving a three-years term as member of the school board, and is a stockholder and director of the Western Arkansas Fair Association. He is a prominent Mason, having served as High Priest of his Chapter and Worshipful Master of his Lodge. He is now in the clothing and gents' furnishing goods business, in which he has been successfully engaged since coming to Fort Smith.

Hon. John S. Little, judge of the Twelfth Judicial Circuit of Arkansas, was elected in 1886 by the Democratic party, having no opposition. His district comprises Sebastian, Crawford, Logan and Scott Counties. Judge Little is a native of Sebastian County, Ark., and was born in 1851, being the son of Jesse and Mary E. (Tatum) Little. Jesse Little was a native of Pitt County, N. C., born in 1818. In 1838 he became a resident of Sebastian (then Crawford) County, Ark., was married in 1845, and located near Jennie Lind, in that county. He was a farmer, was the owner of 200 acres of land, and died in August, 1887. The mother was born in 1829, is still living, and is the mother of two children: John S. and Thomas E. John S. received his education in the common schools, and at Cane Hill, Washington Co., Ark. He remained on the farm until 1872, when he engaged in teaching, and followed this profession three terms, all in his native county. At the time he commenced teaching he began, also, the study of law, his preceptor being Hon. C. B. Neal. In 1873 he was admitted to the bar at Greenwood, and soon after located at Paris, in Logan County, Ark., and engaged in general practice until May, 1877, when he was elected prosecuting attorney for the Twelfth Judicial Circuit. He was re-elected in 1878, 1880 and 1882, serving in all eight years. In 1884 he was elected to the State Legislature, and served on committee of judiciary, and was chairman on county and probate affairs. In January, 1877, he married Miss Elizabeth Irvin, daughter of Pleasant and Elizabeth Irvin, and a native of Logan County, Ark., born in 1861. Three children were the result of this union: Paul, Jesse and Monte. Judge Little is a member of the Masonic order, Master Mason, is a member of the K. of H., and he and wife are members of the Methodist Episcopal Church, South.

George Dallas Loder, builder and contractor, was born in Boone County, Ky., opposite North Bend, Ohio, December 12, 1846, and is a son of George R. and Hannah (Wallace) Loder, natives of Pennsylvania and Ohio, respectively. The father was of German descent, his ancestors having settled in Pennsylvania in an early day, and in connection with farming and trading he was engaged in building and contracting. The mother was born in Ohio, and was a daughter of William Wallace, a native of North Ireland. George Dallas grew to manhood in Kentucky, and before completing the builder's trade engaged in trading upon the Mississippi and Ohio Rivers. He was married in Covington, Ky., to Miss Laura Hedges, daughter of Clayburn Hedges, a native of Virginia, and subsequently located in that city, and for many years was connected with the building interests of that place and Cincinnati, Ohio. In 1887 he was the successful bidder for the building of the new United States Court-house at Fort Smith, which brought him to this place. Himself and wife worship at the Central Methodist Episcopal Church, South. They have reared a family of one son and two daughters, viz.: Florence Pearl, a high-school student; Raymond and Beulah. Mr. Loder is a member of the Blue Lodge in Masonry, and belongs to the National Union and the Hartford Annuity Insurance Company.

Gilbert Looman, proprietor of a livery. and feed stable at Greenwood, was born in Madison County, Ill., in 1829, and is the son of Thomas and Charity (Heddie) Looman. Thomas Looman was born in the State of Tennessee, and was a farmer by occupation. When young he went to Madison County, Ill., married and located there. He was a soldier in the Black Hawk War, and died soon afterward. After his death his widow married John T. Norton, who moved to Dallas County in 1835. Mrs. Norton was born in Kentucky, and died in 1862. She was the mother of four children by Mr. Looman, Gilbert Looman being the second child in order of birth. He was quite small when his father died, and lived with his mother until sixteen years of age. He traveled about for four or five years, visited the "Lone Star State," and then returned to Sebastian County in 1844. In 1853 he married Miss Margaret Byram, who was born in Kentucky in 1831, and seven children were the fruits of this union: Thomas, Mary E. (wife of Virgil McClain), John, Sarah (wife of William Hindman), Ida (wife of William Newsam), Katie and Emma. After marriage Mr. Looman located six miles north of the county seat, where he owned 200 acres of land. In 1885 he moved to Greenwood and established a livery and feed stable; was also proprietor of the Capital Hotel until October, 1888. He keeps six horses, three buggies, a hack, and is the oldest liveryman in Greenwood. He is a Republican in politics, is a Master Mason, and his wife is a member of the Free-Will Baptist Church. In 1863 Mr. Looman enlisted in Company E, First Arkansas Infantry, United States Army, and was in service eight months, being discharged on account of disability.

R. H. McConnell was born March 6, 1815, in Blount County, Tenn. His father, Samuel McConnell, was of Scotch descent, and was born in Pennsylvania. Early in life he went to Tennessee, where he grew up on a farm. He served throughout the entire War of 1812, and in 1820 immigrated to McMinn County. In 1840 that county was divided, and the part he resided in was named Polk County. He died there in 1849. The mother, Mary (McGill) McConnell, was born in Tennessee, and reared on Duck River. She bore seven children, named as follows: Peggy A., Susan, Eliza J., Marella, Elizabeth, Robert H. and Isabella (deceased). The paternal grandfather of our subject was a soldier in the Revolution, and a native of Pennsylvania, as was also his wife. R. H. McConnell grew to manhood upon his father's farm in Tennessee, and received a good common-school education. In 1842 he married Minerva Hawkins, also a native of Tennessee, who died in 1864, and was the mother of eight children: James H., Samuel K., Mary J., Robert H., Jane A., Mary E., William O. and John (deceased). In 1866 Mr. McConnell married Martha Pitts, a native of Madison County, Miss., and daughter of Samuel and Mary (Frazier) Dufful, natives of Tennessee and Kentucky, respectively. This union was blessed with but one child, Alma E., who is deceased. While in Tennessee Mr. McConnell served twelve years as justice of the peace, and for four years was president of the county court. During the war he served a short time in the Confederate army, and at the battle of Pea Ridge he supported a battery. In 1853 he came to Sebastian County, which he represented in the Legislature in the years 1856, 1858, 1874, 1878 and 1883. In 1885 he was elected State senator from the Twenty-eighth Senatorial District, which term of office has just expired. He is one of the influential and highly respected citizens of the county, and himself and wife belong to the Missionary Baptist Church. He has been a Mason over thirty-two years, and is a member of the "Alliance." In politics he is a Democrat.

Dr. John W. McConnell, physician and surgeon for the Kansas & Texas Coal Company, at Huntington, and senior member of the drug firm of McConnell & Brewster, was born in Lawrence County, Mo., in 1855, and is a son of Samuel C. and Catherine (Miller) McConnell, natives of Blount County, East Tenn., and Huntsville, Ala., respectively. The father was born in 1826, and when twenty-eight years of age went to Missouri. The mother was born in 1828, and when young accompanied her parents to Missouri. After their marriage Mr. and Mrs. McConnell lived in Lawrence County until 1858, when they located near Fort Smith, in Sebastian County, Ark., where they are now successfully engaged in farming. During the war Mr. McConnell served in the Confederate army some time as a forage master. His father, John McConnell, came to the United States from Ireland or Scotland after the Revolution, and served in the War of 1812. He was a farmer and hunter, and died in East Tennessee. Our subject is the eldest of three living children, and after receiving a common-school education attended Cane Hill College. At the age of twenty he began the study of medicine, and at the expiration of eighteen months he practiced for two or three years. He then attended the medical department of the Arkansas Industrial Institute, at Little Rock, one year. After practicing two years more he returned to that institution, from which he graduated, in 1884, in a class of fifteen, receiving the first prize for general proficiency. Since that time he has had two students who have graduated from the same college with highest honors. After graduating he lived in Hackett City until 1887, when he came to Huntington, where he enjoys a good town practice. Since November, 1887, he has been engaged in the drug business in connection with his practice. He is a member of the Sebastian County Medical Association at Fort Smith, and is secretary of the Greenwood Medical Association, besides being a member of the State Medical Association. In 1872 he married Sarah, daughter of the Rev. N. B. and Belle McNabb, formerly of Tennessee, where Mrs. McConnell was born. About 1872 the family came to this county. Since the age of eighteen Mr. McNabb has been a minister in the Cumberland Presbyterian Church. The Doctor has a family of two living children, and himself and wife belong to the Methodist Episcopal Church, South. He is a Democrat, and cast his first presidential vote for Hancock in 1880. He belongs to the Masonic fraternity, American Legion of Honor, and Independent Order of Odd Fellows.

John McCray, of Fort Smith, Ark., was born in the State of Mississippi in 1835, and is a son of Alexander and Keziah (Perkins) McCray. The father was born in Alabama, and was one of the pioneers of Mississippi. He was a man of more than ordinary education and intelligence, and a wealthy land owner and slave holder. He died when his son John was quite young, and the latter was left to fight the battle of life for himself. Until he attained his majority he remained with his mother and assisted her in caring for the younger members of the family. He has one sister and one half sister, who are now living; they are residents of Sebastian County, Ark., and Texas, respectively. During the late Civil War he cast his fortunes with the Confederacy, and joined the Fort Smith Rifles, under Capt. J. Spark, participating in the battles of Wilson's Creek, Prairie Grove, Poison Springs, and others too numerous to mention. At the close of the war he began working in the quartermaster's department, continuing one year, and then re-engaged in agricultural pursuits and merchandising, which occupations he has carried on up to the present time. He was married to Miss Mattie Ingles, who died about fourteen months later, having borne one child, who died at the age of five months. She was a daughter of Capt. Ingles, a hero of the Mexican War. Mr. McCray's second wife was Miss Martha Collins, who only lived about one year after her marriage. He married his third wife in Arkansas, in 1879. She was a Miss Florence Rogers, and became the mother of three children: Clarence, Clifford and Mary. Mr. McCray is a Democrat, and a member of the A. F. & A. M. and the I. O. O. F.

A. A. McDonald, circuit court clerk of Sebastian County, Ark., was born in Rhea County, Tenn., in 1863, and is a son of Charles T. and C. E. (Rice) McDonald. The former was born in Virginia in 1831, and January 16, 1859, was married, in Jasper County, Tenn., to Miss Rice. She was born in Tennessee January 12, 1834, and after her marriage removed with her husband to Alabama, thence back to Tennessee, locating near Dayton. Charles McDonald was a soldier in the Confederate army during the late Civil War, being next to the last man to get out of prison at Rock Island, Ill., his exposure there being the cause of his early death. He died about 1868 in Calhoun County, Ark., where he had located previous to the war. His widow then returned with her family to her people in Alabama, but after residing there one year returned to Arkansas in company with her father, George W. Rice. They finally settled in Greenwood, in 1873, where the family have since made their home. The children are as follows: Emma E., A. A., the subject of this biography, and T. B. Owing to their mother's earnest endeavor and good judgment, they have been reared to intelligent manhood and womanhood. A. A. McDonald has grown up principally in Sebastian County, Ark., and secured a good common-school education. He followed various occupations until August 31, 1884, among which was teaching school, and was then appointed chief deputy in the sheriff's office for Greenwood District, of Sebastian County, and filled this position for over two years. He then resigned the office, and March 1, 1887, accepted a position with Rappenhimer Hardware Co., of Fort Smith, where he worked until June of the same year, and then engaged in the livery business, and worked in the county clerk's office at Greenwood until January 29, 1888. He then became candidate on the Democratic ticket for circuit court clerk, received the nomination, and was elected September 3, 1888. He entered upon the duties of his office October 30, 1888, and, owing to his many sterling business qualities, a bright future is predicted for him. He says that if he ever attains to any prominence in years to come it will be owing to the counsels which he received from a good and intelligent mother, whose advice he has always tried to follow.

Blooming W. McDonough, farmer, was born March 20, 1849, in Caddo Parish, La., and is a son of Wesley F. and Serrenia (Smith) McDonough. The paternal grandparents were of Scotch descent, and were born and reared in Baltimore, Md. They afterward moved to Tennessee, where they died. The maternal grandfather was a soldier in the War of 1812, and himself and wife died in Jackson County, Ala. The father of our subject was born in Virginia, when two years old went to Tennessee, from there he went to Alabama, then to Louisiana, and afterward to Texas. After raising one crop in Franklin County, Ark., he came to this county, but in 1880 went to Montgomery County, where he died in 1883 aged sixty-five. During the trouble with the Indians in Florida he was a volunteer soldier, and he served in the late war three years. The mother was born and reared in Jackson County, Ala., where she was married. She was the mother of ten children, six of whom are living: Blooming W., Joseph B., Thomas J., James B., Sterling P. and Margaret L. Those deceased are Walter W., Mary F., Elizabeth and Roan S. Mrs. McDonough died in Chickasaw Nation in 1887. Blooming W. McDonough lived in Louisiana until nine years of age, and then resided in Texas until sixteen years old. He then came to Arkansas by wagon, where he lived upon his father's farm until of age. He received a common-school education, and January 16, 1870, married Martha J. Berry, daughter of Henry Berry, of Tennessee. Mrs. McDonough was born and reared in Franklin County, Ark., and has borne eight children. Those living are Charles S., Hattie E., Edgar A. P. and Addie Lee. Those deceased are Malonia K., John S., William and Poe Bertie. Mr. McDonough settled upon his present farm in 1872, and now has 113 acres of land, fifty of which he cultivates. He also owns 160 acres of prairie and timber land in Texas. Politically he is a strong Democrat, and his wife is a member of the Regular Baptist Church.

Hon. Robert William McFarlane, attorney at law and real estate agent, of Greenwood, Ark., was born in Grayson County, Tex., in 1858, and is a son of Dr. Robert S. and Isabella C. (Norton) McFarlane. The father is of Scotch descent, and was born in Tennessee July 4, 1821, and when about seven years of age was taken to Jackson County, Ala., by his father, Robert McFarlane, where he resided until 1840, when he went to Texas, and for about two years was one of the Texas Rangers. He then returned to Alabama, and from there moved to Arkansas, locating at Dripping Springs, and two years later removed to Sebastian County. He has served as justice of the peace a few years, and was elected to the Arkansas Legislature in 1852, in which body he served with credit. He has been twice married, his first wife, Miss Norton, being born in Tennessee in 1831; she died in 1866. By her he became the father of four children who lived to be grown. He is the descendant of three brothers who emigrated from Scotland to the United States in 1716, two brothers settling in Virginia (from one of whom he is descended) and the other in South Carolina. Hon. Robert William McFarlane is the third child and the only son, and received his rudimentary education in the common schools of Sebastian County, supplemented by a course in the State University at Fayetteville, which institution he entered in 1876, and from which he graduated with the degree of A. B. in 1882, the degree of A. M. being conferred upon him two years later. In 1877 he entered the teacher's profession, his first term being taught in the Indian Territory, and continued that occupation four terms. After leaving college he became a disciple of Blackstone, his studies being carried on under the instructions of Hon. J. S. Little, now circuit judge of the Twelfth Judicial Circuit, and in June, 1885, he was admitted to the bar. He immediately opened an office and entered upon the practice of his profession, and has met with good and well-deserved success. He is well versed in legal lore, and is considered one of the leaders of the legal fraternity in Sebastian County. He is quite an extensive dealer in real estate, which, with his profession, brings him in a handsome annual income. He is a Democrat in politics, and in 1885 was appointed school examiner of Sebastian County, which office he filled to the satisfaction of all for three years. Mr. McFarlane had but $75 when admitted to the bar in 1885, and has since purchased 160 acres of improved farming land and six lots in the heart of Greenwood, upon which he has built a cozy cottage, out of his savings in the law. He is unsuccessful in politics, having, as he remarks, invested $1,000 in politics without any return in the last four years. He is a Master Mason, and is Past Dictator of his lodge in the K. of H. In September, 1885, he became editor and proprietor of the Greenwood *Times*, but at the end of twelve months he sold the paper to H. T. Hampton, and has since confined himself strictly to the practice of law. November 29, 1887, he was united in marriage to Miss Maggie Harris, who was born in Illinois in 1864, and is a daughter of David D. Harris, of Mound City, Ill. She is a worthy and consistent member of the Episcopal Church.

Dr. John McGinty is a native of Indiana, was born in 1859, and is a son of Andrew and Cicely (Conry) McGinty, natives of Ireland. In 1848 the father and mother came to the United States, and located in Indiana, where the father farmed until his death in 1881. They reared a family of three children: Michael, John and Agnes. Our subject received a common-school education in Indiana, which he afterward supplemented by attendance at the high-school in North Vernon, Ind. He then entered the medical college at Cincinnati, graduated from that institution in 1882, and later attended the Kentucky College of Medicine, from which he graduated in 1884. After receiving his diploma he returned to his old home in North Vernon, and for three years and a half practiced his profession at that place successfully. Then in the fall of 1887 he took up his abode in Hackett City, where he has since practiced his profession in partnership with Dr. A. H. Gordon. These gentlemen have a large and extended practice, and enjoy the respect and esteem of the community. Dr. McGinty is a member of the K. of H., and is the examining physician of that order. In politics he is a Democrat.

Henry McGreevy, retail lumber dealer, of Fort Smith, Ark., was born in County Down, Ireland, in 1849. His parents, John and Mary (O'Connor) McGreevy, were also natives of County Down, and were tillers of the soil, the father dying at the age of thirty-five years. The mother is still living in Ireland, and as far back as the McGreevy family can be traced they have resided on the farm on which she now lives. John and Mary McGreevy became the parents of six children, two of whom are living, Henry and John, who are both residents of the United States. The former received a good education in the national schools of Ireland, and in 1869 concluded to come to America to seek his fortune. He landed in the city of New York, and went directly to Chicago, where he spent about two years, and then took up his abode in Little Rock, Ark., where he resided until 1881, when he came to Fort Smith, and in 1883 engaged in his present business. He was married in the town where he now resides to Miss Rebecca Linder, a daughter of Jacob Linder, one of the early settlers of Fort Smith, and a hero of the Mexican War. Mr. McGreevy is a Democrat in his political views, and is a member of the Roman Catholic Church. His wife is of German extraction.

John S. M. McKamey, who has a stock of general merchandise, cotton, hay, etc., at Huntington, valued at about $9,000, was born in Roane County, E. Tenn., in 1849, and is the third of a family of three children born to Capt. John C. and Zerelda (Tunnell) McKamey, natives of East Tennessee, born in 1809 and 1811, respectively. The father served as captain in 1838 in one of the Indian wars, but was a farmer by occupation. He removed to Anderson County, Tenn., when our subject was an infant, and in 1852 went with his brother, Harvey McKamey, on a prospecting tour to Arkansas. He died near Little Rock, and his wife died in 1875 in Sebastian County, Ark. The paternal grandfather, John McKamey, was born in Virginia, and was of Scotch descent. The maternal grandfather, Col. William Tunnell, was also a Virginian by birth, and was of English descent. He served as colonel in the War of 1812, the epaulets and plumes of his uniform now being in the possession of our subject. He represented Anderson County in the Lower House and in the Senate several terms, and died in that county in 1861. John S. M. McKamey came with his mother to Sebastian County in 1867, and November 20, 1873, married Sarah R., daughter of A. T. Bonham, who removed here with her parents from Anderson County, Tenn., in 1870. Mr. Bonham was married twice, his first wife dying in 1881. He commenced business February 19, 1883, under the firm name of McKamey & Davenport. In August of that year Mr. Davenport retired, and the business was continued by J. S. M. McKamey until November 15 of the same year, when Mr. S. E. Smith took an interest, and the firm was McKamey & Smith. Since January, 1885, Mr. McKamey has carried on business alone. He landed here November 22, 1867, with only $4.75, first taught school in the Choctaw Nation, beginning January 5, 1868, and continuing until June of the same year, making in that time over $300. The following fall he went to Cane Hill College, remained till May, 1869, and then taught school, and finally bought and settled a farm January, 1 1870. February 19, 1883, he went into the mercantile business. December 1, 1888, he bought an interest in the Kansas & Texas Coal Co., of Huntington, Ark., the sales of which will average $20,000 per month. He was also elected president of the bank of Huntington. He is a successful man, and has nearly 500 acres of land in different tracts near Huntington, some of which contains coal deposits. Although he began life in humble circumstances, he is now one of the active and enterprising business men of the county. He is an elder in the Cumberland Presbyterian Church, of which his wife is a member. They have a family of six children. Mr. McKamey is a Democrat in politics, and for twelve years has been a member of Pulliam Masonic Lodge No. 133, in which he has served as Master. His oldest brother, William T., served four years in the Confederate army, first in the Nineteenth Tennessee Infantry, and afterward in Thomason's legion of sharpshooters, in the Virginia army. He was wounded at Shenandoah, and died in Sebastian County in 1871.

Edmund McKenna, general merchant and cotton buyer, was born in Manchester, England, February 5, 1843, and is a son of Owen and Bridget (McAdams) McKenna, natives of County Monaghan, Ireland, and descendants of the McKennas of Truke. Edmund lost his father when six years old, and his mother died when he was eleven. She had previously come to America with her children, Edmund and Agnes, her uncle, James McAdams, and an elder brother, Frank, having located in Philadelphia. Mrs. McKenna was buried in a cemetery near Norristown, Penn., and Frank died from a wound received while serving as first lieutenant of the Second California Cavalry. Agnes is now the wife of Matthew Mooney, of Philadelphia. In 1857 Edmund started west in the service of a United States officer, and in 1859, on his return to Philadelphia, stopped at Fort Smith, growing to manhood in the home of J. K. McKenzie. He entered the Confederate army, in Cabell's brigade (Gordon's regiment), and served until wounded at Mark's Mills. He lost an eye, and was laid up in the hospital until previous to Price's raid, in which he participated. After the war he clerked three years at Fort Smith for Capt. H. Stone, and then for seventeen years did business as his partner. He then bought Capt. Stone's interest, and has successfully conducted the business up to the present. In the spring of 1888 he started a store at Cameron, Ind. T., which is paying him a good interest. He is the secretary, treasurer and financial head of the Farmers' Alliance Cotton Yard, and is a stockholder in the Western Arkansas Fair Association. He was foreman of the first hook and ladder company organized in Fort Smith, has served his township as alderman, and in 1884 was a candidate for the mayoralty. For some time he served as president of the board of sewer commissioners, but resigned that office on account of his business interests demanding his attention. In 1870 he married Miss Mildred Bostick, who has borne him four sons and one daughter: Jerry, who works in the store; Frank, deceased at the age of five; Hubbard Stone, Edmund, and Agnes, who died at the age of two. In religion Mr. McKenna is liberal. He is Past Master of the Belle Point Lodge of A. F. & A. M., and is Past Dictator of the Knights of Honor.

T. D. Magness is a son of M. J. and Melvina (McClary) Magness, whose deaths occurred in 1887 and 1858, respectively. In 1881 the father (who was born in 1835) moved from Marion to Washington County, Ark., and two years later to Sebastian County. In 1887 he went to California, and there died the following year. His father, James Magness, was a farmer, born in South Carolina about 1793, and died in 1873. M. J. Magness enlisted in the Confederate army in 1862, but afterward joined the Federal troops, and participated in the battles of Prairie Grove, Corinth, Fayetteville and Springfield. He was captured at the latter battle, and was afterward sent on exchange to Mississippi, and received his discharge in 1864. The following are his children: M. E. (Campbell), Elzetta (Barham), Mary (Wilburn), Lou (Zinn), Laura, Hanse, Cora, Willie, Nora and T. D. The latter was born in Marion County, Ark., in 1857, and spent his boyhood days in his native county, and began the battle of life for himself at the early age of seventeen. In 1876 he was married to his second cousin, Samantha Magness, who was born in Marion County, Ark., in 1862, and by her is the father of two children, Lawrence Edgar and an infant unnamed. Mr. Magness became a resident of Sebastian County in 1884, and two years later purchased his present farm of 300 acres. He has 100 acres under cultivation, and a pleasant and comfortable home. He is a Republican in politics, and cast his first presidential vote for James A. Garfield in 1880. His wife's parents, Hugh and Huldah J. Magness, were born in Tennessee, and subsequently came to Arkansas, where the father followed the occupation of stock raising, and died in 1877. The following are his children who are living: D. A. (Foster), S. J. (Magness), W. T. and Z. M. J. C., C. B. and an infant unnamed are deceased.

Wilson Manus, a successful agriculturist, and the son of Jesse Manus, was born in Hawkins County, Tenn., March 15, 1842. The father was also a native of Tennessee, was reared and married in Tennessee; was a farmer by occupation, and a Democrat in politics. He was married twice, and became the father of children by both wives. Wilson Manus was but three years old when both of his parents died, and he has no remembrance of his parents, brothers or sisters. After the death of his father he was bound out to a man by the name of Debord, with whom he staid but a short time, when an uncle by marriage took him and kept him until the breaking out of the late war. In 1857 he was brought to Scott County, Ark.. and in 1862 he was conscripted in the Confederate army, and served until the fall of 1863, being under seven different captains. With the idea firm in his mind that he was serving a wrong cause, he determined to escape as soon as possible. In September, 1863, he went to Fort Smith and enlisted in Company C, Second Arkansas Volunteer Infantry, United States Army. Soon after he was transferred to Company F, of the same command, and received an honorable discharge August 8, 1865. He participated in the battle of Saline River, Prairie Grove. A considerable portion of the time he was detailed on scouting service, and in a skirmish near Clarksville, Ark., April 11, 1865, he was wounded in the left thigh and hip, the ball passing clear through and crippling him for life. As a partial compensation he gets a pension. After the war he returned to Sebastian County, where, in 1867, he married Miss Julia Anthony, a native of Scott County, and the daughter of Finis Anthony. Nine children were the fruits of this union: Abraham L., Mary E., Henry W., Daniel G., Tennessee J., Archidelphia A., Eva J. L., Audus L. B. and an infant (deceased). Mr. Manus was a Democrat until the war, and since that time he has been a Republican. After marriage he settled upon the farm where he now lives, and where he is engaged in successfully tilling the soil, although he followed merchandising for a short time in connection with his farming interests. He owns 200 acres of land, ninety under cultivation, has been a resident of this county for twenty-one years, and is an honorable man and a good citizen. He is a member of the Masonic fraternity, is also a member of the G. A. R., and he and wife are members of the Free Will Baptist Church. He received very little schooling, and was not able to read or write until about four years ago. He is deeply interested in the education of his children.

Jesse Martin, farmer and real estate dealer of Mansfield, Sebastian Co., Ark., was born in the "Blue Grass State" in 1819, and is a son of Jesse and Jane (Hunter) Martin, who were born in the "Old Dominion," and whose ancestors were among the "F. F. V.'s." Jesse Martin, the father, was born in 1777, and died in Tennessee in 1840. At an early day he removed to Kentucky, and afterward to Tennessee, where he was engaged in farming, and spent the remainder of his days. His wife was born in 1782, and died in 1882, having borne a family of ten sons and four daughters. The paternal grandfather, John Martin, was born in Virginia, and lived to be one hundred and four years old. He was in the War of 1812, and served two years under Gen. Jackson. His father, James Martin, was a soldier in the Revolutionary War, and was on the staff of Gen. Washington. He also lived to be one hundred and four years old. Jesse Martin spent his boyhood days in Tennessee, and received a fair English education, and at the age of twenty-one years began working for himself. In 1866 he removed to Arkansas and settled in Ashley County, removing to Montreal, Sebastion County, in 1869. Here he resided until the winter of 1887-88, when he came to Mansfield. He is real estate agent for the 'Frisco Railroad Company, and for forty-four years has been a member of the Methodist Episcopal Church, South. He is a Democrat, and cast his first presidential vote for Martin Van Buren. In 1841 he was married to Miss Martha Jane McDaniel, who was born in Tennessee in 1824, and is a daughter of Samuel and Rachel (Cox) McDaniel, who were born in North Carolina and Tennessee, respectively. The father was a mechanic and farmer. To Mr. and Mrs. Martin were born nine children: Jane, (deceased), John, a daughter (Mrs. L. P. Powell), Samuel B., James J., Thomas F., Louisa, Wiley O. and Margaret E. In 1861 Mr. Martin enlisted in Company I, Fifth Tennessee Cavalry, and served with Gens. Bragg, Johnson and Hood, and with them participated in the battles of Perryville, Murfreesboro, Missionary Ridge, Chickamauga, Rocky Fall, Resaca, Marietta, Kenesaw Mountain, Peach Tree Creek and Atlanta. He was discharged in 1865, after Johnston's surrender.

Joseph H. Martin, farmer and stock raiser, was born in Maury County, Tenn., in 1844, and is a son of Patrick and Sarah (Lee) Martin, natives of Virginia, who accompanied their parents to Williamson County, Tenn., where they married. They then settled in Maury County, and a few years later removed to Obion County, Tenn., where they still live. Mr. Martin is a well-to-do farmer, and both himself and wife belong to the Methodist Church. Thomas Martin, the grandfather, was of Irish descent, and died in Maury County when Patrick was a small boy. Joseph H. Martin is the fifth of a family of six children, and when young attended school but little. In 1862 he joined Company K, Seventh Kentucky Cavalry, under Gen. Forrest, with whom he remained until the close of the war. He operated in Tennessee, Kentucky, Mississippi, Alabama and Georgia, and participated in the engagements at Nashville, Franklin, Murfreesboro, Shiloh, and was through the Atlanta campaign. He was also at West Plain at the time of the surrender. After the war he returned home, and December 28, 1865, married Lucinda, daughter of Joseph and Ruth Hogan, a native of Virginia, who when young went to Indiana, where they were married and Mrs. Martin was born. Mr. and Mrs. Hogan had a family of nine children, eight of whom are living. About three years after the birth of Mrs. Martin they removed to Obion County, Tenn., where they died in 1884 and 1870, respectively. Mr. Martin lived in Maury County for two years after his marriage, and in 1878 came to Sebastian County, settling upon his present farm, which was then but little improved. This was situated just south of the present site of Huntington, and consisted at first of eighty acres. Mr. Martin since has sold about forty acres for town lots, the tract being known as Martin's addition to Huntington. He has always followed agricultural pursuits. In politics he is a Democrat, and his first presidential vote was cast for Seymour in 1868.

H. P. Mayers, of the firm of Shelby & Mayers, dealers in furnishing goods, hats, etc., at Fort Smith, Ark., was born in 1858, and is the son of Abraham G. and Jane Buchanan (Gilly) Mayers. The father was born in Hagerstown, Md., in 1807, and when a young man made his way southward, and was married at Natchez, Miss., to Miss Jane B. Gilly, who was a native of New Orleans, born in 1814. A romantic story is connected with their courtship and marriage, as Miss Gilly, then a beautiful young woman, eloped with her lover, and they were married on board a steamer on the Mississippi River. When Fort Smith was in its infancy, and still a barrack, containing then a few soldiers, whose duty it was to quell any hostile movement displayed by the savage tribes upon the border, this couple landed here, in 1840, and Abraham G. Mayers was appointed Indian agent, which position he filled for several years. He was one of the earliest and leading merchants of the place. He was editor of the *Thirty-fifth Parallel*, one of the earliest newspapers of Fort Smith. He was also postmaster at Fort Smith at the opening of the Civil War, and during the bloody struggle was stationed at Fort Washita, in the Indian Territory, in charge of the Government commissary. He was one of the pioneers of Fort Smith, was a man of unusual enterprise, and when he died, in 1870, this community mourned the loss of one of its most respected citizens. Jane B. Mayers died August 27, 1885. By her marriage she had become the mother of seven children, three of whom are still living: Howard S., Jennie B., wife of T. J. Cunningham, and H. P., the subject of this sketch. H. P. Mayers was of German extraction. He was taken to Tennessee by his parents, and afterward to New Orleans, where he remained until about 1869. From 1875 to the fall of 1880 he was connected with the post-office in Fort Smith, and afterward traveled for Scott, Jones & Co., of St. Louis, for a year. August 15, 1887, he became a member of the present firm with Mr. Edwin Shelby. He is a member of the Episcopal Church, is a Democrat in politics, and is a Sir Knight and Captain of the uniform rank K. of P., Fort Smith Division, No. 9.

J. H. Mershon, ex-Deputy United States Marshal, and dealer in real estate at Fort Smith, Ark., is a Kentuckian, was born in 1838, and grew to manhood in London, the county seat of Laurel County. He is of French descent, and a son of William and Nancy Mershon, the former being born in Kentucky in 1801. He was the proprietor of a large tan-yard in London, and was a leading politician of Southeast Kentucky, but during the early settlement of Kansas moved westward, and located in that State, where he remained two years. From there he went to Northwest Texas, and there died during the war, in 1863. His wife died in 1870. His father, Titus Mershon, was also a Kentuckian, a Whig in politics, and was one of the leading politicians of the day. J. H. Mershon and his youngest brother served in the Federal army in the late war, being a member of the Second Kansas Cavalry, and was promoted as follows: Corporal, commissary-sergeant, first duty sergeant, orderly-sergeant and first lieutenant. He received his discharge at Lawrence, Kas., August 11, 1865, and went directly to St. Joseph, Mo., where he was married on the 3d of September, 1865, to Ellen M. Roberts, a relative of Gov. Silas Woodson, and removed to Wise County, Tex., where their first child was born and died. On account of the ill health of his wife he returned to Labette County, Kas., where he spent one year, thence to Jasper County, Mo., where he purchased a farm and began tilling the soil. Here another child was born, but only lived a very short time. Shortly after he took his wife to Troy, Kas., where she died of consumption, at the home of her mother. Mr. Mershon then sold out all his property in Missouri, and came to Fort Smith, Ark., with the intention of soon joining his brothers in Texas, but, liking the town, engaged in the grocery business, which he followed about a year. About this time he met Miss Minnie Simmons, a school-teacher, and they were afterward married. Their union has been blessed in the birth of four children, only two of whom are living: Maggie and Arthur. Willie W. died at the age of five and a half years, being very delicate from his birth. After his marriage Mr. Mershon resided on a farm for about two years, and then came to Fort Smith, and became Deputy United States Marshal, serving twelve years, a longer period than any of his successors have served. He was instrumental in bringing many notorious characters to justice, prominent among whom was Bully Joseph. He retired from office in 1887, and has since been engaged in the mercantile and real estate business. He is a Republican, and has been a member of the I. O. O. F. and K. of H. for the past ten years. He rode Lexington, a Kentucky horse, at the great post stake, at New Orleans, when he beat Lacompe, Highlander and Arrow. His brother, F. L. Mershon, served in the Confederate army three years during the late war, and then returned to Wise County, Tex., where he has served two terms as county treasurer, and polled more votes than any other man who has ever run for office in the county. His brother, William H., served in the Twenty-fourth Kentucky Volunteer Infantry, as first sergeant, and was with Sherman on his famous march to the sea. He returned to Wise County, Tex., after the war, and has been county school commissioner several terms.

Rudolph Metzger, contractor and builder, was born in Staufen, Baden, Germany, October 16, 1851. He received his education in Baden, Germany, his parents being Rudolph Metzger and Theresia (Haas) Metzger. The father was a joiner, carpenter and cabinet-maker by trade, and imparted his knowledge to his son. In March, 1881, Rudolph came to America, and until 1882 worked at his trade in Centralia, Ill. He came to Fort Smith April 16 of that year, beginning business for himself, and has since been permanently identified with the building interests of his place. While in his native country he married Amelia Straub, who was buried here December 29, 1886. She was daughter of George and Theresia Straub. They live in Griesheim, Baden, Germany. Amelia (Straub) Metzger was mother of one son and three daughters, viz: Rudolph was born April 20, 1876; Mary Katharine was born April 7, 1878; Annie Amelia was born September 20, 1879, in Staufen, Baden, Germany; Theresia was born December 22, 1884, in Fort Smith, Ark. Mr. Rudolph Metzger afterward married Miss Margarita Geheb, August 16, 1887. Margarita (Geheb) Metzger was born August 15, 1862, in Fort Smith, Ark., her parents being Adam and Margarita (Pfrim) Geheb, both born in Brissberg, Baiern, Germany. Mr. and Mrs. Metzger are both members of the St. Bonifacius Roman Catholic Church, and to them one child has been born, August 6, 1888, named Margarita Theresia. His residence is on the corner of Bryned Street, No. 720. Mr. Metzger has built many residences and store buildings in this city, and he was the builder of the Howard school-house and the Grand Masonic Temple, one of the finest buildings in Fort Smith. He is a member of the church committee, and belongs to the Catholic Knights.

Dr. Julius Meyer, of Fort Smith, Ark., was born in Copenhagen, Denmark, February 16, 1852, and is a son of Dr. Marcus and Mosigne (Rothschild) Meyer, natives of the same city as himself, and born December 9, 1812, and June 14, 1820, respectively. The father was a professor of medicine in a university in Copenhagen, and was the author of Meyer's Dictionary of the Danish Language. He was also translator of Webster's Dictionary into the Danish and German languages, and died June 27, 1885. Dr. Julius Meyer is the only one of his seven children who has crossed the ocean. He reached American soil in 1869, landing at New York City, and came almost directly to St. Louis, Mo. He graduated from the literary department of the Copenhagen University in 1866, and from the medical department in 1868. From St. Louis he went to Peirce City, where he was engaged in keeping books until 1870, then went to Ozark County, where he began practicing medicine in partnership with Dr. Jack Patrick. From 1876 to 1878 he practiced his profession in Jackson County, and then spent several years in traveling, and was manager of a lumber company for some time. He came to Fort Smith, Ark., September 28, 1886, where he has been proprietor of the Cleveland Hotel since January 5, 1887. He is doing a prosperous business, and has a large patronage from the traveling public. He is a Democrat, and cast his first presidential vote for Tilden. December 25, 1886, he was married to Miss Laura Kyle, who was born in Shannon County, Mo., January 23, 1859, a daughter of James and Caroline (Harveson) Kyle. The father was born in Kentucky, and was killed at the battle of Wilson's Creek in 1862. He was first lieutenant under Gen. Price, and was a farmer and stock raiser by occupation. The mother was born in Illinois, and died October 3, 1879. They were the parents of nine children, two living, Mrs. Meyer and Mrs. Mahala West, of Fort Smith.

Capt. Dudley Milam, farmer and stock raiser, is a son of John and Levica (Hamby) Milam, who were born in North Carolina, and when young went to Hickman County, Tenn., where they married, and where the father died at the age of about forty-two years. The mother spent her last days in Boone County, Ark., where she lived to be sixty years of age. The father was a soldier in the War of 1812, being a participant in the battle of New Orleans, and was a blacksmith, wood workman and farmer by occupation. He was an old-time Democrat, and a son of Jordan Milam, who served seven years in the Revolutionary War, and died in Arkansas at the age of one hundred and ten years. Capt. Dudley Milam is the eldest of seven children, and was born in Hickman County, Tenn., February 9, 1826. He was reared on a farm, and received just enough education to enable him to read, and at the early age of fifteen years began earning his own living. He was of a rather roving disposition, and spent several years' earnings in traveling in different States. During the Mexican War he spent nine months in Capt. Whitfield's company, and at the end of that time was discharged from active duty on account of sickness, and then returned to Tennessee, and in 1847 came to Franklin County, Ark., locating soon after in Johnson County, where he was married, in 1852, to Miss Lennet Wood, who was born in North Carolina October 16, 1825. Since 1857 they have resided in Sebastian County, where he owns a fertile farm of 100 acres, with about fifty acres under cultivation. In April, 1862, he enlisted in Capt. Oliver Bassham's company, Confederate service, and at the end of three months joined Capt. Leister's company, but two months later this company split, and Capt. Leister joined the Federal forces. Mr. Milam was then elected captain of the company. At Mark's Mill, in Bradley County, Ark., he was leading a battalion of advance skirmishers, and in the heat of the battle he was struck by a minie-ball in the left ankle joint, the bone being so shattered that his leg had to be amputated a little below the knee. This was done in April, 1863. He has been the hero of two wars, and is yet hale and hearty, and has never had to pay a doctor's bill for himself in his life. He is a stanch Democrat in politics, and is the father of seven children: Emeline P. (deceased), Kansas, William M. (deceased), John, Wood B., Lennet A. and Frances E. Mrs. Milam is a member of the Methodist Church.

John G. Miller, of the lumber firm of Miller & Dyke, Fort Smith, Ark., was born in Indiana in 1842, and is the son of W. B. and Sarah A. Miller. W. B. Miller was a native of England, a miller by trade, and came to America with his parents at the age of eight years, locating in Dearborn County, Ind. A stone mill, erected by him in Dearborn County in 1839, is still in operation, and is run by the youngest son of the family. Mr. Miller was here married, and here passed a long and useful life. The Miller family belonged to the Methodist Church, and were among the higher classes of the English people. John G. Miller was reared and educated in Indiana, and there served an apprenticeship to the milling and flouring business. During the Civil War he was a member of the Sixteenth Indiana Infantry, in which he served three years. After the war he continued in the milling business until he came to Arkansas in 1870, where he located at Georgetown, and in that vicinity ran a saw-mill for several years. The place was subsequently called Piney Station. Mr. Miller moved to Clarksville, Johnson County, in 1877, and from there came to Fort Smith in 1879, entered the saw-mill and lumber business, and now manufactures sash, doors, blinds, etc., on a large scale. He married Miss Mary J. Trester, a native of Indiana, in 1867, and to them were born five children: Carl, Daisy, May and Florence. Their third child, Roy, died at the age of five years. Mr. Miller is a Republican in politics, is a member of the Masonic fraternity, K. of H., and has been a member of the Methodist Episcopal Church since twelve years of age.

Mrs. Mary Miller, of Fort Smith, Ark., was born in the Kingdom of Bavaria, Germany, in 1842, and is a daughter of Conrad and Mary A. Sanger, who were also natives of Bavaria. The father was a cabinet-maker by trade, and in 1846 came to America, landing at New Orleans, and after residing at Louisville, Ky., for a short time, located in Cincinnati, Ohio, where he was residing when the Civil War broke out. He joined the Thirty-second Ohio Regiment, United States Army, and after going to the front was never afterward heard from. His father was also a Bavarian, and belonged to the gentry of Germany. The maternal grandfather, John N. Ragena, was born in Baden, was a talented physician and the highest officer in Baden. Mrs. Mary Miller was brought to America when about fourteen years of age, and became a resident of Fort Smith in 1886. She has been married twice, her first husband being a Mr. Peter Shumes, whom she married when only sixteen years of age. Five children were born to this union: Henry, a manufacturer; Peter, a printer; William, a barber; Philip and Katie, the latter the wife of Theodore Vogel. She was afterward again married. She has given all her children a good start in life, and is now worth about $20,000, which she has made by her own industry and good management.

Dr. Thomas C. Miller, of Dayton, Sebastian Co., Ark., was born in Jennings County, Ind., October 23, 1846, and is a son of Jonathan M. and Helen M. (Thomas) Miller, who were born in Indiana in 1823, and New York in 1828, respectively. They were married in Indiana, August 29, 1844, and were early settlers of that State. In 1856 they removed to Clinton County, Mo., in 1862 went to Effingham County, Ill., and in 1868 went to Caldwell County, Mo. In 1880 they became residents of Dayton. The father died here November 15, 1887, a devoted member of the Methodist Episcopal Church, and the mother died March 1, 1885. The paternal grandfather of our subject, Robert Miller, was of Scotch-Irish descent, and a native of North Carolina. He was an early pioneer of Jennings County, Ind., during the days when, for safety, they attended church carrying a gun on the shoulder. He reared a large family, and died near Paris, Ind., about 1855. The maternal grandfather, Dewitt C. Thomas, was born in New York, settled in Indiana in an early day, and afterward removed to Illinois. Late in life he returned to Indiana, where he died. Dr. Miller is the eldest of a family of seven sons and one daughter. He attended common schools in Indiana, Missouri and Illinois before the age of seventeen, when he joined Company E, Sixty-second Illinois Veteran Infantry. He entered the army February 24, 1864, and served until discharged, March 23, 1866. He served as hospital steward in Arkansas after October, 1865, having joined the army at Little Rock, Ark. He fought in no regular engagements, but participated in many skirmishes. December 3, 1865, he was married at Fort Smith to Eunice, daughter of Michael and Elizabeth Bader, natives of Germany, where they were reared and married. Mr. Bader served in the United States army after coming to America, and died at Fort Smith in 1848. Mrs. Miller is a native of New York, and has borne ten children, five of whom are living. After the war Mr. Miller went to Illinois, and at once began to study medicine at Mason, with Dr. M. McCarty. A year later he moved to Caldwell County, Mo., and then began to practice at Proctorville. In 1869 he located near Dayton, in which town he built the first house, the following year. He soon started a drug store in connection with his medical work, and about 1871 succeeded in having the Hodges Prairie Post-office removed to his place of business. He then named it the Dayton Post-office, and served as postmaster two years. Some years later he also engaged in the general mercantile business. He is one of the leading spirits in all enterprises for the advancement of the country in this neighborhood, and himself and wife are zealous and active members of the Methodist Episcopal Church. He owns a farm of sixty-one acres near Dayton, and is a well-to-do man, although he began life in humble circumstances. He is a strong Republican, and in 1868 cast his first presidential vote for Grant. He belongs to the G. A. R., Pea Ridge Post No. 45, and is a member of the I. O. O. F. Encampment at Huntington. He is a Mason, having joined Reid Lodge No. 163, in Scott County, in 1872.

Charles Milor was born in Floyd County, Ky., October 4, 1818, and died January 12, 1887. He was the son of James Milor and Martha (Boles) Milor, who were married in 1806. James Milor was the son of Charles Milor, an Englishman, who came from England to Rockingham County, Va., in an early day. Martha Boles was the daughter of James Boles and Nellie (Stanley) Boles, who spent most of their lives in Surrey County, North Carolina. They were extensive slave-holders. James Milor and Martha (Boles) Milor moved to Floyd County, Ky., in 1811. He was a farmer on the Big Sandy River. He was murdered August 19, 1822. They were the parents of four children: Mrs. Mary Stevens, Colchester, Ill.; Col. Alfred Milor, Grandview, Ind.; John (deceased), Judge Charles Milor (deceased), being the youngest child. Charles Milor's chances for school were very limited, except when he went to the State University, Bloomington, Ind., a short time. He took advantage of the public library, and by attentive reading and hard studying acquired a good English education, and in time became one of the best read men in the community in which he resided. He was known to have a most remarkable memory. He was a Republican, but never affiliated with the extreme wing of the party. He always ran independently. He cast his first presidential vote for William Henry Harrison. He settled in Arkansas in 1838. He was justice of the peace four years, and was county and probate judge of Sebastian County two terms. In 1864 he was elected to the State Senate, filling the duties of that office with honor to himself and to the entire satisfaction of the constituents. He then returned to his farm. In 1876 he was again elected to represent Sebastian County in the State Legislature, serving one term. From that time until his death he was engaged in agricultural pursuits and stock raising. He was married December 12, 1849, to Miss Emiline Tyree, who was born in Franklin County, Ark., March 14, 1833, and by her became the father of four children, two living: Blanche Mary, who married Samuel H. Rains, son of Gen. James S. Rains, of Dallas County, Tex.; Mrs. Martha J. Tompson, of Washington County, Ark. His wife died on the 14th of October, 1860. December 15, 1862, he married Miss Amanda Largen, who bore him eight children, seven of whom are living: Aurora, Charles, Flora (deceased), Fannie C., Mollie, Alfred W., Lola Pearl, Louis Chester. Mrs. Amanda (Largen) Milor is a native of Corroll County, Va., born May 11, 1839, and is the third child of nine, and a member of the Christian Church; she is a daughter of James and Thersa (Hawks) Largen, who were born in 1810 and 1814, and died in 1858 and 1882, respectively. They moved from Virginia to Georgia, thence to Franklin County, Ark., reaching the latter State in 1848, where they engaged in farming. Their grandparents, William and Nancy (Dalton) Largen, were born and spent their lives in Virginia, and were among the wealthy planters of that country.

Lawrence Mivelaz, proprietor of the LeGrande Hotel at Fort Smith, was born in Switerland in 1848. His parents, Louis and Annie (Bhena) Mivelaz, were both natives of Switzerland. The father owned the stage company in Switzerland before coming to America, and afterward followed agricultural pursuits in New Albany, Ind. He died at the age of fifty-five years. His wife is now alive and residing in Little Rock, Ark. Lawrence Mivelaz attained his growth in Indiana, and was a cook by occupation. He was married in Kentucky in 1870, and went to Memphis, Tenn., where he remained three years, and then came back to the old homestead in Indiana. He here remained for eleven years engaged in agricultural pursuits. In 1883 he went to Little Rock, Ark., where he remained one year, and then came to Fort Smith, where he was in the McKibben's Hotel one year, after which he became the proprietor of the LeGrande, and has remained in that capacity ever since. He was married in Louisville, Ky., to Mary Bardelle, who was born and reared in Kentucky, and who is the daughter of Michael Bardelle, a native of Strausberg, Germany, and Catherine (Hitler) Bardelle. Her father was a miller by occupation, came to America in 1846, located in Kentucky, and is still there. For twenty years he kept a livery stable, and for twenty-two years was a grocer at Louisville, Ky., where he has resided for forty-two years, in his own home. Mivelaz's paternal grandfather was also a miller, and the family have owned a mill, called the Bardelle Mill, for over 100 years. To Mr. and Mrs. Mivelaz were born seven children: Willie, Josephine, Louie, Lena, Maggie, Joseph and Amealia. Mr. Mivelaz is the owner of the old homestead in Northern Indiana, is the owner of eleven lots and four houses in Fort Smith, and the fine hotel is capable of accommodating from sixty-five to seventy individuals. The family are members of the Catholic Church.

George W. Moore, farmer and stock raiser, was born in Giles County, Tenn., in 1832, his parents being John and Lavinia (Kincaid) Moore, who were born in Georgia in 1798, and Tennessee in 1796, respectively. They were married in Maury County, Tenn., and, after two years' residence in Indiana, went to Giles County, Tenn. In 1859 Mr. Moore removed to Lawrence County, of that State, where the father died in 1865. Mrs. Moore died in Giles County in 1846. Mr. Moore was of Irish descent, and lost his father when a boy in Georgia. He afterward accompanied his mother to Tennessee, where he learned the blacksmith's trade and engaged in farming. He was twice married. The maternal grandfather of our subject, David Kincaid, was born in Pennsylvania, and when young went to Giles County, Tenn., where he passed the remainder of his life. George W. Moore is the fifth of a family of eight children. He lived upon a farm during his boyhood, and received a common-school education. Upon attaining his majority he began life for himself by clerking. He worked the first year for $75, the second for $200, and the third year he received $300. He then established himself in business at Mooresville, Marshall Co., Tenn., and remained there until the war, when he sold out and enlisted in Company E, Fifty-third Tennessee Volunteer Infantry, in which he served until discharged in June, 1865, at Johnson's Island, on Lake Erie. He enlisted as a private, but in September, 1862, was made first lieutenant, which position he held until the close of the war. He was captured at Fort Donelson during his first engagement, and for several months was held a prisoner at Camp Chase, Ohio. He was then exchanged at Vicksburg, and in September, 1862, rejoined his company. After participating in the fights at Jackson, Miss., Mission Ridge and New Hope he was captured again, after an all-night struggle. He was then imprisoned at Johnson's Island one year, or until the close of the war. Returning to Marshall County, Tenn., he was, in 1868, married in Madison County to Sarah, daughter of Lieut.-Col. Timothy P. and Catherine Jones, who were formerly from North Carolina. Mrs. Moore was born in Madison County, Tenn., where her mother died. After the war Mr. Moore again engaged in business at Culleoka, Maury Co., Tenn. He remained there until 1872, and then farmed in Jackson County upon land settled by Mrs. Moore's grandfather many years before. In 1880 he came to Fort Smith, and for two and a half years kept a grocery store, since which time he has farmed with success. He is an active and enterprising citizen, and owns a farm of 120 acres, ninety-five acres being under cultivation. Mr. and Mrs. Moore have had eight children, six of whom are living. Two of these belong to the Methodist Episcopal Church, South, as do their parents. Mr. Moore cast his first presidential vote for Buchanan, in 1856, and is a member of the I. O. O. F.

Ira Lain Morris, a wealthy farmer of Sebastian County, Ark., is a son of Enoch and Mary (Sexton) Morris, both of whom were born in North Carolina, the former in 1794 and the latter in 1796. The family first came from Wales at an early day, and located in North Carolina, where the Sextons, who were of English birth, had also settled. Here the parents were married, and lived until 1827, when they moved to De Kalb County, Ga., and made that State their home the remainder of their days. The father was an expert carpenter, and was very handy with tools of all kinds, and in connection with his trade carried on farming. He died while visiting his children in Texas, in 1884, his wife having died in Paulding County, Ga., in 1868. They were devoted members of the Methodist Church, and were the parents of eleven children, six of whom are living. Four sons served in the Confederate army during the late war. The fifth child of the family, Ira Lain Morris, was born in Davidson County, N. C., April 17, 1825, and was reared on a farm, but received but little early education, as his boyhood days were spent on the Cherokee Purchase in Georgia, there being very few schools in the region at that time. He afterward acquired a sufficient knowledge of the common English branches to enable him to acquit himself creditably in the transaction of business, and he is now considered one of the most intelligent men in the community in which he resides. In 1847 he was married to Miss Nancy J. Simes, who was born in De Kalb County, Ga., January 14, 1829, and by her is the father of twelve children: Mary J., Sarah A., James W., William J., Martha E., George L., Frances O., Amanda M. (deceased), Enoch H., Nancy C., Charles H. (deceased), and Jennie L. In 1853 Mr. Morris moved to Texas, and during thirteen years in that State was a resident of the following counties: Cass, Wood and Upshire. In 1866 he came to Sebastian County, where he has since made his home, and is the owner of 220 acres of fertile land. The family are all members of the Methodist Church, and he is a Democrat and Mason. In February, 1863, he enlisted in Company R, Texas Volunteer Cavalry, Confederate States Army, and served until the close of the war. The chief battle in which he participated was Yellow Bayou, and he was neither wounded nor taken prisoner during his service.

George L. Morris, a progressive farmer of Sebastian County, and the owner of 141 acres of land, fifty-six of which are under cultivation, is a son of Ira L. and Nancy J. (Simes) Morris, and was born in Wood County, Tex., January 10, 1860. At the age of six years he was brought to Sebastian County, Ark., and was reared in White Oak Township, his early life being spent in farming and attending the district schools. He received sufficient early education to enable him to transact all his business affairs, and at the age of twenty years was sent to school for the greater part of the year by his father, whose habit had been to give his sons their liberty at the age of twenty, or to school them one year. George L. accepted the latter, and made good use of his time while in school. Having lived a life of single blessedness until March 26, 1882, he was united in marriage to Miss Medora A. Kersey, a daughter of William Kersey, and by her is the father of three children: Clara E., Monta C. and Maud E. Mrs. Morris was born in Greenwood, Ark., March 25, 1861, and she and Mr. Morris are members of the Mount Zion Methodist Episcopal Church, South. Mr. Morris having been a steward in the same since he was seventeen years of age. He is a Democrat politically, and is considered by all an honorable, enterprising and intelligent young man.

Charles Munder, of Fort Smith, Ark., was born in the Kingdom of Wurtemburg in 1821, and is a son of Charles and Dorodtha Munder, who were also natives of Wurtemburg, the former being a civil engineer, and a son of William Munder, who was a farmer and an only son. Charles Munder, the gentleman whose name heads this sketch, learned the stone-cutter's trade in his native land, and at the age of twenty-eight years came to America, landing at New York City. He only remained a short time in this place, then went to Philadelphia, where he worked at his trade for about two months. After a residence of three months in Cincinnati, Ohio, he located in St. Louis, Mo., where he made his home for nearly two years. He next took up his abode in Louisville, Ky., thence to Bradford, Ind., and back again to Louisville, and then to Memphis, Tenn., where he worked in the navy yard. He came to Fort Smith in 1852, and here has since made his home and worked at his trade. During the late war he served in the Confederate army, and is now a Democrat in politics. He was married in Fort Smith to Miss Amelia Euper, by whom he became the father of five children, Paulina, Charley, Amelia, Anton and M. M. Amelia is deceased. The mother and children are members of the Catholic Church.

Hon. Caswell B. Neal, attorney at law and real estate agent, of Greenwood, is a native of Anderson County, Tenn., where he was born in 1829, being the son of John O. and Permelia (Young) Neal, and grandson of Daniel Neal, who was a native of Ireland. John O. Neal was born in Russell County, Va., in 1793, and was a young man when he went to Whitley County, Ky., where Daniel Neal died. About 1820 John O. Neal went to Tennessee, and soon after married Miss Permelia Young, who was born in the State of Virginia, Spottsylvania County, in 1808. She is still living, but her husband died in Tennessee in 1878. They were the parents of eight children, only three now living: Caswell B., John R., who is a member of Congress from Chattanooga District, in Tennessee, and is now serving his second term, and Henry C., who is an itinerant minister in Holston Conference in Tennessee, of the Methodist Episcopal Church, South. Hon. Caswell B. Neal was educated at Strawberry Plains, in Jefferson County, Tenn., and at the age of twenty-one he entered the teacher's profession, receiving $10 per month for compensation, and paying $2 per month for board. This was in Anderson County, Tenn. In 1848 he went to Scott County, Ill., and taught here four terms. In 1852 he returned to his native State, and became employed in the chancery court's office in Madisonville, Monroe Co., Tenn. He was there two years, and during that time became a disciple of Blackstone, his preceptor being Hon. George Brown, who now lives in Knoxville, Tenn. In 1856 he was admitted to the bar at Madisonville, and afterward left his native State, and in January, 1860, he became a citizen of Greenwood, Sebastian Co., Ark., where he resumed his practice. He was a Whig in politics before the war, but since then he has affiliated with the Democratic party. In 1862 he was elected State representative, and in 1864 he was re-elected from Sebastian County, serving on the judiciary committee. In 1870 he was again elected as representative, and it was this Legislature that passed the articles of impeachment against Gov. Powell Clayton and John McClure, chief justice of the State. Hon. C. B. Neal was chosen to present the charges before the Senate and prosecute the same. This service he performed to the satisfaction of his party. He was also complimented by the Democratic vote for speaker of the House. He has devoted his time to his profession, his practice extending from Arkansas to Red River, and is one of the leading legal lights in Sebastian County. He has been wonderfully successful financially, and is the largest land-holder in Western Arkansas. He owns 1,500 acres, and at one time was the owner of 3,000 acres. He also owns fine property in Greenwood, about one-third of the village. In 1858 he married Miss Susan Inge, who was a native of Alabama, born in 1835, and who became the mother of four children: John M., dealer in stock; Caswell B., salesman in Greenwood; William H., attorney with his father, and Thomas W. Mrs. Neal died in 1876, and in 1878 Mr. Neal married Mrs. M. A. Robertson *nee* Brazier. He and wife are members of the Missionary Baptist Church; he is a Knight Templar, and has been a Master Mason for thirty-five years.

Anton Neis, of Fort Smith, Ark., was born in Alsace, France, in 1818, and is a son of Joseph and Susie (Aesanstack) Neis. The former was a butcher by trade, and also kept a hotel. His grandfather came to America with Marquis de Lafayette, and assisted the colonists in their struggle for freedom, returning home in safety. Joseph and Susie Neis died in their native land, having become the parents of five children, Anton being their youngest born. The latter learned the trade of butcher, and at the age of twenty-one years came to the United States, landing at New York City. He soon after went to Frankfort, Ky., where he worked at his trade for two years, and while in that city cast his first presidential vote for Gen. William Henry Harrison. From Frankfort he went to New Orleans, but after a short stay in that city went to Lexington, Mo., where he made his home for two years. Under the bankrupt law, during Harrison's administration, he was entirely broken up, losing about $6,000. After this he left Lexington and returned to New Orleans, where he began following his trade once more. In 1844 he came to Fort Smith, where he has since resided, and where he was married, about one year after his arrival, to Miss Catherine Sengel, by whom he became the father of five children: Susie, widow of Gen. Bonneville; Louise, widow of Charles Robinson; Tony, Albert, and Katie, who died at Albuquerque, New Mexico. Anton Neis was working at his trade in Fort Smith when Gen. Taylor was preparing for the Mexican War, and was requested by the latter to join his command. He did so, and left Fort Smith November 1, 1845, and served throughout the entire war, being accompanied by his wife. He was afterward in a number of fights with the Indians, the principal engagements being with the Pawnees, and in one of their fights on Blue Creek, Neb., killed 130 Indians and lost only one man. The Indians were armed with bows and arrows. In 1849 he was sent to work in a saw-mill, where he met with an accident, and was seriously injured, but received no compensation from the Government until Grover Cleveland was elected President, since which time he has been receiving a pension. He has been engaged in butchering and in hotel-keeping in Fort Smith for many years, and is doing a satisfactory business. The family attend the Catholic Church, and he is a Democrat in his political views.

Wiley Nelson, farmer, was born in Sevier County, Ark., in 1840, and is a son of William and Sarah (Mitchell) Nelson, who were born in North Carolina and Alabama, respectively. They removed from Alabama to Sevier County, Ark., about 1837, where the father died when our subject was three years old, and the mother died during the war. Mr. Nelson was of Irish descent, and Mrs. Nelson was a member of the Methodist Church. Wiley received a very limited education when a lad, and upon the outbreak of the war joined Company F, Nineteenth Arkansas Volunteer Infantry, being first stationed at the Arkansas post. He then spent nearly three months imprisoned at Camp Douglas, now Chicago, after which he was taken to Richmond, Va., where he was exchanged and sent to the Army of Tennessee, at Chattanooga. He participated in the Georgia and Atlanta campaign, returning with Gen. Hood, and after the engagements at Franklin and Nashville joined Johnston's army in North Carolina, with which he surrendered. He then returned to Sevier County, where he was married, in 1865, to Helen, daughter of the Hon. David Carroll and Catherine Price. Mr. and Mrs. Price were born and reared in Alabama and Kentucky, respectively, and Mrs. Nelson is a native of Crawford County, Ark. Mrs. Price died in 1870, but Mr. Price is still a resident of Washington County, Ark. He was a soldier in one of the Indian wars, and represented Crawford County in the Legislature when it included Sebastian County. For many years he served as justice of the peace. Mr. and Mrs. Nelson are members of the Methodist Episcopal Church, South. They have a family of nine children. After the war they settled in Washington County, and in 1873 came to Sebastian County, where Mr. Nelson rented land for five years. He then purchased his present farm of 110 acres, near Huntington. In politics he is a Democrat, his first presidential vote having been cast for Seymour. He is a member of the A. F. & A. M., and one of the self-made and respected citizens of the township.

Richard Nevill was born in Fort Smith, Ark., in 1856, and is a son of James and Mary Nevill, the former being a native of County Leitrim, Ireland. He came to the United States at an early day, and participated in the Florida and Texas Wars. He was a sergeant in the United States Army under Gen. B. L. E. Bonneville, and afterward came to Fort Smith and purchased land, which is now known as the Nevill Addition to Fort Smith, Richard Nevill, his son, grew to manhood in the latter town, and received a good English education. In 1878 he left the paternal roof and went to New Mexico, and worked at the blacksmith's trade, at which he had previously worked in Fort Smith and in Las Vegas. He returned to Fort Smith in the spring of 1882, and soon after engaged in his present business, which is bringing him in a comfortable income. He is unmarried, and in his political views is a Democrat. He attends the Catholic Church.

Willis W. Nolen, farmer and general trader, was born in Madison County, Tenn., in 1827, and is a son of James and Nancy (Anderson) Nolen, natives of South Carolina, who, after their marriage, removed to West Tennessee in an early day. In 1847 they removed to Hempstead County, Ark., where the mother died in 1865 and the father in 1875. They were members of the Methodist and Baptist Churches, respectively. James Nolen, the grandfather of our subject, served in the Revolutionary War and the War of 1812, and was a son of Irish parents. Willis W. was the fourth of a family of four sons and three daughters. At the age of seventeen he left home to work on a farm in Hempstead County, Ark. In 1849 he married Susan, daughter of Andrew and Rachel Henderson, a native of Illinois. Mr. Henderson died in that State, and the family afterward came to Arkansas, prior to 1844. The mother died in Texas. In 1869 Mr. Nolen came to Sebastian County, and until 1880 farmed and traded at various places. He then engaged in the mercantile business at Lavaca with

M. Harwood for two years, after which he continued in business alone until retiring in the winter of 1887–88: He is one of the wealthy business men of the town, and himself and wife are highly respected members of the Methodist Episcopal Church, South. During the war he served nearly four years in the Confederate army. He was one year in Company E, Twentieth Arkansas Infantry, and afterward in Bryant's regiment of cavalry. He operated in Arkansas, Mississippi and Indian Territory, and was discharged in the Territory at the close of the war. Besides many skirmishes he participated in the battles at Vicksburg and Corinth, and accompanied Steele through Arkansas. He was formerly a Whig in politics, and cast his first presidential vote for Gen. Taylor, but since the war has been a Democrat.

Bernard O'Keeffe, merchant of Fort Smith, Ark., was born in County Wicklow, Ireland, in May, 1863, and is the son of Hugh and Mary (Murphy) O'Keeffe, who were among the sturdy yeomanry of County Wicklow. The family have lived on the same farm in the "Emerald Isle" for several generations, and the old homestead is now occupied by Mary (Murphy) O'Keeffe and four of her children. She was formerly a teacher in the national schools of Ireland. Her husband died March 17, 1876, at the age of eighty-three years, both families being devoted members of the Roman Catholic Church. They were the parents of six children: John, Anastasia, Jennie, Pat, Bernard and Joseph. September 10, 1883, Bernard O'Keeffe embarked on the steamer Republic for America, and landed at New York City on the 21st of September, remaining only one day in that city. He came almost immediately to Fort Smith, and here commenced life as a clerk, which occupation received his attention for about three and a half years, and then he engaged in the mercantile business for himself, his brother, Pat O'Keeffe, who came to the United States in 1887, being in his employ. Mr. O'Keeffe took out his naturalization papers in the fall of 1883. He is a member of the Roman Catholic Church.

John L. Oneal was born December 26, 1834, in Bedford County, Tenn., and is a son of Wiley and Phebe (LaRue) Oneal. His paternal grandfather was born in Virginia, of Irish parents, and was a soldier in the Revolution. The maternal grandparents were natives of Virginia, who immigrated to Tennessee in an early day. Wiley J. Oneal, the father, was born and reared upon a farm in Bedford County, Tenn., and during the late war served in the Confederate army. After being discharged in the Indian Territory he went to Texas, where he immigrated in 1860, and there died in 1884, aged seventy-four. Mrs. Oneal was born in Marshall County, Tenn., and died in Sebastian County, Ark., in 1872. She was the mother of eleven children. The following seven are living: John L., Jasper N., Andrew J., Tennessee C., R. J., Mary E. and Wiley I. B. Those deceased are William T., James M., Clara E. and an infant. John L. lived, until October 15, 1854, in his native country, where he received a common-school education; then he immigrated to Newton County, Mo. A year later he settled in Franklin County, Ark., where Charleston now stands, and there farmed until September, 1861. He then went to Texas, and enlisted in Company D, Thirteenth Texas Volunteer Infantry, serving until the close of the war on station duty on the Brazos River. He then farmed in Van Zandt County until 1868, since which time he has been a resident of Sebastian County, Ark. In 1855 there were but few white settlers, and there were few schools and churches. He now owns 160 acres of land, eighty being cultivated, and is exclusively engaged in agriculture. January 30, 1856, he married Nancy M. Johnson, of Newton County, Mo., who was born in Davidson County, Tenn. This marriage has been blessed with seven children: William W. B., Pinkney A., Clara T., Robert L., James T., Phebe E. and Minnie L. Mr. Oneal has been a member of the Missionary Baptist Church over thirty-eight years, and his wife is a member of the same church. He is a strong Democrat, and has served two terms as school director, although not desirous of public office.

Dr. Reeves M. Osborne was born in Johnson County, Tenn., in 1846, and is the eldest of three children born to Dr. John K. and Ellen K. Osborne, natives of Virginia and North Carolina, respectively. The parents were married in North Carolina, and lived in Tennessee until about 1853, when they removed to Whitfield, Ga. In 1874 they went to Johnson County, Ark., where the father died the same year and the mother still lives. Dr. Osborne was a graduate of the Philadelphia Medical College, and for over twenty-two years was a practicing physician. During the late war he served about three years as surgeon of a

North Georgia regiment in the Confederate army. He was a member of high standing in the Methodist Episcopal Church, to which his wife belongs. The grandfather of our subject George Osborne, served as a colonel in the Mexican War, and lived in Virginia his entire life. Reeves M. Osborne is a self-educated man, who paid for his schooling by clerking and teaching. When but eighteen he joined Company A, of a Georgia engineer corps, and served until the close of the war, surrendering in North Carolina. He operated the most of his eighteen months' service in Tennessee and Georgia, occupying the office of sergeant. In 1869 he began to study medicine with his father and Dr. Hunt, of Georgia, and in 1870–71 attended the medical department of what is now Vanderbilt University, of Nashville. Graduating in 1871, he attended a course of lectures the same year at the Atlanta (Ga.) Eclectic Medical College. He has now practiced his profession successfully in Arkansas over seventeen years, having come to Johnson County in 1872. In April, 1887, he left that county to go to Hackett City, and from there he went to Mansfield, where he engaged in the drug business with Dr. Jackson. In 1888 he came to Huntington, where he is already well and favorably known. He is a subscriber and constant reader of the best medical journals of the day, and even when at college he prepared notes and formulas from the most eminent and popular writers. He was married in Johnson County, in 1874, to Johanna Perry, who died in 1878, leaving two children. In 1882 he married Ida, daughter of John M. Adkins, formerly of Tennessee, in which State Mrs. Osborne was born. This marriage has resulted in three children. Mrs. Osborne has been a member of the Methodist Episcopal Church since her youth, and Mr. Osborne worships at the same church. In politics he is a Democrat, and he belongs to the Masonic fraternity.

Capt. George E. Otis, of Mansfield, Sebastian Co., Ark., was born in Wisconsin in 1849, and is a son of Joseph and Maria E. (Smith) Otis. The father was born in the "Green Mountain State" in 1809, and at an early day removed to Wisconsin, thence to Minnesota in 1855. Here he made his home until 1879, when he moved to Dakota Territory, and after residing there until 1888 came to Sebastian County, Ark. They were the parents of two children: George E. and Ada (Mrs. Graves, of Minnesota). George Otis spent his early days in Minnesota, and received his rudimentary education in the common schools, supplemented by an attendance in the high-school at Chatfield, Minn. He studied civil engineering in the field, and began working at that occupation as chainman, and since his residence in Arkansas, has been "locating engineer" on the 'Frisco Railway about six years, the location of the Mansfield branch being a portion of his work. Since taking up his abode in Mansfield he has been engaged in the wholesale flour business, and also in the fruit and cotton business. He is a Mason, and a stanch Republican in politics.

Frank Parke, a resident of Fort Smith, Ark., was born in County Leitrim, Ireland, July 11, 1829, and is the son of Thomas Parke, and grandson of John Parke, who was born in England, and who owned property in that country. Later he immigrated to Ireland, where he died. Thomas Parke, was born in Ireland, and here passed his entire life. He was the owner of considerable property, and married Miss Mary McGarry, who was born in Ireland, and who became the mother of twelve children, of whom Frank Parke is the youngest. The family came to America in 1849, settling in the State of Ohio, and here the mother died in 1875 at the age of ninety-four. The father died when Frank Parke was a young man. Previous to coming to America the latter followed merchandising, which he continued until the time of his leaving his native country. He located in Ohio, remained there three years, and then came to Fort Smith, where he followed merchandising until the outbreak of the Civil War. He then enlisted in the Confederate army as a private, and resigned at the close of the war as a major of the quartermaster's department. After the war he followed mercantile pursuits in the Choctaw Nation for several years. Returning to Fort Smith in 1873, he engaged in merchandising under the firm name of Parke & Sparks. The firm was very prosperous, and was dissolved on account of the ill health of Mr. Parke, who for many years suffered greatly from inflammatory rheumatism, but has been entirely cured by the use of the waters of Biswell Springs, he having erected a cottage there in the summer of 1887, where with his family he has a beautiful summer resort. Mr. Parke is one of the largest real estate owners in the city, and owns valuable suburban property, and over 2,000 acres of the best coal lands in the county of Sebastian. He was married to Miss Sarah J. Ish, a native of Washington County, Ark., and a granddaughter of one of the early pioneers of Tennessee, who was killed by the Cherokee Indians. Her father was one of the early settlers of Washington County, Ark. Nine children were born to Mr. and Mrs. Parke, six of whom are now living : Myrtle, wife of Martin T. Dyke; Frank, Mary, Lady, Phœbe and A. H. Winfield Parke. Myrtle graduated at the Arkansas Female College, Little Rock, Ark., Frank graduated in law in 1888 at the Vanderbilt University at Nashville, Tenn., and Mary was a graduate of Nashville College for Young Ladies in 1887, and took a post graduate course in 1888. Lady is now attending Nashville College for Young Ladies, and the two youngest children are attending the public schools of this city. The children deceased were named Lillie May, Lalla Rookh and Jane. When Mr. Parke discontinued merchandising he turned his attention to the real estate business. He is a Democrat and a Prohibitionist; is a member of the Masonic fraternity, and is a member of the Methodist Episcopal Church, South. His father, grandfather, and his ancestors as far back as the days of the Wesleys, were Methodists.

Hon. Robert T. Powell, of Greenwood, is a native of Bedford County, Tenn., and was born in 1853, to the marriage of Judge Richard H. and Jane Taylor (Temple) Powell. The father was born near Petersburg, Va., in 1826, and is of Irish-Scotch-Welsh extraction. At the age of five years he went to Tennessee with his father, Thomas Powell, who died about 1854. Judge Powell was married in Bedford County, Tenn., to Miss Jane T. Temple, who was born in the last named county in 1831. She died in 1870. The Judge moved to Arkansas, and since becoming a resident of this State has resided in Independence and Izard Counties. He was in the late war, and was a captain; was captured in Independence County, Ark., and was held a prisoner at Johnson's Island during the greater portion of the war. He is an attorney by profession; was educated in law at Cumberland University, at Lebanon, Tenn., and commenced his practice at Louisburg, Tenn. In 1860 he moved to Arkansas, began practicing at Batesville, and soon became distinguished in his profession. He was a member of the Legislature from 1862 to 1866, and was elected circuit judge of the Seventh Judicial District in 1866. In the year 1878 he was re-elected to the same office in the Third Judicial District, and was re-elected in 1882 and 1886, the district now being the Fourteenth. Judge Powell has served constantly for the last ten years, and at the last election had no opposition. He is a man of prominence and a person of eminent legal ability. He has been married three times, and is the father of eight children living, six by the first wife and two by the last. Robert T. Powell was the second child born to the first marriage. He was educated at La Cross Academy, in Izard County, and then attended the North Arkansas College, at Batesville. At the age of twenty-one he became a disciple of Blackstone under his father's instruction, and in 1879 he entered the law department of Vanderbilt University, at Nashville, Tenn., where he remained seven months, being admitted to the bar at Nashville, Tenn., in 1880. The same year he returned to Arkansas, going to Fort Smith, where he was admitted to the bar. On October 3, 1880, he came to Greenwood, Sebastian County, opened an office, and has since been actively engaged in the practice of his profession. Mr. Powell is Democratic in his political opinions, and in October, 1882, was appointed deputy county clerk of Sebastian County, and served two years. He has devoted the greater portion of his time to the practice of law, and in connection he deals in real estate. Hon. Robert T. Powell is one of the leading attorneys of Sebastian County, and a man universally respected. March 21, 1883, he married Miss Ida M. King, a daughter of E. W. King, and a native of Virginia, born in 1855. They are the parents of one child, Arte Lee. Mr. Powell is the owner of 800 acres of land, and good town property in Greenwood and Fort Smith; is a Master Mason, is an ancient member of the I. O. O. F., belongs to the K. of H., and his wife is a member of the Methodist Episcopal Church.

Prendergast, McShane & Co. The topmost round in the ladder of success in any undertaking can only be obtained by individuals of decided character and a masterful knowledge of the business to be undertaken, coupled with steady and persistent energy. All these characteristics can be found in the persons of William Prendergast and P. E. McShane, of the Arcade Dry Goods House of Prendergast, McShane & Co., Fort Smith Ark. This firm occupy a building over 100 feet deep, and proportionately spacious, on Garrison Avenue, in the central mart of the city. They keep an army of hands busy waiting on the crowd of customers that constantly throng their store. This is one of the new and prosperous firms of Fort Smith that have helped to lift it out of the old ruts and make it a prosperous and pleasant city. This firm opened business on March 1, 1887, and after having doubled the original capacity of their building they find it still inadequate to accommodate the trade, and meditate enlarging it. Their first year's business amounted to over $75,000, and the second year will increase that amount by 50 per cent. They carry an average stock of about $40,000. P. E. McShane was born in County Donegal, Ireland, December 25, 1859, and was educated in the national schools of his native country. His natural inclination for mercantile pursuits manifested itself early in life, as he spent four years with his uncle, Con. McShane, merchandising in Carricktown, Ireland, before coming to America. Thus his natural proclivities for his favorite pursuit were early trained by actual application. He bid farewell to home and friends September 15, 1880, and on the 17th of the same month sailed from Londonderry for America, landing in the great metropolis of the United States ten days later. He came direct to Prescott, Nevada Co., Ark., where he met a relative with whom he went to Pittsburg, Camp County, of the "Lone Star State," where he engaged in merchandising for three years. He then sold out his stock of goods at that place and went to Texarkana, where he sold goods for the firm of O'Reilly & O'Dywere for a short period. In March of 1887 he came to Fort Smith, and became a member of the present firm, where marked success has attended his efforts. Mr. McShane is the son of Patrick and Anna (Byrne) McShane, and the McShanes have been farmers in County Donegal, Ireland, for generations back. Patrick and Anna McShane are the parents of ten children, seven sons and three daughters, and are now living in their native country. Four of their sons have come to America, and James and John are merchandising in Texarkana. P. E. McShane is a Democrat in his political views, belongs to the Catholic Church, and is a member of the Catholic Knights of America. William Prendergast, of the above mentioned firm, was born in County Killkenney, Ireland, and is the son of Michael and Kate (Henlohan) Prendergast. The father was a farmer, and followed that occupation through life. The Prendergast family came originally from France, and settled in Ireland at the time of the invasion of the English to that country. Michael and Kate Prendergast became the parents of five children, all now living, and William Prendergast being the youngest. He is the only one of the family who has immigrated to America, and being naturally endowed with a shrewd business talent and a high conception of personal liberty, he resolved to break the ties that bound him to home, and risk his chances in the Republic of the United States of America. He reached this country in 1880, settling in the city of Chicago, where he served as a clerk in one of the principal dry goods houses in that city for two years. Leaving that position he went to St. Louis, from there to Texas, and finally to Fort Smith, where in March, 1887, he entered and became a member of the above mentioned firm. He is a member of the Catholic Knights of America, and is a first-class business man.

Thomas A. Putnam was born April 26, 1845, in Hall County, Ga., and is a son of Berry B. and Martha F. (Tate) Putnam, natives of Georgia. The father was married in his native State, and from there immigrated to Johnson County, Ark., where he remained two years. He then lived four years in Franklin County, Ark., and after spending another year in Grayson County, Tex., settled in Sebastian County, where he has since lived. During the war he served two years in Company H, Second Arkansas Cavalry, being discharged at Memphis, Tenn. He also fought in the Florida War. He is a Republican, and has served as justice of his township. He is now seventy years of age. Mrs. Putnam was born February 23, 1828, married in 1844, and died October 2, 1864. She was the mother of nine children, four of whom are living, viz.: Thomas A., Mary A. (wife of James P. Frye), Nancy M. (wife of John Luck) and Eliza J. (wife of J. A. Wilburn). Those deceased are George R., William E., Leonidas, Martha B. and an infant. In 1866 Mr. Putnam married Sallie Cardin, who has borne him one child, Millie, wife of Lon Carson. The paternal grandparents of our subject were of German-Irish descent, and natives of South Carolina, where they spent their entire lives. The maternal grandparents passed the greater part of their lives in Georgia. Thomas A. Putnam was reared upon a farm in Arkansas, receiving but a common-school education, and when sixteen years old joined Company F, Seventeenth Arkansas Volunteer Infantry, Confederate Army. He fought in the engagements at Pea Ridge, Corinth and Iuka, and after two years' service was discharged at Port Hudson, La., in March, 1863. He then returned to Fort Smith, and after the death of his mother went to Illinois, where he remained one year. He then returned to Sebastian County, and January 20, 1869, married Martha H., daughter of Castleton and Mary Ward, natives of Alabama. Mrs. Putnam was born in this county, and has borne six children: Vanonar V., Larosa L., Annie M., Pearl, Willie O. (deceased), and an infant, now deceased. Mr. Putnam lived within a mile of his present place until 1878, and then bought the farm he now owns. This contains 220 acres, eighty being under cultivation. Both himself and wife belong to the Methodist Episcopal Church.

Bernard Quante, retired farmer in Fort Smith, Ark., was born in the Kingdom of Prussia, Germany, in 1827, and is the son of G. and Theresa (Vieth) Quante. The Quante family lived in Prussia for many generations back, and the family are the descendants of some of the oldest and best families in Germany. G. Quante was born in Prussia in 1789, and was an architect by occupation. His father was also an architect and carpenter by trade. Mrs. Theresa (Vieth) Quante's people have also lived for generations in Germany. Bernard Quante was educated and grew to manhood in his native country, and at the age of twenty-one years entered the German army, and served three years in the German Revolutionary War, in the Prussian army, from 1848 to 1851. When the war closed he came to America, and landed in New Orleans in August, 1852. He remained only two days in New Orleans, and went to Galveston, Tex., but after a few days' absence returned to New Orleans. From there he went to St. Louis, then to Cincinnati, and at the last named place worked at the carpenter's and architect's trade for nearly a year. He then went to Dubois County, Ind., and resided there for seventeen years. He was there at the time of the Know-Nothing massacre, and after that exciting time he engaged in the carpenter's trade, and built St. Ferdinand's Church at Ferdinand, Dubois; St. Joseph's Church at Josephstown, Dubois; St. Henry's Church at St. Henry, Dubois County; St. Boniface, in Spencer County, Ind., and St. Anthony's Church at St. Anthony, Benton Co., Ind. Mr. Quante moved to the last named county, and remained there for ten years. He has traveled over all the Northern States. He was drafted into the Union army, and sent a substitute. He then traveled westward to look at the country, and then northward until the great Father of Waters dwindles to almost nothing, and here he met "Hole-in-the-day," chief of the Chippewas, who said: "Whites have nothing to do here." Mr. Quante replied that he was recommended to come by a missionary, Father Piers. The chief then welcomed him. He came to Arkansas in 1877, and settled on the prairie in Upper Township, Sebastian County, where he is now the owner of over 800 acres of land, besides considerable town property. Mr. Quante was married in Dubois County, Ind., to Catherine Lesch, who was born on the Rhine, in Germany, in 1840, and who became the mother of fifteen children, thirteen now living: Mary, Frank, Henry, Joseph, Kate, Anton, Florenza, Christ., John, Annie, Ernest, May and Bennie. Two are deceased; the eldest son, Benoid, died at the age of about twenty years, and seemed to be a strong and hearty man; Barbara died when an infant. Mr. Quante is a Democrat in politics, and a member of the Catholic Church.

W. T. Quinley, senior partner of the furniture firm of Quinley & Co., was born in Haywood County, Tenn., in 1851, and is a son of R. B. and Amandy J. Quinley. The father served in the Civil War under Col. Adams, participating in a number of skirmishes, and in 1878 located in the northwestern part of Arkansas, where he died in 1882. Two sons and three daughters born to the parents of our subject are now living. W. T. Quinley was educated at Brownsville, Tenn., and after coming to Arkansas for fourteen years worked at the carriage and wagon trade. In 1886 he sold his business, and came to Hackett City in the month of March, where he established a grocery store, doing business under the firm name of McBride & Quinley. A year later this firm was succeeded by Bolton & Lackey, and then Mr. Quinley went into the undertaker's business. In a short time he added furniture to his stock, and he now carries about $4,000 worth of goods, doing the largest furniture business in the city. In 1874 Mr. Quinley married Miss E. E. Peale, of Crockett Mills, Tenn., who died in 1886. She was the mother of one child, also deceased. In 1887 Mr. Quinley married

Mrs. E. G. Clark, of this city, who is a member of the Baptist Church, to which Mr. Quinley also belongs. Mr. Quinley is a Democrat in politics, and in 1886 served as postmaster of this city. In 1887 he was elected alderman. He is a well-to-do citizen, and owns 240 acres of land in Mississippi County, of this State. He is one of the largest land-owners of Hackett City, owning the building he occupies, a half interest in the one adjoining, and a half interest in the brick store occupied by the Kansas & Texas Coal Company, besides being a stock-holder in the hotel at Hackett City. He also has several town lots and a half interest in the brick-yard.

John Ray, farmer and stock raiser, was born in Tuscaloosa County, Ala., in 1832, and is a son of Hamilton and Polly (Moses) Ray, natives of South Carolina and Georgia, respectively. They were married in Alabama, and when our subject was a small boy removed to Itawamba County, Miss., where their respective deaths occurred in 1880 and 1861. Mr. Ray was a farmer by occupation. He lost his father when a small boy living in South Carolina, but his mother afterward married and removed with the family to Georgia. Mr. and Mrs. Ray were members of the Missionary Baptist Church, and to them a family of thirteen children were born, of whom our subject is the second. He, with a brother, Alfred, are the only survivors. He was educated at the country schools of early days, and in 1855 married Martha J., daughter of Ezra and Lucinda Brown, and a native of Ringo County, Ala. This marriage was blessed with ten children, of whom five sons and two daughters are living. One daughter, Mary Lucinda, was killed, while at home, by a cyclone, April 18, 1880. In 1859 Mr. Ray removed to Hempstead County, Ark., and in 1871 located upon his present place in Sebastian County, which was then a wilderness. He owns 200 acres, and has cleared and cultivated 100. He also cleared a farm while in Hempstead County. During the cyclone of 1880 all of his buildings and a great deal of timber was destroyed. The house was blown from the floor, and all the inmates injured to some extent, one daughter being killed, as above mentioned. During the war Mr. Ray served four years in the Confederate army, having enlisted in Company F, Twenty-fourth Arkansas Volunteer Infantry, in 1862. In January, 1863, he was captured at Arkansas Post, and taken a prisoner to Camp Douglas, at Chicago, where he was held three months. He was then taken to City Point, Va., and exchanged, after which he joined his old company in the Army of Tennessee, under Gen. Bragg. He served in the battles of Chickamauga and Mission Ridge, and after the latter battle returned home. He also fought in many skirmishes, but was never wounded. Mr. Ray cast his first presidential vote for Buchanan, and has voted the Democratic ticket since. He has been a Mason for about eighteen years, and joined the Missionary Baptist Church prior to his marriage. Mrs. Ray is also a member of that church.

James H. Reed, superintendent of the United States court-house and post-office, was born in Crawford County, Ark., in 1836, and is a son of Jesse and Sarah (Lloyd) Reed. The former was of Irish descent, and born in McNairy County, Tenn. He was a builder and brick-layer by trade, and in 1839 came to Fort Smith, where he was engaged in building the garrison. In 1833 he, in company with his elder brothers, Hamilton and Stephen, left Memphis and traveled to Little Rock on foot. Gradually journeying west, they came to Fort Smith in the year 1839, as above stated. Passing his youth here, James H. learned his father's trade, since which time he has erected a large number of buildings, among which are the Arkansas Industrial University, of Fayetteville, the Commercial Bank, the Hotel, Main Block and McKibben Hotel and residence, the Opera House and the Morrison Building. He superintended the building of the United States jail and court-house, and has probably erected more buildings than any other man in Fort Smith. During the war he enlisted in the Confederate service, and for six months served as lieutenant in Reed's Battery, under Gen. Benjamin McCullough. He afterward joined the infantry, and served until the close of the war. His first battle was at Elk Horn. Mr. Reed has seen Fort Smith grow from a small settlement into a thriving town. He lighted the first gas lamp in the place, and opened the first mail received in the post-office here. He served in the town council some time, and was assistant postmaster two years. He was united in marriage here to Miss Martha Talula Marshall, a native of Georgia, by whom he has one daughter, Elizabeth, wife of George R. Cook. Mr. and Mrs. Reed belong to the Presbyterian Church, and he is a member of the Blue Lodge in Masonry.

James D. Richmond, farmer, was born in Chester District, S. C., in 1843, his parents being Robert G. and Louisa (Cornwell) Richmond, also natives of that State, where they were reared and married. In 1853 the family moved to Floyd County, Ga., and five years later went to Jackson (now Lincoln Parish), La. In 1867 they came to Scott County, Ark., where the father is now a well-to-do farmer. While in Georgia he served some time as justice of the peace. Gunning Richmond, the grandfather, came to America with his parents, prior to the Revolution, from Ireland, and after attaining his growth lived in South Carolina until his death. Davis Cornwell, the maternal grandfather, lived and died in South Carolina. The parents of our subject were Presbyterians in faith, and reared a family of seven sons and four daughters, of whom James D. was the second child. At the age of eighteen he joined Company I, Twenty-eighth Louisiana Volunteer Infantry, with which he participated in the famous Red River expedition. He fought at Pleasant Hill, Alexandria, Yellow Bayou and other places, and was wounded at Franklin, near New Orleans, April 14, 1862. He was then held a prisoner by the enemy until his recovery, when he was exchanged, and rejoined his company, remaining in service until the same was disbanded at Shreveport. In 1867 he accompanied his parents to Scott County, and was there married, in 1869, to Jane, daughter of Milton and Amanda Larimore, early settlers of Sebastian County, where Mrs. Richmond was born. They are now living in Scott County. Mr. Larimore was in the Government employ during the late war. In 1879 Mr. Richmond left Scott County and settled upon his present farm, which was then a wilderness. He now owns 200 acres of land, 130 of which he has cleared and cultivated. Himself and wife are Methodists. They have had ten children, six of whom are living, and who have enjoyed the advantages of a good education. Mr. Richmond is a Democrat, and his first presidential vote was cast for Seymour in 1868.

William T. Roberts, a well-to-do farmer of Prairie Township, Sebastian Co., Ark., was born in Monroe County, Miss., in 1838, and is a son of Eli and Permelia (Walpool) Roberts. The father was born in Alabama, on the 13th of December, 1808, and when a young man went to Monroe County, Miss., where he married and passed the remainder of his days, dying in 1872. His wife was born in the "Old North State," June 9, 1814, and died October 4, 1878. Five of their eight children are living: Harriet C. (widow of Thomas J. Savage), Annie C. (wife of Andrew Hawkins), William T., John C. and Jasper, all of whom are living in Monroe County, Miss., except William T. After residing with his parents until he was twenty-three years of age, he was married (in 1861) to Miss Martha Jane Gilmore, a daughter of Simeon and Lettie (Reece) Gilmore, who were born and died in Monroe County, Miss., both dying when Mrs. Roberts was quite small. She was born in Yalobusha County, Miss., in 1846, and became the mother of one child, Fannie Ella, born August 5, 1865, married, July 2, 1879, to Dr. W. L. Gillespie, and bore one child, William J., born April 27, 1880. Dr. Gillespie was born in Tennessee July 24, 1848, and died near Fort Smith, Ark., March 3, 1882. His widow was subsequently married, November 20, 1884, to W. B. Milam, who was born February 20, 1861, in this county. They have one child, Claudie Leander, born September 15, 1885. Mr. Roberts resided in Monroe County, Miss., until 1882, when he immigrated to Sebastian County, Ark., and purchased ninety-three acres of land four miles south of the county seat. He is now the owner of 243 acres of land, 120 acres of which are under cultivation. Mr. Roberts is one of the worthy citizens of the county, and in his political views is a Democrat, casting his first presidential vote for Breckinridge in 1860.

Pinckney J. Roberts, farmer and stock raiser, was born in Marion County, S. C., in 1839. His father, William D. Roberts, was born in the same county, August 29, 1806, and there married Miss L. Manning. He still lives in the place of his birth, where he has a large farm. Prior to the war he was a large slaveholder. The great-grandfather of our subject, Roger Roberts, was one of a large family, and when a boy accompanied his parents to America from Wales, prior to the Revolution. He served in that war, and then settled in the South, where many of his descendants now live. His son, Redding Roberts, was born in North Carolina, and served in the War of 1812, under Gen. Marion. He died in Marion County, S. C., in 1873, nearly a century old. The maternal grandfather of Mr. Roberts was a native of Ireland. Our subject is the third child of ten born to his parents, three being sons and the remainder daughters. He received a common-school education during his boyhood, and at the age of twenty-three, in 1862, joined Company E, First South Carolina Volunteer Infantry. He served in the Army of Virginia until the surrender at Appomattox, and was with Gen. Stonewall Jackson at the time of his death. He was wounded in the jaw in the second battle at Manassas, lost a finger at Gettysburg, and was wounded in the hip at the battle of the Wilderness. Among other engagements in which he participated were Antietam, Fredericksburg, Chancellorsville and the Seven-Days' fight. In 1866 Mr. Roberts removed from his native county to Louisiana, and the following year came to Scott County, Ark. In 1871 he married Ruth Ann, daughter of James and Mary Gregory, formerly of White County, Ga., where Mrs. Roberts was born. Mr. and Mrs. Gregory came to Arkansas in 1869, where the father died the same year and the mother is still living. Mr. Roberts settled upon his present farm in 1874, which was then in a wild and uncultivated condition. He has 170 acres in all, and devotes seventy acres to agriculture. Mr. Roberts is a self-made man, his property being the result of hard labor and economy. He is a Democrat, and cast his first presidential vote for Hancock, in 1880. He joined the Masonic fraternity November 17, 1888.

Thomas Franklin Rodden, farmer of Sebastian County, Ark., and native of North Carolina, was born in 1826, and is a son of Spencer H. and Elizabeth (Hill) Rodden. The father was born in the "Palmetto" State (S. C.) June 7, 1799, and afterward moved to Tennessee, locating first in Monroe County, thence to McMinn County. His wife was born in Virginia December 15, 1805, and died in Sebastian County, Ark., in 1880. Thomas was only an infant when his parents moved to Tennessee, and he was there reared to manhood and married, the latter event taking place in 1846. His wife, whose maiden name was Mary C. Morris, was born in 1820, and became the mother of nine children: Eliza Jane (born February 20, 1847, married Andy M. Cameron), James S. (born October 10, 1848, died March 27,1849), Elisha F. (born June 12, 1854, died February 6, 1855), George W., John B., William M., Thomas M., Joseph M., Andrew J., Winnie Berthena (deceased), Mary Jane and Alice. Mrs. Eliza Cameron left two sons at her death in 1872: James F. and Archibald W. George W. is married, and is the father of five children: Cornelius, Mary A., Thomas, Louella and Tennessee. John B. has also five children: Amanda, Eliza, Emma, Thomas and Rosa. William M. has four children: Franklin, Ora J., Charles C. and an infant. Thomas M. has one child, Frederick C., and Andrew J. also has one child, Bertha. Joseph M. is married and has two children. After his marriage Mr. Rodden located in Polk County, Tenn., and in 1850 moved to Cherokee County, N. C., where he resided twelve years, and again returned to Tennessee. In 1867 he came to Arkansas, and the following year purchased 160 acres of land in Sebastian County, on which he is now residing. He and wife have been members of the Missionary Baptist Church for the past forty years, and he has been deacon for eighteen years. He is a good citizen and an accommodating and obliging neighbor. In 1862 he enlisted in Company H, Twenty-ninth Regiment North Carolina Infantry, and was orderly-sergeant of his company. He is a Democrat in politics.

Capt. Hugh L. Rogers, of Fort Smith, Ark., was born in County Armah, Ireland, in 1812, and is an old and prominent citizen of Sebastian County. His parents, James and Alis (Cassly) Rogers, were natives of Ireland, and came to America in 1824, locating in Pittsburgh, Penn., where they both received their final summons. They were the parents of ten children. Hugh L. Rogers received a good practical education in Pittsburgh, learned the engineer's trade, went on the Ohio River, and navigated on the Mississippi and its branches for several years. He was a judicious financier, saved his money, and finally left the river, going to Washington City, where he worked as overseer for his brother, I. C. Rogers, on the Alexander Canal for some time. Abandoning this he went with his brother on the railroad from Hicksford, Va., to North Carolina, where they took a forty-two mile contract on the Raleigh & Garton Railroad. He had by this become the owner of many slaves, and when this contract was finished he moved his force into South Carolina and took a contract on the Louisville, Cincinnati & Charleston Road, and with a brother-in-law of Wade Hampton took a contract on the Central Railroad, the same road being torn up by Gen. Sherman in his march to the sea. He next moved his forces on James River Canal, Va., and took a contract that lasted one year. After this he went through to Raleigh, N. C., and gathered up the blooded horses he had been purchasing. He then made an extensive trip over the South, visiting all the principal marts, and selling all kinds of stock, including negroes. He had become the owner of some of the fastest running horses of the day, and visited the principal race courses of the country, matching races for fabulous sums. In Galena, Ill., he beat O'Kelly and Maurice O'Connell with his stock. He next went to Mineral Point, Wis., won a race and sold stock, selling one filly for $2,000. After this he went to Raleigh, N. C., and rode horseback from Nashville, Tenn., to that place. Mr. Rogers was familiarly known as one of the leading sportsmen of his day. On reaching North Carolina he found his experience as a sportsman had not been very successful financially, so he returned to the river. The first steamer he owned was the "Osprey," and on her he moved the Mormons from Nauvoo, Ill., to Iowa. He finally sunk her. He afterward owned several boats, but finally built the "General Shield," and ran her for many years, doing much shipping on the Arkansas River with her to Fort Smith. After this he made an extensive trip over the West, and saw many of the Mormons, at Salt Lake, whom he had moved some years before from Nauvoo, Ill. Capt. Rogers finally settled down in Fort Smith, where he still resides as an object of interest to all who know him. The Captain is a member of the Catholic Church.

Thomas Rogers, retail liquor dealer of Fort Smith, Ark., is a native of McMinn County, Tenn., and was born on the 30th of January, 1849. His parents, Thomas and Letitia (Wallin) Rogers, were also Tennesseeans, the father's birth occurring on the 5th of October, 1818. He was reared in his native State, and in 1837 assisted in moving the Indians west of the Mississippi River. In 1867 he moved his family to Texas, thence to the Choctaw Nation, and in 1869 reached Fort Smith, where he is spending his declining years. His wife died on the 12th of April, 1888, having borne a family of eight children, six of whom are living. She was a devoted mother, a true wife, and of noble qualities of mind and heart. Their son Thomas was in his eighteenth year when they left Tennessee, and after locating in Fort Smith, in 1879, he was married November 10, 1881, to Miss Alice Neville, who was born in Arkansas, and is a daughter of James and Mary (Nagle) Neville, who came to America from Ireland at an early day, being among the pioneers of Fort Smith. They had two children, who still survive them. Mr. and Mrs. Rogers are the parents of two children, Agnes Letitia and Mollie. Mr. Rogers began business in Fort Smith a poor man, but now owns two retail liquor stores, two business houses on the great business thoroughfare of the city, besides residence property, most of which he has accumulated by industry and close attention to business. He is a member of the K. of P., and has always voted the Democratic ticket. His family are members of the Catholic Church. He is a Protestant in belief.

Robert A. and Styles T. Rowe, attorneys at law, real estate agents and abstractors of titles, are natives of Crawford County, Ga., and Pike County, Ala., born March 5, 1857, and May 28, 1861, respectively. They are sons of Daniel and Margaret A. (Taylor) Rowe, and grandsons of Joshua and Elizabeth (Rigby) Rowe, who were natives of South Carolina, born in 1780, both of whom died on the same day in Crawford County, Ga., in 1840. Joshua Rowe was a Missionary Baptist preacher. Daniel Rowe was born in Georgia in 1822, and was of English descent. He was a farmer, and also a minister in the Missionary Baptist Church. He was married three times, his first wife being Miss Caroline Dearn, his second Miss Sarah Horn, and his third Miss Margaret A. Taylor, who was born in Crawford County, Ga., in 1832, and a descendant of Gen. Zachary Taylor. She was married to Mr. Rowe in 1856. Daniel Rowe resided in Georgia until 1857, when he moved to Pike County, Ala., and in the first of 1872 became a citizen of Sebastian County, Ark., settling one and a half miles east of the county seat. He died November 19, 1876. He was engaged in his ministerial duties the greater part of his life, and had charge of four churches in Alabama, and two in Sebastian County. His wife is yet living, and is the mother of four children: Robert A.; Daniel, who is residing on the old home place; Mary F., wife of John Carter, and Styles T. Robert A. was educated in the common-schools and in the State University of Arkansas, at Fayetteville, where he attended two years. At the age of twenty years he commenced teaching school, and followed this occupation nine terms in all in Sebastian County, meeting with good success. In 1877, or during his teaching, he began the study of law, his preceptor being Hon. C. B. Neal, and was admitted to the bar November 28, 1882, in Greenwood, Ark. He was married to Miss Jennie E. Jarrell, who was born in Rutherford County, Tenn., September 23, 1864, and who bore him one child, Mamie A. Styles T. was educated in the home schools, and at the family fireside, and at the age of nineteen he entered the teacher's profession, which he followed for three terms in Sebastian County. In 1878 he began the study of law under Hon. C. B. Neal, and was admitted to the bar the same year as his brother, Robert A. Immediately after being admitted they opened a law office, with the firm of Rowe & Rowe, and have since been actively engaged in the practice of law. They have met with excellent success, and in connection with their legal pursuits are also handling real estate. They are temperate, and are men much esteemed by all who know them. Styles T. was married May 23, 1884, to Miss Emma C. Patton, who was born in Sebastian County, Ark., August 20, 1859, and who became the mother of three children by her marriage: Prentiss E., Cherub (deceased) and Emma. For the past six years Robert A. Rowe has held the office of deputy circuit clerk for Sebastian County, and is a member of the city council of Greenwood. In 1884 he was a candidate for clerk before primary, and was defeated by nine votes. Styles T. Rowe has also held a commission as deputy court clerk for five years. Both brothers are Democrats in politics, and both are members of the K. of H. Styles T. Rowe and wife are members of the Methodist Episcopal Church, South, and Mrs. Robert A. Rowe is a member of the Cumberland Presbyterian Church. The brothers both clerked in the store of Thomas McCord, Robert A. for a year, and Styles T. for two years.

Elias Russell, farmer, blacksmith and wood-worker, of Big Creek Township, was born in Atalla County, Miss., about 1832, his parents being William and Polly (Williams) Russell, natives of South Carolina. They were married in the Choctaw Nation, Miss., where the father died when our subject was a lad. The mother died in Mississippi in 1850. The grandfather, John Russell, was born in South Carolina and died in Mississippi. The maternal grandfather, James Williams, was a full-blooded Indian, born in South Carolina, and served in the War of 1812 under Jackson. Elias Russell is an only child, and during his youth received but a limited education, as he was obliged to support his mother. When about grown he learned his trade, at which he has worked at different times since. In 1853 he went to California as a wagon-master, and until 1865 remained there working in the mines. He then engaged in teaming and stage-driving, and during the year 1865 went to Adams County, Ill., where he was married the following year to Elizabeth P., daughter of Malavary Inman. Mrs. Russell was born in Brown County, Ill., and to her union with our subject eight children were born, of whom four sons and two daughters are living. Mr. Russell has lived upon his present farm since 1868, and is one of the pioneers of this vicinity. He has 173 acres of good land, and has greatly assisted in the upbuilding of the surrounding neighborhood. Himself and wife belong to the Union Baptist Church, and have taken great pains to educate their children. Mr. Russell is a Republican, and cast his first presidental vote for Lincoln in 1860.

James Russell, superintendent of the Kansas & Texas Coal Company's Works at Huntington, was born in Scotland in 1848, and when four years of age accompanied his parents to the United States. He grew to manhood in Mercer County, Penn., receiving but a limited education, and until 1879 was employed in mines in Pennsylvania, Ohio, Indiana and Illinois. He then passed six years in the Indian Territory as superintendent of the Osage Coal & Mining Company. He then went to Ray County, Mo., and superintended the Scullin Coal & Mining Company's business, in which he still has an interest. He then went to Crawford County, Ark., where he was employed as assistant superintendent for the Western Coal & Mining Company, of the Missouri Pacific Railway, where he remained from May, 1887, until coming to Huntington to accept the above named position. In July, 1870, he married Jane Reid, daughter of Adam Reid, and a native of Mercer County, Penn., and now the mother of six children. Mr. Reid was born in Scotland, and in 1853 came to the United States. He engaged in mining all his life, and died in Mercer County, Penn., about 1874. Mr. Russell is a Royal Arch Mason, a member of the I. O. O. F. Encampment, and belongs to the United Workmen and Select Knights. In politics he is a Republican, having cast his first presidential vote for Grant in 1872. His parents, Robert and Jeanette (Calderwood) Russell, were natives of Scotland. The father was a Democrat, and died at Washington, D. C., March 11, 1862, while serving his country in Company C, One Hundred and First Pennsylvania Volunteer Infantry, aged fifty-two. The mother is now sixty-four years of age, and a member of the Presbyterian Church. Their oldest son, Capt. Thomas Russell, now a farmer at Leavenworth, Kas., was engaged in mining until a few years ago. He commanded Company F, Seventh Missouri Volunteer Infantry, United States Army, during the war, and had charge of the miners at Vicksburg, Miss., when Fort Hill was blown up. He is a member of the G. A. R., K. of P. and the societies to which our subject belongs with the exception of the order of United Workmen. James' youngest brother, John, succeeded him in the management of the Osage Mines, and is now superintendent for the Western Coal Company in Barton County, Mo.

S. M. Rutherford, deputy sheriff of Sebastian County, Ark., is a graduate of Emory and Henry College, Virginia, having completed a classical course and taken the degree of A. B. from that institution in 1883. He graduated with the second honors of his class, and bears with him from his alma mater the "debater's medal." Since leaving college he has been pursuing the study of law, and is now preparing to be admitted to the bar. In 1885 he was appointed deputy sheriff of Fort Smith District, of Sebastian County, and is still filling that position with a marked degree of success. He is a young man of brilliant attainments, and has the promise of a bright future before him. His birth occurred in Lewisville, La Fayette Co., Ark., in 1859, and he is a son of Robert B. and Sallie W. (Butler) Rutherford, grandson of Samuel M. and Eloise M. (Beall) Rutherford, and the great-grandson of W. B. Rutherford, who was born in Virginia, and moved to Tennessee about 1812, settling near Nashville, where he spent the remainder of his days. His son, Samuel M., was born in Virginia in 1797, and removed to Tennessee with his father, and in 1814 enlisted in the War of 1812, being with Jackson at the battle of New Orleans, and after the close of that war remained in New Orleans until 1817. He then sailed up the Mississippi and Arkansas Rivers until he reached a point about four miles above where Fort Gibson is now situated, where he established a trading post among the Osage Indians, and remained two years. He was the first sheriff of Clark County, being appointed September 1, 1819, and served until 1823. He then moved to Phillips County, and acted as clerk of the circuit court from 1823 to 1825, and from that date up to 1830 was sheriff of Pulaski County. He was treasurer of the Territory of Arkansas for three years, but previous to that time had represented Pulaski County in the Legislature. From 1836 to 1840 he was register of the land office at Little Rock, and at the latter date was elected presidential elector on the Van Buren ticket. In the spring of 1846 he was appointed to what was then the western superintendency of Indian affairs, by President Polk, which position he filled until the summer of 1849. He was the first representative from Sebastian County to the State Legislature (in 1851), and was county and probate judge of Sebastian County from 1854 to 1856. The following year he was appointed by President Buchanan as agent for the Seminole Indians, and held this position until the breaking out of the late Civil War, in 1861. He then retired from public life, and died on his farm in 1867 at the age of seventy years, having lived a long, useful and prosperous life. His son, Robert B. Rutherford, was born at Little Rock, Ark., and was reared in Pulaski and Sebastian Counties. He graduated from Arkansas College, at Fayetteville, in 1854, after which he became a disciple of Blackstone, and practiced his profession in LaFayette County from 1857 to 1867. At the latter date he returned to Fort Smith, where he was elected justice of the peace in 1874, and afterward served as county and probate judge two terms, commencing the duties of the office in 1878. From 1882 until 1886 he served as judge of the Twelfth Judicial District, and since that time has been engaged in the practice of law. His wife was born in South Carolina in 1837, and became the mother of seven children: Samuel M., whose name heads this sketch; William B., attorney at law and civil engineer; R. B.; Raymond P.; Jane G., wife of William B. Smith; Emmala Elise and Ethelende Butler. The mother is a daughter of Dr. William Butler, of South Carolina, who represented that State in the United States Congress in 1844, and a niece of the late Senator A. P. Butler, also a niece of the late Gov. P. M. Butler, who was colonel of the Palmetto regiment of South Carolina volunteers, and was killed in the Mexican War. She is a sister of Gen. M. C. Butler, the present United States Senator from South Carolina. Her parents were of English-Irish descent, and she is a worthy descendant of illustrious ancestors. Mrs. Rutherford is also a niece of Commodores Oliver and Matthew C. Perry, her mother being their sister.

Ashley W. Rutherford was born June 8, 1849, in Butler County, Mo., and is a son of Shelby R. and Charity (Thurman) Rutherford. The father was born in Logan County, Ky., and during his youth learned the blacksmith's trade, which he afterward followed. He immigrated to Missouri, and until 1859 lived in Butler County. He then came to Sebastian County, where he died in April, 1879. The mother was born in Blount County, Tenn., and married in Missouri. She is now living in this county, aged fifty, and is the mother of four living children: Harriet, wife of John McDaniel; Taylor, Ashley W. and Shelby R. The children she lost were Archie, James and Catherine. The paternal grandparents of our subject were born in Virginia, and in an early day immigrated to Kentucky. The maternal grandparents were natives of Tennessee, who went to Missouri. The grandfather died in Arkansas. Ashley W. Rutherford came to this county when ten years old, where he received a good education. He began farming on his own account in 1867, and January 30, 1872, married Mollie, daughter of James Lorgen. The latter went to Georgia from Virginia, and in an early day came to Arkansas. Mrs. Rutherford was born in Murray County, Ga., and died here March 8, 1888. Eight children were the result of her union with our subject: Fred, Edgar and Earl (twins), Jennie, Ida, Sammie, Ashley G. and Morton O. Mr. Rutherford is a well-to-do citizen, owning 100 acres, sixty-five of which he cultivates, and in connection with his farming is interested in general milling. Politically he is a Democrat, and as such has served his township as constable. He is a member of the Baptist Church, and belongs to the Masonic fraternity.

George Sengel was born near Strassburg, France, November 11, 1852, and is a son of John and Siloam (Metzger) Sengel, natives of Alsace, France. The father served fourteen years in the French army, and was stationed at France during the deposition of Louis Phillippe. He remained in the army from the age of twenty until thirty-four years old, and when thirty-six years of age married, coming some years after from Alsace directly to Fort Smith, with his wife and three sons, Charles, John and George. Louis, the fourth son, was born at New Orleans, and Edward was born at Fort Smith. Of this family only Charles, George and Edward survive. John Sengel, Jr., died, leaving a family of three sons and two daughters, and Louis was drowned when twelve years of age. The father died at the advanced age of seventy-eight years. When thirteen years old our subject left school to clerk in a hardware store. When twenty-five he went into business, and until 1888 did business under the firm name of Sengel & Schutte, at which time he purchased Mr. Schutte's interest. Mr. Sengel is a self-made man, and is secretary of the Fort Smith Board of Trade, presdent of the Fort Smith Home Land Company, and a director and the secretary of the Fort Smith Gas Light Company. He assisted materially in the organization of the Western Arkansas Fair Association, and until 1888 was one of its directors. He is now the treasurer of the Fort Smith Evaporating Company, president of the Hayes Ferry Company, and was a director of the Merchants' and American National Banks, both of which he helped to organize. Mr. Sengel married Miss Nannie Kirchherr, a lady of fine education, who is now the mother of three sons and one daughter: Ethel, George, Jerome and an infant. Both himself and wife are members of the Presbyterian Church, and for over twenty years Mr. Sengel has taught in the Sunday-school. He is one of the leading merchants of Fort Smith, and controls a business aggregating about $100,000 per annum. He is a member of the Chapter of the Masonic fraternity, and belongs to the German Saengerverein.

Mrs. Elizabeth (Goode) Smith. The agricultural interests of Sebastian County, Ark., are well represented by the lady whose name heads this sketch, and who was born in Alabama January 5, 1827. Her father, Holbert Goode, was also a native of Alabama, and died in 1833, and three years later Mrs. Smith removed with her mother to Arkansas, locating in Franklin County. Here Mrs. Smith spent her early life, and was married in 1845 to Pleasant W. Richardson, who was born in Georgia January 11, 1815, and a son of William Richardson. He died in 1848, leaving a wife and two children to mourn his loss: Mrs. Emily J. Smith, of Texas, and Mrs. Mary E. Colter, now residing in California. In

1851 she was married to her second husband, John W. Putman, a son of Samuel and Mary Putman (the former from Vermont), and three children, Mrs. Sarah J. Hill, Mrs, Lucy Carroll, and John H., blessed their union. Lucy's husband, Hugh Carroll, was a son of Col. John Carroll, of Carroll County, Ark. He (Hugh) and wife are deceased. Mr. Putman died in 1862. Two years later his widow wedded Augustus H. Smith, who was born in Washington County, Ark., October 8, 1832, and by him became the mother of two children, James A. and Ada G. The father of these children died in 1879; he was a son of Burt and Mary Smith. Since 1851 Mrs. Smith has resided on the farm where she now lives. She at first owned 350 acres of land, but has divided it among her children until she now owns only sixty acres. She moved to Kansas in 1864, but returned to Arkansas in the fall of 1865, where she has been contented to make her home since that time. She is a lady of rare good sense, and is noted for her liberality and charity to the poor and unfortunate.

Dr. J. D. Southard, one of the prominent practitioners of Upper Township, is a native of Franklin County, Ark., where he was born in 1861, being the son of M. and Sarah (Murrell) Southard. The father was born and reared in North Carolina, and moved to Tennessee in an early day. He is a minister in the Methodist Episcopal Church, South, and spent about ten years in Tennessee engaged in his ministerial duties. He came to Arkansas in 1858, settling in Franklin County, and here he now resides. Of the eight children born to his union with Miss Murrell, Dr. J. D. Southard is the seventh in order of birth. He entered the medical department of the University of Louisville, Ky., in 1884, and took the degree of M. D. in 1886. He also took a post-graduate course at the New York Polyclinic in 1888. After taking his degree in 1886 he came to Fort Smith, located, and has been practicing his profession since that time. He became a partner with Dr. J. W. Breedlove in April, 1887. He is a member of the county and State medical societies, of the Masonic fraternity, and of the Methodist Episcopal Church, South.

D. B. Sparks, boot and shoe merchant, at Fort Smith, Ark., was born in that city in June, 1850, being the son of Mitchell and Hannah (Bennett) Sparks. The father was a native of Dublin, Ireland, and was educated in Trinity College, Dublin Institute. He graduated in medicine, but never practiced his profession. He immigrated to America when a young man, locating at Fort Smith, where he engaged in merchandising up and down the river, and entered business with a man by the name of Miller, who was one of the leading merchants of Fort Smith for many years. Mr. Sparks was married in New York, in 1847, to Miss Hannah Bennett, a native of Massachusetts. After marriage they moved to Fort Smith, and here Mitchell Sparks died in 1864. Mrs. Sparks is still alive, and is now residing at Fort Smith. She was the mother of six children, four of whom are yet living, three sons and a daughter. D. B. Sparks was educated in Massachusetts, and afterward returned to Fort Smith, where he was for some time connected with the Elporaso Stage Company, was again associated with the transfer, and for two years was engaged in the saddler's business. He has now, for six years, been occupied in the wholesale boot and shoe business. D. B. Sparks was married to Miss Lillie Pryor, daughter of one of the early settlers of Fort Smith. Four children have been the result of this union: George, Jerry, Kate and Bennett. Mr. Sparks is a member of the A. F. & A. M., also the K. of H., and his wife is a member of the Episcopal Church.

John Speaker, retail liquor dealer of Fort Smith, Ark., was born in the Kingdom of Prussia, Germany, May 16, 1848, and is the son of Ernest and Catherine Speaker. Earnest Speaker was also a native of Germany, born in 1825, and served some time in the army in Germany. He came to America when his son John was quite small, settling in Fort Smith, and here followed the stone-mason's trade for some time. He has also followed various avocations in that city. Catherine Speaker died in Fort Smith with cholera. She was the mother of seven children, John Speaker being the eldest: J. H., L. M., Charles, Annie, Mary and Lena. The father is still living, and resides in Fort Smith. John Speaker was reared and educated in Fort Smith, and in early life followed the brick business, being a brick molder by trade. He was married, in 1875, to Miss Bettie Schuster, a native of New York, and the daughter of Anton Schuster. Of the five children born to this union three are now living: John, Mamie and Frank. Two are deceased: Nettie, who died at the age of seven years, and Charley, who died when five years of age. Mr. Speaker is a member of the Lutheran Church, and a Republican in politics.

Benjamin F. Spears, was born in Mecklenburgh County, N. C., April 8, 1836, and is a son of William and Jane (Gray) Spears. The father was born in Cabarrus County, N. C., and there learned the mechanic's trade, although he lived upon a farm until eighteen. He was also a tailor by trade, but worked at the first named trade the greater part of his life. For a short time he kept a tavern at Charlotte. He died in the prime of life, in North Carolina, in the year 1842. The mother was a native of Mecklenburgh County, where she was educated and married. She died, aged eighty-one years, on April 10, 1877, and was the mother of nine children, of whom three are now living: James M., Flornoy G. and Benjamin F. Those deceased are Washington, Wallace, Charles, Edny, Stanhop and Mary. The paternal grandfather, Wallace Spears, was born in Ireland, of Irish parents, and when twelve years old came to North Carolina, where he married Betsy Gilmor. He never heard but one minister after settling in North Carolina. His wife, Betsey Spears, was born in North Carolina, and was of Scotch parentage. Nelson Gray and Olivia his wife, the maternal grandparents, were natives of Wake County, Va. Mr. Gray had a brother who was killed in the Revolution, and two of Mrs. Gray's brothers served in the same war. Benjamin F. lived in his native county until 1847, and then went to Lafayette County, Miss., where he lived until 1879. He received a common-school education, and in April, 1862, enlisted in Company G, Fourth Mississippi Volunteer Infantry, Confederate Army. He was in the fights at Chickasaw, Vicksburg, Port Gibson, Big Black, Resaca, Franklin and Nashville, among many others. At Nashville he was captured, and held a prisoner at Camp Chase for six months. He was paroled at Vicksburg, but was afterward exchanged. He was discharged June 12, 1865, and then resumed farming in Mississippi. January 4, 1859, he married Marina M., daughter of William and Lucinda Giles, natives of North Carolina, who immigrated to Mississippi when Mrs. Spears was a child. She bore three children, McKindrey, Delia and Eugene, and died February 19, 1873, in Mississippi. December 11, 1879, Mr. Spears married Dorcas Ross, also a native of North Carolina, who immigrated to Mississippi. In 1879 Mr. Spears came to Sebastian County, Ark., where he now owns a farm of 200 acres, which he bought after renting land two years. Fifty acres he keeps under cultivation. Politically Mr. Spears is a Democrat, and himself and wife and McKindrey and Delia belong to the Old School Presbyterian Church.

Mrs. Isabella (McKamey) Spessard, of Sebastian County, Ark., was born in East Tennessee in 1841, and is a daughter of John C. and Zerelda (Tunnell) McKamey, both of whom were born in East Tennessee and died in Arkansas, where they moved in 1869. The father was a farmer, but served one year in the army in 1838. Two of their children are living: Isabella (Mrs. Spessard), and John S., a merchant of Huntington, Ark. William T. is deceased. The grandparents, John and Mary McKamey, were born in Virginia, and removed to East Tennessee at an early day. The maternal grandparents, William and Elizabeth (Worthington) Tunnell, were born in North Carolina and Virginia, in 1774 and 1781, and died in 1861 and 1862, respectively. The grandfather was a farmer, and a colonel in the War of 1812. He was sent ten times to the Legislature at Nashville, Tenn. Mrs. Spessard spent her early life in East Tennessee, and received some education in Robertsville Academy. September 12, 1867, she was married to William R. Spessard, who was born in East Tennessee, in 1844, and by whom she became the mother of seven children: Zerelda A. Lipard, William M., Nancy E. and Mary E., living, and John F., Robert L., Ada D. and William R., deceased. Mr. Spessard was a Master Mason in good standing when he died, March 22, 1880. His parents, William and Delana (Leach) Spessard, were both born in Tennessee. In 1862 he enlisted in Col. Cain's Artillery, and was captured at Cumberland Gap, and taken to Camp Douglas, Ill., but was not exchanged until near the close of the war. He then returned home and resumed farming.

Lieut. George N. Spradling, merchant of Greenwood, and ex-county clerk of Sebastian County, Ark., is a native of Hickman County, Tenn, born in 1840, and the son of Leonard and Elizabeth (Norris) Spradling, and grandson of David and Ann Spradling. Leonard Spradling was born in the State of North Carolina in 1806, and was of German descent. At the age of twelve years he moved with his parents to Alabama, and about 1822 he moved to Hickman County, Tenn., where David Spradling and wife received their final summons. Leonard Spradling was a young man when he went to Hickman County, Tenn., and here he was married about 1829. In 1842 he became a resident of Crawford (now Sebastian) County, Ark., and located eight miles north of Greenwood. He was a farmer, and entered 200 acres. In 1845 he moved and settled seven miles north of the county seat, where he passed the remainder of his days. He was commissioner of the county, and was one of three men who located the county seat, the other two being Jeremiah Bell and Green F. Bethell. This was in 1856, and was the second location of the county seat. Leonard Spradling died in November, 1858. His wife was born in North Carolina in 1806, and died two weeks previous to the death of her husband. They were the parents of nine children who lived to be grown, four of whom are now living: Ephraim, Nancy E., George N., and Martha M., wife of Thomas Wingfield. George N. Spradling was but one and one-half years old when his parents moved to Sebastian County, Ark., was reared and grew to manhood on a farm, and remained with his parents until their deaths. In 1859 he attended school, and afterward became employed as book-keeper in Fort Smith, about the time of the breaking out of the late war. In February, 1863, he went to Springfield, Mo., where he enlisted in Company E, First Arkansas Infantry, in the Federal army, and in the summer of the same year he returned with the army to his home. In October, 1863, he raised a company for the Second Arkansas Infantry, went out as private, and in a few months was commissioned as second lieutenant, and served during the remainder of the war. He was in the battle of Prairie Grove, at Jenkins' Ferry, and at the last fight was acting aide-de-camp for Gen. Edwards, who commanded the brigade. He was in the Federal army, and was discharged at Clarksville, Ark., August 8, 1865. After the war Mr. Spradling established a general store at Clarksville, Ark., but later engaged in merchandising at Greenwood, Ark. He sold out at Clarksville, and returned to Sebastian County in February, 1867, where he again engaged in merchandising at Greenwood. In 1872 he sold out, and was elected county clerk, holding that position two years. The following six years he was proprietor of a grist-mill at Greenwood, but sold the mill in 1879 and again resumed merchandising, which he has since continued. In January, 1865, he married Miss Mary A. King, of Johnson County, Ark., where she was born in 1845. To them were born nine children, four of whom are still surviving, viz.: Maggie, wife of W. J. Hodgens; Lulu, George B. and Rebecca McCord. Mr. Spradling lost his wife in February, 1888. She was a member of the Cumberland Presbyterian Church, and was an excellent woman. Mr. Spradling is a member of the Masonic order, of the K. T., a member of the K. of H., and is a Republican in his political views.

Joseph Cole Stalcup, of the firm of Garrett, Stalcup & Co., liverymen, was born in McMinn County, Tenn., February 20, 1851, and is a son of Moses and Nancy (Black) Stalcup. The father was a native of Virginia, and one of the first settlers of McMinn County, Tenn. He lived upon the farm he first cleared and located upon in that county for over half a century, and there reared a family of eleven sons and two daughters. One son was killed during his youth, while on duty at Vicksburg, serving as lieutenant of Company F, Thirty-first Tennessee Infantry. Another died at the close of the war at Jeffersonville, Ind. Seven of his sons were soldiers in the Confederate army. The Stalcup family originally came from Massachusetts and settled in Virginia, where they became well-to-do planters. The family upon the side of our subject's mother were influential people of Greene County, Tenn., being early settlers of that place. Joseph C. lived in his native county until 1869, when he left home and spent three years in Southwestern Missouri and one year in Kansas. He then engaged in farming in Sebastian County, near Fort Smith, and in 1880 was chosen by his friends to fill the position of deputy circuit clerk, and took charge of the office at Fort Smith. In 1882 he was elected circuit clerk, to which he was successively elected until 1888. He then retired from public life, and went into the livery and transfer business with Mr. Garrett. He was united in marriage at Bolivar, Mo., to Miss Fannie A. Miller, a native of McMinn County, Tenn., and daughter of the Rev. John W. Miller, a minister in the Baptist Church. Mr. and Mrs. Stalcup have one son and two daughters: Ada, a student at Baird College, Clinton, Mo.; May and Hugh. Mr. and Mrs. Stalcup have buried two children in Hackett City Cemetery, named Frank and Lilly. Both himself and wife are members of the Baptist Church, in which the latter is an active worker. He is a Master Mason.

J. R. Stephens was born near Petersburg, Va., August 8, 1858, his parents being William and Mary (Stacey) Stephens. The father was a native of Virginia, and a builder by occupation and trade. In 1839 he removed to Tennessee, and there J. R. Stephens grew to manhood and began to learn his father's trade. At the age of seventeen he went to Sherman, Tex., and there, with an elder brother, completed his trade, which he followed until the breaking out of the war. He then enlisted in Company C, Eleventh Texas Volunteer Cavalry, and served throughout the war, being on detached duty in the South and West the last two years. After peace was declared he returned to Sherman, but in 1868 came to Fort Smith, where he has since been prominently identified with building interests. Among the many buildings he has erected may be mentioned the Belle Grove school-house, the Peabody school, the New Hope school building and the residences of D. B. Sparks, Herman Bair, Frank Bolinger and F. J. Klein. Mr. Stephens was united in marriage in Texas to Miss Mary Akhalt, a native of Maryland, and daughter of M. L. and Elizabeth Akhalt, also natives of Maryland. Mr. and Mrs. Stephens are active members of the Methodist Episcopal Church, South. They have one daughter, Lillie, a young lady of excellent literary and musical attainments. Mr. Stephens is a K. of H.

Elam H. Stevenson, M. D., was born in Giles County, Tenn., near Pulaski, July 22, 1856, and is a son of Willis M. and Eliza T. (Abernathy) Stevenson, and is of Scotch-Irish descent. His ancestors first settled in North Carolina before the Revolution, and his grandfather, Elam Stevenson, was a minister of high standing in the Methodist Episcopal Church. The maternal grandfather was one of the pioneer settlers of Giles County, Tenn. Our subject was one of a family of five sons and four daughters. He passed his boyhood at home, and first began to study medicine with W. Slaughter, M. D., a physician of high standing, A year later he entered the Eclectic Medical Institute, at Cincinnati, from which he graduated in the winter of 1879–80. He then practiced his profession in Kerrville, Tenn., until 1881, at which time he located in Beebe, Ark. Since 1883 he has enjoyed a lucrative practice in Fort Smith. He is a self-made man, having paid his own way through college, and is one of the respected citizens of this place. While but a young man he became identified with the Methodist Episcopal Church, South, and is one of the active members of that denomination at Fort Smith. He was married in Tennessee to Miss Cleopatra, a daughter of Dr. Slaughter, and an accomplished lady. They now have two children; Eugene and Wyatt. Mrs. Stevenson is deeply interested in the progress of the women's temperance work in this city, and also belongs to the Methodist Episcopal Church. Dr. Stevenson belongs to the I. O. O. F., the National and State Eclectic Associations and the American Legion of Honor.

Adam Stinebaugh, farmer, of Prairie Township, was born in Lincoln County, Mo., in 1821, his parents being Jacob and Nancy (Cannon) Stinebaugh, who were born in Pennsylvania and Kentucky, respectively. They were married in the latter State, and in 1819 removed to Lincoln County, Mo., living there until 1850, from which time they made their home in Dallas County until the war. They then returned to Lincoln County, and after peace was declared removed to Texas. There the father died, about 1882, aged eighty-seven. The mother died some years previous. Both were members of the Baptist Church. Mr. Stinebaugh was a skillful mechanic. The grandfather, Jacob, was born in Germany, and with nineteen others joined the English army during the Revolution, with the intention of coming to America, and as soon as possible deserting the English army to join forces with the colonists, in which project they were successful. Mr. Stinebaugh settled in Pennsylvania when the father of our suject was a boy; he next went to West Tennessee, and later settled in Kentucky, where he died. The maternal grandfather was born in South Carolina, and became a pioneer of Lincoln County, Mo., where many of his descendants now live. Adam Stinebaugh is the oldest of a family of ten children, and during his youth received a common-school education. In 1884 he married Mary Daniels, in Lincoln County, who was a native of Fauquier County, Va. She died in Sebastian County in 1876, leaving seven daughters and two sons, who married and reared families. Two have since died. In 1882 Mr. Stinebaugh married Mary E. Cloppon, who was born in Arkansas, and is the mother of four children. In 1845 Mr. Stinebaugh removed to Dallas County, Mo., and in 1850 spent some months in California. He returned home on account of his health, making the trip via the Isthmus of Panama. During the winter of 1850–51 he traveled in

Central America, familiarizing himself with the customs and social habits of the people of that country. After an interesting and eventful journey homeward, he taught school a few years in Dallas County, and engaged in cattle dealing. From 1859 until 1868 he farmed and dealt in stock in Texas, and then came to Sebastian County. He has always lived in the same vicinity, and by the exercise of business ability and industry has accumulated a fortune. He is an experienced cattle dealer, and for fifteen years drove cattle and horses from Texas to this county, sometimes making four trips in one season. He probably handles as much stock as any other man in the county, and is the owner of 600 acres of land, besides property in Dayton, where for a year he sold goods. He is a Democrat, as his father was before him, and although a public-spirited man has never desired public office. He has been a member of the Baptist Church over forty years, and holds a license to preach, but has never done so. He is a member of the Masonic fraternity of thirty years' standing, and has taken most of the degrees conferred by that order.

Capt. Hubbard Stone, merchant, was born in Cincinnati, Ohio, February 20, 1827. His father, Wilmot Stone, was born in Guilford, Conn., of an old New England family, and in after life engaged in shoemaking in Cincinnati. The mother was Miss Ann Eddy, a native of Vermont, and a lady of character and energy. Our subject was reared in the place of his birth, and in 1850 joined a company of 130 who started by water for California. He remained in that State, engaged in mining and merchandising, until April, 1854, when he returned home and sold goods until 1856. He then went into the hardware business at Keokuk, Iowa, and in 1857 began to deal in real estate. Upon the outbreak of the war he joined the Union army as a private. He was afterward made sergeant-major and then first lieutenant of Company A, Fifty-Seventh Ohio Volunteer Infantry. After the fall of Vicksburg he was made captain of Company H of the same regiment. He was wounded by a shell at the battle of Resaca, and was disabled at the battle of Ezra Church, near Atlanta, Ga. After the war he again returned to Cincinnati, and in 1865, on April 1, landed at Fort Smith, where he has since been engaged in the mercantile business. He is a well-to-do man, although he has twice suffered heavy losses. He was married in Cincinnati to Miss Miriam E. Meader, daughter of Daniel F. Meader, a furniture manufacturer and dealer of Cincinnati. Mr. and Mrs. Stone have an adopted daughter, Bettie, now the wife of Howard B. Wier, and a lineal descendant of Wade Hampton, of South Carolina. She has two children, Hubbard Stone and Mary. Mr. Howard B. Wier is a son of the Rev. Wier, of the Methodist Episcopal Church, South (of Mississippi). For twelve years he served as a school director of Fort Smith, during which time he assisted in obtaining from the Government a donation of 365 acres of land in the Government reservation for school purposes. He is a director and stockholder in the First National Bank and the Water Works Company, and has served as secretary of the latter association. He is treasurer of the Western Arkansas Fair Association, and one of its leading spirits. Both himself and wife are active members and liberal donators to the Presbyterian Church. He is a member of the G.A.R., K. of H. and A. F. & A. M.

Henry Suratt, captain of police at Fort Smith, was born at Corinth, Miss., June 12, 1850, and is a son of William and Amanda (Harris) Suratt. The father was born in France, and came to America with his parents, who settled near Huntsville, Ala., where he grew to manhood. In 1844 he was married, and in 1872 came to Arkansas, locating at Arkadelphia, where he still lives. He served throughout the entire war. Capt. Suratt attained his growth in Mississippi, and early in life engaged in farming near Corinth. He served two years during the war in company A, Nineteenth Tennessee (Confederate)Cavalry, commanded by Col. Jeff. Forrest. After 1870 he farmed in Arkansas five years, and then for nine years clerked for William Breen at Fort Smith. He then was employed as receiving and billing clerk by Echols & Johnson for two years. In 1885 he was elected city marshal, which position he held two terms, or until made captain of the police. Mr. Suratt married Miss Belle Harrison, daughter of Willis Harrison, of Alcorn County, Miss., a descendant of Gen. W. H. Harrison. His parents, Luke and Mary Harrison, were from Ireland, and early settlers of Alabama. They died in Alabama. To Mr. and Mrs. Suratt three sons and two daughters have been born: Clara, Willie, Ernest, Mary and Albert. Mrs. Suratt is a member of the Methodist Episcopal Church, South, and Capt. Suratt is a Knight of Honor.

Col. Mark T. Tatum, general merchant of Greenwood, is a native of Dallas County, Mo., where he was born in 1836, and is the son of Eaton and Charlotte B. (Reynolds) Tatum. Eaton Tatum was born in South Carolina in 1792, and was of Scotch descent At the age of eighteen years he went to West Tennessee with his brother, Wilkins Tatum, and here married Miss Charlotte B. Reynolds, who was born in West Tennessee in 1810. About 1828 they moved to Dallas County, Mo., and in 1843 became a citizen of Sebastian County, Ark., locating at Jenny Lind, five miles northwest of the county seat. He here entered 160 acres of land, and here resided until 1862, when he sold out, and moved two miles east. He was a trader and speculator in lands, and owned about 500 acres the greater portion of the time. He died in 1872. His wife died in 1852, and after her death Mr. Tatum married Mrs. Josie Little, who is now living on the old homestead. Eaton Tatum was the father of eight children by the first wife and two by the second, all now living but one. Col. M. T. Tatum was the fourth child by the first marriage, and was only seven years of age when his parents moved to Sebastian County, and virtually he has passed his entire life in that county. He remained on the farm until eighteen years of age, dealt in stock for four years, and in 1858 he was appointed deputy sheriff of Sebastian County, serving four years. In 1861 he made the assessment of Confederate taxes of Sebastian County, and May, 1862, he enlisted in Company D, Thirty-sixth Regiment Arkansas Infantry. He went out as third lieutenant, and in 1863 was promoted to the rank of major of his regiment. Later, for his bravery and meritorious conduct, he was promoted to lieutenant-colonel. He was in the fights at Helena, Jenkins' Ferry and several severe skirmishes. He was in service over three years, being paroled at Marshall, Tex. After the war he taught a term of school in Jefferson County, Tex., and in 1866 returned to Sebastian County. In 1867 he taught the public schools in Greenwood, and became employed as salesman in a general store of Neal & Kersey, for whom he worked five years. In 1874 he established a general store of his own in Greenwood, at which business he has since been engaged. In 1860 he married Miss Lucinda Cauthron, of Scott County, Ark., and daughter of Col. Walter and Bashiwa Cauthron. Mrs. Tatum was born in Scott County, Ark., in 1843, and by her marriage became the mother of twelve children, eight now living: Walter E., Marshall, Mary E. (wife of E. W. Yates), Pearl R., Tennessee, Louisa May, Thaddie and Eddie. Col. Tatum began business in Greenwood as a poor man, but by economy and industry has met with good success. He deals largely in buying cotton and produce of all kinds. In 1879 he purchased 1,628 bales of cotton, and on an average he buys 1,000 bales per year. He is doing the largest business of the kind of any man in Greenwood. He is Democratic in his politics, was postmaster for seven years at Greenwood, is a member of the Masonic order, having taken the Blue Lodge, Royal Arch and Commandery degrees, and is a K. of H. He and wife are members of the Methodist Episcopal Church, South, and he is steward and Sunday-school superintendent of the same.

William J. Teaver, farmer, was born June 27, 1862, in Little River County, Ark., his parents being James and Sarah (Jetton) Teaver. The father was a farmer by occupation, and served during the greater part of the Civil War, being a Confederate soldier. He passed the greater part of his life in Little River County, and died in 1865. The mother was born in Tennessee, but received her early education in Franklin County. After moving to Little River County she was married and bore three children: William J., Martha and Juan (deceased). The maternal grandparents of our subject were natives of Tennessee and early settlers of Arkansas. They died in 1870 and 1883, respectively. William J. came to this county when three years old with his mother, and until the death of his grandparents made his home with them. He then lived with his mother until his marriage, in 1885, to Rosa S., daughter of Robert and Josephine McClendon, and born January 5, 1870. Mrs. Teaver was born and reared in Franklin County, and her father and mother were natives of Tennessee and Alabama, respectively, the latter being reared in Arkansas. Mr. and Mrs. Teaver are members of the Missionary Baptist Church, and the parents of one child, Bertie Lee, born September 18, 1887. His mother being left a widow when he was a lad, Mr. Teaver had few educational advantages, and as he was reared on the farm, he learned no trade. He is a young man of industry and enterprise, and he is now the owner of 135 acres of land, eighty-five of which he cultivates. His home place is well improved, and he also owns 100 acres of land in Little River County. Mr. Teaver is a strong supporter of the present public school system, being a school director, and in politics he is a Democrat.

Mrs. M. J. (Byrd) Thomas, an enterprising and successful lady farmer of Sebastian County, Ark., was born in Hardin County, Tenn., October 17, 1840, and is one of ten children, seven living, born to the marriage of Thomas Byrd and Maria Smith, and is a granddaughter of William Byrd, who was born in the "Palmetto State," and who removed with his family to Tennessee at an early day. His wife's maiden name was Lovey Cherry. John Smith, the maternal grandfather, was a farmer, a soldier in the War of 1812, and died in Tennessee in 1854. His father was a Revolutionary soldier. Mrs. Thomas' parents were born in South Carolina in 1812, and Tennessee in 1814, and died in the latter State in 1884 and 1864, respectively. The names of their children who are living are as follows: William R., Emeline (Bryson), Susan (Counts), Calvin C., Thomas J., Elizabeth and M. J. (Thomas). The last named was reared in Tennessee, and was there married in 1856 to James Thomas, a native of the State, born in 1837, and a son of James and Adaline (Young) Thomas, who were early immigrants to Tennessee. James, the son, was a farmer by occupation, and in 1863 enlisted in the Confederate States army, and served until the close of the war, when he returned home and resumed the peaceful pursuit of farming. In 1875 he came to Sebastian County, Ark., where his death occurred in 1881. He was a Mason, a Democrat, and cast his first presidential vote for John C. Breckinridge. He and wife became the parents of seven children: Newton S., Walter E., Mattie M., James A., Maude, Claude and Nellie.

John Marion Thompson was born in Perry County, Tenn., in 1834, and is a son of William G. and Elizabeth C. (Hagan) Thompson. The father was of Irish and Scotch descent, and was born in Mecklenburgh County, N. C., in 1804, and at the age of nine years was taken by his father, John Thompson, to Bedford County, Tenn., where he received the education and rearing of the average farmer's boy of that period, and was married in 1825. In 1852 he located in Henry County, Tenn., and in January, 1880, became a resident of Sebastian County, and on the 23d of the same month died at the home of his son, John M., having contracted a cold on his way here. His wife was born in Middle Tennessee in 1804, and died October 10, 1874, having borne a family of ten children, five of whom are living: Margaret, wife of W. L. Cole; Rebecca J., wife of Thomas Ary; John Marion, Martha K., and Amanda, wife of W. W. Holden. John Marion resided under the paternal roof until twenty-two years of age, and during the late war was one of the boys in gray. May 20, 1861, he enlisted in Company D, Fifth Regiment Tennessee Volunteer Infantry, Confederate States Army, and was a participant in the battles of Shiloh, Perryville, Murfeesboro, Chickamauga, Missionary Ridge, Atlanta, Jonesboro and many severe skirmishes. He was neither wounded nor captured during the war, and was only sick when he had the measles. He was paroled at Johnsonville, Tenn., May 23, 1865, but surrendered at Greensboro, N. C. His service extended over a period of four years and three days. After the war he returned to Henry County, Tenn., and February 22, 1866, was united in marriage to Miss Mary Ann Cole, a daughter of Joseph and Polly Cole. She was born in 1834 or 1835, and died in Sebastian County, Ark., April 24, 1885, having borne a family of five children: Emma B., wife of Harvey Oliver; Joseph E.; Lulu D., who is keeping house for her father; Albert S. and Mary M. In 1870 Mr. Thompson moved to Calloway County, Ky., and seven years later came to Sebastian County, Ark., and the following year purchased eighty-seven acres of some of the most fertile land in the county. He has since increased his land until he now owns 105 acres, and throughout the county is considered one of its foremost farmers. His farm is about six miles from the county seat, and he has a pleasant and comfortable residence. He is a Democrat in his political views.

Col. F. W. Tillay, contractor and builder, at Huntington, was born in Louisville, Ky., in 1831, his parents being F. B. and Mary E. (Gwathmey) Tillay. The father was born in Ohio, and when a boy went to Louisville, where he engaged in the wholesale mercantile business until his death, in 1851. The grandfather, John B. Tillay, came to America from France in an early day. The mother of our subject was born in Louisville, Ky., and was of Virginian descent. She died at St. Louis in 1876, where she had lived since 1853. During his youth the Colonel attended the schools of Louisville, and when his mother removed to St. Louis he accompanied her. There he married Mary, daughter of Col. Robert Renick, who has borne him two children. While in St. Louis Mr. Tillay engaged in the commission business the greater part of the time. Mrs. Tillay's father was one of the prominent citizens of St. Louis, and at the time of his death was serving as a water commissioner. He was a banker, and having graduated from West Point, he served during the war as colonel of the Missouri State Militia. Mrs. Tillay and her husband, while in St. Louis, became members of St. George's Episcopal Church. The latter is a member of the Blue Lodge in Masonry, having belonged to the fraternity since 1852. He is also a K. of H., and belongs to the L. of H. In politics he is a Democrat, his first presidential vote having been cast for Pierce in 1852.

William Franklin Turner, M. D., of Milltown, Sebastian Co., Ark., is a son of William J. and Mary A. (Nance) Turner, grandson of James Turner, and great-grandson of Jesse Turner, who was born in the "Old North State," and settled in Stewart County, Tenn., at an early day. He was a soldier in the War of 1812. Both James and his son, William J., were reared in Tennessee. After the latter had reached manhood he went to Benton County, Tenn., where he was married January 9, 1845, to Miss Nance, a native of South Carolina, born in 1824, by whom he became the father of five sons and one daughter. In 1858 his wife died, and the following year he married Hannah A. Lynch, who was born in Benton County, Tenn., October 30, 1829. Six children were also born to this union, three sons and three daughters. Mr. Turner has made farming his chief calling through life, but for two years was deputy sheriff of the county, and served as magistrate of Benton County, Tenn., three terms. In 1877 he moved to Jackson County, Ill., and four years later to Sebastian County, Ark. He has always supported the principles of the Democratic party, is a member of the Masonic fraternity, and during the late war espoused the cause of the Confederacy, and for about six months was on post duty. He was born in Stewart County, Tenn., March 20, 1821, and although sixty-seven years of age is yet strong and healthy. The youngest child by his first wife, William Franklin, was born in Benton County, Tenn., on the 9th of October, 1852, was reared on a farm, and received his literary education in the district and the Camden public schools. When about twenty-two years of age he began teaching school, and after accumulating some means began attending school again, and was alternately engaged in teaching and attending school until he acquired a thorough English education. In 1872 he was wedded to Cornelia E. Elmore, a daughter of William P. Elmore. She was born in Benton County, Tenn., January 16, 1855, and became the mother of five children, three of whom died in infancy. Those living are Clemett W. and Bertha May. The Doctor and his wife came to Sebastian County, Ark., in 1880, but after a short time returned to Tennessee, where he remained until the fall, and again took up his residence in Sebastian County. For about fifteen years he had been engaged in the study of medicine, and in 1884 entered the medical department of the Arkansas Industrial University, and after taking lectures in this institution he began practicing his profession at Milltown, Ark., and has by his own energy and meritorious effort built up a most lucrative and increasing practice. He deserves much credit for the prosperity which has attended his footsteps, as he is essentially a self-made man, and has surmounted many difficulties in his walk through life. He belongs to the Masonic, I. O. O. F. and K. of H. fraternities, and is a Democrat politically. The family attend the Methodist Episcopal Church, South.

William M. Tyler, farmer, was born in Gibson County, West Tenn., in 1837, and is a son of Roderick and Tampa (Williams) Tyler, natives of North Carolina, where they were married and lived until 1845. They then went to Gibson County, and in 1858 settled in Dayton Township, this county, where their deaths occurred in 1872 and 1887, respectively. They had for many years been members of the Christian Church. The father was a carpenter by trade, and was of Irish descent, his grandfather having come to America from Ireland and located in South Carolina, where he taught school. William M. is one of a family of eight children, of whom two sons and two daughters are living. He received but a limited education, and accompanied his parents to this county, where in 1861 he married Caroline, daughter of Hansel and Louisa Caleb, who came here from Tennessee in 1856. They died in Scott County. Mrs. Tyler was born in Tennessee, and is the mother of eleven children, eight of whom are living. Since his marriage Mr. Tyler has lived near Dayton, but has only been a resident of his present farm about a year. He owns 150 acres in two farms, all of which he has become the possessor of since the war, as he lost all his property at that time. He served a short time in the Confederate army with Capt. William Oosley, under Col. William Brooks, but was discharged at Fayetteville in 1862 on account of disability. He voted for Breckinridge in 1860, and in politics is a Democrat. Himself and wife are worthy members of the Baptist Church, and he is a member of the Farmers' Alliance. He is now a well-to-do citizen, and has given his children the advantages of good educations.

Theodore and Francis Vogel, of the grocery firm of Vogel Brothers, at Fort Smith, Ark., were born in that city in 1851 and 1860, respectively. Their parents, Trangott and Appelinia (Fink) Vogel, were both natives of Germany. Trangott Vogel was born in the Kingdom of Prussia in 1819, and is the son of William Vogel, who was also a native of Prussia, and who was forced to join the army of Napoleon when but seventeen years of age, and served under him four years. Trangott Vogel served his time in the Prussian army, and came to America at the age of twenty-four years. After staying two years in New Orleans he came to Fort Smith, where he located in 1845. He is one of the sturdy citizens now living who witnessed the gradual growth and development of the country, and who, by his unswerving energy and perseverance, amassed considerable wealth, owning some of the best property on Garrison Avenue, the central part of the city. By his marriage to Miss Fink he became the father of four children: Theodore, William, Frank and Henry. Trangott Vogel is now living a retired life in Fort Smith. He is a member of the Lutheran Church, and his wife and sons are members of the Catholic Church. Theodore Vogel supplemented his common school education with a literary course at Cane Hill College, at Boonsborough, Washington Co., Ark. On leaving school he commemced life as a clerk in a store, and in 1876 he engaged in the grocery business for himself, which he has since continued. He was married to Miss Kate Shumes, who bore him three children: Lena, Kate and an infant (deceased). Mr. Vogel is a member of the Catholic Knights of America. Francis Vogel is one of the competent business men of the city, was educated and reared in Fort Smith, where he also served an apprenticeship at the shoemaker's trade, and afterward followed agricultural pursuits for five years. He then clerked in a grocery store for two years, after which he became a member of the present firm.

Mrs. Martha J. Walker is a native of Winchester, Tenn., born on the 6th of January, 1822, and is a daughter of Capt. William M. and Martha (Baldwin) Raines. The former was a Virginian, born near Richmond, and was a merchant by occupation. At an early day he left his native State and went to Georgia, and during the Creek War acted as captain under Gen. Jackson. After the close of the War of 1812 he moved to Winchester, Tenn., being one of the pioneers of that place. Here he was engaged in agricultural pursuits, and followed the occupation of merchant tailor for many years. While in Virginia he was married to Miss Baldwin, by whom he had seven children, only four of whom are now alive: Dr. C. B. (of Mineral Wells, Tex.), Col. Henry A. Raines (deceased), Martha (Mrs. Walker), Mrs. M. B. Ake (of Las Cruces, N. Mex.) and Mrs. A. M. Ward (of Little Rock, Ark). R. P. was an eminent lawyer of Trenton, Tenn., and is now deceased. Mrs. Martha Walker came to Arkansas in 1838, and has been prominently connected with the schools of Sebastian County ever since. She has been married twice, her first husband being Dr. C. B. Ake, and in 1854 she was married to Calvin Walker, who was killed during the late war, while at home. She has one living child, Mollie, who is the wife of Edward Pennington, editor and proprietor of the Deming *Head Light*, of Deming, N. Mex. One of Mrs. Walker's grandchildren is living with her.

James S. Weaver, who has been an agent for the Kansas & Texas Coal Company, at Huntington, since 1887, was born in Maryland in 1837, and is a son of Daniel and Sarah (Wetzel) Weaver, who were born in Pennsylvania and Maryland, respectively, and married in the latter State. The father died there in 1883, and the mother in 1886, in the city of Baltimore. The father was a farmer by occupation, and of German descent. His father, Daniel Weaver, passed his life in Adams County, Penn. James S. Weaver is the eldest of a family of fourteen children, of whom eleven are living. All with the exception of one have families. James is the only one living West. He received a common-school education during his youth, and in 1858 went to Alton, Ill., where for a number of years he was interested in the grocery and grain business. While there he was married, in 1868, to Mary E., daughter of John Darneille, of Madison County, Ill., where Mrs. Weaver was born. Mrs. Weaver's father was one of the well-to-do farmers, traders and pioneers of Madison County, Ill. Since that time Mr. Weaver has been engaged in the grain or grocery business, one year at Des Moines, Iowa, Oswego, Kas., six years, and two years, at Salina, Kas. From 1879 until 1887 he engaged in the grain business at Stanberry, Mo., when he removed to near Kirkwood, St. Louis Co., Mo. Since the fall of that year he has been employed in Huntington, as above stated. Mr. Weaver has a nice home in town; in politics he is a Democrat, and his first presidential vote was cast for Douglas, in 1860.

Hon. John F. Weaver was born at Fort Smith September 11, 1849, and is a son of W. J. and Catherine (Minmier) Weaver, natives of Philadelphia, Penn., and Germany, respectively. His father was a tradesman, and was a son of Emmor T. Weaver, born in Chester County, Penn., of English parents; he was a goldsmith or jeweler. The great-grandparents of our subject were of Quaker faith, and early settlers of Pennsylvania, landing with William Penn. They were people of temperate habits and fine physique, and were engaged in agricultural pursuits. Their descendants were mostly farmers, but many became ministers and lawyers. Catherine Minmier was born in Prussia, near Minden. John F. Weaver grew to manhood on a farm in Henry County, Ill., where he received a common-school education. At the age of sixteen he began to learn the printer's trade, at Salem, Ohio, working in the office of the Salem *Journal.* After having learned his trade, he worked two years on a farm, and in 1871 came to Fort Smith, Ark. Here he worked three years at his trade in the office of the *New Era*, and then spent five years on the *Western Independent.* In 1880 he assumed the management of the paper, which became known as the *Independent Democrat*, with which he remained until 1885. He then took an active interest in the publication of the *Elevator*, with which he is now connected. Mr. Weaver has always been an active politician, and is now a representative of his county in the Legislature. He is a member of the Knights of Honor, and an honored and respected citizen.

Thomas J. Webb was born near Nashville, Tenn., in 1821, and is the oldest of four children born to Kendall and Mary (Dugal) Webb, natives of Maryland and Pittsburgh, Penn., respectively. They were married in Tennessee, where the mother died about 1834. The father re-married two years later, and then removed to where Ozark, Ark., now stands. In 1853 he went to California, where he spent about three years, after which he located in Franklin County, Ark. He was left an orphan when young, and being bound out to a Quaker in Philadelphia, learned the shoemaker's trade, which he afterward engaged in extensively. He was a prominent Mason, and died near Ozark in 1873. Thomas Webb, the grandfather, came with a brother to the United States at an early day. The maternal grandfather was of Irish origin, the name formerly having been McDugal, but it was changed by the Pennsylvania Legislature. Thomas J. Webb passed his boyhood in Nashville, Tenn., and when fifteen accompanied his father to Arkansas. In 1846 he enlisted in the Mexican War for twelve months, and served in Company D, Arkansas Cavalry, under Gen. Taylor. He was captured previous to the battle of Buena Vista, and taken on foot to the City of Mexico, a distance of 1,000 miles, where he was held a prisoner six months. In 1852 he crossed the plains to California, where he remained until 1883, engaged in mining and farming. During the late war he served three years and one month in Company L, First California Cavalry, being engaged the greater part of the time in fighting the Indians in Arizona. He had charge of supply stations several times. After returning to Arkansas from California he engaged in cattle trading for some time in Franklin County, but since 1885 has farmed in Sebastian County. By the exercise of industry and economy Mr. Webb has become a well-to-do man, and in partnership with his brother he owns 1,200 acres of choice land in this county. He is devotedly fond of reading, being well-informed on all current topics, and his library contains a number of good works by well-known authors.

J. C. Welch was born in Sevier County, Ark., on the 4th of March, 1861; was principally reared in Scott and Yell Counties, Ark., on the farm. In 1879 he entered school at Booneville, Logan Co., Ark,, and remained in school the better part of three years. After quitting school he went to Brazil Station, I. T., and entered into the mercantile business in connection with his father, D.

R. Welch, who had been doing a large business at that place as merchant and planter since 1871. After carrying on a very successful business at Brazil Station for three and one-half years, he came to Hackett City, Ark., and in September, 1886, opened a general merchandise store, and has since been one of Hackett City's leading merchants, carrying a stock of from $12,000 to $15,000, owning the store building in which he is doing business, and, besides, quite a number of valuable town lots, a fine residence, etc. October 30, 1887, he was united in marriage to Miss Mollie Forbes, daughter of Dr. J. H. Forbes, one of Hackett's leading physicians and oldest residents. One child is the result of the happy union, named Gussie.

O. D. Weldon, local editor and business manager of the Fort Smith *Weekly Elevator*, was born near Cleveland, Ohio, September 23, 1847, and is a son of Oliver and Augusta A. (Smith) Weldon. Oliver Weldon was a native of Connecticut, and a clock-maker by trade, though in his younger days he followed the life of a sailor. He was one of the inventors of the spring clock. During his early married life he lived in Connecticut, but being of a roving disposition moved to Ohio, and thence to the State of Michigan. In 1854 he traveled extensively as a peddler, and, with his two horses and watch dog as companions, made his way from Michigan to the line of the Indian Territory, and here set up a store in a log hut and engaged in trading with the Indians. While at this point he became interested in lead mine discoveries, and sent for his family, who traveled the entire distance from Dewajack, Mich., to Polk County, Ark., in a two-horse wagon, being about eight weeks on the road, his son-in-law, A. L. Strong, accompanying them. After living in Polk County about one year he drifted to Fort Smith, where he died in 1872. Augusta A. (Smith) Weldon is still living, is seventy-six years of age, and a resident of Fort Smith, so well preserved that a casual observer would not take her to be more than fifty-five or sixty. She was the mother of seven children, O. D. Weldon being her youngest child and only son, five of whom she survives. The paternal grandmother of the subject of this sketch was twelve years of age at the time of the signing of the Declaration of Independence, and lived to be one hundred years old. She was one of twelve who organized the first Baptist Church in the then town of Hartford, Conn. O. D. Weldon began learning the printer's trade in 1861, just at the breaking out of the war, in the office of the *Thirty-fifth Parallel*, a weekly paper edited and published by Gen. A. G. Mayers at Fort Smith. This paper only survived a short time after the beginning of hostilities between the North and South. Weldon remained in the Confederate lines until 1863, when the Federals, under command of Gen. Blunt, captured the place, and occupied it until after the close of hostilities. During the war he learned the butcher's trade, and assisted in slaughtering beef for the army. In 1866 he again went to work at the printing business in the office of the Fort Smith *Herald*, owned by Judge John F. Wheeler, and from that time engaged alternately in the butchering and printing business until 1877, having spent one year at Fort McKavett, on the Texas frontier, furnishing beef to the soldiers under command of Gen. Clitz. He has been constantly connected with his present paper for ten years, and previous to that was connected with the *New Era*, the late V. Dell being editor and proprietor. He was first married to Miss Elona Haag, of Fort Smith, and one child, Lorena A., was the result of this union. Mrs. Weldon died in 1876, and in 1880 Mr. Weldon married Miss Lue Brown, who bore him three children, one now living, Jimmie. One child, John Carnall, died at the age of two years, and Ollie D. at the age of five months. Mr. Weldon is the regular correspondent at Fort Smith for the New York *Herald*, Chicago *Times*, *Globe Democrat*, Fort Worth, Tex., *Gazette*, and Little Rock, Ark., *Gazette*, and occasionally writes for other papers. He is a Democrat in his political views, and his wife and eldest child are members of the Baptist Church. Mrs. Weldon is a member of the Ladies' Aid Society, and was educated at Tuscaloosa, Ala. Their daughters, Lorena and Jimmie, are members of "The Little Helpers" society.

Master Lewis Joseph White, only son of Edward S. White, deceased, was born June 27, 1881, in Louisville, Ky. His father was a native of New York City, born October 14, 1856, and was the son of Lewis Joseph White, a very prominent and wealthy capitalist, of New York, who in his younger days had been a very extensive and successful wholesale merchant in the hide and fur trade. Edward S. White came West, when a young man, to Fort Smith, and engaged in the cattle business in the Indian Nation a short time. He there met and married Miss Bessie Hurley, who was born February 19, 1860, in Ottawa, Canada, and is of Irish ancestry. Mrs. White's parents died when she was quite young, and she married Mr. White, whom she survives. One child is the result of this union. He is named Lewis, and is the heir to a large estate, consisting of all kinds of property in New York, Louisville and Fort Smith.

James C. Wilkinson, dairyman and breeder of Jersey cattle, in Sebastian County, Ark., was born in England in 1843, and is a son of Joseph and Mary (Beard) Wilkinson, who were also born in England. In 1863 James C. Wilkinson crossed the ocean as a volunteer in the United States army, and enlisted in the Sixteenth Kansas Volunteers, operating in Kansas and Missouri until the close of the war. He then went to New Mexico, as agent in charge of the Comanche Indians, and was afterward appointed sub-agent to the Cheyennes and Arapahoes. He next located in Fort Smith, Ark., where he was United States Marshal for fourteen or fifteen years, and then moved to the country in Sebastian County, where he purchased 245 acres of land, which he fenced and made into a fine dairy farm. He resides in a large two-story frame house, and his barns are commodious and convenient, there being ample room for fifty cows. He finds a ready sale for dairy products in Fort Smith, and also handles pedigreed Jersey cattle. In 1876 he was married to Miss Mary J. Majors, a daughter of Robert T. and Nancy (Petty) Majors. She was born in Sebastian County, and is the mother of five children: James C., Cassius E., Robert, Mary J. and Bertha Catherine. Mr. Wilkinson is a Knight Templar in the Masonic fraternity, and belongs to the K. of H. and the G. A. R. He is a stanch Republican, and cast his first presidential vote for Abraham Lincoln. The family worship at the Episcopal Church.

Harvey D. Wilkinson, farmer, was born July 9, 1863, in Polk County, Ark., and is the son of Benjamin J. and Sallie A. (Arbuckle) Wilkinson. Benjamin J. Wilkinson was born in Mississippi, and there lived to be grown, and was by profession a lawyer, graduating, both in the academic and law department, at Lebanon, Tenn., and establishing himself in the profession at Fort Smith with Judge Walker as his law partner. He had previously read with Judge Brown, of Van Buren, and subsequently continued in practice in Fort Smith until the breaking out of the war. Then he went to Texas, and remained there until his death in 1864. Sallie Arbuckle was born and reared in Sebastian County, on Arbuckle Island, and was educated by private tutor. Here she grew to womanhood, and married Mr. Wilkinson, and bore him one child, Harvey D. After Mr. Wilkinson's death she was married to John Jacoway. James A. Wilkinson, the paternal grandfather, was a native of Tennessee, and was there reared and married, going thence to Mississippi and Texas, returning finally to Tennessee. He is now living in Texas. John D. Arbuckle, the maternal grandfather, was born near Hopkinsville, Ky., leaving there when about twenty years of age. He remained in Missouri some time teaching school, and then came to Sebastian County, having married, however, in Missouri, Louisa Jones. On coming to Arkansas he settled on Arbuckle Island, which now bears his name. During his early life he was elected colonel in the State Militia in Kentucky. He and wife both died on the farm where our subject now lives, he at the age of sixty-five, December 8, 1873, and while occupying the senatorial seat from the Eighth District, having been elected over Col. B. J. Brown, and in an article taken from the Fort Smith paper we find the following: "The noble old man, whom the people all delighted to honor, passed away from earth to an assembly where we trust he will wear brighter than any earthly honors. Arkansas has lost a valuable representative, the community an estimable citizen, and the family a loving husband and father." Gen. Mathew Arbuckle, of Kentucky, was an uncle, and a graduate of West Point, and it was through him that Arbuckle Island was acquired by a patent from Martin Van Buren in 1839. The first court-house site of the county is now on land owned by Harvey Wilkinson, he having acquired the property through his grandfather, John D. Arbuckle. Harvey D. Wilkinson was principally reared in this county, being cared for after the death of his parents by his grandfather and grandmother, Mr. and Mrs. Arbuckle. He lived with them until their deaths, and from 1879 until 1886 attended the Fayetteville University. He is the owner of 700 acres of land, 200 of which he cultivates, the old homestead being included. In connection with his farming he is engaged in milling and ginning. In politics Mr. Wilkinson is a Democrat, and he belongs to the Masonic fraternity.

Charles H. Willhaf, manager of the mammoth store of the Kansas and Texas Coal Company, at Huntington, was born in Crawford County, Ark., in 1848, and is a son of Leonard and Mary (Beckel) Willhaf, who were born in Wurtemburg and Hesse-Darmstadt, Germany. When young they came to the United States, and after their marriage at Fort Smith they settled at Van Buren, where for years Mr. Willhaf kept a bakery and grocery store. He was a lieutenant in Yell's Arkansas regiment during the Mexican War, and one of the first merchants of Van Buren, where he died in 1866, and the mother still lives. Our subject was an only child and passed his youth in Van Buren, receiving but a limited education, and at an early age began life for himself by clerking. In 1868 he went to Oswego, Kas., where he clerked until 1881, and since that time has been employed by the Kansas and Texas Coal Company, with the exception of two years at Pittsburg, Kas., Monett, Mo., Hackett City and Huntington, Ark. He has been a resident of the last named place since August, 1887. Mr. Willhaf was married in 1876, at Oswego, Kas., to Caroline J., daughter of Isaac A. Marks, formerly of Crawfordsville, Ind., where Mrs. Willhaf was born. Mr. and Mrs. Willhaf have but one child. The former is a Republican in politics, and is a member of the Masonic fraternity.

James A. Williams was born at Dripping Springs, Crawford County, Ark., in 1836, and is a son of Hansford and Cyntitha (McDonald) Williams. His parents were married in Arkansas in 1830, and have reared a family of fourteen children. All lived to be grown with the exception of one. In 1839 the father left Tennessee and came to Crawford County, locating on Lee's Creek, where he farmed until after the war. He then engaged in the mercantile business near Hackett City until a few years ago when he again resumed farming. He now lives upon his farm with his wife, enjoying in his old age the fruits of his youthful industry. James A. Williams passed his youth in Crawford County, where he farmed until 1870. He then embarked in the dry goods business at Greenwood, but ill health compelled him to give it up. He afterward established the *Horse-Shoe*, a newspaper, of which he is still editor. In August, 1862, he entered the Southern army. He served in Company H of the Thirty-third Texas throughout the entire war, and was in the quartermaster's department, a brother of his serving in the Sixth Kansas during the war. Mr. Williams is now interested in the real estate business and owns five town lots and a handsome residence. In 1886 he was elected to the Legislature by a majority of 1,465, his opponents being Dr. H. W. Fanner and Cash Barnes, and in 1888 was re-elected to the same office by a majority of 1,100, his opponents being Thomas Lathern and Robert Claybourne. Mr. Williams is a member of the Masonic fraternity, and has for five terms served his lodge as Worthy Master. In 1858 he married Miss Malvina F. Kelly, of Kentucky, a niece of the late Winright Flanagan, of Texas. This union has been blessed with eleven children, seven of whom are living: Hansford A., Philander M., James W., Lillie E., Joseph F., Noval A. and Pauline M. Mr. Williams is a K. of H., and himself and wife belong to the Christian Church.

Hon. S. A. Williams, present mayor of Fort Smith, was born in Charleston, S. C., January 24, 1841. His grandfather, Charles Williams, though of Scotch descent, was a native of Hamburg, Germany, from whence he immigrated with his family about the year 1789 to this country, and settled in South Carolina. In religion he was a Lutheran, which faith is adhered to by the family to this day. He was a soldier in the War of 1812. His son Andrew, the father of our subject, was born in 1799, who, when twenty-five years of age, paid a visit to Hamburg, Germany, the former home of his father, and while there married, and upon his return established himself at Charleston, S. C., as merchant tailor. Samuel A., when about ten years of age, came, by consent of the parents, with his uncle, John H. Williams, to California, where the latter engaged in mining. Schools in those days being something unheard of in the mining regions of California, the uncle taught the boy at night and rainy days as best he could. About four years after their arrival in California an accident caused the death of the uncle, and Samuel A., at the age of barely fourteen, found himself, without any relatives, in a strange land with no means whatever, the uncle having been unfortunate in all his mining ventures. Making his way on foot to Sacramento City (170 miles), Samuel A. worked at anything he could get to do during the day, and with a portion of these earnings educated himself at night schools. In 1860 he went to Virginia City, Nev., and found employment as book-keeper. After the outbreak of the war in the spring of 1862, the Second

California Volunteer Cavalry passed through Virginia City on their way to the front (as they were told and believed), and Mr. Williams left his desk, and together with a number of others joined that regiment as privates. When arriving at Salt Lake City, greatly to the disgust and sore disappointment of all the troops, they were ordered to stop and build quarters, and never afterward during the war got further east than Fort Laramie, where, after four years of hard fighting with Indians on the plains, Mr. Williams was mustered out. After leaving the army Mr. Williams engaged some in grain dealing in Chicago, and in 1867 went to Kansas City, where he carried on a small mercantile business. He arrived in Fort Smith in January, 1869, where he has since resided. Here he has been engaged as deputy clerk of the State Circuit Court and of the United States Court until elected mayor of the city in 1887. He has filled a great many honorary positions in the city, among them six terms as alderman and four years as director and secretary of the school board. All public enterprises received his hearty support. He assisted in organizing and putting in operation the Fort Smith Evaporating Company, the Fort Smith Canning Company, two building and loan associations, of one of which he is still the president; also the fair association, which he served as secretary for eight years, an enterprise acknowledged to have contributed more than any other one agency to the growth and prosperity of the city. He is a charter member of the K. of H. lodge, and an active member of a number of other societies and organizations. The family, back to the great-grandfather, being practically of German descent, that language is no foreign tongue to Mr. Williams or his family, all of whom worship at the German Lutheran Church. Mr. Williams married Miss Paulina Geiger, daughter of the late Mr. William Geiger, and is the father of four sons and two daughters: Benjamin C., Annie E., Pauline M., Elias J., Oscar G. and Andrew H. In politics Mr. Williams is a Republican.

John F. Williams, sheriff of Sebastian County, Ark., was born in Ste. Genevieve County, Mo., in 1847. His father, I. O. Williams, was born in Terre Haute, Ind., in 1827, a mechanic by trade, and moved to Missouri soon after his marriage to Miss Sarah Lee. He located in Ste. Genevieve County, where he was engaged in farming, and in 1850 came to Arkansas, dying in Sebastian County in April, 1887. His wife was born in Illinois in 1829, and died in Arkansas April 1, 1888, their union resulting in the birth of seven children, four living. The paternal and maternal grandparents were of Scotch and German descent, respectively. John F. Williams was reared in Sebastian County, Ark., and worked at the mechanic's trade until he was elected to the office of sheriff in 1884, and is now filling his third term. He was married to Miss Alice Jones, of Tennessee, a daughter of Henry Jones, who died in 1861, and was an extensive planter in Weakley County, Tenn. Mrs. Williams became the mother of the following children: Beulah, Minnie, Hervey, Jim and Effie. The family attend the Methodist Church, and Mr. Williams is a member of the A. F. & A. M., the K. of H., and is a stanch adherent of the Democratic party. He is one of the best informed men of the county relating to the agricultural condition of the country, and has one of the finest stock farms in the county, and is preparing to engage in the stock business on a large scale in a short time. Mrs. Williams belongs to the Eastern Star Lodge, and is a member of the Ladies' Christian Association.

Constant P. Wilson, farmer of Upper Township, Sebastian Co., Ark., and native of the county, was born in 1856, being a son of Thomas E. and Mary A. (Dillard) Wilson, who were born in Kentucky and Virginia, July 6, 1804, and April 27, 1822, respectively. The father removed from Kentucky to Fort Gibson, and in 1832 located at Fort Smith, Ark., where he was engaged in surveying, and acted as sutler for the soldiers. He owned a large farm of 1,200 acres, and from fifteen to twenty slaves. The following are his children: Neosho L. (deceased), Thomas E., Virginia T. (Baxter), John D., Constant P., Sallie P. (Falconer), and Macha M. He has one step-daughter, Mrs. Marcus Boyd. Mr. Wilson's death occurred September 11, 1880, his wife dying on the 11th of January, seven years later. Her parents, John and Sallie P. (Moore) Dillard, were born in Virginia, and in 1822 removed to Arkansas, where the father engaged in merchandising, farming and stock dealing. He was one of the prominent men of his section of the country, and represented his county in the State Legislature. He died in 1846. His maternal grandparents, Benjamin and Polly (Price) Moore, came from Virginia to Arkansas in 1821, and the descendants of this noble couple are among the leading citizens of Arkansas. Constant P. Wilson, whose name heads this sketch, has spent his entire life in Sebastian County. He was married on the 30th of May, 1881, to Miss Nellie Collins, who was born July 4, 1860. From 1877 to 1885 he was in the saloon business at Fort Smith, but since that time has been manager of the Wilson and Collins farms, comprising 1,600 acres of land, and is the most extensive planter in Northwestern Arkansas. Throughout life Mr. Wilson has been the architect of his own fortune, and is of a very energetic and determined disposition. He is a member of the Episcopal Church, and in his political views is a Democrat, casting his first presidential vote for Samuel J. Tilden. Mrs. Wilson's father, James M. Collins, was born in Virginia in 1830, and died on the 2d of March, 1887. He was reared and educated in Pennsylvania by his grandfather, Christopher Riley, and after attaining man's estate went to Texas and engaged in the stock business on a large scale. While in the "Lone Star State" he became acquainted with and married Mary J. Whitsett, a daughter of Dr. William C. and Elizabeth L. (Edmunds) Whitsett. Although not in the army, Mr. Collins gave valuable assistance to the Confederate cause in furnishing the army with provisions. In 1866 he came to Fort Smith, and engaged in the mercantile business, and also purchased 1,200 acres of land in Sebastian County, on which he located in 1869. Here he died March 2, 1887. His parents, John and Elizabeth (Riley) Collins, were natives of Virginia. His wife's parents were born in Kentucky August 7, 1812, and December 15, 1815, and died January 9, 1882, and January 22, 1883, respectively, and her paternal great-grandparents, Gen. William and Emily (Haden) Whitsett, were Virginians, the former dying in 1841. Her maternal grandparents, William and Mary A. (Penn) Edmunds, were Virginians, Mary A. being a descendant of William Penn, of historical renown.

Green B. Wimberley, land agent of the Kansas & Texas Coal Company, at Huntington, has held that position since the location of the company at that place. He was born in Choctaw County, Ala., in 1846, and is the second of a family of twelve children (nine of who are living) born to William and Susan (Needham) Wimberley, natives of Enterprise, Miss., and Greensboro, Ala., born in 1814 and 1820, respectively. They were married in Choctaw County, Ala., where they still live. In younger days the father was an overseer, but he is now a well-to-do farmer and planter. When a boy he lost his father, John Wimberley, who was of Irish origin. The great-grandfather of our subject, Capt. William Wimberley, came to America with Gen. La Fayette, and served as a captain in the Revolution. The maternal grandfather, Benjamin Needham, was of Scotch descent, born in North Carolina, and died in Choctaw County, Ala. In 1862, at the age of fifteen, Green B. Wimberley joined Company G, Fortieth Alabama Infantry, in which he served until discharged in September of the same year for disability. The following December he enlisted in Company E, Ninth Alabama Cavalry, as second sergeant, and operated afterward in Mississippi, Alabama, Tennessee, Kentucky and Georgia. June 24, 1864, he was captured at La Fayette, Ga., and taken to Camp Morton, Ind., where he was held ten months. He was paroled in Virginia a few weeks before the general surrender, and then returned home. In the winter of 1865–66 he went to Louisiana and was there married, in November, 1867, to Mary Ann, daughter of C. C. and Mary Brewster, who were formerly from Mississippi, the State of Mrs. Wimberley's birth. Mr. and Mrs. Wimberley have been members of the Methodist Episcopal Church, South, for over twenty years. To them four sons and four daughters have been born. In December, 1869, our subject settled near the present site of Huntington, and until the establishment of that town made farming his sole occupation. His farm now consists of 200 acres, all of his property being the result of his own labor. He is a Democrat, and since 1884 has held the office of deputy sheriff of Sebastian County. He is a member of Pulliam Masonic Lodge No. 133, of which he was Master six years.

T. P. Winchester, attorney at law, of the law firm of Winchester & Bryant, at Fort Smith, Ark., was born in Sumner County, Tenn., in 1850, and is the son of George W. and M. H. (Gaines) Winchester. George W. Winchester was born May 14, 1822, in Sumner County, Tenn. He was an attorney, was in the State Legislature before the war, and was a member of the secession convention. He was a Confederate soldier, was a major on Gen. W. B. Bates' staff, and was captured at Missionary Ridge. He was imprisoned at Johnson's Island until the close of the war. He was the seventh son and the youngest child of Gen.

James Winchester, an officer of the Revolutionary War and of the War of 1812, and one of the pioneers of Middle Tennessee. The family is of Welsh descent. T. P. Winchester was reared in Sumner County, Tenn., and lived there until 1865, read law under his father, and also studied one year in the University of Virginia. He practiced law in Memphis, Tenn., seven years, and in 1880 located in Fort Smith. The present law firm was organized in September, 1883. In Albemarle County, Va., he was married to Miss Nanna Thurman, in the year 1874, and to them have been born three children, one (Agnes) now living. Two died in infancy. Mr. Winchester is a member of the K. of P. and the Methodist Church, South.

Edgar E. Bryant, also a member of the above mentioned firm, was born in Paris, Miss., December 9, 1861, and is the son of A. A. and Margaret (Stein) Bryant. A. A. Bryant was a native of Virginia, is a physician, and immigrated to Mississippi with his father when a boy. He there married Miss Margaret Stein, and seven children were the result of the union, of whom Edgar D. is the eldest. The paternal grandfather was a native of Virginia, and the paternal great-grandfather was a Scotchman. The maternal grandmother was a Pope. The Pope family located in Westmoreland County, Va., and Pope's Creek was named after them. A. A. Bryant is still alive, and is now a planter in Mississippi. Margaret Bryant died on Christmas of 1885. Edgar E. Bryant attained his growth in Mississippi, and in 1880 graduated with the degree of A. B., from the University of Mississippi, with the honors of his class. He afterward graduated in law from Vanderbilt University, at Nashville, Tenn., and also graduated in law from the Columbia University, of Washington City, in 1883. In August of the same year he came to Fort Smith, and September 7 became a member of the present firm, having practiced at this place since. He is president of the Young Men's Democratic Club at Fort Smith, Ark., and is a member of the order of K. of P.

Capt. William J. Witcher, postmaster and farmer at Witcherville, was born in Surrey County, N. C., in 1829, and is a son of Lacy and Elizabeth (Lyon) Witcher, natives of North Carolina, where the father passed his entire life, dying when William J. was an infant. The mother afterward married Edward Crossen, and about 1835 moved to Johnson County, Ark., going from there to Sebastian County, where Mr. Crossen died at Fort Smith during the war. Mrs. Crossen was a daughter of Col. William Lyon, who always lived in North Carolina. She was a member of the Christian Church, and died at Witcherville in 1860. Her grandfather, Col. Lyon, was an officer in the Revolution, and among his descendants is the Hon. Frank Lyon, a cousin of our subject, who, for many years, was a member of Congress from Alabama. William J. has a twin sister, who, with himself, was reared and educated by their maternal grandfather, in Virginia. In 1848 they came to Johnson County, Ark. In 1849 Capt. Witcher married Mary E., daughter of Abram L. Lester, formerly of Wilson County, Tenn., where Mrs. Witcher was born. There are seven living issues of this marriage. In 1850 Capt. Witcher located upon 160 acres of land in Sebastian County, where he was one of the early settlers. The town of Witcherville was afterward built upon his farm, and received its name in his honor. In 1862 he organized Company D, of Col. W. H. Brooks' infantry regiment, and after serving some time as first lieutenant he was made captain of the company. In the fall of 1863 he was captured while at home, and until February, 1864, was held a prisoner at Fort Smith and Little Rock. Finding it impossible to rejoin his company he joined Gen. Shelby's army, with whom he operated in Missouri and Arkansas, and participated in the engagements at Perry Grove and Helena. In the fall of 1864 he joined his family in the Choctaw Nation, and soon after the surrender returned to Sebastian County. From 1868 until 1884 he engaged in the mercantile business at Witcherville, and since March, 1888, has been the postmaster of that place, Prior to the war he was twice elected internal revenue collector, which position he resigned to enter the army. Mr. and Mrs. Witcher and three of their children are members of the Cumberland Presbyterian Church, in which the former has been an elder since 1854. He is a charter member of Pulliam Lodge, No. 133, and in politics is a Democrat, his first presidential vote having been cast for Cass in 1848.

H. C. Wyman, chief of police at Fort Smith, was born in Rock County, Wis., June 16, 1855, and is a son of C. L. and Emily (Adams) Wyman, natives of New York State. Our subject attained his growth in Knox County, Ill., whither his parents had removed, and in 1869 went to Jefferson County, Iowa, spending four years at Fairfield. He then ran a stage line in Henry County, Mo., three years, went to New Albany, Ind., and spent two years in Kansas, after which he located at Fort Smith. In 1878 he established a stage line, which ran from Fort Smith to Muskogee, and engaged in the liquor business. He spent some time in Kansas and Texas before Fort Smith became a thriving city. In 1887 he was appointed sergeant of the police, and upon the resignation of John Nevil, in 1887, became the chief. He was married in 1882, at Fort Smith, to Miss Eliza Dodson, daughter of Joseph Dodson. [See sketch.] Mrs. Wyman is a member of the Church of the Immaculate Conception. They have a family of two children: Mamie and Henry. Mr. Wyman's father was born in Syracuse, N. Y., and traced his ancestry to a period prior to the Revolution, in which war the grandfather of our subject, John Wyman, participated.

John C. Yadon is one of the enterprising farmers of Sebastian County, Ark., and was born in East Tennessee in 1835. His father, Thomas Yadon, was born in Washington County, Va., March 27, 1801, and when a small boy was taken by his parents to East Tennessee, where he met and espoused Nancy Haynes, October 14, 1819, who was born in North Carolina March 1, 1803, and moved with her to Missouri in 1839, and to Sebastian County, Ark., in 1849. Here he entered 160 acres of land and spent the remainder of his days, dying January 18, 1886. He served as justice of the peace for twenty years, and held the office of postmaster for a number of years. The following are his children who are living: M. A. (Long), M. J. (Condran), Minerva A. (Douglas) and John C. The mother of these children died February 14, 1881. Joseph Yadon, the grandfather, was born in County Down, Ireland, December 17, 1856, and during the early part of the Revolutionary War crossed the ocean as a soldier in the British army, and served in Burgoyne's command until the latter surrendered to Gen. Gates on the 17th of October, 1777. He then took the oath of allegiance to the colonies and joined the American army, fighting for its interests until the close of the war. He was discharged in 1782, at the falls of the Ohio, and went to Virginia, where he met and married Mary Pennabaker, and moved to Tennessee in 1805. His death occurred September 8, 1838. The maternal grandfather, John Haynes, was born in North Carolina, and was married to Mary McCarver. He died in 1842 or 1843. John C. Yadon spent his boyhood days in Tennessee and Missouri, and on the 17th of March, 1859, was married to Susan A. Douglas, who was born in East Tennessee August 31, 1836, by whom he became the father of six children, four of whom are living: William Thomas, Margaret L. (Williamson), John P. and Joseph M. Those deceased are Nancy E. and Samuel H. The mother of these children died January 11, 1879. Her parents, William R. and Margaret A. (McConnell) Douglas, were born in East Tennessee, October 24, 1796, and December 22, 1806, respectively. The father died in August, 1864, but the mother is still living, and is a resident of Sebastian County. W. R. Douglas was an old-line Whig, during the Civil War was an uncompromising Union man, and though too old and feeble to be in the service, he gave substantial aid to the Union cause and Union sympathizers. He was a member of the Old School Presbyterian Church, and for a number of years a colporteur for the American Tract Society. Mr. Yadon owns 346 acres of land, 115 of which are under cultivation and well improved. In 1863 he enlisted in company E, First Arkansas Infantry, United States Army, and served until the cessation of hostilites in 1865. He is a member of the Old School Presbyterian Church, belongs to the Republican party, and cast his first presidential vote for James Buchanan.

D. J. Young, resident agent for the Anheuser-Busch Brewing Association, of St. Louis, for Fort Smith and adjacent territory, was born in Illinois September 4, 1848, and is the son of William and Sarah (Wells) Young, who were married in Ohio, and soon afterward went to Illinois, where they were pioneer settlers of Bureau County. Here they both died, William at the age of seventy-one, and Sarah at the age of sixty-eight. The Young family were of old New England stock. Sarah (Wells) Young was also a native of Ohio, was of German descent on the mother's side, and on the father's side for several generations back were Americans. She was the mother of nine children, of whom D. J. Young is next to the youngest in order of birth. He grew to manhood on a farm in Illinois, and received a good education for the chances he had. At the age of twenty he left Illinois, went to Missouri, and here followed the railroad business for nine years, being conductor for six years. He ran a train, principally in Missouri, on the St. Louis, Salem & Little Rock Railroad. In 1877 he quit the railroad, and engaged in merchandising for about three years, when he became agent for the Anheuser-Busch Brewing Association, of St. Louis, residing at Seligman, Mo., while that was a railroad point. He left that city and moved to Fort Smith in 1883, though he had an agency here in 1882. Mr. Young has also been engaged in the brick business, under the firm name of Braden & Young, and furnished all the large contracts in the city while in the business, principally the United States court-house, the county court-house, the Anheuser-Busch building, Masonic Temple and others. He is sole proprietor of the Fort Smith Steam Bottling Works, in Fort Smith, and has enlarged the business to its present proportions. He became sole proprietor in March, 1888. Its capacity will supply a trade of 50,000 inhabitants. Mr. Young has been the prime mover in having the Anheuser-Busch Brewing Association invest nearly $60,000 in buildings in the city. He was married in Steelville, Mo., to Miss Angie Jamison, June 16, 1873, daughter of Preston and Mary (Early) Jamison. This union resulted in the birth of four children: James Roswell, Imogene, Maude and Agnes Early. Maude died at the age of four months and eight days. Mr. Young is a Republican in politics, and is a stockholder in the American National Bank, of Fort Smith. He is also a stockholder in the Fort Smith Canning Company, Fort Smith Building & Loan Association No. 3, Fort Smith Journal Publishing Company, Fort Smith Fair Association, Van Buren Ice & Coal Company, Border City Ice & Coal Company, of Fort Smith, and Border City Soap Factory, and is a member of the Chamber of Commerce. He is a member of the Masonic fraternity, being a Knight Templar of that order in four lodges; a K. of P., both subordinate and uniform rank; A. O. U. W., and uniform rank of the order, in which he carries $5,000 life insurance. He is also insured for $2,000 in the Masonic fraternity, and the same amount in the New England and New York Mutual. Mr. Young owns business property on Townsen Avenue and on Rogers Avenue, and residence property on Fifth Street and Twelfth Street, and has great confidence in the future prospects of Fort Smith. He avoids serving as a director in any of the many enterprises he is interested in, as he has enough business of his own to look after.

Joseph W. Young, mayor and postmaster of Huntington, was born in Pickens County, S. C., in 1853, and is a son of Archibald M. and Margaret E. (Sewright) Young, natives of South Carolina, born in 1826 and 1824, respectively. The father served during the entire Civil War as a blacksmith in Ferguson's Fying Artillery, having charge of the battery. He was captured at Missionary Ridge, and died a prisoner at Nashville March 2, 1864. The grandfather, Joseph Young, was of English descent, and born in Kentucky in 1785. He passed his entire life, after becoming seventeen years of age, in South Carolina, and served many years as justice of the peace and postmaster at Branch Island. He died in 1870. His father, Levi Young, was born in Pennsylvania in 1750, and after serving in the Revolution settled in Kentucky. He died in South Carolina in 1845. He was quite a writer, having written many poems besides a history of his life. Our subject is the eldest of a family of four sons and one daughter, and consequently, his help being needed at home, he attended school but five months during his youth. He was but eleven when he lost his father, and notwithstanding the many difficulties which beset his way, he became a well-informed man by persistent application when the opportunities offered. In 1874 he married Mrs. Martha M. Looper, daughter of Robert and Jane McWhortor, of South Carolina, where Mrs. Young was born. Her paternal grandfather was a native of Ireland. In 1882 Mr. Young sold goods at Excelsior, and in 1883 bought a farm in Center Township, and remained on the farm till October, 1886. He then went into the drug and grocery business at Witcherville, and remained at Witcherville till January, 1888, when he came to Huntington. His grocery stock is valued at $1,800, and he has a well-improved farm of 280 acres in Center Township, stocked with several head of horses, mules and cattle, and besides this owns a lot on Broadway, in Huntington, besides a two-story frame house. All this is the result of his own industry and good management. He is a public, spirited man, and in April, 1888, was elected mayor of Huntington, and the following September made postmaster. Mr. and Mrs. Young belong to the Missionary Baptist Church. Mr. Young has a family of seven sons and three step-sons. In politics he is a Democrat, and he has been a member of the Masonic fraternity four years. Since December, 1887, he has been the Worshipful Master of Pulliam Lodge No. 133, at Witcherville. He is also a K. of L.

www.ingramcontent.com/pod-product-compliance
Lightning Source LLC
LaVergne TN
LVHW061240100826
845148LV00008B/998

* 9 7 8 0 7 8 8 4 9 8 7 5 6 *